CAPITAL IN MANUFACTURING
AND MINING
Its Formation and Financing

NATIONAL BUREAU OF ECONOMIC RESEARCH

Studies in Capital Formation and Financing

1. Capital Formation in Residential Real Estate: Trends and Prospects
   Leo Grebler, David M. Blank, and Louis Winnick

2. Capital in Agriculture: Its Formation and Financing Since 1870
   Alvin S. Tostlebe

3. Financial Intermediaries in the American Economy Since 1900
   Raymond W. Goldsmith

4. Capital in Transportation, Communications, and Public Utilities: Its Formation and Financing
   Melville J. Ulmer

5. Postwar Market for State and Local Government Securities
   Roland I. Robinson

6. Capital in Manufacturing and Mining: Its Formation and Financing
   Daniel Creamer, Sergei P. Dobrovolsky, and Israel Borenstein

Capital in Manufacturing and Mining

ITS FORMATION AND FINANCING

BY

DANIEL CREAMER
NATIONAL INDUSTRIAL
CONFERENCE BOARD

SERGEI P. DOBROVOLSKY
RENSSELAER
POLYTECHNIC INSTITUTE

AND ISRAEL BORENSTEIN
BUREAU OF ECONOMIC AFFAIRS, UNITED NATIONS

ASSISTED BY MARTIN BERNSTEIN

A STUDY BY THE
NATIONAL BUREAU OF ECONOMIC RESEARCH, NEW YORK

PUBLISHED BY
PRINCETON UNIVERSITY PRESS, PRINCETON
1960

Copyright © 1960, by Princeton University Press

All Rights Reserved

L.C. CARD NO. 60-12233

Printed in the United States of America

NATIONAL BUREAU OF ECONOMIC RESEARCH
1960

OFFICERS
George B. Roberts, *Chairman*
Arthur F. Burns, *President*
Theodore W. Schultz, *Vice-President*
Murray Shields, *Treasurer*
Solomon Fabricant, *Director of Research*
Geoffrey H. Moore, *Associate Director of Research*
Hal B. Lary, *Associate Director of Research*
William J. Carson, *Executive Director*

DIRECTORS AT LARGE
Wallace J. Campbell, *Nationwide Insurance*
Solomon Fabricant, *New York University*
Crawford H. Greenewalt, *E. I. du Pont de Nemours & Company*
Gabriel Hauge, *Manufacturers Trust Company*
Albert J. Hettinger, Jr., *Lazard Frères and Company*
H. W. Laidler, *League for Industrial Democracy*
Shepard Morgan, *Norfolk, Connecticut*
George B. Roberts, *Larchmont, New York*
Harry Scherman, *Book-of-the-Month Club*
Boris Shishkin, *American Federation of Labor and Congress of Industrial Organizations*
George Soule, *Washington College*
J. Raymond Walsh, *New York City*
Joseph H. Willits, *The Educational Survey, University of Pennsylvania*
Leo Wolman, *Columbia University*
Donald B. Woodward, *Vick Chemical Company*
Theodore O. Yntema, *Ford Motor Company*

DIRECTORS BY UNIVERSITY APPOINTMENT
V. W. Bladen, *Toronto*
Arthur F. Burns, *Columbia*
Melvin G. de Chazeau, *Cornell*
Frank W. Fetter, *Northwestern*
H. M. Groves, *Wisconsin*
Gottfried Haberler, *Harvard*
Walter W. Heller, *Minnesota*
Maurice W. Lee, *North Carolina*
Lloyd G. Reynolds, *Yale*
Theodore W. Schultz, *Chicago*
Jacob Viner, *Princeton*
Willis J. Winn, *Pennsylvania*

DIRECTORS APPOINTED BY OTHER ORGANIZATIONS
Percival F. Brundage, *American Institute of Certified Public Accountants*
Harold G. Halcrow, *American Farm Economic Association*
Theodore V. Houser, *Committee for Economic Development*
Stanley H. Ruttenberg, *American Federation of Labor and Congress of Industrial Organizations*
Murray Shields, *American Management Association*
Willard L. Thorp, *American Economic Association*
W. Allen Wallis, *American Statistical Association*
Harold F. Williamson, *Economic History Association*

DIRECTORS EMERITI
Oswald W. Knauth, *Beaufort, South Carolina*   N. I. Stone, *New York City*

RESEARCH STAFF
Moses Abramovitz
Gary S. Becker
Gerhard Bry
Arthur F. Burns
Phillip Cagan
Morris A. Copeland
Frank G. Dickinson
James S. Earley
Richard A. Easterlin
Solomon Fabricant

Milton Friedman
Raymond W. Goldsmith
Millard Hastay
Daniel M. Holland
Thor Hultgren
F. Thomas Juster
C. Harry Kahn
John W. Kendrick
Simon Kuznets
Hal B. Lary
Ruth P. Mack

Ilse Mintz
Geoffrey H. Moore
Roger F. Murray
Ralph L. Nelson
G. Warren Nutter
Richard T. Selden
Lawrence H. Seltzer
Robert P. Shay
George J. Stigler
Herbert B. Woolley

Relation of the Directors to the Work and Publications of the National Bureau of Economic Research

1. The object of the National Bureau of Economic Research is to ascertain and to present to the public important economic facts and their interpretation in a scientific and impartial manner. The Board of Directors is charged with the responsibility of ensuring that the work of the National Bureau is carried on in strict conformity with this object.

2. To this end the Board of Directors shall appoint one or more Directors of Research.

3. The Director or Directors of Research shall submit to the members of the Board, or to its Executive Committee, for their formal adoption, all specific proposals concerning researches to be instituted.

4. No report shall be published until the Director or Directors of Research shall have submitted to the Board a summary drawing attention to the character of the data and their utilization in the report, the nature and treatment of the problems involved, the main conclusions, and such other information as in their opinion would serve to determine the suitability of the report for publication in accordance with the principles of the National Bureau.

5. A copy of any manuscript proposed for publication shall also be submitted to each member of the Board. For each manuscript to be so submitted a special committee shall be appointed by the President, or at his designation by the Executive Director, consisting of three Directors selected as nearly as may be one from each general division of the Board. The names of the special manuscript committee shall be stated to each Director when the summary and report described in paragraph (4) are sent to him. It shall be the duty of each member of the committee to read the manuscript. If each member of the special committee signifies his approval within thirty days, the manuscript may be published. If each member of the special committee has not signified his approval within thirty days of the transmittal of the report and manuscript, the Director of Research shall then notify each member of the Board, requesting approval or disapproval of publication, and thirty additional days shall be granted for this purpose. The manuscript shall then not be published unless at least a majority of the entire Board and a two-thirds majority of those members of the Board who shall have voted on the proposal within the time fixed for the receipt of votes on the publication proposed shall have approved.

6. No manuscript may be published, though approved by each member of the special committee, until forty-five days have elapsed from the transmittal of the summary and report. The interval is allowed for the receipt of any memorandum of dissent or reservation, together with a brief statement of his reasons, that any member may wish to express; and such memorandum of dissent or reservation shall be published with the manuscript if he so desires. Publication does not, however, imply that each member of the Board has read the manuscript, or that either members of the Board in general, or of the special committee, have passed upon its validity in every detail.

7. A copy of this reservation shall, unless otherwise determined by the Board, be printed in each copy of every National Bureau book.

(Resolution adopted October 25, 1926
and revised February 6, 1933 and February 24, 1941)

This monograph is part of a larger investigation of trends and prospects in capital formation and financing made possible by a grant from the Life Insurance Association of America.

CONTENTS

ACKNOWLEDGMENTS   xxi

INTRODUCTION, by Simon Kuznets   xxiii
    Trends in Output and in Capital   xxvi
    Trends in the Capital-Output Ratios—the Findings   xxx
    Trends in the Capital-Output Ratios—Some Hypotheses   xxxiv
    Trends in Financing—External and Internal   xliii
    Trends in the Structure of External Financing   xlvii
    Bearing upon Future Prospects   l

PART I

CAPITAL AND OUTPUT TRENDS IN MANUFACTURING AND MINING

by Daniel Creamer and Israel Borenstein
assisted by Martin Bernstein

I. THE MEASUREMENT OF MANUFACTURING AND MINING GROWTH   3
    Growth of Manufacturing Activity   3
    Growth of Mining   7
    Sources and Methods of Measurement and their Limitations   11
    Definition of Capital   12
    Definition of Output   15
    Selection of Benchmark Years   17
    Comparability of Industrial Classifications   18
    Adjustment for Price Changes   19

II. LONG-TERM GROWTH OF CAPITAL IN MANUFACTURING AND MINING   22
    Manufacturing, 1880–1953   22
    Mining, 1870–1953   31
    Summary of Findings   36

III. TRENDS IN CAPITAL-OUTPUT RATIOS   38
    Capital-Output Ratios in Reported and Constant Prices, All Manufacturing (1880–1953) and Mining (1870–1953)   38
    Effect of Data Deficiencies on Trend   43
    Effect of Changes in the Composition of Manufacturing Industries   46
    Price Adjustments and their Effect   47
    Ratios in Constant Prices, by Minor Industries, 1880–1948   51

CONTENTS

Trends in the Ratios of Industries Classified by Ultimate Use of Output	52
A Measure of the Effect of Changing Composition	53
Effect of Changes in the Composition of Mining Industries	55
Size of Firm and the Capital-Output Ratio	60
Summary of Findings	65

IV. TRENDS IN RATIOS OF FIXED AND WORKING CAPITAL TO OUTPUT — 67

Manufacturing, 1890–1948	67
Mining, 1870–1948	74
Total Capital-Output Ratios, by Industries	79
The Record in Manufacturing, from 1948 to 1953	83
The Record in Mining, 1948–1953	87
Changes between 1953 and 1957 in Capital-Output Ratios for Manufacturing	88
Summary of Findings	91

V. SOME RELATIONSHIPS BEARING ON CHANGES IN THE CAPITAL-OUTPUT RATIOS — 93

Pattern of Change in Capital-Output Ratios in Individual Manufacturing Industries	93
Relation between Labor and Capital per Unit of Output and Capital per Man-Hour	94
Manufacturing	94
Mining	99
Mining: Factors Contributing to Interindustry Differences in the Rate of Change of the Capital-Output Ratios	101
Comparison with Manufacturing	103
Summary of Findings	105

PART II
LONG TERM TRENDS IN CAPITAL FINANCING
by Sergei Dobrovolsky
assisted by Martin Bernstein

VI. INTERNAL AND EXTERNAL FINANCING — 109

Concepts and Definitions	109
Sources of Data	112
Asset Growth and Profit Retentions	113
Gross Internal Financing and Security Issues	120
Gross Internal Financing and Expenditures on Plant and Equipment	124

CONTENTS

Components of Gross Internal Financing	130
Depreciation and Depletion	130
Net Profit Retention	134
Total Short-Term and Long-Term External Financing	141
Gross External Financing	141
Net Balance of External Financing	146
Summary of Findings	154
VII. DEBT AND EQUITY FINANCING	**156**
Definitions	156
Total Debt	156
Long-Term Debt: New Bond Issues	161
Bond Issues and Equity Financing	166
Total Bond Debt Outstanding	169
New Types of Long-Term Financing	172
Private Placement of Securities	172
Bank Term Loans	179
Short-Term External Financing	182
Summary of Findings	189

PART III
Appendixes

A. NOTES ON ESTIMATES OF CAPITAL, OUTPUT AND EMPLOYMENT IN MANUFACTURING, 1880–1953	195
A. Sources and Adjustments of Reported Values	195
B. Capital and Output in 1929 Prices	221
C. Total Number of Persons Employed in Selected Manufacturing Industries, 1900–1953	239
D. Supporting Tables	241
B. NOTES ON ESTIMATES OF CAPITAL, OUTPUT, AND EMPLOYMENT IN MINING, 1870–1953	274
A. Census Remarks and Definitions on Capital Invested in Mining	274
B. Coverage	280
C. Level of Business Activity in Year of Census Canvass	284
D. Estimate of the Value of Leased and Total Land Used in Mining, 1909 and 1919	284
E. Notes on the Statistical Reliability of the Major Findings	293
F. Notes on the Comparability of the Benchmark Years with Regard to Employment Levels	299
G. General Remarks on Table B-6	301
H. Supporting Tables	304
I. Adjustment of Capital Estimates for Manufacturing and Mining to Eliminate Duplication	324

C. FINANCIAL SERIES: NOTES AND SUPPORTING
   TABLES 326
   A. Estimates of External Financing by Manufacturing and
      Mining Corporations, 1900–1953 326
   B. Estimates of Internal Financing by Manufacturing and
      Mining Corporations, 1900–1953 328
   C. Estimates of Expenditures for New Plant and Equipment by
      Manufacturing and Mining Corporations, 1900–1953 329
      1919–1953 329
      1900–1918 329
   D. Ratios of Selected Balance Sheet Items to Total Assets of
      Manufacturing and Mining Corporations, by Asset Size,
      1937 and 1948 330
   E. Supporting Tables 331

INDEX 341

TABLES

1. Income Originating in Mining and Manufacturing as a Per Cent of National Income or Aggregate Payments, Selected Periods, 1870–1953 — 3
2. Selected Measures of the Growth of Manufacturing, Selected Years, 1880–1953 — 4
3. Mineral Production and Consumption and Gross and Net National Product, Selected Ratios, by Major Mining Industries, 1870–1953 — 8
4. Level of Business Activity in Year of Census Canvass, 1880–1919 — 17
5. Total Capital and Gross National Product per Worker, All Manufacturing, Dates of Peaks and Troughs in Secular Swings, 1873–1953 — 22

Total Capital in Manufacturing Industries:
    6. Rates of Change per Year between Benchmark Years, 1880–1953 — 25
    7. Comparison with All Manufacturing of Alternating Periods of High and Low Rates of Change between Benchmark Years, 1880–1953 — 26
    8. Percentage Distribution, by Minor Industry Groups, Selected Years, 1880–1948 — 28

Mining Industries, 1870–1953:
    9. Total Change in Capital between Selected Years — 33
    10. Capital (Excluding Land) and Output, Rates of Change per Year between Selected Years — 34
11. Ratios of Capital to Output and to Value Added, Selected Valuations, All Manufacturing, Selected Years, 1880–1953 — 40

Capital-Output Ratios:
    12. All Mining, Selected Valuations, Selected Years, 1870–1953 — 43
    13. Manufacturing Industries Classified by Use of Product, Selected Years, 1880–1948 — 52
    14. Effect of Changes in Internal Composition of Industries, All Manufacturing, Selected Years, 1880–1937 — 54
15. Share of Major and Minor Mining Industries in Total Mining, Selected Years, 1870–1947 — 56

Capital-Output Ratios in Mining:
    16. Major and Minor Industries, Averages for Selected Groups of Years, 1870–1947 — 58
    17. Actual and Hypothetical, and Ratio of Actual to Hypothetical Capital, Selected Years, 1870–1948 — 59

TABLES

Fixed Capital-Output Ratios of Net Income Corporations, by Manufacturing Industries:
- 18. By Asset Size, 1947 — 62
- 19. Largest Firms Compared with Smallest Firms, 1937 and 1947 — 64

Ratios of Fixed and Working Capital to Output:
- 20. All Manufacturing, Selected Years, 1890–1953 — 67
- 21. By Minor Manufacturing Industries, 1929, 1937, and 1948 — 68
- 22. Ratios of Inventories to Output, by Major Manufacturing Industries, Selected Years, 1919–1948 — 72

Capital-Output Ratios in Mining:
- 23. Major Industries, Selected Years, 1870–1953 — 73
- 24. Minor Industries, Selected Years, 1870–1947 — 75
- 25. Working Capital and Components, Major Industries, Selected Years, 1929–1948 — 77

Major Manufacturing Industries:
- 26. Ratios to Output of Selected Capital Components, 1948 and 1953 — 84
- 27. Fixed Capital and Selected Capital-Output Ratios, Per Cent Change between 1948 and 1953 — 85
- 28. Ratios of Selected Short-Term Assets to Output, 1948 and 1953 — 86

29. Selected Capital-Output Ratios, by Major Mining Industries, 1948 and 1953 — 87

30. Change in Fixed Capital and Its Ratio to Output, by Major Manufacturing Industries, 1948–1953 and 1953–1957 — 90

31. Coefficient of Variation of the Capital-Output Ratios in Thirty-seven Manufacturing Industries, Selected Years, 1880–1948 — 93

Indexes of Selected Ratios:
- 32. Man-hours, Capital, and Output, All Manufacturing, Selected Years, 1880–1957 — 95
- 33. Number Employed, Capital, and Output, by Major Manufacturing Industries, Selected Years, 1900–1953 — 97
- 34. Wage Earners, Man-hours, Capital, and Output, by Major Mining Industries, Selected Years, 1880–1953 — 100

35. Total Change in the Capital-Output Ratio, Output, and Wage Earners per Unit of Output, by Major Mining Industries, 1880–1919 and 1919–1953 — 101

Comparison of Manufacturing and Mining:
- 36. Output and Capital, Selected Years, 1880–1953 — 104
- 37. Capital and Value Added, Selected Years, 1880–1948 — 105

TABLES

Growth of Corporate Assets and the Relative Importance of External and Net Internal Financing:
    38. All Manufacturing and Mining Corporations, Selected Years, 1900–1953   114
    39. Large Manufacturing Corporations, 1900–1954   117

All Manufacturing and Mining Corporations, 1900–1953:
    40. Gross Internal Financing, New Security Issues, and Plant and Equipment Expenditures   121
    41. Depreciation and Depletion Allowances and Retained Net Profit   131

Ratio to Net Plant and Equipment Expansion of Retained Net Profit and of New Security Issues, and Ratio of New Security Issues to Retained Net Profit, 1900–1954:
    42. All Manufacturing and Mining Corporations   137
    43. Large Manufacturing Corporations   139

Internal and External Sources of Funds:
    44. Large Manufacturing Corporations, 1900–1954   142
    45. All Manufacturing Corporations, 1946–1953   146

Capital Expenditures on Physical Assets, Gross Internal Financing, and Net Balance of External Financing:
    46. Large Manufacturing Corporations, 1913–1953   148
    47. All Manufacturing and Mining Corporations, 1923–1953   150

All Manufacturing and Mining Corporations:
    48. Components of Net External Financing Related to Gross and Net Internal Financing, Selected Periods, 1923–1952   152
    49. Ratio of Debt to Assets, Selected Years, 1890–1952   157
50. Ratios of Total Debt to Operating Assets and Relative Change in Operating Assets, by Manufacturing Industries, Selected Years, 1919–1948   159
51. New Security Issues, Retained Net Profit, and Net Plant and Equipment Expansion, All Manufacturing and Mining Corporations, 1900–1953   162
52. Net Bond Issues during Cycles in Business Activity, All Manufacturing and Mining Corporations and Major Manufacturing Industries, 1900–1943   163
53. Ratios of New Stock Issues and New Long-Term Debt Financing to Retained Net Profit, Large Manufacturing Corporations, 1900–1953   168
54. Operating Assets and Par Value of Bonded Debt Outstanding, All Manufacturing Corporations, Selected Years, 1900–1952   170

TABLES

55. All Corporate Securities, Total and Private Placements, 1934–1951 — 173
56. Distribution of Privately-Placed Corporate Debt, by Type of Investor, 1947, 1949, and 1950 — 174
57. Distribution of Privately-Placed Securities, by Major Manufacturing Industries, during 1951–1952 — 175

Manufacturing Industries:
    58. Distribution of New Plant and Equipment Expenditures and of Privately Placed Loans, during 1951–1952 — 176
    59. Distribution of Privately-Placed Securities, by Type, during 1951–1952 — 178

60. Corporate Short- and Long-Term Loans Outstanding Held by Commercial Banks, All Corporations, 1932–1952 — 180
61. Business Term Loans Outstanding Held by Member Banks, by Year of Final Payment, as of November 20, 1946 — 181
62. Debt Excluding Tax Liability and Total Assets Excluding Government Securities, All Manufacturing and Mining Corporations, Selected Years, 1929–1952 — 188

Appendix A

A-1. Assets as Percentage of Invested Capital, Sample Drawn from *Moody's* of Manufacturing and Mining Corporations, 1919 — 199
A-2. Derivation of Total Invested Capital in All Manufacturing Corporations, by Major Industries, 1919 — 200
A-3. Derivation of Estimates of Capital in Major Manufacturing Industries and in Mining, 1919 — 202
A-4. Comparable Industrial Classifications, *Census of Manufactures*, *1919* and *Statistics of Income*, *1929* and *1930* — 208
A-5. Investment in Emergency Facilities; Amortization in Excess of Normal Depreciation, All Manufacturing, as of 1948 — 219
A-6. Derivation of 1937 Index for Expressing Book Values of Machinery and Equipment for Food and Kindred Products Group in 1929 Prices — 222
A-7. Computation of the Ratio of Net to Gross Fixed Capital, Corporations with Balance Sheets, All Manufacturing, 1937–1948 — 225

Supporting Tables

By Major and Minor Manufacturing Industries:
    A-8. Total Capital in Book Values and in 1929 Prices, Selected Years, 1880–1948 — 241

TABLES

A-9. Fixed Capital in Book Values and in 1929 Prices, Selected Years, 1890–1948   248
A-10. Value of Output in Current and in 1929 Prices, Selected Years, 1880–1948   252
A-11. Price Indexes for Deflating Book Values of Fixed and Total Capital, by Major Manufacturing Industries, Selected Years, 1880–1948   259
A-12. Indexes of Wholesale Prices of Output, by Major and Minor Manufacturing Industries, Selected Years, 1880–1948   261

By Major and Minor Manufacturing Industries:
A-13. Ratios of Total Capital to Output, Selected Years, 1880–1948   265
A-14. Ratios of Fixed Capital to Output, Selected Years, 1890–1948   268
A-15. Basic Data for Capital-Output Ratios in 1929 Prices, by Major Manufacturing Industries, 1948 and 1953   270
A-16. Total Number of Persons Employed, by Major Manufacturing Industries, Selected Years, 1900–1953   273

Appendix B

B-1. Industry Coverage of Mining Data, Selected Years, 1870–1919   281
B-2. Items Reported and Transcribed from the *Census of Mining*, Selected Years, 1870–1919   283
B-3. Assumed Average Length of Life for Royalties on Leased Mineral Lands, by Mineral Groups, 1919 and 1909   292
B-4. Value of Output: Benchmark-Year Estimate as Percentage of Five-Year Average, by Major and Minor Mining Industries, Selected Years, 1870–1948   300
B-5. Capital: Ratio of Benchmark-Year Estimate to Five-Year Average of Output, by Major Mining Industries, Selected Years, 1870–1948   300

Supporting Tables

B-6. Capital, Value of Output, and Related Measures, by Major and Minor Mining Industries, Selected Years, 1870–1919   304

By Major Mining Industries, Selected Years, 1870–1953:
B-7. Value of Output in Current Prices   315
B-8. Value of Output in 1929 Prices   316
B-9. Book Value of Capital (Including Land)   317
B-10. Book Value of Plant and Working Capital   318
B-11. Book Value of Capital (Excluding Land)   319

TABLES

B-12. Indexes for Deflation of Output, by Major Mining Industries, Selected Years, 1870–1953 — 321

B-13. Indexes for Deflation of Book Values of Mining Capital, by Components, 1870–1953 — 322

B-14. Implicit Price Indexes for Deflation of Capital (Excluding Land), by Major Mining Industries, Selected Years, 1870–1953 — 322

B-15. Employment and Man-Hours, by Major Mining Industries, Selected Years, 1880–1953 — 323

B-16. Unduplicated Total of Capital (Including Land), in Book Values and in 1929 Prices, in All Manufacturing and Mining, Selected Years, 1880–1953 — 325

Appendix C
Supporting Tables

All Manufacturing and Mining Corporations, 1900–1953:

    C-1. External Financing through Net Capital Stock and Net Bond Issues — 331

    C-2. Internal Financing — 332

    C-3. Expenditures for New Plant and Equipment — 334

C-4. Selected Balance Sheet Items as Percentages of Total Assets, All Manufacturing and Mining Corporations, 1937 and 1948 — 335

CHARTS

1. Indexes of Output by Mining Industries, and Index of Gross National Product, 1870–1953 6
2. Total Capital, by Major Manufacturing Industries, Rate of Change per Year between Benchmark Years, 1880–1953 23
3. Value of Capital Excluding Land, by Major Mining Industries, Selected Years, 1870–1953 32
4. Ratios of Capital to Output and to Value Added, Selected Valuations, All Manufacturing, Selected Years, 1880–1953 39
5. Indexes of Ratios of Capital to Output and to Value Added, All Manufacturing, Selected Years, 1880–1948 41
6. Capital-Output Ratios, by Major Mining Industries, Selected Years, 1870–1953 42

Major Manufacturing Industries:

   7. Price Indexes (Book Value) of Total Capital, Selected Years, 1880–1953 48
   8. Price Indexes of Output, Selected Years, 1880–1948 49
   9. Capital-Output Ratios, Selected Years, 1880–1953 50

10. Internal Financing, New Security Issues, and Plant and Equipment Expenditures, All Manufacturing and Mining Corporations, 1900–1953 122
11. Ratios of New Security Issues to Gross Internal Financing, All Manufacturing and Mining Corporations and Sample, 1900–1953 123

Gross Internal Financing and New Security Issues as Percentages of Plant and Equipment Expenditures:

  12. All Manufacturing and Mining Corporations, 1900–1953 125
  13. Large Manufacturing Corporations, 1914–1953 126

All Manufacturing and Mining Corporations, 1900–1953:

  14. Relation between New Security Issues as a Percentage of Total Long-Term Financing and Gross Internal Financing as a Percentage of Plant and Equipment Expenditures 128
  15. Depreciation and Depletion Allowances, and Retained Net Profit, 1900–1953 133
  16. Retained Net Profit and New Security Issues, 1900–1953 135

17. Ratios of Gross Internal Financing to Capital Expenditures on Physical Assets, All Manufacturing and Mining Corporations and Sample, 1913–1954 147
18. Ratios of Debt to Total Assets, All Manufacturing and Mining Corporations with Balance Sheets, by Total-Asset Classes, 1937 and 1948 160

CHARTS

19. New Bond and New Stock Issues, All Manufacturing and Mining Corporations, 1900–1953 165
20. Ratios of Selected Liabilities to Total Assets, Large Manufacturing Corporations, 1900–1954 171
21. Ratios of Short-Term Debt to Total Assets, All Manufacturing and Mining Corporations with Balance Sheets, by Total-Asset Classes, 1937 and 1948 184

Ratios of Selected Assets to Total Assets:
    22. Large Manufacturing Corporations, 1900–1954 185
    23. All Manufacturing and Mining Corporations with Balance Sheets, by Total-Asset Classes, 1937 and 1948 187

ACKNOWLEDGMENTS

PART I is essentially a combining of the materials first published in National Bureau Occasional Papers 41 (*Capital and Output Trends in Manufacturing Industries, 1880–1948*) and 45 (*Capital and Output Trends in Mining Industries, 1870–1948*). The material comprising Part II and all three appendixes is published for the first time in this volume. Accordingly we should like to acknowledge the generous assistance given to us in the preparation first of the Occasional Papers and more recently of the monograph.

We are all greatly indebted to Simon Kuznets for posing the general problems dealt with in this volume and for his continuous counsel along the way. At one stage or another helpful critical comments were gratefully received from Moses Abramovitz, Harold Barger, Solomon Fabricant, Michael Gort, Raymond Goldsmith, Millard Hastay, Geoffrey Moore, Anna J. Schwartz, Eli Shapiro, George Stigler, Alvin Tostlebe, and Melville J. Ulmer, all of the National Bureau Staff, and from Bureau Directors Harold Halcrow, Frank W. Fetter, and Oswald W. Knauth. To others outside the National Bureau, we are also obligated for assistance: to those who made unpublished data available—the Internal Revenue Service, in particular Mr. E. J. Enquist, Jr., and Raymond C. Peacock; Stanley S. Schor, University of Pennsylvania—and to those who graciously permitted us to benefit from their experience in related studies: Frederick J. Moore, Sidney Sonenblum, and W. H. Young of the Bureau of Mines, Arnold C. Harberger when he was engaged on the President's Materials Policy Commission, and Lawrence Bridge of the Office of Business Economics.

Special thanks are due the members of the National Bureau Advisory Committee of the American Institute of Certified Public Accountants. Among them were Messrs. C. W. Bastable, Percival F. Brundage, Albert E. Hunter, J. J. Kesselman, C. H. Martin, Maurice E. Peloubet, A. C. Tietjen, Hassel Tippit, and Edward B. Wilcox, who broadened our understanding of the nature of the changes in accounting practices in the valuation of assets. We are also grateful for the general guidance and review performed by the Advisory Committee on the Study of Capital Formation and Financing. Members of the Committee were Leo Wolman, chairman; Sherwin C. Badger, Donald R. Belcher, Claude L. Benner, Percival F. Brundage, Arthur F. Burns, W. Braddock Hickman, Edgar M. Hoover, Delong H. Monahan, and Geoffrey H. Moore.

There are still other debts: to those who diligently performed the tedious and lengthy transcriptions from the volumes of the *Census of Manufactures*—Madeline Edelstein, Martin Segal, and Ibson Wu; to

ACKNOWLEDGMENTS

those who processed the statistical data with skill, patience, and imagination—Martin Bernstein, Nancy Byrne, and John Myers; to Elizabeth Jenks, whose critical reading of various drafts has rescued us from committing innumerable errors; and to those who prepared the volume for the printer—Ester Moskowitz for her editing and H. Irving Forman for his charts. To all, our sincere thanks.

Daniel Creamer
Sergei Dobrovolsky
Israel Borenstein

Introduction

By Simon Kuznets

This monograph is part of an inquiry into trends and prospects in capital formation and financing initiated by the National Bureau of Economic Research in 1950, with the financial assistance of the Life Insurance Association of America.[1] The inquiry examines long-term trends in capital formation and financing in the United States and is organized primarily around the principal capital-using sectors of the economy—agriculture, mining and manufacturing, the public utilities, residential real estate, and governments. The analysis for each sector summarizes the major trends in real capital formation since 1870 (or the earliest year for which data are available), in financing since 1900 (the earliest practicable date), and the factors determining these trends; and, so far as possible, it suggests the significance of these factors for the future. In addition to the five sector studies, the inquiry includes two others. One deals with trends in financing channeled through intermediate financial institutions and attempts to link the major types of institutions with the various groups of capital users. The second utilizes the results of all the other studies within a framework provided by countrywide estimates of national product and relevant components as well as of assets and debts.

Some of the findings have been presented, in part or in preliminary form, in a series of Occasional and Technical Papers.[2] This monograph, like the four preceding, presents the full results of a specific study, together with the supporting data.

The task the authors of this monograph set themselves appears

NOTE: I am indebted to the authors of the monograph and to Dr. Solomon Fabricant for valuable comments.

[1] Monographs already published are: *Capital Formation in Residential Real Estate: Trends and Prospects*, by Leo Grebler, David M. Blank, and Louis Winnick, 1956; *Capital in Agriculture: Its Formation and Financing since 1870*, by Alvin S. Tostlebe, 1957; *Financial Intermediaries in the American Economy since 1900*, by Raymond W. Goldsmith, 1958; and *Capital in Transportation, Communications, and Public Utilities: Its Formation and Financing*, by Melville J. Ulmer, 1960.

[2] Leo Grebler, *The Role of Federal Credit Aids in Residential Construction*, Occasional Paper 39 (1953); Daniel Creamer, *Capital and Output Trends in Manufacturing Industries, 1880–1948*, Occasional Paper 41 (1954); Raymond W. Goldsmith, *The Share of Financial Intermediaries in National Wealth and National Assets, 1900–1949*, Occasional Paper 42 (1954); Melville J. Ulmer, *Trends and Cycles in Capital Formation by United States Railroads, 1870–1950*, Occasional Paper 43 (1954); Alvin S. Tostlebe, *The Growth of Physical Capital in Agriculture, 1870–1950*, Occasional Paper 44 (1954); Israel Borenstein, *Capital and Output Trends in Mining Industries, 1870–1948*, Occasional Paper 45 (1954); David M. Blank, *The Volume of Residential Construction, 1889–1950*, Technical Paper 9 (1954); all published by the National Bureau of Economic Research.

INTRODUCTION

simple. First, they undertook to compare trends in stock of capital and in output of mining and manufacturing—on the obvious assumption that capital is needed to produce output; and in the reasonable hope that observation of past trends in the relation between the two, via the capital-output ratio, would provide a basis for a better understanding of the factors that determine the demand for capital, in the past and therefore in the future. Second, they attempted to measure the changing contribution of various sources of financing—internal and external, equity and debt—in providing funds for capital formation in mining and manufacturing, again on the reasonable assumption that if past trends could be established, better understanding would be gained of the factors that determine choices among various sources of funds for needed additions to capital assets.

But in this field of capital formation and financing, as in other fields of economic research, tasks that seem simple and obvious when laid out often prove difficult and not at all obvious in execution. The reasons are not hard to find. The present study requires continuous, comparable data over long periods, with the measured quantities geared to clearly defined economic concepts—of capital, output, internal funds, external financing, etc.—and available for a variety of significant divisions within the wide mining and manufacturing aggregates. What one finds for most decades are data only at long intervals, with varying definitions and coverage; and for some important aspects, such as sources of financing relative to total uses, comprehensive, long-term data are not available, and reliance must be placed on samples (some of them small) of large corporations. By dint of laborious and patient effort, the authors secured usable records of stock of capital (at selected dates) back to 1880 or 1870 and of sources of financing back to 1900. But, as they themselves stress, these records leave much to be desired with respect to continuity, comparability, completeness, and detail.

As these incomplete data are examined, the initially simple task is further complicated by a variety of pertinent questions. Granted that capital is needed to produce output, should we take capital gross or net of accumulated depreciation, confine it to real assets or include financial assets; and if the latter, should all financial assets be included or should they be limited to some "working minimum"? Should the denominator of the capital-output ratio be gross value of output, or net value added (i.e., net of cost of materials and fuel), or net income originating (i.e., compensation of productive factors net of all payments to other industries)? On the financing side: Is the gross retention total for an industry aggregate a true measure of funds internal from the viewpoint of each firm, given the possibility of intraindustry, inter-

INTRODUCTION

firm, borrowing and lending? Can gross retention be compared with capital formation alone, or must it always be related to total uses? Is it correct to interpret accumulated tax liabilities, which are treated as short-term debt, as short-term external financing provided to the enterprise by the government? The authors of this monograph, like all scholars in the field of economic research, were forced to revise and sharpen their initial concepts in the light of the variety of questions raised by the empirical data.

Finally, even if questions of the kind suggested are resolved—and the way they are answered will affect the cast of the findings, even if the available data are brought to bear upon the concepts thus revised and specified—the problem of establishing significant long-term trends still remains. For the interest here, as in the other monographs in the series, lies not in the year-to-year or short-term changes. The search is for persistent, underlying trends suggesting long-term factors that could be used in a more informed view of the present and, under reasonable assumptions, of the future. Even with continuous and comparable records stretching over long periods, it is not easy to segregate long trends from the complex of all changes, nor to secure characteristic measures of the former that would permit cogent analysis. When the data are discontinuous and do not cover a long period, and the short-term changes are varied in magnitude and impact, the task becomes difficult indeed. Significant long-term trends are particularly elusive for the financing flows; the financial data extend back only to 1900 and reflect the disturbances of two world wars, the Great Depression (itself partly a postwar maladjustment), and several years of "cold war."

The difficulties just noted—with respect to the quality and quantity of available data, the specification and revision of initially oversimplified concepts, the establishment of orderly patterns of change over time—are quite familiar to those who have ever tried to add to the stock of tested economic knowledge. They may not be so familiar to the wider body of readers for whom, it is hoped, this monograph will be of interest. But they go far to explain why, in this monograph as in others in the series, so much emphasis had to be placed on collating and organizing the relevant data to permit some clear pattern of past trends to emerge, and on establishing the broad movements. They also explain why, for some aspects of the subject, the results are uncertain, forcing the authors to present their conclusions in a hesitant and qualified fashion. And this concentration on securing an acceptable record of past trends means, in view of the limited resources at the disposal of the study, less emphasis on the explanatory framework; a greater emphasis would necessitate additional detail that would carry the study beyond feasible scope.

INTRODUCTION

For these reasons, the present monograph, like the others, emphasizes empirical findings buttressed by detailed evidence. It does not reach out, as deeply as one might wish, into analysis of the underlying factors. This is stated not by way of apology, but as an indication of the priority given to establishing an acceptable record of what would, otherwise, be speculative analysis. On the contrary, we owe a heavy debt to the authors for having persisted in their efforts to wrest testable conclusions from recalcitrant data. It is altogether too tempting to evolve analytical hypotheses unrestrained by empirical evidence: the human imagination abhors the vacuum of ignorance and, for lack of facts, fills it with speculation. It is a more difficult, and often an exasperating, task to organize a vast and inchoate body of raw data in such a way that it may be brought to bear meaningfully upon a series of significant questions.

The following sections of this lengthy introduction present an attempt to summarize the findings in sufficient detail so that the reader can turn to the monograph proper adequately oriented. In pursuing this aim, we try to avoid technicalities and qualifications, courting the danger of oversimplification for the sake of a relatively clear, roughly true, picture. But the discussion goes beyond a summary of empirical findings. It tries to sketch out some explanatory hypotheses, and concludes with comments on the problem of using the findings for analyzing the prospects of capital formation and financing in this country.

Trends in Output and in Capital

In a democratic society, capital is needed to produce final goods, rather than accumulated by the state as a symbol of pride or a weapon of power. Hence, before considering trends in capital formation in the mining and manufacturing sector, we must take account of trends in the output of that sector.

Familiar though these output trends may be, three of their characteristics, observed over the past seven to eight decades, deserve note in the present connection.

First, the rate of growth of output in the mining and manufacturing sector has been high—appreciably higher than that of the economy's total output as measured by national product. In 1880, the first year for which we have figures on capital in mining and manufacturing, the total value of output of the sector was $8.73 billion in 1929 prices (all figures for 1953, here and elsewhere in this summary, have been adjusted for comparability with those for prior years). By 1953, the value of product amounted to $173.66 billion, again in 1929 prices, an increase to almost twentyfold the 1880 level. Over the same period, gross

INTRODUCTION

national product in 1929 prices rose from $18.0 billion to $185.0 billion, or to only about tenfold.[3] This comparison is affected, however, by the fact that the national product is gross only in that consumption of fixed capital is not deducted. Thus, it is a much "netter" total than value of product for manufacturing and mining, which includes costs of raw materials and other goods produced in other industries. A more direct comparison can be made if, instead of value of product, we use either net income originating or payments to factors in the sector—the net return to labor, capital, and enterprise in the sector. The contribution of mining and manufacturing to national income or aggregate payments (all are totals in current prices) was 15.4 per cent in 1880 and almost 30 per cent in 1944–1953. Thus, we are dealing here with a major sector of the country's industrial structure, one that grew over the last three-quarters of a century at a rate almost double that of national product.

Second, the rate of growth of mining and manufacturing output was subject not only to cyclical fluctuations, which do not concern us here, but also to long-term retardation. Between 1880 and 1900, total output grew from $8.73 billion to $23.16 billion (all figures here and below are in 1929 prices), or at the rate of 62.9 per cent per decade; from 1900 to the average of 1919 and 1929 (centered in 1924), it grew further to $61.40 billion, or at the rate of 50.1 per cent per decade; then it rose to $173.7 billion in 1953, or at the rate of 43.1 per cent per decade. The particular sequence of percentage rates of growth over successive long periods, and the extent of retardation revealed by them, depend partly upon our choice of the dates. These should relate to years not too far from secular levels and should distinguish intervals long enough so that the effects of the cycles and long swings that characterize rates of economic growth in this country can be canceled out. But, even without recourse to elaborate curve fitting, any justifiable selection of dates and periods would reveal a significant slowing down in the percentage rate of growth of mining and manufacturing output measured in constant prices.

Third, among the various industries within the sector, there were marked differences both in the rate of growth of output over the period as a whole and in the patterns of these secular rates of growth over time. Thus, while the output of the mining industries rose from $363 million in 1880 to $6,460 million in 1953, an increase to almost eighteenfold the 1880 level, the growth in coal output was from $225 million to $989 million, or to over fourfold; in metals, from $76 million

[3] See *Capital in the American Economy: Its Formation and Financing* (forthcoming), Appendix A, Table R-2 and Appendix C, unpublished extension of Table R-22.

INTRODUCTION

to $731 million, or to almost tenfold; and in petroleum and natural gas, from $33 million to $3,939 million, or to well over a hundredfold. Likewise, value of product in total manufacturing rose from $8.36 billion in 1880 to $167.20 billion in 1953, a rise to twentyfold the 1880 level. But in the more slowly growing branches the rise was smaller. Thus, in leather and its manufactures, the rise was only from $0.93 billion to $1.98 billion, or to over twofold; and in forest products, from $1.54 billion to $4.27 billion, or to less than threefold. By contrast, in the more rapidly growing branches, the rates were far higher: the output of chemicals and allied substances increased from $0.29 billion to $11.52 billion, or to more than fortyfold; iron and steel products, from $0.46 billion to $13.83 billion (in 1948, comparable data for 1953 not being available), or to thirtyfold; and transportation equipment, from $0.051 billion to $17.76 billion, or to nearly three hundred fiftyfold. Even more extreme differences in rates of growth over the period would be found were we to deal with the *minor* industry branches within mining and manufacturing; we would find industries that have ceased growing and whose output had declined by 1953 to a vanishing point, and others that sprang up after 1880 and whose percentage rates of growth have been astronomically high.

With such large differences in rates of growth of output among the various industries within the sector, it would be surprising not to find also differences among them in the pattern of growth rates over time. To be sure, retardation in the rate of growth is a common feature: it is found both in the older industries and also in the young and emergent industries. In the older industries, exhaustion of domestic natural resources, the slowing down of the rate of technological change, and the competition of the newer industries all make for damping of the rates of growth. In the younger industries, the very high early rates of increase—a doubling or tripling in a few years—just cannot be sustained once the production base, from which the percentage increase is calculated, widens. But the formal similarity—the retardation commonly observed—is overshadowed by differences in the absolute level of the rates: a shift in the rate of growth from 20 to 19 per cent per decade in a large and already mature industry, and from 1,000 to 100 per cent per decade in a young and rapidly growing industry, are both instances of retardation; but, for many realistic purposes, particularly for estimating the effect on capital formation and capital-output ratios, they are worlds apart. And in some cases, exceptions emerge in the very pattern in which retardation occurs. Thus, from 1880 to 1900, the output of all textile materials (excluding carpets, knit goods, and clothing) rose by 36.9 per cent per decade; from 1900 to the average of 1919 and 1929 (centered in 1924), by 47.5 per cent per

INTRODUCTION

decade; and from the latter point to 1948, by 17.7 per cent per decade. In this case, there was *acceleration* between the first and second interval followed by a sharp retardation in the third. By contrast, in the forest products group, the rate of growth per decade in the first interval was 46.7 per cent; in the second, there was a *decline* of more than 6 per cent per decade; and in the third, a rate of increase of 17.2 per cent per decade. Here, then, growth accelerated from the second to the third interval. Thus, even where retardation is the dominant pattern, different combinations of rates over the three intervals can be found.

Since growth of output is a major factor in the growth of capital, we would expect that the three features just observed—a high rate of growth, significantly in excess of that in the countrywide total; a distinct retardation in the rate of growth over time; and marked diversity among industries in the rate of growth over the period and in the time pattern of that rate—would be true also of the stock of capital used in the mining and manufacturing sector. And this is what we find. In 1880, the unduplicated total of capital assets in the sector, including fixed capital, inventories, and cash and receivables, was, in 1929 prices and for the coverage comparable with that in recent years, $5.55 billion; by 1948, it amounted to $82.68 billion—a rise to almost fifteenfold the earlier level. Over the same period, the total stock of all tangible wealth in this country, including land and international assets but excluding consumers' inventories and military goods, increased from $69.5 billion in 1880 to $429.5 billion in 1948, a rise to over sixfold.[4] But here, again, the comparison is affected in that capital assets for the mining and manufacturing sector include domestic financial claims, and the countrywide wealth totals do not. A more defensible comparison can be made between the growth of fixed capital (structures and equipment, including land) in the mining and manufacturing sector and in the country. If we use, as always, totals in 1929 prices and coverage comparable with that in 1919–1948, fixed capital in the sector (not adjusted for duplication between manufacturing and mining) can be set at $3.23 billion in 1880 and $42.85 billion in 1948, a rise in level to over thirteenfold. The roughly comparable figures for the country are $60.2 billion in 1880 and $350.7 billion in 1948,[5] a rise to less than sixfold. Thus, the share of the country's fixed capital accounted for by the sector rose from about 5.4 per cent in 1880 to over 12 per cent in 1948—a more than doubling of the share.

[4] See Raymond W. Goldsmith in "Income and Wealth of the United States," *Income and Wealth, Series II* (International Association for Research in Income and Wealth, Bowes and Bowes, Cambridge, England), Table II, p. 310.
[5] *Ibid.*, Tables I and II, pp. 306–307 and 310.

INTRODUCTION

We find also, as in the case of output, a marked retardation in the rate of growth of capital. For total capital assets in the sector (adjusted to eliminate duplication between manufacturing and mining), the rise from 1880 to 1900 was as high as 92.7 per cent per decade; from 1900 to the average of 1919 and 1929 (centered in 1924), the rise was down to 61.0 per cent per decade; from 1924 to 1953, it was as low as 17.8 per cent per decade. The estimates of fixed capital including land (not adjusted to eliminate duplication) tell a similar story of marked slowing down in the rate of growth. The rate of rise from 1880 to 1900 was 92.5 per cent per decade; from 1900 to the average of 1919 and 1929, 59.4 per cent per decade; from 1924 to 1953, 12.3 per cent per decade. It will be noted that the rate of growth of capital in the early periods was appreciably higher than that of output, but lower in the later period. As a result, the retardation in the rate of growth of capital is much more marked. We shall return to this point below in dealing with the movement of the capital-output ratios.

Finally, just as in the case of output, there are wide interindustry differences in the rate of growth of capital over the period and in the pattern of growth over time. Thus, total capital assets in mining rose from $1.03 billion in 1880 to $8.87 billion in 1953, or to less than ninefold the 1880 level. Over the same period, capital in manufacturing (unadjusted for duplication between manufacturing and mining) rose from $4.52 billion to $98.6 billion, an increase to almost twenty-twofold. Within mining, the value of capital (excluding land) in coal rose over the period from $147 million to $1,069 million, or to over sevenfold; in metal, from $174 million to $1,019 million, or to almost sixfold; but in petroleum and natural gas, from $68 million to $5,550 million, or to over eightyfold. Within manufacturing, the rise over the period ranges from that for leather and its products to that for transportation equipment. In the former, total capital rose from $298 million in 1880 to $819 million in 1953, or to less than three times the 1880 level; in the latter, the rise was from $18 million to $8,771 million, or to almost five hundredfold. And, while retardation in rates of growth of capital was widespread, the differences in absolute levels of the growth rates were persistently important.

Trends in the Capital-Output Ratios—The Findings

In the capital-output ratio the numerator may be capital either including or excluding land and financial assets, net or gross of accumulated depreciation, in current valuation or translated to constant prices. The denominator may be gross value of output, or net value added, or net income originating, in current or constant prices,

INTRODUCTION

and may cover output for a month, a year, or a decade. Finally, the ratio may be of the stock of capital at some point of time to the output during the period to which this point is relevant (*average* capital-output ratio); or it may be of the *change* in capital over some interval to the *change* in output over the same or another relevant interval (*marginal* or incremental capital-output ratio).

Our summary here will be largely in terms of the *average* capital-output ratio, relating either total or fixed capital, net of depreciation, to value of product, all in 1929 prices. This choice is due partly to the availability of detailed data, partly to analytical considerations. In general, movements of the ratio will reflect the similarities in or differences between the trends of output and of capital measured in constant prices. If these trends are similar, the capital-output ratio will show long-term constancy; if the trends in output and capital differ in some systematic way, there will be corresponding systematic movements in the capital-output ratios. If the ratios show long-term constancy, the finding is of obvious importance both analytically and in projecting capital formation as a simple function of projected output (projected output for a sector being, in turn, a function of projected national product). If the capital-output ratios for a sector show systematic long-term movements, the finding throws into relief both the analytical problem—how to explain these movements—and the problem of prognosis—how the factors advanced in the explanation bear upon future prospects of capital formation. In either case, the use of constant price data in calculating the ratio removes the distortion due to lags between changes in valuation of capital and prices of output.

1. In both manufacturing and mining, the ratio of capital to output based on values in 1929 prices rose markedly from 1880 through 1919 and then declined just as markedly. Thus, in manufacturing, the ratio of net total capital to gross value of product rose from 0.54 in 1880 to 1.02 in 1919 and then dropped to 0.61 in 1948 (and, still further, to 0.59 in 1953); ratio of capital to value added moved from 1.51 in 1880 to 2.55 in 1919 and down to 1.55 in 1948. In other words, whereas in 1880 it took 0.54 dollar of capital to produce one dollar of manufacturing output (or 1.51 dollars of capital to produce one dollar of manufacturing value added), in 1919 it took almost double that capital to produce a dollar of output or of value added. Then the situation changed, and by 1948 the capital needed to produce a dollar's worth of output or of value added dropped back to levels only slightly higher than those of 1880. In mining, the ratio of capital (excluding land) to value of output rose from 0.7 in 1870 to 2.3 in 1919 and then declined to 1.3 in 1948 (and 1953). These movements mean, as already indicated, that up through 1919, capital in both manufacturing and mining grew

INTRODUCTION

at rates significantly higher than those of output, whereas after 1919 the reverse was the case.

2. These long-term rises and declines in the *average* capital-output ratios imply an even more conspicuous reversal in the levels of the *marginal* or incremental capital-output ratios. If the average capital-output ratio rises from time 1 to time 2, the marginal ratio over the interval must necessarily be *above* the higher of the two average ratios (i.e. above that for time 2); if the average capital-output ratio declines from time 1 to time 2, the marginal ratio over the interval must necessarily be *below* the lower of the two average ratios (i.e. below that for time 2).[6] Thus, when the average capital-output ratios are rising, the marginal ratios for each interval must be above the higher of the two terminal average ratios. Then, when the average capital-output ratio turns downward, the marginal ratios must drop below the lower of the two average ratios in each interval. The resulting violent movement of the marginal ratios can be illustrated by the estimate for total manufacturing. The average capital-output ratio was 0.54 in 1880, rose to 0.79 in 1900, and the mean of the two values for the period was 0.66. The marginal capital-output ratio for that interval was as high as 0.95. From 1900 to 1919, the average ratio rose again, from 0.79 to 1.02 (the mean thus being 0.905). Over that interval, the marginal ratio was as high as 1.24. Then, from 1919 to 1948, the average ratio dropped from 1.02 to 0.61 (the mean being 0.815, as compared with that of 0.905 for 1900–1919). But the marginal ratio for 1919–1948 was as low as 0.38, less than a third of the level of the marginal ratio for 1900–1919. With the detailed series available in the monograph, it is easy to calculate the marginal capital-output ratios for successive intervals and to show how widely they vary over time. The significance of these findings is that through 1919 it took much larger net additions to capital to produce a dollar of net additions to output than was the case after 1919.

[6] This can be shown by simple algebra. Assume that C_2/O_2 is larger than C_1/O_1, i.e. the average capital-output ratio at time 2 is larger than that at time 1. Then:

$(C_2/O_2 : C_1/O_1)$ is larger than 1, and it follows that
$C_2 O_1$ is larger than $C_1 O_2$. (1)

The marginal capital-output ratio over the interval is:

$(C_2 - C_1)/(O_2 - O_1)$

It can be shown that under the condition stated above (viz. that C_2/O_2 is larger than C_1/O_1), this marginal ratio will be larger than C_2/O_2. Thus:

$[(C_2 - C_1)/(O_2 - O_1)] : C_2/O_2 = (C_2 O_2 - C_1 O_2)/(C_2 O_2 - C_2 O_1)$ (2)

Since, as we know from expression (1) above, $C_1 O_2$ is smaller than $C_2 O_1$, it follows that the right-hand side of expression (2) must be larger than 1 and, hence, the marginal ratio larger than C_2/O_2.

The same reasoning will show that if the average capital-output ratio declines, i.e., if C_2/O_2 is smaller than C_1/O_1, the marginal ratio over the interval will be smaller than C_2/O_2.

INTRODUCTION

3. The long-term rise of the average capital-output ratio through 1919 and the equally marked long-term decline thereafter were general, i.e., these movements characterized the distinguishable subgroups of capital as well as the different industrial branches within mining and manufacturing. For manufacturing, we can distinguish between fixed capital (plant and equipment) and working capital (inventories, cash, and receivables) for selected dates between 1890 and 1953. The ratio of fixed capital to output rises from 0.36 in 1890 to 0.47 in 1904, drops slightly to 0.43 in 1929, and then declines to 0.285 in 1948 (falling still further to 0.27 in 1953). The ratio of working capital to output rises from 0.36 in 1890 to 0.45 in 1929, and then declines to 0.32 in 1948 (and 1953). Thus, in both cases, we have the rise to the twenties and then the decline. Significantly, the drop in the ratio of working capital to output is not as great as the decline in the ratio of fixed capital to output. For mining, we can distinguish between plant (net value of structures and equipment) and working capital (defined as in manufacturing), for the full period, from 1870 to 1953. The ratio of plant to output rises from 0.61 in 1870 to a peak of 2.00 in 1919, and then drops to a trough of 0.84 in 1953. The ratio of working capital to output rises from 0.11 in 1870 to a peak of 0.57 in 1929, and then declines to 0.42 in 1953. Here again, both components show the rise and decline in the ratio to total output; but the ratio of working capital to output declines less, and the relative excess of its level in 1953 over that in the earliest year is greater. It follows that in both manufacturing and mining, at least since the twenties, the share of working capital in total capital increased, and the share of fixed capital decreased.

4. Even more important is the fact that this long-term rise and decline in the capital-output ratios is observed, with fair synchronism, in the great majority of the industrial branches within both manufacturing and mining. This can be demonstrated by calculating the proportion of the movement in the capital-output ratio for total manufacturing and mining due to such movement *within* each industry, i.e., eliminating the effects of changes in weights *among* the industries by holding industry weights constant. The calculation for manufacturing, for 1880–1919, using thirty-eight minor industries weighted by 1919 output, shows that as much as 83 per cent of the rise in the capital-output ratio for all manufacturing was due to the rise in the ratios *within* each industry, and only 17 per cent to interindustry shifts. A similar calculation for 1880–1909, using 1909 output weights, again shows that 85 per cent of the rise in the ratio for total manufacturing over the interval was due to the movement of the ratios *within* the minor industries, and only 15 per cent to shifts in industry weights. The results of a similar analysis for the phase of secular

decline of the ratio are even more striking. From 1919 to 1937, the capital-output ratio for all manufacturing declined by about a quarter. The effect of shifts *among* industries, using 1937 output weights, would have been to *raise* the ratio slightly; it follows that *all* of the decline in the ratio for total manufacturing was due to the decline in the minor industry ratios.

The results of an analogous calculation for mining suggest similar conclusions. The capital-output ratio for total mining rose from 0.72 in 1870 to 2.30 in 1919, or by 1.58. Over this same interval, with the industry ratios held at their 1890 levels, the changing weights of the industries within mining would have produced a rise of 0.66 in the ratio. This shows that the movement of the ratios *within* the industries accounted for about six-tenths of the rise in the ratio for total mining. In the declining phase, the ratio for total mining dropped from 2.30 in 1919 to 1.34 in 1948. The shift in weights among industries would have made for a *rise* in the ratio for total mining. Hence, all of the decline in the capital-output ratio for mining after 1919 was due to the decline of the ratios *within* the industries.

5. For manufacturing, both theoretical expectation and empirical observation indicate that the capital-output ratios are higher for the larger than for the smaller plants and firms. From 1880 onward, large plants and firms became increasingly important. This must have been a factor contributing to the observed rise in the capital-output ratio for total manufacturing. However, we have no data by which to measure the effect of this factor, nor can we assume that the growth of large plants and firms was independent of the whole complex of forces (some of which will be suggested below) that made for the secular rise in the capital-output ratio. But large plants and firms continued to increase in importance after 1919. This means that the decline in the capital-output ratio for total manufacturing since 1919 occurred *despite* the rise in the indicated trend toward larger firms. Indeed, data for 1937–1947 indicate that the fixed capital-output ratios of large firms declined more than did the ratios of small firms.

Trends in the Capital-Output Ratios—Some Hypotheses

The findings above reveal that, at least for manufacturing and mining, a secular rise in the capital-output ratio, extending from the 1870's and 1880's through 1919 or 1929, and a secular decline thereafter, were generally observed throughout the sector, and could hardly have been either a statistical or historical accident. While it is not possible to provide a tested and thorough explanation of these trends, tentative analysis should be illuminating, particularly for the use of these findings as bases for assaying future prospects.

INTRODUCTION

In such a tentative explanation, a secular *decline* in capital-output ratios may be easily ascribed to the pressure for reducing costs and maximizing profits. A high capital-output ratio may contribute to higher costs in several ways. First, and most obvious, are the interest charges—overt or imputed—on the capital thus tied up. If the capital-output ratio is 2 instead of 1, two dollars of capital investment are tied up in producing one dollar of output (i.e., gross recovery). If the interest rate is, say, 6 per cent, the cost to be recovered out of the proceeds of output—in whatever form such recovery appears (interest on equity may appear as a component of total net profits)—is 12 cents instead of 6 cents. Second, to the extent that capital is consumable and depreciable, which is true of plant and equipment, a higher capital-output ratio means either a higher ratio of depreciation charges to cost of output, or a longer life over which depreciation, i.e., recovery of capital assets, is spread. In the former case, there is a larger cost element in current output; in the latter case, the enterprise is exposed for a longer period to risks of obsolescence, loss of markets, and any other economic danger implicit in a slow recovery of investment. Third, there is a limit to the size of capital that any single firm can secure—if only because of the necessary balance between equity and debt. If, then, the maximum capital of an enterprise is set at X, a lower capital-output ratio would mean that much more output and sales volume. Since profits are, at least in part, a function of sales volume, a lower capital-output ratio would mean a higher rate of profit for total capital—and an even higher rate on the equity share of it.

These arguments could be expounded further, but it is hardly necessary to labor this obvious point. The economic incentive to minimize the stock of capital tied up per unit of output is clear and strong—just as is the incentive to minimize the inputs of other costly factors of production. But there is this significant difference in the case under consideration: capital *stock* rather than flow is involved; for this stock (unlike the stock of labor services), the firm carries the risk and responsibility. Thus, one could assume that, *unless* other factors intervened, economic incentives would bring about a persistent reduction and consequently, a secular decline in the capital-output ratios.

The other factors are numerous: technological and related social inventions, whose application requires tangible capital goods of large size and long life, and changes and innovations in financing, which may require a higher ratio of financial assets to output. The technological innovations are perhaps most important and, certainly, most conspicuous. If a small machine costing $100,000 can, because of

INTRODUCTION

a new invention, be replaced by one costing $1 million, with somewhat larger capacity but much longer life and much lower cost per unit of product, the replacement will be made. However, unless output can be immediately increased tenfold (which is rarely the case), the capital-output ratio will rise, and may remain at a higher level for a long time. Much of modern technical change inherently involves larger volumes of power, more costly construction materials, and more elaborate functions (mechanical or chemical). Thus, it requires plant and machinery of ever increasing size, and the rise in the volume of capital thus tied up exceeds, for a long period, the possible rise in the volume of output. Furthermore, there are always changes in the capacity for organizing large plants and large firms—partly necessitated by, partly inherent in, the changing technology of production proper—which call for an ever increasing scale of operation. Insofar as it is feasible to have larger plants and firms—to the extent that the limit upon the maximum amount of capital that can be tied up in a single firm is lifted—a higher capital-output ratio can be tolerated, and the pressure for reducing the ratio for any of the reasons suggested above is lessened. Also, new forms of credit and new types of financial institutions may facilitate growth in the size of firms and the volume of capital, for they may permit easier mobilization of equity funds and a higher ratio of debt (particularly long-term) to equity.

As compared with these technological, and closely related organizational, innovations that make for higher capital-output ratios, those that contribute to the building up of financial assets seem less important. As plants and firms grow in size, and as the division of labor increases among them in various industries, conditions may develop under which the producing units must, in order to facilitate output and sales, extend short-term credit to the buyers of their products. As a result of such practices, receivables may grow more rapidly than output. Likewise, a need may develop for cash balances. With the economic size of such firms increasing, and the cost of cash to them declining, cash balances may rise not only absolutely but also proportionately to output. Thus, it is likely that, during some periods of an industry's growth, its financial assets may grow at a greater rate than the volume of its output. In a rapidly expanding industry, an expansion of short-term credit to buyers may facilitate the high rate of growth of the market for its products. At the same time, the rate of growth of its cash balances may be high as a by-product of the rapidly increasing volume of its net profits and total turnover.

Thus, the life span of an industry, as reflected in the secular movement of its capital-output ratio, may be envisaged as the result of continuous competition between technological and other innovations, many of which serve to raise the ratio, and economic incentives which, again through technical changes and managerial improvements, just as continuously operate to depress the ratio. In general, in the earlier phases of a modern industry's vigorous growth, the ratio-raising factors seem to preponderate. It is in these phases that capital-demanding technological innovations come thick and fast; that the optimum scale of plant and firm increases rapidly; that, with the rapid growth of the market, as evidenced by high percentage rates of growth of the industry's output, the main pressure upon enterprises is for rapid expansion of capacity and volume of output—under relatively favorable price-cost relations in a growing market. Then, as the industry reaches large size and comparative maturity, accompanied by a much higher ratio of capital to output than that characterizing it in its early decades, the pressure for economy in the use of capital increases. The very slowing down in the rate of growth of output that typically ensues permits greater concentration upon a host of refinements in the use of capital, with resulting economies for which there is great scope within the already existing network of plant and equipment. Thus, after a certain phase in the life of an industry is reached, the ratio-depressing factors are likely to begin to outweigh the ratio-raising forces, and a secular decline in the capital-output ratio begins.

Several comments supplementing this rather sketchy picture of an industry's life cycle of capital-output ratios can be made.

1. The first relates to the role of undercapacity utilization of fixed capital in the early phases of an industry's growth and to the effects of an increasing ratio of capital replacement (consumption) to total capital in the later phases. Both conditions accentuate the secular movement of the capital-output ratios. In the early phases of an industry's growth, the construction of new capacity, because of indivisibilities and prospective long life of the plant and equipment, may result in additions geared to the longer future. Suppose the optimum scale is a plant whose full capacity is 10 million units per year. Further suppose that the market will not warrant full capacity output for several years to come. Nevertheless, it may pay to build such a full-capacity plant rather than a less economical plant capable, at full utilization, of producing only 1 million units per year. In the early phases of an industry's growth, when rapid and large increases in the market are expected, such large additions to capacity that are bound to be temporarily underutilized may be fully warranted by economic calculation. *If* such additions to what is temporarily overcapacity constitute an increasing fraction of total capital, the result would be not only relatively high but *rising* capital-output ratios; such additions

INTRODUCTION

would raise the ratios over and above the technological and related changes that would warrant higher capital-output ratios under the assumption of full utilization of capacity. Then, as the industry matures and the percentage rate of its growth declines, the economic justification for such future-oriented additions to capacity is weakened, and the effects of such additions on high and rising capital-output ratios slacken.

As the rate of growth of capital diminishes, another factor comes into play that may contribute to a secular decline in the capital-output ratio. Given a constant life period of depreciable capital, a high rate of growth of gross fixed capital formation means a low ratio of current capital consumption to total stock of fixed capital; conversely, a low rate of growth of gross fixed capital formation means a high ratio of current capital consumption to the total stock of fixed capital. Assume a life span of, say, twenty years, straight line depreciation, and a million units of gross fixed capital formation in the first year. Assume that no growth takes place during the following twenty years, i.e., annual gross fixed capital formation is exactly a million units per year. Then in the twenty-first year, capital consumption will equal current gross fixed capital formation and will be a tenth of the total net stock of accumulated fixed capital. If any growth in annual volume of gross fixed capital formation is assumed, capital consumption in the twenty-first year will be smaller than gross capital formation in that year and will be below a tenth of the total accumulated stock of fixed capital. Hence, with constant life, a slowing down in the rate of growth of gross capital formation means a rising ratio of capital consumption to total fixed capital (whether gross or net of depreciation). An additional relevant consideration is that, with the growth of an industry to maturity, a slowing down in the rate of growth of capital formation is often accompanied by a decline in the share of long-lived construction in total fixed capital and a rise in the share of shorter-lived equipment. The resulting reduction in the weighted average life of depreciable capital contributes further to an increase in the ratio of capital consumption to fixed or total capital.

Capital replacement, under conditions of modern technology, raises the productive capacity of capital, even when the calculation is in constant prices, since the adjustment for price changes does not correct for growth in the productive power of the dollar spent on plant and machinery. Hence, the same stock of capital in constant prices will be capable of turning out a larger volume of output if a larger proportion of that stock is replaced during the year. Assume that replacement means an increase of 100 per cent in productive power, not an unrealistic figure if the life span involved is as long as twenty years; and

INTRODUCTION

that fixed capital remains the same both in years 1 and 2 and years 51 and 52. However, in year 2, capital consumption (replacement) is 5 per cent of fixed capital, and in year 52 it is 10 per cent. The increase in the productive power of the capital of the same volume (as measured by us in the numerator of the capital-output ratio) is, therefore, 5 per cent from year 1 to year 2 and 10 per cent from year 51 to year 52. If output in both intervals rises by the same percentage, say, 5 per cent, and if the capital is geared to capacity use, the average fixed capital-output ratio will remain the same in years 1 and 2, but will decline from year 51 to year 52.

The relevance of these comments to the model of secular movements of capital-output ratios is obvious. This is evidenced by our earlier finding that the rate of growth of capital, particularly fixed capital, declined in both mining and manufacturing. The overcapacity additions in the early phases of an industry's life span, and the secular rise in the ratio of capital consumption (replacement) to total and fixed capital may accentuate the secular movement of the capital-output ratios, both the rise in the upward phase of the secular swing and the decline in the downward phase.

2. The preceding discussion clearly suggests that the extent to which the secular capital-output ratios can rise during the upward phase and fall in the downward phase is fairly narrowly limited. To begin with, there is a limit to the impact of technological changes in enlarging the scale of operations and increasing the intensity of capital as measured by the ratio of capital to output. An industry is a circumscribed framework of operations. After the major technological innovations have been made in it, much less room remains for additional *economical* major inventions and improvements. Furthermore, no single industry can long grow at constant percentage rates of increase of output. Eventually, the rate of growth must retard. Retardation reduces the raising effects of advance overcapacity construction on the level of the capital-output ratio. Thus, even without capital-saving innovations, there would be an upper limit to the capital-output ratio. And the level of such a limit is all the lower because, as the capital-output ratio rises, the room and incentive for capital-saving innovations increases; and as growth of capital slackens, the effect of the rising ratio of replacement to stock of capital begins to come into play.

If, in any given industry (or complex of industries), there is an upper limit, a ceiling, to the secular rise of the capital-output ratio there must likewise be a lower limit, a floor, to the decline. To begin with, the economic incentive for capital-saving innovations and improvements slackens as the capital-output ratio declines. Furthermore, there are always technological and other changes that make for a higher

INTRODUCTION

capital-output ratio even in the mature industries with slowly growing output; changes may originate in the technology of other sectors. (Witness the effect of innovations in packing and quick-freezing on some of the oldest and most mature food industries.) It is, thus, unlikely that the secular decline of the ratios, even of the fixed capital-output ratio, will reach fractions close to the impossible zero level. With reference to the total capital-output ratios, the same point is strengthened by consideration of the working capital components, whose ratios to output need not decline as much as those of durable and depreciable capital.

3. The model sketched out so far implies a positive correlation between the rate of growth of an industry's output and its capital-output ratio. In the earlier phases of an industry's life, when the rate of growth of its output is high, its capital tends to grow at an even higher rate, and the capital-output ratio rises. In the later phases, the percentage rate of growth of output is much lower, capital grows at an even lower rate, and the capital-output ratio declines.

Of course, the association is rough, rather than continuous: the percentage rate of growth of an industry's output retards even in the early decades when the capital-output ratio is still rising. Here, I comment upon this association not because of its importance for the analysis of secular changes in the capital-output ratios of the type summarized in the preceding section, but because of its much greater relevance to the analysis of shorter, though still secular, movements—specifically, the long swings of about twenty years, which have been noted in so many series relating to output and other aspects of the economy of this country. There is reason to argue that such shorter-term accelerations and decelerations in the rate of growth of output would tend to be accompanied by even greater rises and declines in the rate of additions to capital and, hence, by alternations in the capital-output ratios. The estimates of capital in manufacturing suggest the existence of these twenty-year swings in the rate of its growth, but the data are not sufficiently continuous to permit an analysis of them in comparison with the long swings in the rate of growth of output.

4. Finally, one may note that the implications of the model for the fixed capital-output ratio differ from those for the ratio of working capital to output. A great part of our discussion applied to the ratio of fixed capital to output. Some implications relevant to the ratio of inventories to output may be drawn. Thus, one could expect that high and rising ratios of fixed capital to output in the earlier phases of an industry's growth would, all other conditions being equal, make for high and rising ratios of inventories to output (relatively larger sup-

plies of raw materials, goods in process, etc.). Likewise, the greater economy in the use of capital in the later phases of the growth of an industry might make for declining inventory-output ratios. But the effect of indivisibilities and the requirements of large-scale operation do not apply to inventories with the same force as they do to fixed capital; nor does the argument relating to the effect of a rising ratio of capital replacement to stock of capital apply to inventories. It is quite likely, therefore, that both the rise of the inventory-output ratio in the upward phase (if there be a rise at all) and the decline of this ratio in the downward phase are milder than the secular movement of the fixed capital-output ratio. Data for manufacturing, available from 1919 on, do tend to suggest that the decline of the inventory-output ratio up to 1948 was much less than that of the fixed capital-output ratio.

Few of the arguments adduced above apply to the ratios of financial assets (cash and receivables) to output. To be sure, there would always be an incentive to minimize both the absolute volume of funds tied up in these assets and the volume per dollar of output. Technological and related organizational changes can make for larger scale operation, enormously larger units of long-lived capital equipment, and rising fixed capital-output ratios. Just so, changes in the business and credit structure of industries can make for larger volumes of cash and receivables, absolutely and even in relation to output. In a purely formal way, the model of the secular movement of the financial assets-output ratio may, like that of the fixed or the total capital-output ratio, appear to be a combination of factors, some of which press for a higher ratio of capital to output, and others, for a lower ratio. But the relative strength and timing of the ratio-raising and -depressing factors that act on the financial assets-output ratio need not be the same as those that act on the fixed capital-output ratio. One may argue, in particular, that the very increase in the size of firms, which accompanies the coming of an industry to maturity, facilitates, and sometimes necessitates, increases in cash holdings and in short-term credit extensions through receivables (in many cases, the big firms have assumed a sort of banking and financial function to meet their own needs and those of their customers). Thus, in the downward phase of the life-cycle of capital-output ratios, the ratio of financial assets to output need not decline as drastically as does the ratio of fixed capital to output.

The brief discussion above can hardly be considered an adequate explanation of the findings concerning the secular movements of the capital-output ratio in mining and manufacturing. An adequate explanation would require more statistical and other documentation that would draw heavily upon the historical records of the major

INTRODUCTION

branches within the sector.[7] Such an undertaking is beyond the scope of the present monograph. But the hypotheses suggested do bear directly upon the major findings. Moreover, they carry some validity in that the major arguments are closely associated with the generally observed characteristics of industrial growth in dynamic economies, such as that of this country. After all, the retardation in the growth of output has been found in several studies of industrial growth in this country, and much of the structure of the hypotheses above is anchored in the broad differences between the early and the later phases of the life-cycle of an industry's growth.

The discussion above suggests, then, that the mining and manufacturing sector of the United States grew most rapidly from the 1870's to the 1920's. During this time, its share in national income rose from about 16 to 25 per cent; and, in this typical period of early and rapid growth, the capital-output ratio-raising technological and social changes tended to preponderate. High capital-output ratios were reached by the twenties. Since then the share of the sector in national income has risen by only five to six points, the rates of growth of output have been much lower than in the decades preceding 1919, and the capital-saving, capital-output ratio-reducing factors have tended to preponderate.

The consideration of these capital-output ratio-raising and -depressing factors led to some suggestions concerning secular trends in the structure of capital assets and to some implications concerning the trends in financing. We turn now to a direct consideration of this aspect of capital formation in mining and manufacturing.

---

[7] Thus, no explicit consideration was given to the relative prices of other factors of production—raw materials and labor—regarding which various speculative hypotheses could be advanced. For example, it could be argued that an industry in the early period of its growth has to draw labor for its rapidly growing working force away from other industries. Such labor is more expensive relative to prevailing rates. This higher cost, combined with the limited experience of the working force in what is, essentially, a new process, provides further stimulus for the use of capital. Consequently, the capital-output ratios must rise. Likewise, any difficulties in obtaining an adequate supply of raw materials to feed a rapidly expanding industry would exert pressure for greater economies in the use of materials. Such economies might be attained by a more elaborate, and more capital-demanding, way of utilizing the materials. But these are, necessarily, speculations. Equally speculative are considerations relating to possible changes, in the course of an industry's growth, in the functions that it will retain, and those that it may transfer to others, e.g., the transfer of the manufacture of power from the manufacturing industry to central power stations. Clearly, the purpose of the brief discussion in the text is not to provide a complete and tested theory of industrial growth that could be used to derive the pattern of movement of the observed capital-output ratios; rather, the purpose is to suggest particular factors that seem most likely to account for the actual trends in the capital-output ratios as they have been revealed by the empirical investigation on which this monograph reports.

INTRODUCTION

Trends in Financing—External and Internal

The data on financing of capital formation in mining and manufacturing are far less adequate than those on long-term changes in the stock of capital. To begin with, the former extend back only to 1900. Second, they relate to corporations alone. However, the exclusion of unincorporated firms is not too damaging a limitation since, even in the decade before World War I, corporations accounted for over 80 per cent of total output and, probably, for an even greater share of capital.[8] Third, even for corporations, estimates relating to the total include, for the full period since 1900, only gross retention (depreciation and depletion charges plus net retained profits) and new security issues; for other forms of financing, particularly short-term, we have to rely on samples of large corporations with a coverage that becomes distressingly thin as we go back in time. Finally, the structure of financing is subject to rapid and violent fluctuations, associated with business cycles, wars, and changes in tax policy. As a result, long-term trends in financing are more difficult to establish and are subject to greater error than are those in capital in constant prices or even in capital-output ratios. The findings summarized below should, therefore, be taken with great caution—particularly in their possible use as bases for analyzing future prospects.

1. Gross internal financing (gross retention)—depreciation and depletion charges plus undistributed net profits—in manufacturing and mining represents a much greater proportion of total new financing than do external funds. For all corporations, gross internal financing during 1900–1953 totaled $180 billion, over five times as much as the total net amount of new security issues ($33.6 billion) of these companies over the same period. For a sample of large corporations (of varying coverage during successive periods), the share of internal financing in total financing (including here both long- and short-term external financing) was 70.4 per cent in 1900–1910, and 71.6 per cent in 1915–1953.[9] And the relatively small share of external financing was, in large measure, offset by the outflow of funds resulting from the acquisition of financial assets, so that the *net* balance of external financing, in most periods, was even smaller.

2. Although it is not realistic to identify specific sources of funds with specific uses, it may be significant that internal funds have been an increasing percentage of expenditure on plant and equipment. For all corporations, the ratio was 0.87 in 1900–1914, 1.08 in 1919–1929, and 1.10 in 1946–1953. In other words, gross additions to fixed capital

---

[8] Raymond W. Goldsmith, *A Study of Saving in the United States*, Vol. I, Princeton University Press, 1955, Table P-11, line 1b, p. 889.

[9] Using dollar volumes, shown in Table 44, cumulated over the period.

could be financed to an increasing extent out of the internal funds of corporations.

3. The two components of gross internal funds (gross retention)—depreciation and depletion charges, and undistributed profits—are available separately. The ratio of the former to plant and equipment expenditures was 0.42 in 1900–1914, 0.79 in 1919–1929, and 0.58 in 1946–1953; the ratio of the latter to the same expenditures was 0.45, 0.29, and 0.52, respectively. Thus, both depreciation charges and retained net profits, particularly the former, are responsible for the rise in the ratio of internal funds to plant and equipment expenditures. It should be noted that these gross retention components are unadjusted for the effects of changes in inventory valuation and for differences between depreciation charges based on cost and those based on replacement values. However, in the analysis of financing flows, such unadjusted totals in current prices are perhaps the most useful.

4. While there was a rise in the ratio of internal funds to expenditures on plant and equipment, no such rise appears in the ratio of internal funds to total capital expenditures or uses (sources). This cannot be shown in the data for all corporations, for which new security issues are the only external financing source that can be estimated back to 1900. Even so, if we take the share of gross internal funds in a total that combines them with new security issues, it moves from 0.74 in 1900–1914, to 0.75 in 1919–1929, and to 0.83 in 1946–1953 (Table 40, below)—a rise to be sure, but quite moderate. But when we use the sample of large corporations (Table 44, below), in which all external financing is included, we find that the share of internal funds in total financing is 70 per cent in 1900–1910, 89 per cent in 1919–1927, and 67 per cent in 1946–1953. If any inference can be drawn, it is that there was no significant long-term trend, either upward or downward, in the share of internal funds in total sources (uses) of funds.

5. The combination of an upward trend in the ratio of internal funds to both plant and equipment expenditures and to the sum of internal funds plus new security issues, on the one hand, with the absence of such secular rise in the share of internal funds in total uses (sources), on the other, leads to one obvious inference. The share of short-term external financing in total financing must have increased, and so must have the share of short-term assets in total assets. The first conclusion can be checked directly in the evidence provided by the sample of large corporations. The share of short-term external in total financing was only 2.4 per cent in 1900–1911; it was negative during the twenties; and as high as 20 per cent in 1946–1953. A large contribution to this rise is made by income tax accruals, which are treated here as short-term financing provided to corporations by the government. If

INTRODUCTION

these accruals were to be considered a kind of short-term income retention and included in internal funds, the ratio of internal to total financing would show a slightly upward trend over the period. But, even so, the trend would involve a rise of just a few percentage points over a period longer than half a century, and its significance would be greatly reduced by lack of continuity over time. It should be noted that the increase in tax accruals was accompanied by a rise in holdings of government securities.

We may now sketch an explanation of the findings just summarized. The first of these is that gross internal funds constitute a large proportion of total financing—in the long run, well above two-thirds. In any attempt to explain this pattern, one naturally turns to the capital-output ratio, as well as to the general argument that any growing sector of the economy that uses a great deal of capital will, in order to avail itself of the favorable opportunities provided by an expanding market, consistently retain and reinvest some fraction of net earnings. What are the proximate quantitative determinants involved? We know that in manufacturing the ratio of total capital, net of depreciation reserves, to value added was, at most, 2.6. Assume that with capital gross of depreciation reserves, the ratio was 3.0; that about six-tenths of the capital is durable and depreciable capital, of which seven-tenths is plant, with an average annual depreciation rate of 2 per cent, and the balance is equipment, with an average annual depreciation rate of 8 per cent. This means that the combined depreciation charges would amount to 3.8 per cent of the depreciable part of capital, 2.28 per cent of total capital, or 6.84 per cent of annual net value added (i.e., 2.28 per cent multiplied by the capital-value added ratio of 3.0). Assume next that value added grows at the rate of 5 per cent per year, and that the marginal ratio of gross capital to value added is, like the average, 3.0. The gross additions to capital must, therefore, be 15 per cent of value added (i.e., 5 per cent multiplied by the capital-value added ratio), and depreciation charges, equal to 6.84 per cent of value added, would contribute about 46 per cent of the total funds needed to finance gross capital additions. Assume further that total net profits, after interest and taxes, are 10 per cent of value added, and that a third of total net profits is retained. Then, retained profits would provide funds equivalent to 3 per cent of value added, or another fifth of the funds needed to finance gross capital additions. In this illustration, then, internal funds account for about 66 per cent, or two-thirds, of the total financing needed.

The specific figures used in the illustration above are not important, even if there be a rough and ready realism about them. What *is* important is the demonstration of the connection between the

INTRODUCTION

capital-output ratios and the structure of financing in its distribution between internal and external funds. A difference between the average and marginal capital-output ratios, which means movement over time in the average, will affect the share of internal funds, because the marginal ratio bears directly upon the volume of *total* financing, and the average ratio determines (given the depreciation rate) the contribution of depreciation charges to *internal* financing. Given a functional relation between output, volume of total net profits, and volume of expected profit retention, the average and the marginal capital-output ratios will also determine the share of total financing that would be contributed by undistributed net profits. It follows that much of the previous discussion concerning the levels of, and trends in, capital-output ratios bears upon the levels of, and trends in, the share of internal funds in total financing. With the inclusion of a few additional variables (such as length of life and other elements in setting depreciation charges, and the ratio of retained profits to output), a single model could be devised for the analysis of secular movements in both the capital-output ratios and the share of internal funds in total financing.[10]

This point bears directly upon the second major finding presented above, the long-term rise in the ratio of internal funds to expenditures on plant and equipment. We have argued above that a retardation in the rate of growth of fixed capital formation means a rise in the ratio of capital consumption to current gross fixed capital formation (plant and equipment expenditures). Capital consumption is measured by current depreciation charges. We know that the rate of growth of capital and, hence, of capital formation, in the mining and manufacturing sector has declined. We should, therefore, expect that the ratio to plant and equipment expenditures of internal funds contributed by depreciation charges would rise, and this is what we find. However, the rise in the ratio is relatively modest, partly because the underlying data are available only since 1900 (and the rate of growth of capital formation had largely slowed by then), partly because we use deprecia-

[10] The model is complete, but only on the severely limiting assumption that external funds are always available to fill the gap left by internal financing. If they are not, or are in excess of the demand for external capital funds as determined by the model sketched out in the text, the system will not be in equilibrium. As a result, the cost of capital funds will change, with consequent changes in all the variables of the system; finally, the entire level of economic activity will change—with effects on the distribution between external and internal financing not accounted for by the model. The model could, perhaps, be completed by making savings other than those internal to an industry a function of total output and making part of such savings available to an industry as external funds, i.e., as a function of the industry's share in countrywide output. But the purpose of the model is to indicate the relation between capital-output ratios and shares of internal funds in total financing. No claim is made that such relation fully determines the actual trends in the share of internal funds in total financing.

INTRODUCTION

tion charges based on original-cost valuation, and partly because we deal with a disturbed period over which long-term trends are difficult to establish.

Furthermore, it may be argued that, to a substantial extent, retained net profits are a function of output, i.e., of the volume of sales. Hence, if the marginal fixed capital-output ratio declines, the share that retained net profits would contribute to the financing of plant and equipment expenditures should rise—all other conditions being equal. Because the average fixed capital-output ratio declined from the twenties onward, the marginal fixed capital-output ratios since then should be much lower than they were from 1900 to about 1920. In turn, this should have made for a secular rise in the ratio of retained profits to plant and equipment expenditures. Here again, long-term movements in factors affecting the stock of capital and its ratio to output are connected with the findings relating to the upward trend in the ratio of a component of internal funds (this time, retained profits) to a major category in the uses of funds (plant and equipment expenditures).

Given a long-term rise in the ratio of internal funds to expenditures on plant and equipment, a rise in the ratio of such funds to net new issues is probable. For one would expect the trend in the latter to be geared to the trend in expenditures on new plant and equipment—even though one should not push too far the association between specific uses and sources of funds.

The last of the findings summarized above—absence of a rise in the share of internal funds in total financing—appears to be due to forces outside those considered in connection with the capital-output ratios, namely (as already indicated), to a rise in the share of short-term external financing. Hence, the explanation can be more easily sought in a direct examination of the trends in the structure of external financing.

Trends in the Structure of External Financing

1. Within total external financing, the share of short-term funds was much higher in the post-World War II period than during the earlier periods back to 1900, excluding the World War I and World War II years. In the sample of large corporations, the share of short-term in total external financing was 8 per cent in 1900–1910, over 65 per cent during the World War I period (1915–1919), negative in the twenties and early thirties, almost 90 per cent during the World War II period (1939–1946), and 61 per cent during 1946–1953 (Table 44, below). For all manufacturing corporations, the share of short-term in total external financing in 1946–1953 amounted to 57 per cent. Though the

trend is disturbed by major fluctuations during depressions and wars, there is some semblance of a rise in the share of short-term in total external financing.

2. The substantial proportions of short-term financing during 1915–1919, 1939–1946, and 1946–1953 were, in large part, due to increased accruals for income tax purposes. The increase in the latter accounted for between 33 and 54 per cent of total short-term financing, as shown by the sample of large corporations. Yet, if we deduct these increases from both numerator and denominator, the share of short-term financing in external financing is still almost 50 per cent during 1915–1919, almost 85 per cent during 1939–1946, and almost 44 per cent during 1946–1953. Thus, the upward trend in the share of short-term in total external financing still remains, if we compare the post-World War II period with either the twenties or 1900–1910.

3. There was some rise in the ratio of debt to operating assets (total assets minus investment in government and corporate securities). In manufacturing, the ratio of interest-bearing debt to total capital invested in operating assets (in book values) rose from over 14 per cent in 1890 to 18 per cent in 1952. The ratio of total debt to total assets increased from 23 per cent in 1929 to 36 per cent in 1952. Similar tendencies are revealed by the data for mining.

4. This rise in the ratio of debt to assets was due partly to the rise in the relative importance of short-term external financing, with such financing all taking the form of debt obligations partly to the rise, within long-term external financing, of debt obligations relative to equity issues. For all manufacturing and mining corporations, the share of new bond issues in total new security issues was 46 per cent during 1900–1914, 20 per cent during 1919–1929, and 62 per cent during 1946–1953 (Table 51, below). The ratio of total bonded debt to current value of operating assets of all manufacturing corporations fluctuated, but it was 3.7 per cent in 1900, 4.5 per cent in 1919, and 6.3 per cent in 1952 (Table 54, below). Again, granting the marked variation in the shares over time, there is some semblance of an upward trend in the relative weight of debt obligations within long-term external financing—although the sharp rise occurred largely in the post-World War II years.

The paragraphs above summarize the major findings on the long-term changes in the structure of external financing. There are many other changes, e.g., the increased share, in recent years, of privately placed long-term financing compared with that chaneled through public security markets. But the summary will suffice for the present purposes, the more detailed findings being available to the interested reader in the chapters that follow.

INTRODUCTION

Among the factors that may have made for these trends in the structure of external financing, two somewhat different groups may be distinguished. One lies in the realm of government policy, which is, in turn, affected by the changing internal problems of our society and the vicissitudes of war and other changes in international relations. The increased weight of income taxes, and the resulting rise in the share of income tax accruals in short-term financing of business corporations is a clear illustration. Obviously, we deal here with a factor that is beyond the control, the decision power, of the private sector. Also among the extraneous factors, which business enterprises adjust to but do not determine, is the effect of corporation taxes on the relative attractiveness of bonds or other long-term debt obligations as compared with equity issues. The interest payments on debt can be treated as costs and deducted for tax purposes, but the dividend payments on equity issues cannot be so treated. Finally, one must not overlook the government policy, during World War II and some of the postwar years, of keeping long-term interest rates low to provide an adequate market for government obligations. As a consequence, bonds and other interest-bearing debt were more attractively priced than new stock issues. Thus, it would not be difficult to explain, in terms of government policy, the high levels, in recent decades, of the share of short-term in total external financing, of the share of debt obligations in that total, or of the share of bonds in total new security issues.

Yet, it would be an oversimplification to limit our consideration to government policy, induced by war and other necessities. There are factors within the private sector that might have contributed to the same trends. In discussing the secular movement of the capital-output ratios through the life span of an industry's growth, we have noted that, in the downward phase of this movement, the decline in the ratio of working capital to output need not be as great as the decline in the ratio of fixed capital to output; indeed, the estimates strongly suggest this conclusion. It follows that during this downward phase, which begins in the mining and manufacturing sector in the twenties, the average ratio of working to total capital is bound to rise, and the marginal ratio even more so. Working capital represents short-term assets, so that a rise in its share means a rise in the share of short-term in total assets. While no specific assignment of short-term funds (which are external funds by definition, because we classify gross retention with long-term funds) to short-term assets is fully warranted, it stands to reason that, all other conditions being equal, a rise in the share of short-term in total assets would be accompanied by a rise in the share of short-term in total financing. The latter would also mean a rise in

INTRODUCTION

the share of short-term financing in total external financing, so long as the share of the latter in total financing is constant or does not materially rise. Finally, such a rise in the share of short-term in total external financing will, in turn, serve to raise the ratio of debt to external financing and, probably, of debt to operating assets.

Another factor lies in the relation between debt and assets for corporations classified by volume of assets. In general, cross-section analysis for 1937 and 1948 reveals that the ratio of debt to assets is lower for the large corporations and higher for the small corporations. But this relationship holds only for the range of assets from less than $50 thousand to the asset class of $5 million to $10 million. The ratio of long-term debt to assets rises, if anything, with the size of the corporation, from the $1 million class upward—particularly in the data for 1948. This latter positive relationship between corporation size and the ratio of long-term debt to assets can be easily explained in terms of the greater economic stability and credit-worthiness of the larger units. It may have contributed also, if in a minor way, to the slight upward trend, which we found among manufacturing and mining corporations, in the ratio of long-term debt both to equity issues and to assets.

Finally, we should note that the complexes of factors, suggested above, in both government policy and the private sector, affect not only the structure of external financing, but also the division between internal and external financing. Thus, the economic conditions that prevailed immediately after World War II, characterized, on the one hand, by active consumer demand and rising prices, and on the other, by government policy with respect to taxes and debt management, influenced the earning position of corporations and their outlook for the future. These economic conditions influenced the extent to which corporations could earn both depreciation charges and retained net profits, their capacity and willingness to provide internal funds for reinvestment, and their choice, in seeking external funds, between debt and equity funds and between short- and long-term debt.

Bearing upon Future Prospects

What is the bearing of the empirical findings and explanatory hypotheses discussed above upon prospects for capital formation and financing in the mining and manufacturing sector over the next two to three decades? The period is designedly set at this duration, because both our analysis of the past record and our interest in future prospects emphasize secular movements—not the transient changes associated with business cycles and other short-term alarums and diversions.

INTRODUCTION

Furthermore, over a short period, changes in the rate of secular movement are too small to be either clearly discernible or of much importance for practical policy. For example, if the secular level of the stock of capital in the sector in 1958 is X, and the secular rate of change suggested by past experience is, say, 4 per cent per year, the projections for 1959 and 1960 will be $1.04X$ and $1.082X$, respectively. If the projection is in substantial error in that the actual secular rate of change declines to, say, 3.5 per cent (a truly large decline in a single year), the difference between the projection and the actual rate will be only between $1.04X$ and $1.035X$, and between $1.082X$ and $1.071X$—hardly significant for practical purposes. It is only in a long extension from the starting point in time that projected and actual secular trends can diverge significantly, and we are interested in these long-term extensions so that the slowly made changes in institutional patterns and policies can at least be considered. The period ahead must be long enough to permit the emergence of significant possible differences in secular movements.

When such long-term prospects are considered, two aspects of the findings and analysis above become directly relevant. The first is that, whatever patterns of order we find in the past trends in capital formation and financing in the sector (and it is only such orderly patterns that can be projected), the empirical coefficients involved were quite variable over the decades. For example, the ratio of capital to output in manufacturing declined from 1.02 in 1919 to 0.61 in 1948, and to 0.59 in 1953. In view of such past movements, there is no immediate reason to assume that, over the next two decades (to the late seventies) the ratio could not continue to rise to, say, 0.8, or decline to 0.5. If, then, we project output of the manufacturing sector as a function of some projected gross national product, the annual rate of capital formation required by such future output may vary within a wide range indeed. In other words, there is no empirically observed *constancy* of the capital-output ratio that would justify simple statistical extrapolations using fixed coefficients. And this comment applies even more strongly to trends in financing—discontinuous, as they have been over time, and distorted, as they have been in the past, by wars and major depressions.

Second, the factors suggested, even in this brief and tentative explanation of past trends, have been diverse and, while identifiable, not easily measurable. Most important, our knowledge of the characteristics of these factors, particularly their persistence over time and susceptibility to change, is deficient. For example, we can identify many of the technological and other capital-demanding innovations that made for a secular rise in the capital-output ratio in the sector, as well as many of those capital-economizing changes that made for a decline. But, considering the long, and still unexplored, sequence of causal connection running from scientific discoveries to inventions to technological innovations to the use of capital, how can we translate the patterns of the past record into a basis for prognosis of the future? Clearly, we do not know enough of what makes for scientific discovery, invention, and innovation to derive from this line of analysis firm bases for projecting capital demand into the future. Likewise, we can clearly recognize the forces that made for the changed role of government in our economy during the recent decades. Thus, we can indeed understand some of the government policies that had a direct effect on the structure of financing in the sector. But, given the connection between government policy and the state of international relations—with the latter likely to loom large in the future of this country over the next two to three decades—how can we project into the future the changing and complex patterns of past relations?

These comments obviously do not mean that the statistical estimation and economic analysis embodied in this monograph are futile exercises in scholarly ingenuity for the gratification of antiquarian whimsy. To begin with, the indication of the variability over time of the empirical coefficients and of the variety of factors impinging upon trends in capital formation and financing should have at least the negative value of discouraging oversimplified extrapolations. It may be debated whether wrong projections are worse than none, but it can hardly be denied that too much faith in simple extrapolations of constant coefficients may lead to distressing policy results. Such faith is far worse than skepticism, which should lead, if projections are needed, to experimentation with a wide range of values and assumed changes. Insofar as the monograph, through its findings and analysis, contributes to such healthy skepticism, it will have performed a useful service.

But there is also a substantial positive result. The very task of establishing long-term trends in capital formation, in their relation to output, for the different minor industries within the sector, serves to provide a series of starting points, otherwise nonexistent, for any projection into the future. Also, whatever points of light have been shed on the connection between technological changes, changes in size of firms, changes in industry mix, and changes in the relation between gross capital formation and consumption, are so many guideposts for any contemplated projection that would try to translate some reasonable assumptions concerning movements of population and per capita, or per worker, productivity into a structure of manufacturing and mining output and, thence, into prospective demand for capital in the

INTRODUCTION

sector. Likewise, whatever the estimates have shown concerning trends in the structure of financing, and the analysis concerning the factors at play, are indispensable to a projection that must *assume* some plausible complex of domestic and international conditions and then translate these assumptions into inferences concerning prospects of financing.

In short, the empirical findings and the analytical discussion in the monograph provide raw materials for an evaluation of prospects of capital formation and financing in the sector. Such an evaluation can be sensibly undertaken only as part of an explicit projection of the prospects for the economy as a whole. But the findings and discussion are no more than raw materials, for two reasons. First, we deal here with just one sector of the economy, though an important one, and it is not meaningful to project its future without making a whole host of assumptions relating to the economy as a whole. Second, in making these assumptions for the country, as well as the more specific ones relating to the sector proper, we have a choice between two alternatives. One is to formulate the assumptions quite restrictively by saying "if conditions remain much the same as in the past." In such a case, we can extrapolate past trends, provided we are successful in establishing them, but the projections are likely to be puerile, since the future is rarely a replica of the past. The second is to formulate the assumptions quite permissively, by allowing for major changes in future conditions. However, we must be able to specify these changes, gauge their magnitude relative to the past changes upon which we established trends and, thus, estimate their probable effect. But this requires an elaborate specification and analysis of the assumptions on which the projection relies—both those for the economy as a whole and those specific to the given sector or sectors. This is an entirely new study, in which the empirical findings of the type provided by this and other monographs are combined with such specification and analysis of future changes in underlying conditions as are deemed probable.

The broader aspects of this topic can be, and are, discussed more effectively in the summary monograph. But it can be suggested here that, among the complexes of general conditions that would have to be taken into account in any projection into the future, three stand out clearly: the changed position of the country in the world, which imposes upon it a set of obligations of a continuity and magnitude unparalleled in the past—a task not merely of assuring external security, but also of providing economic leadership in the free and uncommitted part of the world; the accelerated pace of technological change and, evidently, a new power revolution; and what is, apparently, a major acceleration in the rate of growth of our population, at least

INTRODUCTION

in comparison with the decades immediately preceding World War II. These groups of changes are hardly coordinate; there are some parallels to them in the past; and they are not offered here as a fully thought out selection. They are cited here to illustrate the kind of general changes, concerning which assumptions are needed to provide the framework for projections not only for the economy, but also for any major sector in it. In addition, there are, of course, the more specific assumptions, such as those relating to the possible effects of automation on capital demand in manufacturing, the impact of a continuing high level of income taxes and inflationary pressures on the structure of financing in the sector, and the possible trends and changes in credit and financial institutions and policies.

All of this is to say that the present monograph, like all the others, has necessarily concentrated on only one part, and that the *prior* part, of the job of interpreting the past as a basis for understanding the future—i.e., finding the order in the past, and some rationale for that order. Without such an understanding of the past, no intelligent view of present problems or of future prospects is possible. But there is another part, in which reasonable alternative specifications of future changes are set down and combined with the past order to yield some tentative insights. However, such specification is definitely beyond the scope of this group of monographs.

In such a translation of past order into future prospects, and in any understanding of the present, it is extremely important—indeed indispensable—to be quite sure what the order was, and to know how secure the bases are for statements concerning past trends. One would need to have at hand all the detail the authors of this monograph have accumulated and organized with such skill and effort, all the analytical links suggested, and, most important, all the qualifications, when the apparent long-term movements are too insecure to be given much weight. The present monograph adds richly to our store of tested information, reveals movements in the capital-output ratios and in the financing flows that have barely, if ever, been hinted at before, and is a storehouse of organized information in an important field. One can only hope that it will be used widely in the many studies that are concerned with the relation between capital and output and between uses and sources of capital funds.

PART I

Capital and Output Trends in Manufacturing and Mining

BY

DANIEL CREAMER AND ISRAEL BORENSTEIN
ASSISTED BY MARTIN BERNSTEIN

CHAPTER I

The Measurement of Manufacturing and Mining Growth

NATIONAL income statistics (Table 1) readily establish the importance of mining and manufacturing in the economy of the United States. In the first years (1869 and 1879) of the period under study, nearly 16 per cent of national income originated in mining and manufacturing. Barring periods that include the Great Depression, the proportion increased steadily and accounted for about 30 per cent of national income during 1944–1953.

Growth of Manufacturing Activity

Since the movement of the combined share is dominated by net income originating in manufacturing, it may be taken to represent

TABLE 1

Income Originating in Mining and Manufacturing as a Per Cent of National Income or Aggregate Payments, Selected Periods, 1870–1953
(based on current prices)

	Per Cent Originating in—		
Period of Average	Mining	Manufacturing	Mining and Manufacturing
R. F. MARTIN'S ESTIMATES (AGGREGATE PAYMENTS)			
1870 and 1880	1.8	13.9	15.7
1880 and 1890	2.1	16.6	18.7
1890 and 1900	2.5	18.2	20.7
1900–1908	3.1	18.4	21.5
1904–1913	3.3	18.9	22.2
1909–1918	3.3	20.8	24.1
1914–1923	3.3	22.2	25.5
1919–1928	3.1	22.2	25.3
NBER ESTIMATES (NATIONAL INCOME)			
1919–1928	2.5	21.9	24.4
1924–1933	1.9	19.6	21.5
1929–1938	1.7	19.4	21.1
1934–1943	1.7	24.2	25.9
1939–1948	1.6	27.1	28.7
1944–1953	1.9	28.0	29.9

Source: 1869–1948: Simon Kuznets, "Long-term Changes in the National Income of the United States of America Since 1870," in International Association for Research in Income and Wealth, *Income and Wealth of the United States, Trends and Structure*, Income and Wealth Series II, Cambridge, England: Bowes and Bowes, 1952, p. 89, Table 14; 1944–1953: based on Department of Commerce figures relating to income originating (excluding corporate taxes and including interest on government debt) from *National Income, 1954 Edition, A Supplement to the Survey of Current Business.*

TABLE 2

Selected Measures of the Growth of Manufacturing, Selected Years, 1880-1953

	1900 Comparable with—						1948 Comparable with—		
	1880[a]	Following Year[b]	1880[a]	1909[b]	1919[c]	1937[c]	Preceding Years[c]	Following Year[c]	1953[c]

A. ABSOLUTE QUANTITIES (DOLLARS IN 1929 PRICES)

1. Total assets (mill. $)	4,821	18,626	17,452	31,563	46,094	55,319	77,982	78,357	99,040
2. Fixed capital (Do.)	n.a.	9,651	n.a.	n.a.	n.a.	25,851	36,526	36,685	45,258
3. Working capital (Do.)	n.a.	8,975	n.a.	n.a.	n.a.	29,468	41,456	41,672	53,782
4. Value of product (Do.)	8,820	23,182	21,984	32,648	45,090	74,687	128,124	128,604	167,821
5. Value added (Do.)	3,201	9,916	9,275	13,674	18,042	30,581	50,326	n.a.	n.a.
6. No. of establishments (thous.)	213	457	205	265	270[b] / 210[c]	167	241 (1947)	n.a.	n.a.
7. No. of persons engaged (Do.)	2,808	5,457	5,063	7,226	9,665	10,615	15,333	15,468	17,414
8. Horsepower per reporting establishment	40	65	75	99	129	281 (1939)	n.a.	n.a.	n.a.

B. RATE OF CHANGE PER YEAR BETWEEN BENCHMARK YEARS (PER CENT)

	1880-1900	1900-1909	1909-1919	1919-1937	1937-1948	1948-1953
Total assets	+7.0	+6.4	+3.9	+1.0	+3.2	+4.8
Value of product	+4.9	+4.2	+3.3	+2.8	+5.0	+5.5
Value added	+5.8	+4.1	+2.8	+3.0	+4.6	n.a.
Number of establishments	+3.9	+2.7	+0.2	−1.3	+3.4[d]	n.a.
Number of persons engaged	+3.4	+3.8	+3.0	+0.5	+3.4	+2.4
Horsepower per reporting establishment	+2.5	+2.9	+2.7	+4.4[e]	n.a.	n.a.

Line	Source
1-5	Based on data in Appendix A. Same index used to deflate value of output and value added.
6	1880 and comparable 1900 data from *Census of Manufactures, 1900*, Vol. I, p. 23; the lower 1919 figure from *Census of Manufactures, 1939*, Vol. I, p. 20. Adjustments were made to exclude industries not covered by this study; 1948 from *Census of Manufactures, 1947*, Vol. II, Table I, p. 21.

n.a. = not available.
[a] Includes custom and neighborhood shops.
[b] Factories producing annual value of $500 or more.
[c] Factories producing annual value of $5,000 or more. Figures for 1953 include shipbuilding; whenever possible, comparable figures were compiled for 1948.
[d] 1937 to 1947.
[e] 1919 to 1939.

also the relative growth of manufacturing in the economy. Table 2 clearly reveals two aspects of this growth. One is the tremendous expansion over the seventy years of all measures except the number of establishments (the least reliable of the six measures shown). For example, between 1880 and 1948, total assets (the sum of fixed and working capital) and value added by manufacturing (both in constant prices) grew to more than sixteen times the 1880 level. Despite the rapid increase in labor productivity, the number of persons in manufacturing grew to more than five times the original figure.

The other aspect, as clearly evident as the impressive growth, is the slowing up in the rate of growth after 1900 (Panel B). That is, the percentage change per year between benchmark years is lower after 1900 than during 1880–1900. These rates of change continue to diminish through 1919–1937. The first reversal appears in the decade that includes World War II and the postwar boom. It is significant that the rate of growth in the use of horsepower per establishment did not follow the general pattern. The rate of growth was virtually constant between 1880 and 1919 and accelerated between 1919 and 1939, when the series ends. The divergence in rates of growth between capital (total assets) and horsepower per establishment has an intimate connection with our findings on the trends in output and capital.

The slackening of the rate of growth was most pronounced in number of establishments. The annual percentage increase in the first decade of this century was one-half the rate of growth in the preceding twenty years and was negligible between 1909 and 1919. An absolute decrease actually occurred between 1919 and 1937. This trend suggests that during the later decades of the nineteenth century, entrepreneurial ability in manufacturing was primarily directed toward organizing new enterprises. During 1900–1937, entrepreneurial energies shifted, on balance, enlarging the scale of operations and promoting technological and managerial measures that resulted in a more efficient utilization of resources. This consideration also may help to explain our principal finding: an initial period of rising capital-output ratio has been followed by a period of decline.

Notes to Table 2, concluded.

7   1880: estimated by using percentage change from 1890 to 1880 in number of wage earners as given in the *Reports on Manufacturing Industries in the United States, Tenth and Eleventh Censuses, 1880 and 1890*; 1900–1919: census data used; 1937, 1948, and 1953: sum of average number of full-time and part-time employees and number of active proprietors of unincorporated enterprises from *Survey of Current Business, National Income Supplements*, various years, Tables 25 and 27. The data were adjusted to exclude ship- and boatbuilding and repair, except in 1953.

8   Horsepower data from *Census of Manufactures, 1939*, Vol. I, p. 275, Table 1.

CHART 1

Indexes of Output by Mining Industries, and Index of Gross National Product, 1870–1953

(centered nine year moving averages based on values in 1929 prices)

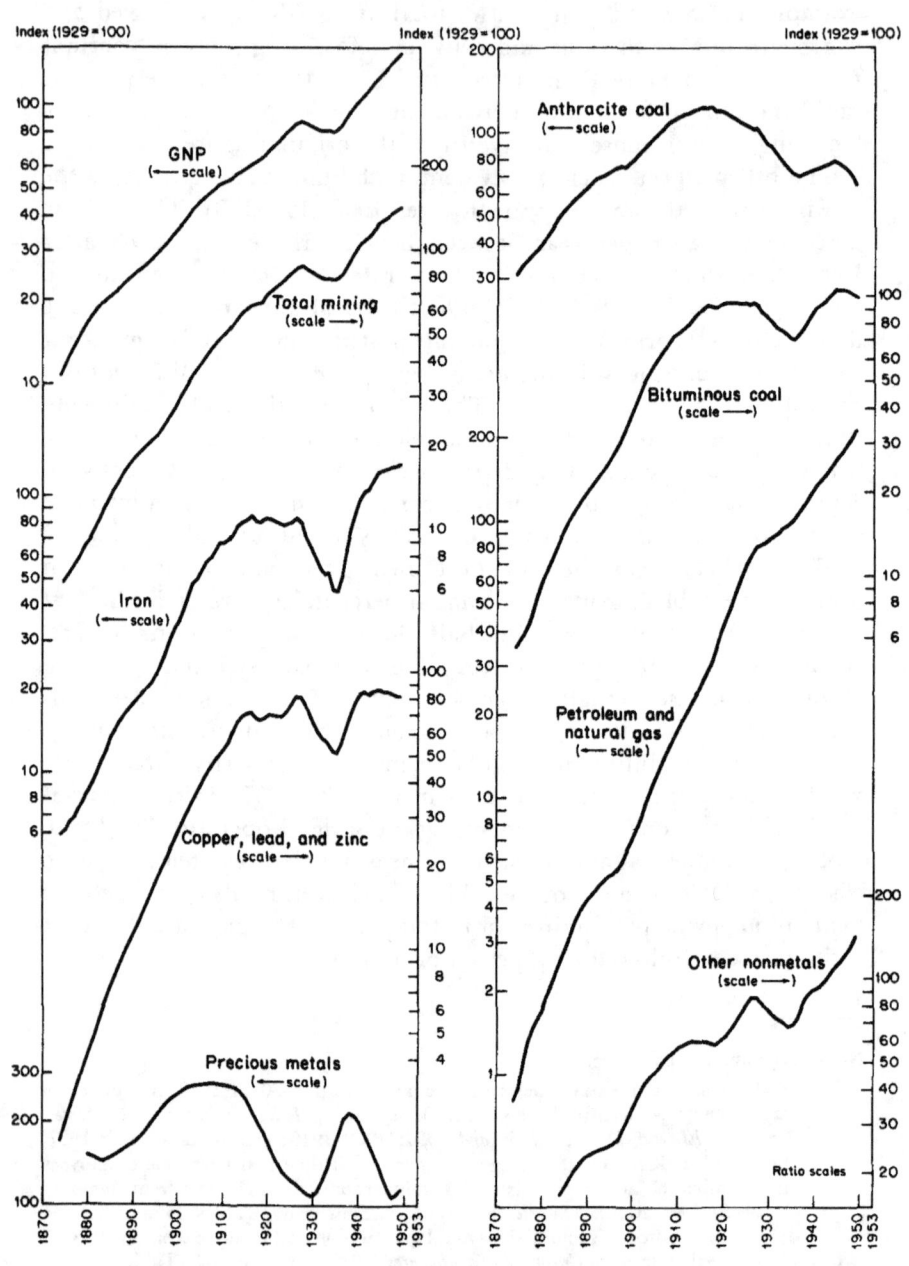

MEASUREMENT OF GROWTH

Growth of Mining

The trends in mineral output are presented in Chart 1. The chart reveals a characteristic common to many of the mining series and one that seems to have an important bearing on the movement of the capital-output ratios. This common feature is the sharp retardation in the secular growth of output that occurred in the second decade of this century. As we shall find in the next section, the turning points in the movement of the capital-output ratios occurred at about the same time. Hence, except for the petroleum and natural gas industry and, possibly, other nonmetals,[1] high rates of growth in output have tended to coincide with increases in the capital-output ratio, and comparatively low rates of growth (or declines) with declines in the ratio.

We can see the growth of mineral output in better perspective by comparing output with consumption and relating mineral consumption to gross or net national product in constant prices. We describe such a ratio as a "mineral coefficient." This ratio is interesting as a measure of the nation's mineral consumption in relation to its product. Because of a high degree of substitutability among minerals, such

---

[1] Growth in output of other nonmetals was close to, if not below, zero between 1909 and 1919. The other nonmetals series is heavily weighted by construction materials and shows swings in the rate of growth similar to those in construction. Simon Kuznets dates the swings in the secular growth of gross construction as follows: troughs—1897, 1917, and 1935; peaks—1909, 1926, and 1945 ["Swings in the Rate of Secular Growth," Work Memorandum 37, Capital Requirement Study (mimeographed, National Bureau of Economic Research, 1952)]. A similar timing of swings in the other nonmetal series can be determined by inspection of Chart 1.

Notes to Chart 1.

Source: The gross national product series is based on Simon Kuznets' unpublished estimates.

The nine-year moving averages of mineral output are based on annual series derived by interpolating between census years. The interpolation procedures for 1929–1953 are similar to those described in the notes to Tables B-7 and B-8. The interpolations for the earlier years are based on the following annual series:

Anthracite and bituminous coal, and iron ore: Quantities reported by the Bureau of Mines (except 1870–1880, when pig iron production, reported by the same source, is used instead of iron ore.

Copper, lead, and zinc; petroleum, natural gas, and natural gasoline; gold and silver: As above; each combined group index is the sum of the individual annual quantities weighted by the price of the given mineral in 1929.

Other nonmetals: 1880–1929: Leong's index for this group (Y. S. Leong, "Index of Mineral Production," *Journal of the American Statistical Association*, March 1950, p. 28)

Total mining: 1880–1929: as above [the results are similar to the Barger and Schurr index, Harold Barger and Sam H. Schurr, *The Mining Industries, 1899–1939: A Study of Output, Employment and Productivity* (National Bureau of Economic Research, 1944)]; 1870–1880: Persons' Index of Mineral Production, Warren M. Persons, *Forecasting Business Cycles* (Wiley, 1931), p. 170.

Note: Data for Total Mining, Petroleum and Natural Gas and Other Non-Metals available through 1953 only.

TABLE 3

Mineral Production and Consumption and Gross and Net National Product, Selected Ratios, by Major Mining Industries, 1870–1952
(*per cent based on decennial averages in 1935–1939 prices*)

Period of Average	Consumption as Percentage of—		Production as Percentage of—			Consumption as Percentage of—		Production as Percentage of—		
	GNP	NNP	GNP	NNP	Consumption	GNP	NNP	GNP	NNP	Consumption
	ALL MINERALS (EXCEPT GOLD)					ALL METALS (EXCEPT GOLD)				
1870–1879	n.a.	n.a.	n.a.	n.a.	n.a.	n.a.	n.a.	n.a.	n.a.	n.a.
1880–1889	n.a.	n.a.	2.72	3.08	n.a.	n.a.	n.a.	0.44	0.50	n.a.
1890–1899	n.a.	n.a.	3.16	3.65	n.a.	n.a.	n.a.	0.55	0.63	n.a.
1900–1909	3.67	4.20	3.74	4.28	1.02	0.68	0.77	0.65	0.75	0.97
1910–1919	4.30	5.00	4.46	5.18	1.04	0.77	0.90	0.80	0.93	1.03
1920–1929	4.23	4.90	4.23	4.89	1.00	0.66	0.77	0.59	0.68	0.89
1930–1939	4.17	4.88	4.13	4.84	0.99	0.59	0.70	0.41	0.48	0.70
1940–1949	4.44	5.31	4.28	5.11	0.96	0.78	0.93	0.54	0.64	0.69
1949–1952	4.44	5.38	4.04	4.91	0.91	0.73	0.88	0.44	0.54	0.61
	ALL FUEL					OTHER NONMETALS				
1870–1879	n.a.	n.a.	1.68	1.89	n.a.	n.a.	n.a.	n.a.	n.a.	n.a.
1880–1889	n.a.	n.a.	1.91	2.16	n.a.	n.a.	n.a.	0.37	0.42	n.a.
1890–1899	n.a.	n.a.	2.23	2.58	n.a.	n.a.	n.a.	0.38	0.44	n.a.
1900–1909	2.51	2.88	2.66	3.04	1.06	0.48	0.55	0.43	0.49	0.88
1910–1919	3.02	3.52	3.20	3.72	1.06	0.50	0.58	0.46	0.53	0.91
1920–1929	3.04	3.52	3.14	3.63	1.03	0.52	0.61	0.50	0.58	0.94
1930–1939	3.06	3.58	3.22	3.77	1.05	0.52	0.61	0.50	0.59	0.96
1940–1949	3.05	3.65	3.15	3.76	1.03	0.61	0.73	0.59	0.71	0.97
1949–1952	2.99	3.62	2.91	3.53	0.97	0.72	0.88	0.69	0.84	0.96

n.a. = not available.

Source: Gross National Product (GNP) and Net National Product (NNP): Simon Kuznets' unpublished estimates in 1929 prices converted to 1935–1939 price values.

Production and apparent consumption, 1900–1952: *Raw Materials in the United States Economy 1900–1952*, Bureau of the Census, Working Paper No. 1 (apparent consumption is defined as primary production plus imports minus exports).

Production, 1870–1900: coal (anthracite and bituminous), petroleum, natural gas and natural gasoline, iron, copper, lead, zinc, and silver, as reported in *Raw Materials, op. cit*, extrapolated on the basis of the quantities reported by the Bureau of Mines; other metals and other nonmetals, as reported in *ibid.*, extrapolated by Leong's index (Y. S. Leong, "Index of Mineral Production," *Journal of the American Statistical Association*, March 1950, p. 28) for the appropriate group.

mineral coefficients can be based only on broad groups of minerals. For this purpose, we divide mineral output into three groups, metals (except gold),[2] fuel, and other nonmetals (Table 3). Such historically determined mineral coefficients can be applied, in a rough way, to projected national product aggregates to obtain projections of mineral consumption; projection of these aggregates is virtually independent of the output projection of any single component.

For all major mining categories the ratio of production to both gross and net national product rose until about the decade ending in 1919. The same was true of the ratio of consumption to Gross National Product and Net National Product, as can be inferred from the record for the two decades between 1900 and 1919. The increase in the ratio of mineral consumption to national product reflects the ever-greater use of metals and other minerals in the output of goods and services. Except for other nonmetals, this steadily growing use seems to have reached a climax during 1910–1919. In this period a sharp retardation occurred in the rate of growth of all branches of mining, except petroleum and natural gas, other nonmetals, and other metal mining.

Although the factors working for a decline in mineral use per dollar of national product were certainly present before World War I, the rapid industrialization of the time—the development of railroads, public utilities, and manufacturing—seems to have had the greater impact on mineral use. It was only when the forces acting to increase mineral-use lost their impetus that other factors acting to decrease it began to play an important role in shaping the long-term movement of the ratio of mineral consumption to national product. The increasing use of scrap metals is one of the important factors. The more efficient use of mineral products, for instance, the reduction in the amount of coal required to produce a kilowatt-hour of electricity, is another. Also, the more extended fabrication which minerals undergo before reaching the final consumer generally adds to aggregate output without causing a commensurate increase in mineral input. Still another factor is the substitution of raw materials that are not mined, such as plastics and rubber products, for minerals.

This helps to explain the reversal in the movement of the ratio of mineral consumption to national product after 1919. For other nonmetals only did the ratios of consumption to GNP and NNP continue to rise after 1919; even for that group, no increase occurred during the twenties and thirties. Fuel consumption per unit of GNP remained

---

[2] The concepts used for consumption (changes in inventories are neglected) and for the mineral coefficient call for separate treatment of gold. The reason is that, even during the period covered by ten-year averages, the monetary uses of gold may cause large changes in gold inventories.

virtually constant, and fuel consumption per unit of NNP increased only negligibly between 1910 and 1952. Consumption of metals other than gold per unit of GNP and NNP declined drastically after 1919. The increase in the consumption of these minerals per unit of national product during the forties was no more than sufficient to bring it back to the 1909–1919 level. During 1950–1952, the most recent years for which we have data, the consumption of metals as a percentage of GNP and NNP declined once again.

Similarly, consumption of all minerals per unit of GNP and NNP declined during the twenties and thirties. However, the consumption rate was somewhat higher during the forties than during 1910–1919. In the early fifties, this higher rate was maintained with respect to GNP and was even somewhat increased with respect to NNP. During the twenties and thirties, the decline in the ratios of total mineral production to GNP and NNP was more marked than the decline in the ratios of consumption to these national product aggregates. Similarly, the rise during the forties was less pronounced and, apparently, temporary; the decline in the most recent years appears to be a continuation of the long trend starting about 1919.

Fuel production ratios to GNP and NNP after 1919 moved about the same way as, though more erratically than, the ratios of consumption to these aggregates. During 1950–1952 there is, nonetheless, a marked decline in these ratios, though the decline in the rate of consumption is almost negligible. For metals other than gold, there was a much sharper drop in the production, than in the consumption, ratio to GNP and NNP. Only other nonmetals registered an increase in the ratios of production to GNP and NNP.

After World War I, net imports of minerals became more important. The metal mining industries changed, at that time, from surplus producer to net importer. In recent decades, less than 70 per cent of demand has been met by domestic production. The fuel group continued to be a net exporter up to the late forties. Reduction of the export surplus was slight.[3] During the most recent years, however, this group has become a net importer. The ratio of production to consumption of other nonmetals continued to increase until World War II. In recent decades, however, the ratios suggest that the share of imports in domestic consumption has been stable.

Two features in the relationship between mining output and aggregate output of more general interest should be mentioned. The first,

---

[3] The trends are different, however, for the two components, coal, and oil and gas. Coal exports have steadily increased over imports. Surplus production of oil and gas has decreased throughout the period until, beginning with the forties, there were virtually no net exports.

MEASUREMENT OF GROWTH

indicated by Chart 1 and by the rise and subsequent decline in the ratio of mining output to aggregate output, is that retardation has been greater in mining output than in national product. This behavior bears out Burns'[4] observation that the retardation rate of the majority of individual industries is higher than the retardation rate of total production.

A second interesting feature is the timing of the turning point in the movement of the ratio of mining output to national product. The turning point occurred around 1919, and thus coincides with the turning points in the capital-output ratios of most of the mining and manufacturing industries[5] and with the retardation in the rate of growth of many branches of mining. Expressed another way, the period in which technological and other developments favored rising capital-output ratios was also the period of increased material use, while the period of declining capital-output ratios coincides with the period of reduced material use. There is no doubt that each of the trends has influenced the other.

Sources and Methods of Measurement and their Limitations

The sources of the raw data and the estimating procedures used to derive the capital-output ratios in mining and manufacturing are, for the most part, so similar that many of the estimating problems can be discussed by reference to only one of the industries. To minimize repetition, we shall base this part of the discussion mainly on the problems encountered in developing the estimates for the manufacturing branch.[6] We have no choice in selecting the basic data on output and capital. They are derived from the *Censuses of Manufactures* for 1880–1919 and from the corporation income tax returns to the Internal Revenue Service (formerly Bureau of Internal Revenue) in 1929 and in selected years thereafter. While the use of these data poses difficult problems, it is possible to obtain a workable degree of comparability over the entire span of seven decades beginning with 1880.[7]

---

[4] Arthur F. Burns, *Production Trends in the United States since 1870* (National Bureau of Economic Research, 1934), see esp. Chap. 6.

Mining output, of course, is an aggregate also, and its rate of growth is sharply influenced by the development of new industries. For example, recent developments in aeronautics and nuclear physics have transformed the "rare" metals into a "new" industry, just as the growth of automobile transportation made a new industry out of petroleum production. However, mining output is less comprehensive an aggregate than total production, and includes fewer new industries.

[5] For manufacturing industries, see Chapter III, below.

[6] For a discussion of similar and other problems encountered in the preparation of the estimates for mining industries, see Appendix B.

[7] See Appendix A, section A1 for our refutation of the census allegation that capital is grossly understated in the *Censuses of Manufactures*.

11

Definition of Capital

In the *Census of Manufactures* for 1900, the definition of capital is given in the following terms:

"Capital invested: The answer must show the total amount of capital both owned and borrowed. All the items of fixed and live capital may be taken at the amounts carried on the books. If land or buildings are rented, that fact should be stated and no value given ... The value of all items of live capital, cash on hand, bills receivable, unsettled ledger accounts, value of raw materials on hand, materials in process of manufacture, and finished products on hand, etc., should be given as of the last day of the business year reported."[8]

In the following census years up to and including 1919, there are only minor alterations in this definition, although on some points the instructions become more explicit. While, in the earlier census years, the query on invested capital is not fully articulated, the census authorities in 1900 express the judgment that "the statistics of capital invested at the two censuses (1890 and 1900) show totals which are perfectly comparable...."[9] Again, in the preceding decade, the census authorities conclude that "the questions of 1880 apparently cover the same ground as the more detailed questions in 1890." However, the qualification is added "that materials on hand, goods in process of manufacture and other items were, to some extent, overlooked."[10] This qualification bears on our analysis of the trend in the capital-output ratios. The deficiency in reported capital results in a capital-output ratio lower than the "true" ratio and exaggerates the rise in the ratio between 1880 and 1890.

In balance sheet terms, the census definition of invested capital is equal to fixed capital (land, buildings, machinery, and equipment) and working capital (cash, inventories, and accounts receivable), all in book values. This definition of invested capital can be closely matched with the balance sheet data reported to the Internal Revenue Service and published in *Statistics of Income*.[11] The equivalent definition is total assets minus investments in government and other securities.[12]

---

[8] *Census of Manufactures, 1900*, Part I, p. XCVII.
[9] *Ibid.*, p. XCVIII.
[10] *Census of Manufactures, 1890*, Part I, p. 10.
[11] Unpublished tabulations, called the "Source Book," show these data in greater industry detail.
[12] A formal difference in definition exists: The census definition excludes such intangible assets as patent rights and good will that are included in *Statistics of Income* for 1929 and 1937 in "other assets" and in "capital assets" for later years. However, for total manufacturing, intangible assets in 1939 represented only 3.7 per cent of total assets excluding investment in securities. As we show in Chapter III, this minor conceptual difference imparts a bias that adds to the firmness of our findings.

MEASUREMENT OF GROWTH

That there is continuity in the figures on invested capital from the two sources is suggested by the closeness of the reconciliation of the 1919 data on capital from the *Census of Manufactures* and from *Statistics of Income.* The adjustments necessary to carry out the comparison are detailed in Appendix A, section A1, part a. The two totals differ by only 6.4 per cent, the higher total being reported by *Statistics of Income.*[13] This difference, moreover, is in the expected direction. The 1919 reports to the Internal Revenue Service are on a consolidated basis. As a result, more nonmanufacturing activity was reported under manufacturing than vice versa.

It is reassuring, also, that in benchmark years, beginning with 1919, the estimates of fixed capital stock in manufacturing based on balance sheet data were very close to estimates independently derived from cumulative annual expenditures on structures and equipment.[14]

Estimates of capital derived from *Statistics of Income* are net of depreciation. Since the reconciliation of the capital estimates as of 1919 from the two sources is close, we infer that capital reported in the 1919 *Census of Manufactures* also is net of depreciation. However, a definitive answer cannot be given concerning the treatment of depreciation reserves in the earlier censuses. In the 1890 census, the respondents were instructed to make "such allowance for depreciation as may be suitable in the individual case," and the schedule for that year called for "average annual allowance since June 1, 1880, for depreciation of buildings and machinery."[15] Although "the data furnished in the individual reports relating to depreciation of manufacturing were not sufficient to form a basis for correct computations,"[16] the very presence of the query suggests that depreciation accounting was being practiced in 1890 by some firms, presumably the larger corporations. Probably, depreciation accounting was less widely practiced in 1880 and used ever more widely after 1890. Undoubtedly, the inception of the corporate income tax in 1909 caused still more firms to set aside depreciation reserves. By 1919, this practice must have been followed by virtually all manufacturing firms. In the light of these presumptions, our estimates of capital become progressively more and more net of depreciation as we come forward from 1880 to 1919. This

---

[13] Although the differences are larger for some of the major industrial divisions, the largest difference did not exceed 15 per cent; and in six of the ten groups the differences were 10 per cent or less.
[14] For the reconciliation of these two estimates, see Appendix A, section A, part 1b.
[15] *Census of Manufactures, 1890,* Part I, p. 10.
[16] *Loc. cit.*

13

possible bias in the capital estimates strengthens the analysis of Chapter 3.[17]

However, this is only a supposition, but it is the one that seems most reasonable to us. It is also conceivable that before the use of formal depreciation accounting, many capital expenditures were treated as current operating expenses and so were fully depreciated within a year or two. It is not clear how this practice would affect the figures reported to the Bureau of the Census. The respondent did not submit his balance sheet to the Bureau; he was asked, in effect, how much he paid for his assets less suitable depreciation. A reasonable answer would include those assets that were fully depreciated because they were treated as an operating expense less suitable depreciation. In this event, the capital estimates are subject to the same bias as under the first supposition. Our estimates of invested capital between 1880 and 1909 are understated to the extent that any such assets were excluded from the reported capital figures. If it is true that the use of formal depreciation accounting was gradually spreading, the relative understatement of capital diminishes, resulting in an opposite bias in the trend of the capital-output ratios between 1880 and 1909. How these suppositions could affect the interpretation of the statistical results we discuss in Chapter III.

In summary, we have estimates of capital in book values based principally on original cost less depreciation. During periods of substantial price changes or waves of company mergers, the book values doubtless reflect revaluation of assets.

The merger movement between 1889 and 1904 was extensive, and individual mergers were frequently accompanied by extravagant and highly arbitrary upward revaluations of assets. These revaluations were excluded from the 1900 census by the census authorities.[18] However, by 1904, the census authorities were no longer able to insist in all cases on their own definition of invested capital.[19] The effect of these arbitrary

---

[17] Several other adjustments were made to improve comparability. For example, we had to make allowance for the fact that the *Statistics of Income* data relate only to corporations submitting balance sheets, and in 1948 exclude emergency plant and equipment subject to accelerated depreciation. The biases in both adjustments strengthen the firmness of our results. (The procedure for correcting for accelerated depreciation is described in Appendix A, section A, part 2b iii.)

Capital used in manufacturing as we define it excludes rented plant and equipment. From a time series on rental payments by manufacturing firms, we infer that there has been no significant trend in the use of rented capital.

[18] Thus, for the 185 combinations formed before June 30, 1900, the census reported invested capital of $1,462 million, although these combinations had issued stocks and bonds of $3,093 million (*Census of Manufactures, 1900*, part I, pp. lxxvii–lxxviii).

[19] Although "incorporated companies were requested to report the value of land, buildings, machinery, etc., as distinct from their capitalization, . . . a number con-

revaluations is to raise total capital above the "true" amount and thus to raise the capital-output ratio above its "true" level. However, only a minor qualification of our results is necessary because of this consideration.[20]

The same is true of revaluations caused by price changes. Fabricant argues that, in the long run, they have the same effect on the value of assets as a secular change in price level. In the short run, Fabricant's evidence for large industrial corporations for 1925–1934 shows that the maximum change represented only 3.3 per cent of capital assets.[21]

Definition of Output

Value of product is the operational definition of output for 1880–1919, when this information is taken from the *Censuses of Manufactures*; for 1929, 1937, and 1948, when the data are taken from *Statistics of Income*, it is the sum of sales, gross receipts from other operations, and the change in physical inventories valued in current prices.[22] These operational definitions are equivalent. For some purposes, particularly for dealing with total manufacturing, an output concept that eliminates or at least minimizes interfirm transactions is more meaningful. Value added (value of product minus cost of purchased materials, fuels, and containers) is one such concept. It is reported in the *Census of Manufactures* and can be readily estimated for the years when the ratios are based on *Statistics of Income*.

For the mining industries we use the *Census of Mining* classification of mining output and adjust all other estimates for comparability with census coverage. The census classifies output according to the main

---

tended that such a segregation was impracticable . . ." [*Manufactures*, 1905 (Special Report of the Census Office; hereafter, *Census of Manufactures*, 1905), Part I, p. lxviii].

Again in 1909 the census authorities note: "Some corporations engaged in manufacturing industries have issued capital stock and other securities in excess of the actual cost of their properties and assets, or even in excess of the capitalization of the present earning capacity of their plants according to prevailing capitalization rates. In such cases it frequently happens that an arbitrary value is assigned to the assets of the corporation in order to balance its securities, and this arbitrary value is likely to be reported to the Census Bureau rather than the actual value" [*Thirteenth Census of the United States, 1910*, Vol. VIII: *Manufactures*, 1909 (hereafter, *Census of Manufactures, 1909*), p. 22].

[20] Our reasons are given in Chapter III.

[21] Solomon Fabricant, *Capital Consumption and Adjustment*, National Bureau of Economic Research, 1938, pp. 238–240.

[22] The estimate of change in physical inventories valued at current prices is actually made by the National Income Division of the Department of Commerce on the basis of data derived from *Statistics of Income*. This item can be estimated only for total manufacturing and for the major industry groups. In none of the three years did this item amount to as much as 3 per cent of output. Output based on *Statistics of Income*, as in the case of capital, is adjusted to a level that represents all firms (see Appendix A, section B4).

mineral extracted.[23] Output includes, in addition to the main product, by-products or joint products. It excludes, however, the given mineral extracted as a by-product of other minerals. Our working definition of industrial output specifically includes the value of power sold, of miscellaneous services to other enterprises, and the value of minerals produced and used by the operating companies.[24]

Earlier censuses were not quite consistent in drawing a demarcation line between mining and manufacturing operations. However, these inconsistencies do not seriously impair the comparability of the data. Beginning with 1919, duplication of the *Census of Mining* by the *Census of Manufactures* became negligible, so that a uniform definition can apply to the data reported in the 1919, 1929, and 1939 censuses. The census definition of mining in this later period includes, generally, all activities through the point at which a marketable product is obtained. Thus, the figures include preparation activities that are frequently carried on at the mine or quarries, but do not include those that are more frequently carried on at the manufacturing plants. Specifically, the data include concentration of metallic ores; washing and sizing of coal; and crushing, grinding, pulverizing, and drying of stone, clay, gypsum, phosphate rock, etc., done at plants operated in conjunction with the quarries, pits, or mines, or at custom plants. They exclude blast furnaces, metal smelters, metal and petroleum refineries, coke ovens, plants engaged in dressing or polishing stone, etc. It should be noted that this greater uniformity of definition in the later censuses does not affect our estimates of capital during that period. Beginning with 1929, we use capital values reported by the Internal Revenue Service, after adjusting them to census coverage. This adjustment is proportional to the difference in value of product reported by the two sources. It does not take into account, however, the somewhat different character of the product reported by the two sources. The unconsolidated returns to the Census Bureau make possible a finer distinction between manufacturing and mining than do the more consolidated returns to the Internal Revenue Service. The latter uses the principle of the "predominant operation" as a basis for classification of returns. For instance, data pertaining to the smelting of metals will appear under mining statistics if the predominant activity of the given company consisted of *mining* operations; data pertaining to mining operations will appear under *manufacturing* statistics if the predominant activity of the given corporation consisted

---

[23] The Bureau of Mines, on the other hand, classifies output on a minerals basis in its reports on production.

[24] However, with respect to some minor items, our estimates for the period up to 1909 do not strictly correspond to this definition.

MEASUREMENT OF GROWTH

of manufacturing processes. This fact affects somewhat the comparability of the capital data between 1919 and 1929.[25]

Selection of Benchmark Years

Value of output is more sensitive to cyclical changes in business activity than is book value of capital. Consequently, the capital-output ratio is relatively high during business contractions and relatively low during business expansions. For the analysis of long-term movements it is important, therefore, to select benchmark years representing similar positions in business cycles. However, between 1880 and 1919,

TABLE 4
Level of Business Activity in Year of Census Canvass, 1880–1919

Period Covered by Census	Level of Business Activity According to National Bureau of Economic Research Business Cycles Chronology
June 1, 1879–May 31, 1880	A trough occurred in March 1879, terminating a depression of 65 months. The subsequent peak is dated March 1882. This census year represents the first third of a business expansion.
June 1, 1889–May 31, 1890	Between this census and the preceding one, there had been two complete cycles and an expansion phase of a third with a peak in July 1890. This census year covers the last half of a two-year expansion.
June 1, 1899–May 31, 1900	Business activity traced three complete cycles (measuring from peak to peak) between 1890 and 1900. The beginning of this census year coincides with a peak. The following trough is dated December 1900. This census year extends over the first year of an 18-month contraction.
January 1, 1904–December 31, 1904	There was one business cycle from 1901 to 1904, with the terminal trough dated August 1904. Two-thirds of this census year, then, coincides with the last stages of contraction, and one-third with the first stage of expansion.
January 1, 1909–December 31, 1909	In the quinquennium between this and the preceding census there was one business cycle and an expansion phase of another with a peak in January 1910. This census year spans the last two-thirds of that expansion phase.
January 1, 1914–December 31, 1914	A full cycle (peak to peak) and a contraction phase of a second with a trough in December 1914 are found in the 1910–1914 period. This census year covers the second half of that contraction.
January 1, 1919–December 31, 1919	The expansion phase initiated in December 1914 extended to August 1918. The next contraction was brief, ending in April 1919, followed by an equally brief expansion ending in January 1920. This census year covers the last stages of contraction and virtually the entire subsequent expansion.

[25] For an appraisal of this and other inconsistencies resulting from the change from census capital figures to values reported in *Statistics of Income*, see Appendix B.

the requisite data are available only in census years—1880, 1890, 1900, 1904, 1909, 1914, and 1919. Beginning with 1929, annual data are available. The choice of years, beginning with 1929, depends then on the cyclical position most frequently represented by the census years. This information is set out in Table 4 using the business cycle chronology of the National Bureau.

On this evidence the census years fall into the following classifications:

Extending wholly in expansion phase—1880, 1890, 1909.

Extending into contraction and expansion phases, but predominantly in expansion phase—1919.

Extending into contraction and expansion phases, but predominantly in contraction phase—1904.

Extending wholly in contraction phase—1900, 1914.

Census years 1880, 1890, 1909, and 1919 may be taken as years of business expansion. This is essentially true, also, of the census year 1900 (June 1899 to May 1900), since indexes of industrial activity for the contraction of 1899–1900 show a plateau movement from June 1899 to June 1900 and then a sharp but brief contraction. The fact that the census year 1880 represents the early stages of expansion serves as some offset to the depressive effect on the ratio of the under-reporting of capital in that year. Since all except two census years, 1904 and 1914, are years of business expansion or are near peak levels of business activity, we select years of business expansion for the more recent period, namely, 1929, 1937, 1948 and, for a more limited set of comparisons, 1953.[26] Although we present ratios for all available years before 1919, the main reliance for determining trend movements should be placed on the ratios computed from the decennial censuses between 1880 and 1919 and extended forward by ratios derived from *Statistics of Income* for peak years 1929, 1937, 1948, and 1953.[27]

Comparability of Industrial Classifications

To understand the relationship between capital and output for total manufacturing or mining, we should observe it for significant subdivisions of the total. This approach raises the problem of establishing comparable industry classifications over the seven or eight decades.

---

[26] Although business activity reached a cyclical peak in 1937, the scanty evidence available suggests that capacity utilization in 1937 was generally lower than in 1929. This also gives a conservative bias to our results, as we shall point out in Chapter III.

[27] The Census of Mines was not taken in all of these years and was taken in other years. A comparable listing for mining is given in Appendix B, section D.

The difficulties of achieving a workable degree of comparability for manufacturing for the census years 1880 to 1919 were relatively minor; since more than 200 individual industries are distinguished in those census reports, regrouping is facilitated. Moreover, acceptable groupings for this period appear in an unpublished manuscript by the late Daniel Carson, which we have used. The more troublesome questions arise in establishing comparable groupings after 1919 when we draw upon Internal Revenue data. The "Source Book" distinguishes only 45 manufacturing industries in 1929 and 1937 and 122 in 1948. In arranging comparable classifications over the seven decades, we are restricted, of course, by the smallest number of classes in any one benchmark year. Over the entire span, then, we are able to distinguish only 41 minor industries classified into 15 major industry groups. For a more highly selected series of benchmarks, census years 1880 to 1919 and 1948, the greater industry detail of the "Source Book" in recent years makes it possible to compare 66 minor industries within the same 15 major industry groupings. The extension of the estimates to 1953 was based on published statistics of the Internal Revenue Service, which distinguishes only the major groupings.[28]

Adjustment for Price Changes

Comparison of capital as a factor input with the associated output should be free from the distortions imposed by price changes, which have a different impact on capital than on output. To minimize the effect of price changes, we express both the numerator and the denominator in 1929 prices, in keeping with other studies in this series.

The precision of the price adjustment is conditioned, of course, by the availability of time series on prices for detailed commodity classifications. Much larger deficiencies attach to capital items than to output; hence, the adjustments for price changes in the book value of capital are cruder.

Our general procedure for deflating capital is to derive a composite index of prices underlying book values of buildings, machinery and equipment, and working capital for each of the fifteen major industrial groups.[29] For the manufacturing industries, for example, a construction cost index weighted by volume of construction depreciated over fifty years is used to represent the changes in the book value of land and

[28] The composition of the major mining groups in terms of minor industries is given in Appendix B, Table B-7.
[29] The details of constructing the deflators for book values of capital in manufacturing and mining are set forth in Appendix A, section B2 and Appendix Table B-11.

buildings.[30] This component of the composite index is identical for all fifteen groups. For machinery and equipment we are obliged to use a price index of general machinery and equipment for all fifteen groups. In each group, however, the index is weighted by volume of machinery and equipment produced, depreciated according to the length of life typical for a given industry as reported by the Internal Revenue Service.[31] Because of these changing industry weights we obtain a different deflator for machinery and equipment in each major group. The wholesale price index of the output of a given major industry is used to deflate the third component, working capital which consists of cash, inventories, and accounts receivable.

These three components are combined into a composite index, one for each major group. The weights used in the composite measure the relative importance of the three elements in the capital structure of each major group. The weights are those reported by the *Census of Manufactures* in 1890, 1900, and 1905, the only years in which the value of buildings is reported separately. Constant weights are used for all benchmark years between 1880 and 1937 because, to judge by all manufacturing, fixed capital as a percentage of total capital varied within a narrow range, from 46 to 49 per cent. In 1948 and 1953, however, fixed capital represented only about 40 per cent of total capital and the weights were appropriately adjusted. In this manner, we obtain fifteen composite price indexes for eliminating price changes in the book values of total capital. To deflate fixed capital, we use a composite index based on the index of construction costs and on the price index of machinery and equipment; again, one composite for each major industry group. The respective price deflators for total and fixed capital are identical for all minor industries within a major industry classification. At best, this procedure eliminates only the changes in book values that result from price changes affecting the original cost of capital. To our knowledge, there are no data that would make possible the elimination of changes in book values caused by a revaluation of assets.

No such problem exists, however, in dealing with output, since it is valued at current prices received by manufacturers. These price changes

---

[30] It is inappropriate to deflate land value by a building construction cost index, but we know of no alternative procedure and have no choice except to deflate, because the value of land, in half of the benchmark years, is not separately reported. We take some comfort from the fact that land constituted only 8 per cent of total capital in 1900, about 4.5 per cent in 1937, and about 2 per cent in 1948. In mining land presents a special problem which is discussed in Appendix B, section E.

[31] *Depreciation Studies—Preliminary Report of the Bureau of Internal Revenue* (January 1932) and *Bulletin F*, "Income Tax, Depreciation and Obsolescence, Estimated Useful Lives, and Depreciation Rates," (rev. January 1942).

are approximated by changes in quoted wholesale prices. The procedure, then, is to compile for each minor industry a wholesale price index composed of as many commodity price series as we can find that are representative of a given minor industry. The coverage, in each instance, becomes more adequate as we approach the recent decades.[32]

An alternative procedure, at least through 1937, would be to use the indexes of physical output prepared by Frickey and Fabricant.[33] As indexes of physical output our estimates are of inferior construction. However, as components of capital-output ratios our estimates are preferred, because it is essential that both the numerator and the denominator have the same industrial coverage and be derived from the same source material. These conditions would not be satisfied by using the output indexes of other investigators. As we show in Chapter III, the general conclusions are the same regardless of the output indexes used.

These indexes, in common with most price indexes, do not allow explicitly for quality changes. This does not detract from their usefulness in the making of capital estimates. Our interest centers on whether capital has become more efficient, which would result in large part from quality changes in capital itself. It is important, therefore, not to eliminate quality changes by deflation. Our procedure attempts to eliminate only the changes in book values that result from price movements. In the case of output, however, the inability to correct for quality changes is a limitation, and it probably causes output to be cumulatively understated over the period that we analyze.

[32] For the price deflators of output and the details of their construction, see Appendix A, section B4.
[33] Edwin Frickey, *Production in the United States, 1860–1914*, Harvard University Press, 1947; and Solomon Fabricant, *The Output of Manufacturing Industries, 1899–1937*, National Bureau of Economic Research, 1940.

CHAPTER II

Long-Term Growth of Capital in Manufacturing and Mining

Manufacturing, 1880–1953

The development of manufacturing industries is a familiar story in terms of output and employment,[1] and the broad outlines of the story are not altered when it is told in terms of the stock of capital. For this reason, we show only two measures of the development of manufacturing industries since 1880. One is a measure of the annual rate of change between benchmark years of book value of total capital in 1929 prices, in all manufacturing industries and in the fifteen major groupings (Table 5 and Chart 2).

TABLE 5

Total Capital and Gross National Product per Worker, All Manufacturing, Dates of Peaks and Troughs in Secular Swings, 1873–1953
(*based on values in 1929 prices*)

	Dates of Level		Rate of Change Per Year (*percentage*) (3)
Level	GNP Per Worker (1)	Total Manufacturing Capital (2)	
Trough	1873		
Peak	1884	1880–1890	+8.8
Trough	1892	1890–1900	+5.3
Peak	1903	1900–1904	+6.5
Trough	1912	1909–1914	+3.0
Peak	1926	1914–1919	+4.6
Trough	1932	1929–1937	−1.6
Peak	1945	1937–1948	+3.2
		1948–1953	+4.8

GNP = Gross National Product.
Source: Column 1: Simon Kuznets, "Swings in the Rate of Secular Growth," Work Memorandum No. 37, p. 19, Table 6 (mimeographed, National Bureau of Economic Research, March 1952); Columns 2 and 3: Table 6, below.

The highest annual rate of growth of the stock of manufacturing capital occurred during 1880–1890, the first decade covered by the statistics, when modern manufacturing in general was emerging from

---

[1] See, for example, two monographs by Solomon Fabricant, *The Output of Manufacturing Industries, 1899–1937*, and *Employment in Manufacturing, 1899–1939*, National Bureau of Economic Research, 1940 and 1942, respectively.

CHART 2

Total Capital, by Major Manufacturing Industries, Rate of Change per Year between Benchmark Years, 1880–1953

(values in 1929 prices)

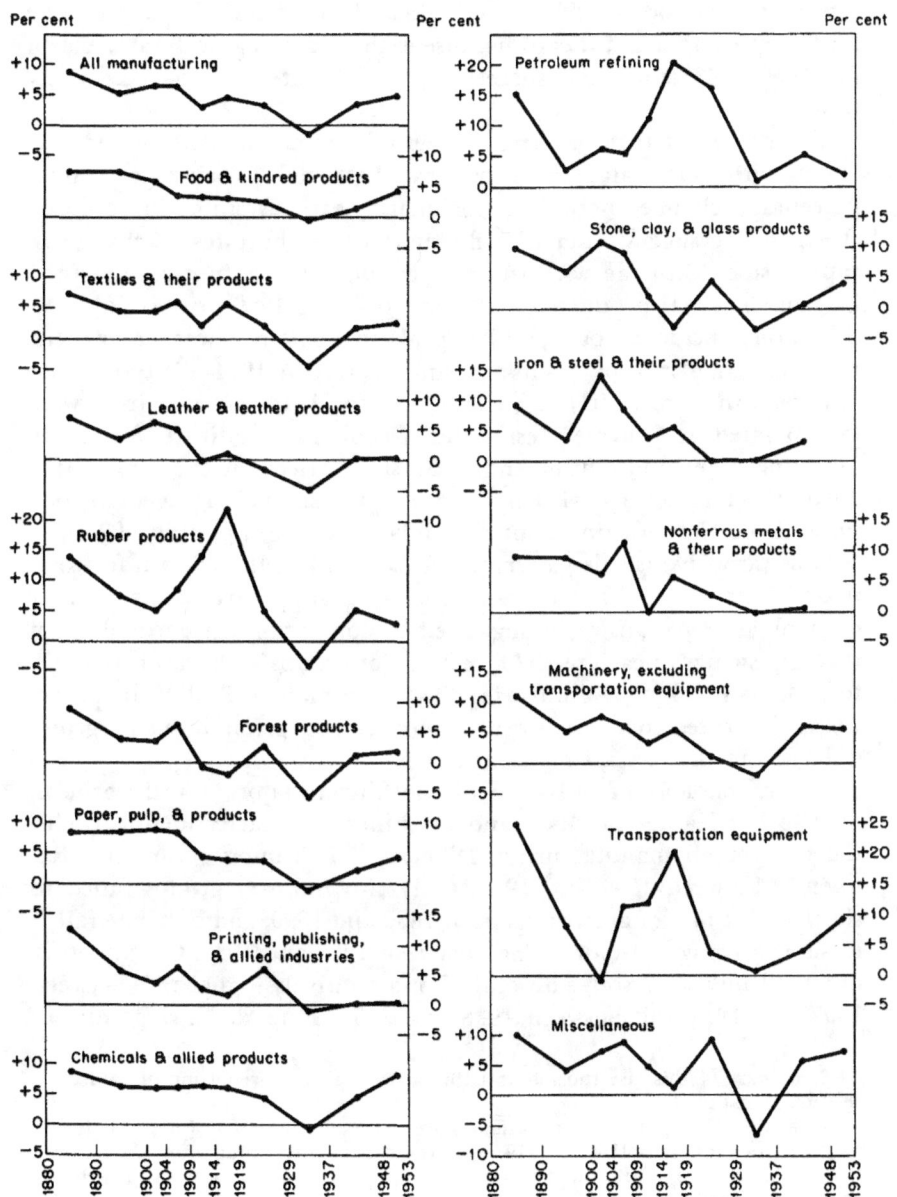

Source: Table 6.
Note: Data for iron and steel and their products and Nonferrous metals and their products are not available separately in 1953.

its earlier beginnings.[2] The annual rate of growth has tended to decrease as we approach the present period.[3] However, it would be wrong to infer from this that the rate of growth decreases continuously and never reverses itself. Certainly, the stock of capital has undergone alternating periods of relatively high and low rates of increase. The long-term trend is downward because each succeeding peak rate, except for 1948–1953, and each succeeding trough rate is at a successively lower level.

The dating of these alternating periods cannot be determined precisely with our data, since we are restricted to average annual percentage changes between benchmark years. Despite this crudity, the evidence suggests that the fluctuations in the rates of change in capital stock coincide with those in countrywide output as measured by gross national product (GNP) per worker in 1929 prices (Table 5). The noncoincidence of the 1926 peak in GNP per worker and the relatively high rate of manufacturing capital in 1914–1919 are more apparent than real. If the latter figure for 1914, for example, were extrapolated by Chawner's estimates of capital expenditures for manufacturing plant and equipment in constant prices for the years 1915–1940,[4] the long-term peak based on a nine-year moving average computed from the resulting annual estimates would appear in 1926.

How pervasive is this pattern of fluctuation? Is the pattern for total manufacturing capital a result of averaging diverse or similar chronologies? An answer is suggested by comparing the chronology of the long swings in each of the fifteen major groups with the chronology for all manufacturing industries (Tables 6 and 7). A date in parentheses indicates that the turning point for a given industry group differs from that for all manufacturing.

The chronology of only two of the fifteen major industry groups, leather and leather products and machinery, is exactly identical with the one for all manufacturing. Differences in timing occur most frequently between 1890 and 1919. Only two industry groups failed to show a peak rate of growth between 1880 and 1890, and only one failed to show a trough rate of change between 1929 and 1937. On the other hand, all industry groups developed at a relatively higher rate between 1937 and 1948 and between 1948 and 1953. Extended swings due to

---

[2] Some part of this rise must be attributed to the under-reporting of capital in 1880 (see Chapter I).

[3] If, as we assume, the capital estimates are more and more net of depreciation as we move forward from 1880 to 1919, this would have a damping effect on the rate of growth; if the opposite has been true, which we doubt, the rate of growth has been exaggerated.

[4] Lowell J. Chawner, "Capital Expenditures for Manufacturing Plant and Equipment—1915 to 1940," *Survey of Current Business*, March 1941, p. 11.

TABLE 6

Total Capital in Manufacturing Industries: Rates of Change per Year between Benchmark Years, 1880–1953

(per cent based on values in 1929 prices)

	1880–1890	1890–1900	1900–1904	1904–1909	1909–1914	1914–1919	1919–1929	1929–1937	1937–1948	1948–1953
All manufacturing	+8.8	+5.3	+6.5	+6.4	+3.0	+4.6	+3.2	−1.6	+3.2	+4.8
Food and kindred products	+7.4	+7.4	+5.8	+3.5	+3.4	+3.1	+2.4	−0.5	+1.2	+4.1
Textiles and their products	+7.3	+4.5	+4.3	+5.9	+2.2	+5.5	+2.0	−4.6	+1.8	+2.6
Leather and leather products	+6.9	+3.4	+6.2	+5.0	−0.1	+0.9	−1.5	−5.0	+0.1	+0.1
Rubber products	+13.7	+7.5	+5.1	+8.4	+13.8	+21.6	+4.9	−4.0	+5.2	+3.0
Forest products	+8.7	+3.9	+3.7	+6.2	−0.7	−1.9	+2.6	−5.7	+1.3	+2.0
Paper, pulp, and products	+8.3	+8.6	+8.9	+8.4	+4.5	+4.1	+3.9	−1.0	+1.7	+4.4
Printing, publishing, and allied industries	+12.5	+5.6	+3.5	+6.1	+2.7	+1.5	+5.8	−1.1	+0.2	+0.3
Chemicals and allied products	+8.8	+6.2	+6.0	+6.2	+6.3	+6.0	+4.3	−0.8	+4.6	+8.3
Petroleum refining	+15.1	+2.6	+5.9	+5.2	+11.0	+20.1	+16.0	+0.8	+5.1	+2.0
Stone, clay, and glass products	+10.1	+6.1	+10.9	+9.1	+2.0	−2.9	+4.5	−3.3	+0.7	+4.0
Metals and metal products	+10.4	+5.1	+9.3	+8.0	+3.6	+7.1	+1.2	−0.4	+4.1	+6.1
Iron and steel and their products	+9.2	+3.3	+13.8	+8.3	+3.7	+5.4	−0.1	+0.1	+3.3	+4.6
Nonferrous metals and their products	+9.1	+8.9	+6.2	+11.3	−0.1	+5.8	+2.7	−0.1	+0.7	+4.6
Machinery, excluding transportation equipment	+10.9	+5.2	+7.6	+6.2	+3.3	+5.4	+1.0	−1.9	+6.3	+5.8
Transportation equipment	+24.8	+8.0	−1.0	+11.2	+11.8	+20.1	+3.4	+0.7	+4.0	+9.2
Miscellaneous	+10.0	+4.1	+7.2	+8.8	+4.7	+1.1	+9.1	−6.6	+5.8	+7.3

Source: Based on data in Appendix Tables A-8 and A-15.

TABLE 7

Total Capital in Manufacturing Industries: Comparison with All Manufacturing of Alternating Periods of High and Low Rates of Change between Benchmark Years, 1880–1953

(based on values in 1929 prices)

All Manufacturing	High 1880–1890	Low 1890–1900	High 1900–1904	Low 1909–1914	High 1914–1919	Low 1929–1937	High 1948–1953
Food and kindred products	(1890–1900)a					1929–1937	1948–1953
Textiles and their products	1880–1890	(1900–1904)	(1904–1909)	1909–1914	1914–1919	1929–1937	1948–1953
Leather and leather products	1880–1890	1890–1900	1900–1904	1909–1914	1914–1919	1929–1937	1948–1953
Rubber products	1880–1890	(1900–1904)			(1919–1929)	1929–1937	(1937–1948)
Forest products	1880–1890	(1900–1904)	(1904–1909)		1914–1919	1929–1937	1948–1953
Paper, pulp, and products			1900–1904	(1914–1919)		1929–1937	1948–1953
Printing, publishing, and allied industries	1880–1890	(1900–1904)	(1904–1919)		(1919–1929)	1929–1937	1948–1953
Chemicals and allied products	1880–1890	(1900–1904)	(1909–1914)			1929–1937	1948–1953
Petroleum refining	1880–1890	1890–1900	1900–1904	(1904–1909)	1914–1919	1929–1937	(1937–1948)
Stone, clay and glass products	1880–1890	1890–1900	1900–1904	(1914–1919)	(1919–1929)	1929–1937	1948–1953
Metals and metal products	1880–1890	1890–1900	1900–1904	1909–1914	1914–1919	1929–1937	1948–1953
Iron and steel and their products	1880–1890	1890–1900	1900–1904	1909–1914	1914–1919	(1919–1929)	1948–1953
Nonferrous metals and their products	1880–1890	(1900–1904)	(1904–1909)	1909–1914	1914–1919	1929–1937	1948–1953
Machinery, excluding transportation equipment	1880–1890	1890–1900	1900–1904	1909–1914	1914–1919	1929–1937	1948–1953
Transportation equipment	1880–1890	(1900–1904)			1914–1919	1929–1937	1948–1953
Miscellaneous	1880–1890	1890–1900	(1904–1909)	(1914–1919)	(1919–1929)	1929–1937	1948–1953

a A date in parentheses indicates that the turning point for a given industry group differs from that for all manufacturing.
Source: Based on data in Appendix Tables A-8 and A-15.

prolonged expansions occurred in two industry groups related to the revolution in road transportation: transportation equipment, which includes automobiles, and rubber products. In these industries expansion was initiated in 1900–1904 and continued until 1914–1919. Other groups that reached a peak during World War I, rather than in the twenties, were petroleum refining, the metal industries, textiles, and leather products. In all these industries, substantial military orders were added to regular civilian demands. The groups closely connected with building construction—such as forest products and stone, clay, and glass products—were depressed during World War I, when these activities had a low priority, but were booming during the twenties when restrictions were removed.[5]

Thus, the development of manufacturing has not always proceeded at an even pace, and at certain periods some branches of manufacturing have lagged behind and others have forged ahead. This uneven rate of growth is shown by our second measure of relative changes in manufacturing development. For selected benchmark years, total capital in each minor industry is expressed as a percentage of total capital in all manufacturing industries (Table 8). We have selected 1880, the first year for which comparatively reliable statistics are available, the beginning of the century, and years that closely follow the termination of World Wars I and II.[6] For these particular years it is possible to distinguish sixty-five minor industries.

Even by 1900, the industries that had been among the first to be mechanized were losing ground to newly developed products and to familiar commodities newly produced by the factory system with mechanical power and manipulation. Thus, the textile, leather, and forest products industries failed to expand as rapidly as all manufacturing industries on the average. Capital in these three major industry groups constituted 45 per cent of all manufacturing capital in 1880 and 34 per cent at the turn of the century. Within these old industries, new branches were emerging, particularly in textiles, as a result of the transfer of household activities to the factory. This was the case with women's, children's and infants' clothing, and knit goods, and these two minor industries had a better than average rate of expansion between 1880 and 1900.

The same sort of transfer explains the relative rise in food products; bakery products, canning, and slaughtering and meat packing were being rapidly shifted from the household to the market economy.

[5] In Clarence Long's investigation there is a trough in 1917–1919 and a subsequent peak in 1924–1927. (*Building Cycles and the Theory of Investment*, Princeton University Press, 1940, p. 136, Table 11.)

[6] At the time of writing, the basic data by minor industries for 1953 are not available.

TABLE 8

Total Capital in Manufacturing Industries: Percentage Distribution, by Minor Industry Groups, Selected Years, 1880–1948

(*per cent based on values in 1929 prices*)

	1880	1900	1919	1948
All manufacturing	100	100	100	100
Food and kindred products	18.5	20.6	16.4	13.8
Bakery and confectionery products	1.0	1.5	2.4	1.5
Canned products	0.3	0.8	1.0	1.5
Mill products	6.7	2.5	2.1	0.9
Packing house products	1.8	2.5	3.1	1.7
Sugar refining	1.0	2.7	1.2	0.7
Liquors and beverages	5.0	6.7	2.0	2.7
Nonalcoholic beverages	0.1	0.3	0.3	0.7
Malt liquors and malt	3.9	5.9	1.6	1.0
Wines	0.1	0.1	a	0.1
Distilled liquors	0.9	0.4	0.1	0.9
Other food products	1.2	2.5	3.0	2.8
Tobacco products	1.5	1.5	1.6	2.0
Textiles and their products	20.6	16.4	14.5	9.1
Cotton goods	8.4	6.3	5.0	b
Silk and rayon goods	0.7	1.0	1.2	b
Woolen and worsted goods	4.0	3.2	2.0	b
Carpets, floor coverings, etc.	0.8	0.6	0.4	0.4
Knit goods	0.6	1.0	1.2	0.8
Clothing	3.9	3.1	3.4	2.6
Hats, except cloth and millinery	0.3	0.3	0.3	0.1
Men's and boys' clothing, except fur and rubber	3.0	1.9	1.9	1.2
Women's clothing, children's and infants' wear except fur and rubber	0.3	0.6	1.0	1.3
Millinery	0.3	0.3	0.2	a
Textiles, n.e.c.	2.2	1.2	1.2	b
Cotton + silk and rayon + woolen and worsted goods + textiles, n.e.c.	(15.4)c	(11.7)c	(9.5)c	5.2
Leather and leather products	6.8	4.6	3.0	1.1
Boots and shoes	1.9	1.4	1.2	0.6
Other leather products	4.9	3.2	1.8	0.5
Leather, tanned, curried, and finished	3.2	2.4	1.3	0.3
Leather products, n.e.c.	1.8	0.8	0.5	0.2
Rubber products	0.3	0.6	2.1	1.8
Forest products	17.6	12.9	6.8	3.9
Sawmills and planing mill products	10.7	7.7	4.3	2.4
Other wood products	6.9	5.2	2.5	1.5
Wooden containers	1.2	0.9	0.5	0.2
Wood products, n.e.c.	5.7	4.3	2.0	1.3
Paper, pulp, and products	1.9	2.6	3.3	3.2
Paper, pulp, and paperboard mills	1.6	2.0	2.5	2.1
Paper bags, containers, and boxes	0.1	0.3	0.4	0.6
Other paper products	0.2	0.3	0.4	0.5
Printing, publishing, and allied industries	3.0	4.6	3.3	3.4
Book and job, including lithography	2.5	1.6	1.3	1.1
Newspapers and periodicals	d	2.6	1.7	1.8
Allied industries	0.5	0.4	0.3	0.5

(*continued*)

TABLE 8 (concluded)

	1880	1900	1919	1948
Chemicals and allied products	4.3	5.0	6.0	8.3
Fertilizers	0.6	0.7	0.7	0.3
Chemicals proper, acids, compounds, etc.	1.5	1.7	2.2	2.4
Allied chemical substances	2.2	2.7	3.1	5.5
Drugs, medicines, and cosmetics	0.4	0.6	0.7	1.2
Soaps, cleaning and polishing preparations	0.5	0.4	0.5	0.5
Paints and varnishes	0.5	0.6	0.6	0.8
Other chemical substances	0.8	1.0	1.3	3.0
Petrolum refining	0.8	1.1	3.0	14.2
Stone, clay, and glass products	3.2	4.0	3.6	2.8
Cement, lime, and concrete products	0.2	0.6	1.1	0.9
Clay and pottery products	1.4	1.8	1.2	0.5
Glass and glass products	0.8	0.8	0.7	0.6
Cut stone and products	0.7	0.6	0.3	0.1
Stone, clay, and glass products, n.e.c.	0.1	0.2	0.3	0.7
Metals and metal products	21.1	25.6	35.9	35.3
Iron and steel and their products	9.8	9.1	14.5	11.9
Iron and steel	7.9	6.9	11.4	8.7
Blast furnaces, steel works, and rolling mills	7.1	6.0	9.0	5.6
Ordnance and accessories	0.3	0.2	0.6	0.2
Tin cans and other tinware	d	d	0.6	0.5
Iron and steel, n.e.c.	0.5	0.6	1.2	2.4
Metal building materials and supplies	0.3	1.0	1.7	2.1
Hardware, tools, etc.	1.5	1.2	1.4	1.1
Nonferrous metals and their products	2.4	3.5	3.9	3.1
Clocks, watches, and parts	0.2	0.3	0.2	0.2
Jewelry, silverware, and plating	0.6	0.6	0.7	0.3
Smelting, refining, and alloying	0.7	2.0	2.4	2.2
Nonferrous metal products, n.e.c.	0.9	0.6	0.6	0.4
Machinery excluding transportation equipment	8.6	11.0	12.0	13.3
Electrical machinery and equipment; radios, complete or parts	0.1	1.0	2.5	4.4
Agricultural machinery	2.2	1.9	0.9	1.6
Office equipment	0.2	0.3	0.4	0.8
Factory, household, and miscellaneous machinery	6.1	7.8	8.2	6.5
Transportation equipment	0.4	2.0	5.3	7.0
Motor vehicles, complete or parts	d	0.4	4.2	5.2
Locomotives and railroad equipment	0.4	1.6	1.1	0.8
Aircraft and parts	d	d	d	1.0
Miscellaneous	1.8	1.9	2.0	3.1
Professional, scientific, photographic, and optical equipment	0.1	0.2	0.3	1.1
Miscellaneous, n.e.c.	1.7	1.7	1.7	2.0

n.e.c. = not elsewhere classified.

a Less than one-tenth of one per cent.

b Included in the published source in a new classification, "textile mill products," and entered here in the last category under "textiles and their products."

c Sum of component percentages to provide figures comparable to those for 1948.

d Not covered by the source.

Source: Based on data in Appendix Table A-8; 1948 data are adjusted to exclude investment in emergency facilities.

Milling, on the other hand, which had been a factory process for many decades, declined sharply in relative importance during these two decades.

The largest relative expansion occurred in new industries that were still at the threshold of tremendous growth: transportation equipment; electrical machinery and equipment; metal building materials and supplies; smelting, refining, and alloying of nonferrous metals; cement, lime, and concrete products; paper bags, containers, and boxes; and rubber products. In the succeeding twenty-year period this same group of industries, together with petroleum refining and iron and steel, nearly doubled their share of manufacturing capital (from 15.5 per cent in 1900 to 29.9 in 1919). The relative decline of the old industries —textiles, leather, and forest products—continued. They accounted for a third of the total in 1900 and a quarter in 1919.

Some of the industries with a better than average rate of capital expansion up to and including 1919 had turned down by 1948. This was true of the basic metal industries, both ferrous and nonferrous, and rubber tires and tubes. Some of the metal-using industries, on the other hand (electrical machinery and equipment including radios and television sets; automobiles; airplanes; office equipment; professional, scientific, and optical instruments; and metal building materials and supplies) continued to expand at a better than average rate. However, the largest relative gains occurred in petroleum refining, followed by chemicals and allied products.[7]

The paper and printing industries accounted for about the same percentage of manufacturing capital in 1948 as in 1919. Food and kindred products as a group declined in relative importance, although the minor industries of canning and deep-freezing, and tobacco products continued their capital formation at a faster rate than that for all manufacturing industries. The older industries continued to wane, using only a seventh of all manufacturing capital in 1948 compared with a fourth in 1919. Indeed, the decline in leather and in forest products had proceeded to the point where, in absolute terms (constant prices), less capital was being utilized after World War II than after World War I. In textiles, the rise of synthetic fabrics, which cannot be shown separately, failed to offset the relative and absolute loss of capital in the primary textile industries. Throughout this period the only textile industry of growing importance in terms of capital was the manufacture of women's, children's, and infants' clothing.

In sum, the older industries, such as textiles, leather, and forest products, have declined in importance over this seventy-year period.

---

[7] The percentage distribution in 1948 is based on estimates that exclude investment in emergency facilities. We find that this doesn't change the basic trend.

The newer ones, such as the metal-producing and -using industries, chemicals, and petroleum refining, have increased in importance.[8]

Mining, 1870–1953

In mining, the depreciated net value of structures and equipment is designated "plant," and the sum of inventories, cash, and receivables, "working capital." The net value of surface land and mineral resources owned by the mining establishment, excluding leased land,[9] is termed "land." The sum of plant and working capital is called "capital," and the sum of capital and land, "total capital."[10]

Chart 3 shows the growth of mining capital (book values adjusted for price changes) by major industries. Like output, capital grew rapidly in all industries to about 1909, but the rate of growth dropped sharply between 1909 and 1919 in all industries except oil. However, because of the continued rapid growth of capital in the oil industry, the rate of growth of capital in all mining was substantial until 1929. The depression of the thirties caused a shrinkage of capital in all branches, and there has been only a partial recovery since then. In none of the major mining industries did capital in 1953 exceed the 1929 level. In anthracite, the 1953 level was only one-third of the 1929 total.

These trends and, in particular, the absence of net capital formation in mining during the last two and a half decades, are brought into even sharper focus by the changes in the deflated value of capital between selected years (Table 9).

Little or no evidence exists that the long-term rate of growth of capital in mining has undergone cyclical fluctuations in the manner of capital growth in manufacturing. The evidence indicates rather that the rate of growth began to retard early in this period and, typically, was not arrested until the decade of World War II or even later.

---

[8] The relation between differential rates of growth and differential movements in capital-output ratios is discussed in Chapter V.

[9] The value of leased land is excluded because of difficulties in estimating it for the period after 1919. For the narrower purpose of this study the omission is not significant. Primarily, our concern with the book value of land stems from its importance in determining the capital dimension of a mining enterprise, for example, its asset structure as compared with its liability structure. No such importance can be ascribed to the value of leases. Moreover, the only way to approximate the value of leases is to capitalize royalties. Royalties are strictly dependent upon the value of output in a given year. Hence, the value of leases is directly related to the value of output and is of limited interest for our purpose. For a more extended discussion, see Appendix B, section E.

[10] The basic estimates of total capital in book values and of capital in 1929 prices, and a short description of the methods used to derive them, are given in Appendix Tables B-9 and B-11.

CHART 3

Value of Capital Excluding Land, by Major Mining Industries, Selected Years, 1870–1953

(values in 1929 prices)

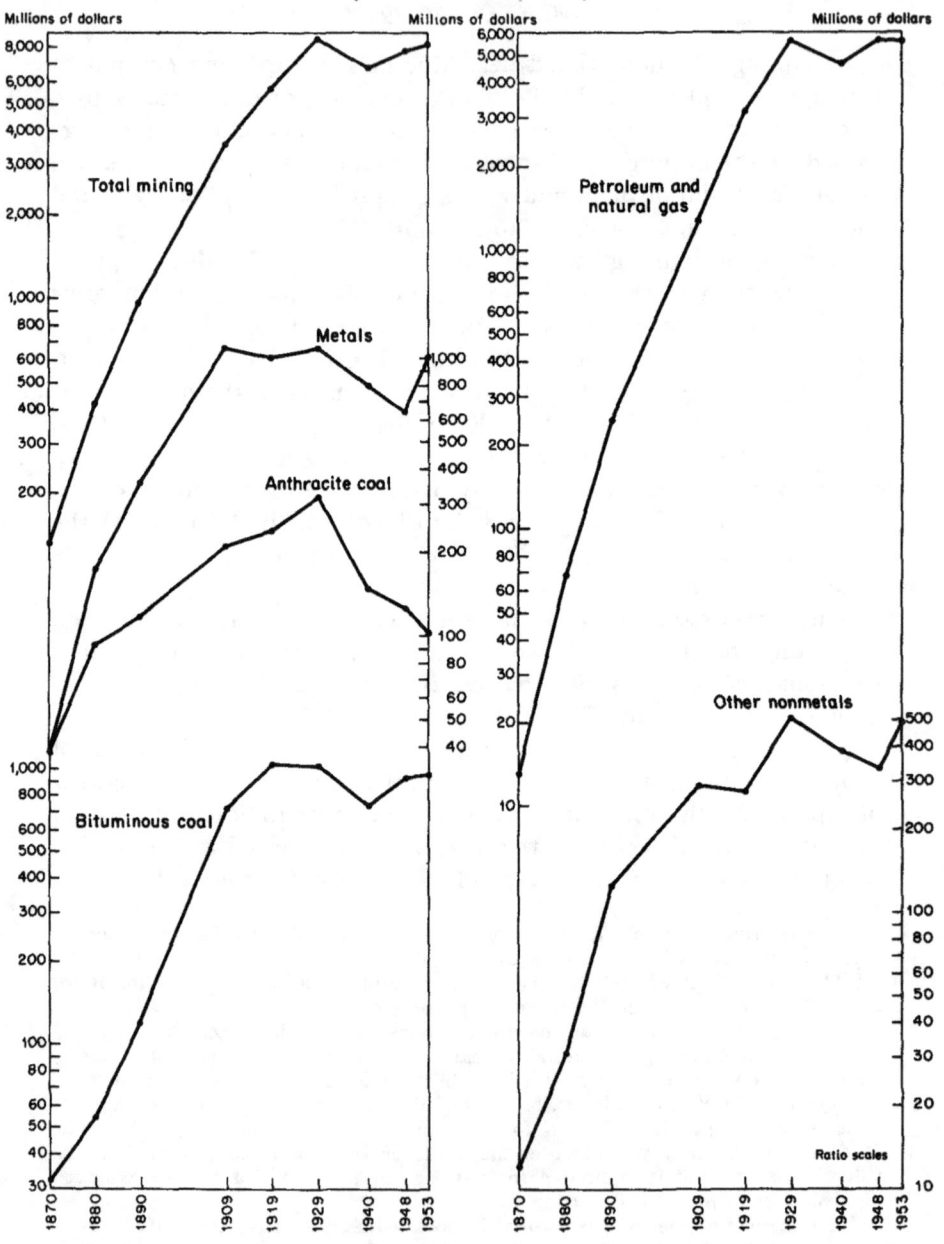

Source: Based on Appendix Table B-11.

TABLE 9
Mining Industries: Total Change in Capital between Selected Years, 1870–1953
(millions of dollars in 1929 prices)

	All Mining[a]	Metals	Coal		Petroleum and Natural Gas	Other Nonmetals
			Anthracite	Bituminous		
1870–1880	+283	+136	+55	+22	+55	+13
1880–1890	+508	+183	+24	+64	+176	+62
1890–1909	+2,558	+736	+94	+595	+1,020	+111
1909–1919	+2,120	−89	+29	+323	+1,869	−10
1919–1929	+2,846	+82	+78	−10	+2,468	+228
1929–1940	−1,833	−288	−170	−296	−964	−116
1940–1948	+1,074	−147	−19	+229	+1,059	−48
1948–1953	+354	+368	−26	+7	−146	+151

[a] Because of rounding details may not add to total.
Source: Appendix Table B-11.

Table 10[11] shows that the highest rate of growth for total mining took place between 1870 and 1880 and that in all major branches except bituminous coal capital grew faster than output.[12] In the next decade, total mining output continued to grow rapidly, at a rate slightly lower than that during 1870–1880. Capital increased more than output in all major industries except anthracite mining.[13] The pattern of rapid mining growth continued at an only slightly lessened rate in the third period, 1890–1909. Capital grew faster than output in all the major industries except metals.[14]

During 1909–1919, capital continued to increase at a faster rate than output in the three major industries enjoying relatively high rates of

---

[11] The comparison given here and in Tables 23, 24, and 33 is somewhat affected by differences between the bench marks with respect to employment levels. For a discussion of this problem, see Appendix B, section G.

[12] The rates of growth for this period are probably somewhat overstated because the coverage of the 1870 census is incomplete, particularly in the case of precious metals.

[13] Note that during this decade the growth of capital in bituminous coal conformed strictly to the growth of output and that in copper mining the increase in output was steeper than that in capital. However, the statistical record for copper mining is unreliable in the earlier years.

The high capital figure reported for anthracite in 1880 seems to have worried the census authorities (*Report on the Mining Industries of the United States: 1880*, Bureau of the Census, p. 639). The inclusion of the value of nonproducing mines of the then largest anthracite mining company—the Philadelphia and Reading Coal and Iron Company—may have contributed to the overstatement (*ibid.*, p. 631). Chart 3 shows that the 1880 figure lies far above a smooth curve connecting the 1870 figure with the later figures. This would be the case even if we made a reasonable allowance for any possible understatement of the figures for 1870. This suggests that the 1880 census overstates the value of capital in anthracite mining.

[14] The latter is affected by the shifts in industry weights (Table 10).

TABLE 10

Mining Industries: Capital (Excluding Land) and Output, Rates of Change per Year between Selected Years, 1870–1953
(per cent based on values in 1929 prices)

A. MAJOR INDUSTRIES

	Total Mining		Metals		Anthracite		Bituminous		Petroleum and Natural Gas		Other Nonmetals	
	Capital	Output	Capital	Output	Capital	Output	Capital	Output	Capital	Output	Capital	Output
1870–1880	+12.4	+7.1	+16.5	+10.0	+9.5	+5.0	+5.5	+8.3	+18.2	+16.2	+10.5	n.c.
1880–1890	+8.4	+6.6	+7.4	+5.6	+2.3	+4.7	+8.2	+8.3	+13.6	+7.0	+14.6	+13.3
1890–1909	+6.8	+5.4	+5.8	+6.2	+3.0	+2.9	+9.4	+7.1	+8.6	+7.0	+4.4	+3.9
1909–1919	+4.9	+2.4	−0.9	+0.6	+1.3	+0.9	+3.8	+2.0	+9.5	+7.9	−0.5	+0.1
1919–1929	+4.1	+4.7	+0.8	+3.2	+2.8	−1.7	−0.1	+1.6	+6.0	+11.3	+6.3	+6.8
1929–1940	−2.2	+0.5	−2.8	+0.1	−7.2	−3.3	−3.1	−1.4	−1.7	+2.5	−2.4	−0.4
1940–1948	+1.9	+4.1	−2.7	+0.1	−1.8	+1.3	+3.5	+3.5	+2.6	+5.6	−1.7	+4.9
1948–1953	+0.9	+2.2	+9.4	+2.4	−4.6	−13.1	+0.1	−5.6	−0.5	+4.4	+7.7	+5.9
1870–1919	+7.9	+5.4	+6.8	+5.7	+3.8	+3.3	+7.2	+6.6	+11.6	+9.0	+5.6a	+4.1a
1919–1953	+1.1	+2.8	0.0	+1.3	−2.5	−3.1	−0.2	+10.0	+1.7	+6.0	+1.7	+3.8

B. MINOR METALS INDUSTRIES

	Iron		Copper		Lead and Zinc		Precious Metals	
	Capital	Output	Capital	Output	Capital	Output	Capital	Output
1870–1880	+13.6	+7.7	+17.3	+8.2	+10.2	+11.0	n.c.	n.c.
1880–1890	+9.9	+7.3	+6.4	+14.6	+4.0	+3.7	+7.1	+1.4
1890–1909	+8.5	+6.6	+12.2	+9.0	+11.0	+7.3	+2.9	+2.9
1909–1919	+0.4	+1.7	+5.3	+0.1	+5.3	+7.0	−11.6	−6.3

n.c. = not comparable.
a 1880–1919.
Source: Based on Appendix Tables B-8 and B-11 and worksheets.

growth—oil and gas, bituminous coal, and anthracite. The other two industry groups—metals and other nonmetals—show an absolute decline in the amount of capital invested and a very moderate increase, if any, in output. Has this decline in capital been a result of shifts in the relative importance of component industries or a result of lessened use of capital in each of the industries? In the case of other nonmetals the answer cannot be readily given. For metals, a glance at Table 10 suggests that the declining output of the precious metals mining industry, an unusually large capital user, was as much responsible as the decreasing use of capital per unit of output in iron, lead and zinc, and precious metals mining.

What appeared in 1909–1919 to be an exceptional relationship (the faster growth of output than of capital in metals and in other nonmetals) became the rule during 1919–1929. In metal mining, capital increased slightly, while output increased substantially. In bituminous coal, a moderate increase in production was accompanied by a slight decline in capital. In oil and other nonmetal mining, there was a substantial increase in output with a relatively smaller increase in capital. The only exception to the new growth relationship was in anthracite mining, where capital increased and output fell.[15] By comparison, the shrinkage of capital in anthracite during the thirties appears unusually rapid.

The story of the thirties is one of capital shrinkage in all mining industries, accompanied by a less than proportional shrinkage in production, and even, in the case of oil, an increase. In the forties, the relationships are more varied. Capital declined and production increased in metals, anthracite, and other nonmetals; bituminous coal output increased in proportion to the increase in capital; and the increase in output of natural gas and petroleum was more than proportional to the increase in capital. In the five years between 1948 and 1953, a marked reversal in pattern developed. Only in the petroleum industry did capital decline while output increased. In metals and in other nonmetals, the increase in capital was substantially higher than in output. In anthracite, on the other hand, the decline in capital was less than the decline in output. In bituminous coal mining, a slight increase in capital occurred along with a considerable decline in output.

During 1870–1919, when growth was rapid, capital grew at a steeper rate than output in all mining industries. During 1919–1953, when growth was at a much lower rate, production rose at a faster rate

[15] This somewhat strange increase in capital at a time of a sustained downward trend in production is also indicated by the capital figures reported by the Pennsylvania State Bureau of Statistics in its *Report on Productive Industries*.

when capital expanded. When capital contracted, output was either stationary or declined at a less rapid rate than capital.[16]

Summary of Findings

1. In manufacturing industries, the highest annual rate of growth in the stock of capital, expressed in 1929 prices, occurred during 1880–1890, the first decade covered by the statistics, when modern manufacturing in general was emerging from its earlier beginnings. The evidence of subsequent retardation in the rate of growth of capital is unmistakable, but it is equally clear that the decreases in the rate of growth have not been continuous. Rather, the evidence suggests, there have been alternating periods of relatively high and low rates of increase.

2. This uneven pace of development was even more apparent in the individual branches of manufacturing; at certain periods, some branches have lagged behind and others have forged ahead. This is revealed by expressing total capital in each branch as a percentage of total capital in all manufacturing industries for each benchmark year. Even by 1900, textiles, leather, and forest products, industries that had been among the first to be mechanized, were losing ground to familiar commodities then newly produced by the factory system and to newly developed products. The largest relative growth occurred in new industries that were still at the threshold of tremendous growth: transportation equipment; electrical machinery and equipment; metal building materials and supplies; nonferrous metals; cement, lime, and concrete products; paper bags, containers, and boxes; and rubber products. The basic metal industries, and rubber tires and tubes, industries with a better than average rate of capital expansion up to 1919, had a less than average rate by 1948. Some of the metal-using industries, on the other hand, continued to expand at a better than average rate. The largest relative gains, however, occurred in petroleum refining, followed by chemicals and allied products.

3. In mining, capital (book values adjusted for price changes) grew rapidly in all branches to about 1909, but the rate of growth dropped sharply between 1909 and 1919 in all industries except oil. The depression of the thirties caused a shrinkage of capital in all branches, and there has been only a partial recovery since then. In none of the major branches did capital in 1953 exceed the 1929 level.

4. There is little or no evidence that the long-term growth of capital in the total of all mining industries has undergone alternating periods

---

[16] For long-term trends in employment, hours, horsepower, and supplies in mining industries, see Appendix Table B-15; see also, Israel Borenstein, *Capital and Output Trends in Mining Industries, 1870–1948*, Occasional Paper No. 45, pp. 19–28.

of high and low rates of growth similar to those in manufacturing. The evidence indicates, rather, that the rate of growth began to retard early in this period and, typically, was not arrested until the decade of World War II, or even later.

5. In the period 1870–1919, when growth was rapid, capital grew at a steeper rate than output in all mining industries. In the period 1919–1953, when growth was at a much lower rate, output grew at a faster rate when capital expanded and was either stationary or declined at a less rapid rate when capital contracted.

CHAPTER III

Trends in Capital-Output Ratios

THE relationship between capital and output can be investigated by relating either the change in capital to the associated change in output (the marginal ratio of capital to output) or the stock of capital existing in a given period to the total output of the period (average ratio of capital to output). When output is increasing—which generally has been the case during these decades—the movement of one ratio can be inferred from the movement of the other. There is no need, therefore, to analyze changes in both.[1] We use the average ratios.[2]

Capital-Output Ratios in Reported and Constant Prices, All Manufacturing (1880–1953) and Mining (1870–1953)

In all manufacturing industries the amount of capital invested per dollar of output rose steadily from 1880 through 1914 (see Chart 4 and Table 11; capital is measured in book values and output in current prices, magnitudes that owe little to our statistical processing). The amount of capital invested per output dollar began to fall after 1914 and continued to do so through 1948. The capital-output ratio for 1919 was sharply below the peak ratio because the inflation of output prices greatly exceeded the inflation of capital in book values. Similarly, the inflation of post-World War II caused a sharp drop in the ratios between 1937 and 1948. Contributory factors were the unusually high rate of capacity utilization and the inability of management to expand capacity to desired levels because of continued shortages. The substantial expansion in capital between 1948 and 1953 eliminated many of the bottlenecks of the early postwar years and exceeded the sharp rise in output. As a result, the 1953 capital-output ratio, without adjustment for price changes, exceeded that for 1948 by nearly 7 per cent.

The 1937 ratio is of critical importance in establishing the downward trend. Although business activity in 1937 was at a cyclical peak, the rate of capacity utilization in 1937 was less than that in 1929. Were

---

[1] It can be shown algebraically that if output increases, a rise in the average ratios means that the marginal ratio is higher than the larger of the two average ratios bounding the interval; if output increases, a decline in the average ratios means that the marginal ratio is lower than the smaller of the two average ratios. It follows from this that the marginal ratios fluctuate more widely than the average ratios. These relationships were brought to our attention by Simon Kuznets (see Introduction, note 5, above).

[2] The use of average ratios obviates the problem of dealing with negative changes in one term of the ratio.

CAPITAL-OUTPUT RATIOS

this the only factor that had changed, then the 1937 ratio would be higher than the 1929 ratio. Since it is lower, other factors may have been operative.

Since price changes are incorporated more rapidly into the value of output than into the book value of capital, they should be eliminated for a truer perspective. This is most effectively accomplished by deflating both output and book values of capital. We express them in

CHART 4

Ratios of Capital to Output and to Value Added, Selected Valuations, All Manufacturing, Selected Years, 1880–1953

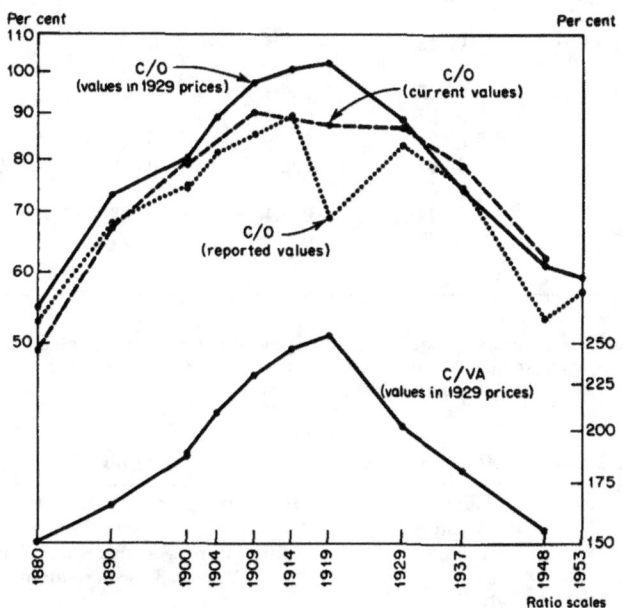

C/O = capital-output ratio.
C/VA = capital value added ratio.
Source: Table 11.

1929 prices. Introduction of the constant price base raises the level of the ratios for 1919 and 1948 and produces smoother trend movements. With price changes eliminated (but not revaluations of capital assets), the capital-output ratio rises through 1919 at a faster rate than the uncorrected ratio, and declines thereafter (until 1948), again at a faster

CAPITAL AND OUTPUT TRENDS

TABLE 11
Ratios of Capital to Output and to Value Added, Selected Valuations,
All Manufacturing, Selected Years, 1880–1953

	Ratio Of			
Benchmark Years	Capital (book value) to Output (current prices) (1)	Capital to Output (1929 prices) (2)	Capital to Output (current prices[a]) (3)	Capital to Value Added (1929 prices) (4)
1880	0.528	0.547	0.489	1.506
1890	0.679	0.730	0.670	1.651
1900				
Comparable with preceding years	0.748	0.803	0.795	1.878
Comparable with following years	0.743	0.794	0.790	1.882
1904	0.815	0.891	n.a.	2.093
1909	0.851	0.967	0.900	2.309
1914	0.894	1.008	n.a.	2.460
1919	0.688	1.022	0.873	2.555
1929	0.829	0.885	0.867	2.020
1937	0.744	0.741	0.787	1.809
1948	0.532	0.609	0.621	1.550
1953[b]	0.570	0.590	n.a.	n.a.

n.a. = not available.

[a] Capital in current prices is equivalent to replacement costs in the given year.
[b] If privately operated, government-owned facilities are excluded from total capital, the respective ratios are 0.549 and 0.570 (see Table 26, note b).

Source

Column	Appendix Table	Remarks
1	A-8 and A-15	1953 output from worksheets
2	A-13 and A-15	
3	A-10 (output only)	capital from worksheets (see App. A, sec. B, part 3 for derivation)
4	A-10	

rate than the uncorrected ratio.[3] Despite the rapid expansion in real capital between 1948 and 1953, the ratio decreased by about 3 per cent.

Some might argue that the appropriate denominator of the capital-output ratio is value added, in order to eliminate interfirm transactions

---

[3] Another way to minimize price distortion is to relate capital in current prices (i.e., replacement cost) to output in current prices. This procedure reduces the errors of estimate, because no adjustments are made in the reported value of output. Significantly, the path traced by the ratios in current prices is very similar to the one traced by the ratios in constant prices, except for 1919 (Chart 4 and Table 11).

from the value of product. Since this claim has some merit, we show (Chart 5) the ratio of capital to value added in manufacturing, both in constant prices. This ratio, too, traces virtually the same pattern as the capital-output ratio based on values in constant prices.[4] However, ratios based on the indexes of manufacturing output prepared by Frickey

CHART 5

Indexes of Ratios of Capital to Output and to Value Added, All Manufacturing, Selected Years, 1880–1948

(*based on values in 1929 prices*)

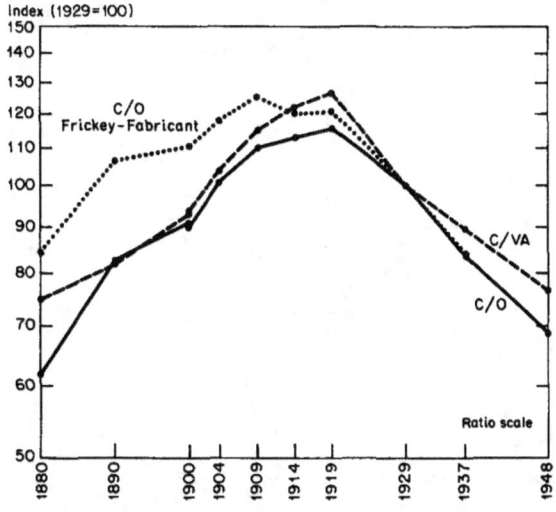

C/O = capital-output ratio.
C/VA = capital-value added ratio.
Source: Appendix Tables A-8 and A-10.

and Fabricant show a definite reversal in direction beginning in 1909 instead of 1919.

On the basis of this evidence, we can say that manufacturing has developed along the following course: In the earlier decades, an increasing fraction of a dollar of capital was used to produce a dollar of output; in more recent decades, a decreasing fraction of a dollar of capital has been sufficient to produce a dollar of output. This is consistent with the interpretation that, in the earlier decades, capital

[4] In mining, also, the trend movements are similar whether the denominator is value of product or value added (Table 36, below).

innovations on balance probably served more to replace other factor inputs than to increase output. More recently, the balance has been in the other direction—capital innovations serve more to increase the

CHART 6

Capital-Output Ratios, by Major Mining Industries, Selected Years, 1870–1953

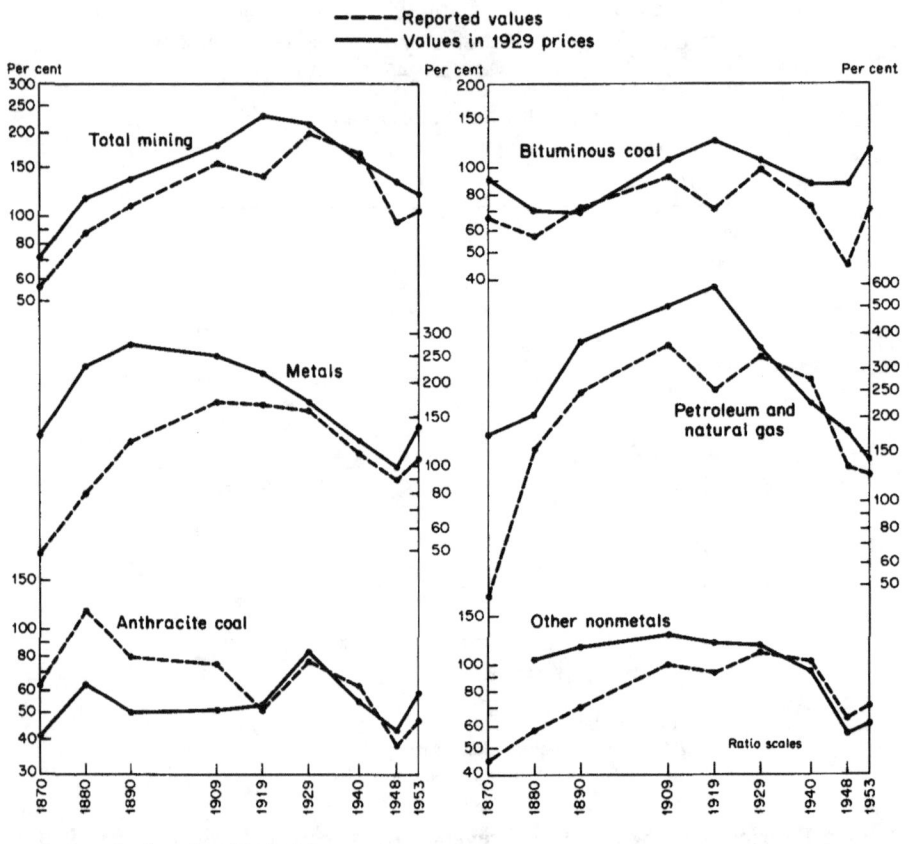

Source: Based on Table 23.

efficiency of capital and hence, to increase output, rather than to replace other factor inputs.

Trend movements in the capital-output ratio were much the same in mining as in manufacturing. The general configuration of the trend movements is similar whether the ratios are based on reported values or on values in 1929 prices (Chart 6 and Table 12).[5] However, the ratio

[5] See Chapter II, note 9

based on deflated values reached a peak around 1919. It has continued downward through 1953, the final year of our estimates. On the other hand, the ratios based on reported values have a steeper rise, a sharper decline, and a hollow in 1919. The reason for these differences is that 1870, 1919, and 1940–1948 were years of war or postwar inflation, when price increases were incorporated into the market value of the product

TABLE 12

Capital-Output Ratios: All Mining, Selected Valuations, Selected Years, 1870–1953

Benchmark Years	Capital-Output Ratios based on:	
	Values in 1929 Prices	Reported Values
1870	0.72	0.56
1880	1.16	0.87
1890	1.36	1.09
1909	1.80	1.55
1919	2.30	1.39
1929	2.14	1.99
1940	1.59	1.68
1948	1.34	0.96
1953	1.26	1.16

Source: Appendix Tables B-7 to B-11.

more promptly than into the book value of capital. Thus, the ratios based on reported values are too low in those years. The capital-output ratios, especially the plant[6]-output ratios, based on reported values are useful chiefly as a check on the results of the adjustment for the variation in price levels. Their only virtue is that they are based on figures obtained by less statistical processing than those based on values in 1929 prices.

Effect of Data Deficiencies on Trend

The apparent reversal in the trend of the capital-output ratio is our cardinal finding, and it is important, therefore, that its empirical validity be above challenge. For this reason, we consider the probable impact on this finding of some of the deficiencies in the data and in our procedures.

The reversal in trend cannot be attributed to the adjustment for price changes because the reversal also appears in the ratios based on

[6] Net value of structures and equipment.

reported values. Moreover, the adjustment for price changes alters the ratios in the direction demanded by logic.

If the downward movement in the ratios between 1919 and 1929 is suspect because of the shift in the source of our data—from the *Census of Manufactures* to *Statistics of Income*—we point to the continued decline in the ratios between 1929 and 1948, when all the ratios are based on data from *Statistics of Income*.

While the precise impact of the shift in the treatment of depreciation on the trend in capital-output ratios is difficult to assess because of serious gaps in our information, some important conclusions can be made with certainty. For example, beginning with 1919, no significant changes have taken place in the treatment of depreciation. Therefore, the fall in the capital-output ratios after 1919 cannot be due to changes in the treatment of depreciation.[7]

What of the rising trend in the ratios between 1880 and 1909? There is no reason for believing that any important shift in the practice of depreciation accounting occurred before the inception of the corporate income tax, i.e., before 1909. Whatever bias stems from the situation, however, minimizes the rise in the capital-output ratio and thus strengthens our finding. If, as we believe, capital was increasingly reported on a net basis, as formal depreciation accounting became more widespread, then the rise in the capital-output ratio is understated. Between 1909 and 1914, this understatement should be especially pronounced because of the widespread acceptance of depreciation accounting following the introduction of the corporate income tax. If capital expenditures treated as operating expenditures were excluded from the reported figures on invested capital in 1909 and earlier years, the level of the capital-output ratios in those years would be lower than the "true" level. The trend of the ratios before 1909 would not be affected unless there was a trend in the percentage of these expenditures to the stock of capital. Since the important changes in capital accounting in manufacturing occurred after 1909, we conclude that there probably was no strong trend in this direction and that the estimates of capital-output ratios are, consequently, understated.

Can the rise in the ratios for manufacturing between 1900 and 1904 be attributed to the inflation of capital assets resulting from the mergers of that period? Undoubtedly, part of the rise can be traced to this development. Mergers were most important in iron and steel and their products, and in tobacco products, and these were the only industries in which the rise from 1900 to 1904 in the capital-output ratios based on reported values was spectacularly large (39 per cent for

---

[7] For the effect of another aspect of depreciation during recent decades, see p. 46.

iron and steel and their products and 133 per cent for tobacco).[8] However, even if we exclude these two major groups from the computation, the capital-output ratio for 1904 is still 4 per cent higher than the 1900 ratio, and for 1909 the ratio is 10 per cent above 1900. With these two major groups included, the percentage increases were 10 and 15. This suggests that not all of the rise between 1900 and 1904 or 1909 can be explained by promoters' revaluation of the assets of industrial combinations.

Thus, the rising trend in the ratios between 1870 or 1880 and 1909–1919 is no accounting mirage, and the declining trend after 1919 cannot be attributed merely to the shift in depreciation practices.

Statistics of Income for 1929 and later years includes intangible assets such as patent rights and good will. Exclusion of these intangible assets in the earlier years raises the level of the ratios for 1929 and after but does not affect the direction of movement. Our finding of a decline in the capital-output ratios for this period is not, therefore, affected by the slight shift in the definition of capital.

The ratios for 1929, 1937, 1948, and 1953 are based on balance sheet data of corporations only. The ratios for earlier years are based on data for all firms, incorporated and unincorporated alike.[9] However, unincorporated firms have smaller assets per firm than the average corporation, and the smaller the firm, the smaller the capital-output ratio. Therefore, the lack of comparability adds to the firmness of our results.

And this is also the effect on the 1948 ratio of our treatment of the wartime emergency facilities subject to accelerated amortization.[10] We assume that these facilities are subject only to normal depreciation; but because of the specialized character of some of them, the rate of obsolescence must have been above average. Thus, the 1948 estimate of capital is overstated by a small amount; and on this score, too, the "true" capital-output ratio would be slightly lower than our estimate.

---

[8] The relative importance of mergers in major industry groups is measured by relating the cumulative authorized capital stock by major groups as reported by Myron W. Watkins (*Industrial Combinations and Public Policy* [Houghton Mifflin, 1927], Appendix II) to the 1905 *Census of Manufactures* figure on capital by major groups. In iron and steel and their products, authorized capital stock was 98 per cent of census capital in 1904, and in tobacco products 128 per cent. For all other industries, authorized capital stock amounted to one-third of capital reported in the 1905 census.

[9] Unincorporated firms accounted for 8.5 per cent of value added in manufacturing in 1929 and for 8.1 per cent in 1947 (see *Census of Manufactures* for these years). In mining, the unincorporated firms accounted for 9 per cent of total value of output in 1939 (see *Census of Mining, 1939*).

[10] In mining, the value of wartime emergency facilities subject to accelerated amortization was negligible. At its peak in 1943, accelerated amortization amounted to only 5 per cent of normal depreciation.

Depreciation accounting since 1929 beclouds our view of the secular movement of capital. Some argue, for example, that statutory depreciation charges in manufacturing are too high (length-of-life estimates are too low). Consequently, net capital is understated, and the understatement becomes progressively larger as the stock of capital expands. Could this understatement cause the capital-output ratio to decline after 1929? This possibility could be explored in the following way. In each benchmark year, we would add the amount of the understatement of the stock of capital to the reported values. We would then compute the capital-output ratios. However, we cannot estimate the true amount of the understatement, and we are obliged to assume varying amounts of understatement. We start with the extreme assumption that there is no capital consumption and that the understatement is equal to the entire depreciation reserve. The resultant ratios of gross total capital to output (both in constant prices) are 1.199, 0.998, and 0.856 for 1929, 1937, and 1948, respectively. The downward trend is clear and substantial, and it would be pointless to experiment with smaller amounts of understatement of net capital. Therefore, the downward trend of the ratios based on capital net of depreciation cannot be attributed to a progressive understatement of the net capital accounts.

Our appraisal of the statistical materials we are obliged to use is reassuring. It fails to disclose any weakness large enough to shake our confidence in the validity of the trend in the capital-output ratios, particularly when our interest in centered on the broad pattern of movement.

Effect of Changes in the Composition of Manufacturing Industries

Thus far, we have presented ratios based on aggregative data—fixed and working capital combined, all industries, and all firms regardless of size. Could the reversal in the trend of the ratios have been caused by the shifting importance of the components of the aggregates? Fortunately, we have sufficient evidence to give definitive answers on the effects of changes in the type of assets and of interindustry differences in growth.

A casual inspection of the deflated capital-output ratios (in percentages) by minor industries for 1880 (Appendix Table A-13) is sufficient to indicate their wide range—from 8.5 (packing house products) and 25.7 (boots and shoes) at the lower end, to 207.8 (agricultural machinery and equipment) and 211.4 (chemicals proper, acids, compounds, etc.) at the upper end. We can infer from Table 6 that the various industries have grown at different rates. Thus, the possibility exists that industries with relatively high capital-output ratios in

1880 expanded more rapidly until 1919 than those with relatively low ratios and, thus, caused the ratio for all manufacturing to rise. Similarly, after 1919, did industries with relatively low ratios become more important than those with high ratios, and so cause the ratio for all manufacturing to decline?

Price Adjustments and Their Effect

Before we investigate the foregoing problems, we must consider whether our method of deflating the book value of capital would in itself impose a common pattern of change on the ratios of the minor industries. Our method was to derive a set of composite indexes, one for each of fifteen major industry groups, from (1) an index of building costs (identical for all industries) based on a fifty-year life; (2) an index of prices of machinery and equipment differently weighted in each major group according to the length of life typical of the industry; and (3) as a deflator of working capital, an index of wholesale prices of the output of each major industry group. The composite index for a given major industry was applied to all minor industries classified under the given major industry.

Chart 7 shows the indexes used for each of the fifteen groups to adjust book values of capital to 1929 prices. The strong resemblance among these indexes cannot be denied, and this result is to be expected in view of the procedure. However, it does not necessarily follow that these indexes differ by substantial margins from the movements of indexes based on more complete price data, since producers' prices of many commodities move in sympathy over the longer term. The movement of the implicit price indexes used to express output in 1929 prices also supports this view (Chart 8). Here, also, the individual indexes, except for rubber products, show only small deviations from a common pattern, despite the fact that each group index is based on wholesale price quotations for a different roster of commodities.

In Chart 9 we show, for each major industry, two sets of capital-output ratios, one based on reported values and one on 1929 prices. As a result of the price adjustments, the 1919 and 1948 ratios have been raised. These ratios are "too low" when based on reported values because, in both years, the culmination of rapid price rises affected the value of output more than it did the book value of capital.

Only in 2 of the 15 groups, rubber products, and petroleum refining, is it probable that the price adjustments have seriously distorted the movements of the ratio before 1929. It is important to note that the reversal in direction of the capital-output ratios exists in the unadjusted ratios, and the price adjustment has the effect, in many cases, of dating the peak at 1919 rather than at an earlier benchmark year.

CHART 7

Major Manufacturing Industries: Price Indexes (Book Value) of Total Capital, Selected Years, 1880–1953

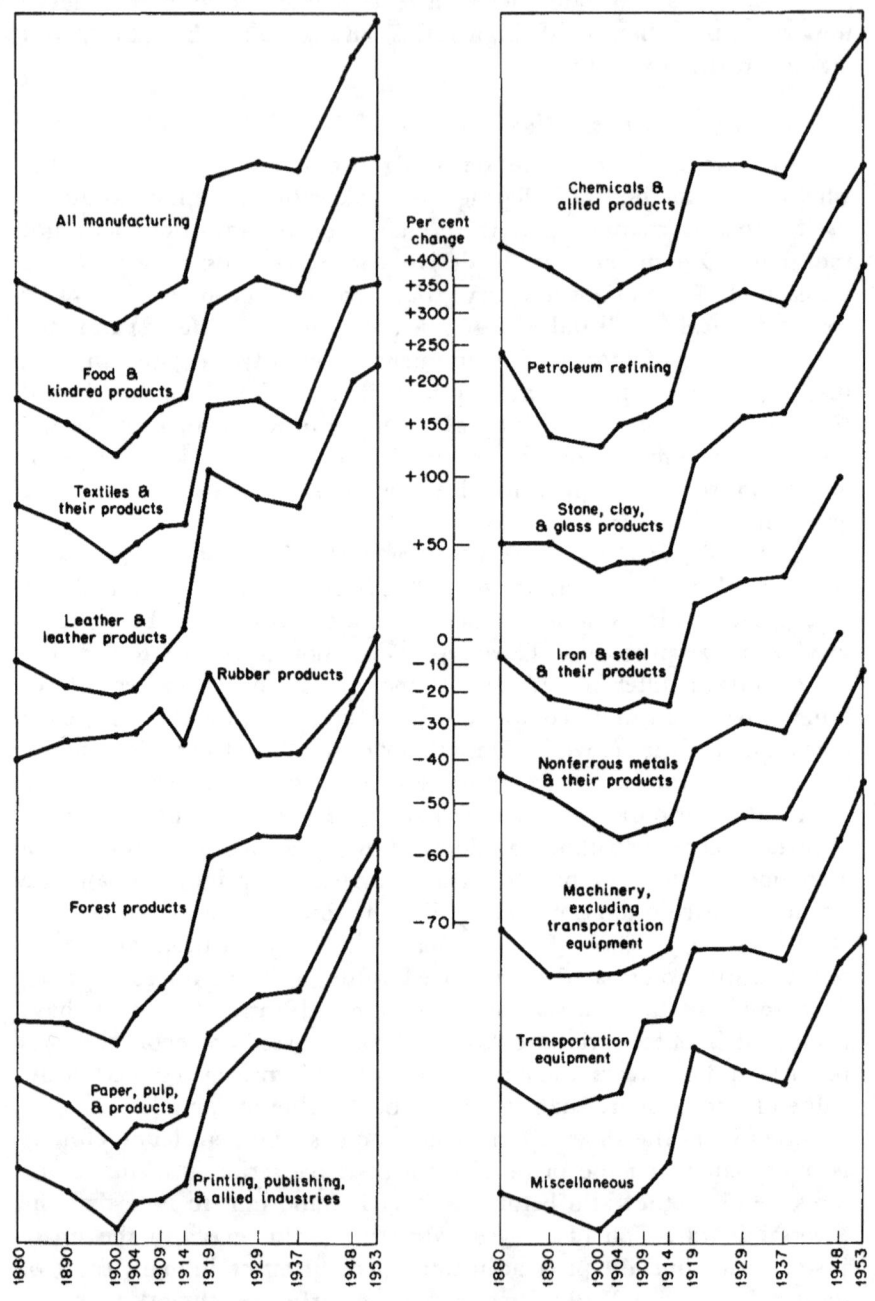

Source: Appendix Table A-11.
Note: Data for iron and steel and their products and nonferrous metals and their products are not available separately in 1953.

CAPITAL-OUTPUT RATIOS

CHART 8

Major Manufacturing Industries: Price Indexes of Output, Selected Years, 1880–1948

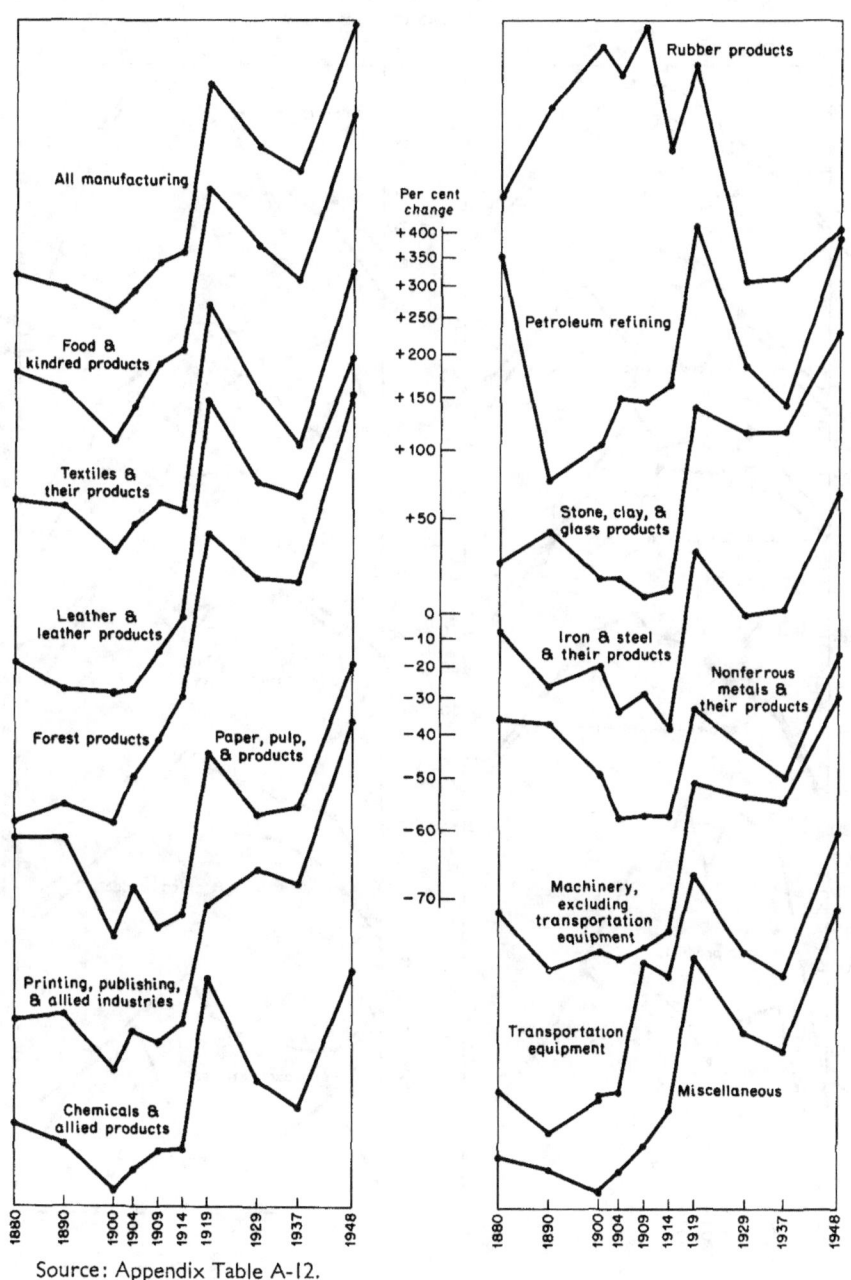

Source: Appendix Table A-12.

CHART 9

Major Manufacturing Industries: Capital-Output Ratios, Selected Years, 1880–1953

----- Reported values
——— Values in 1929 prices

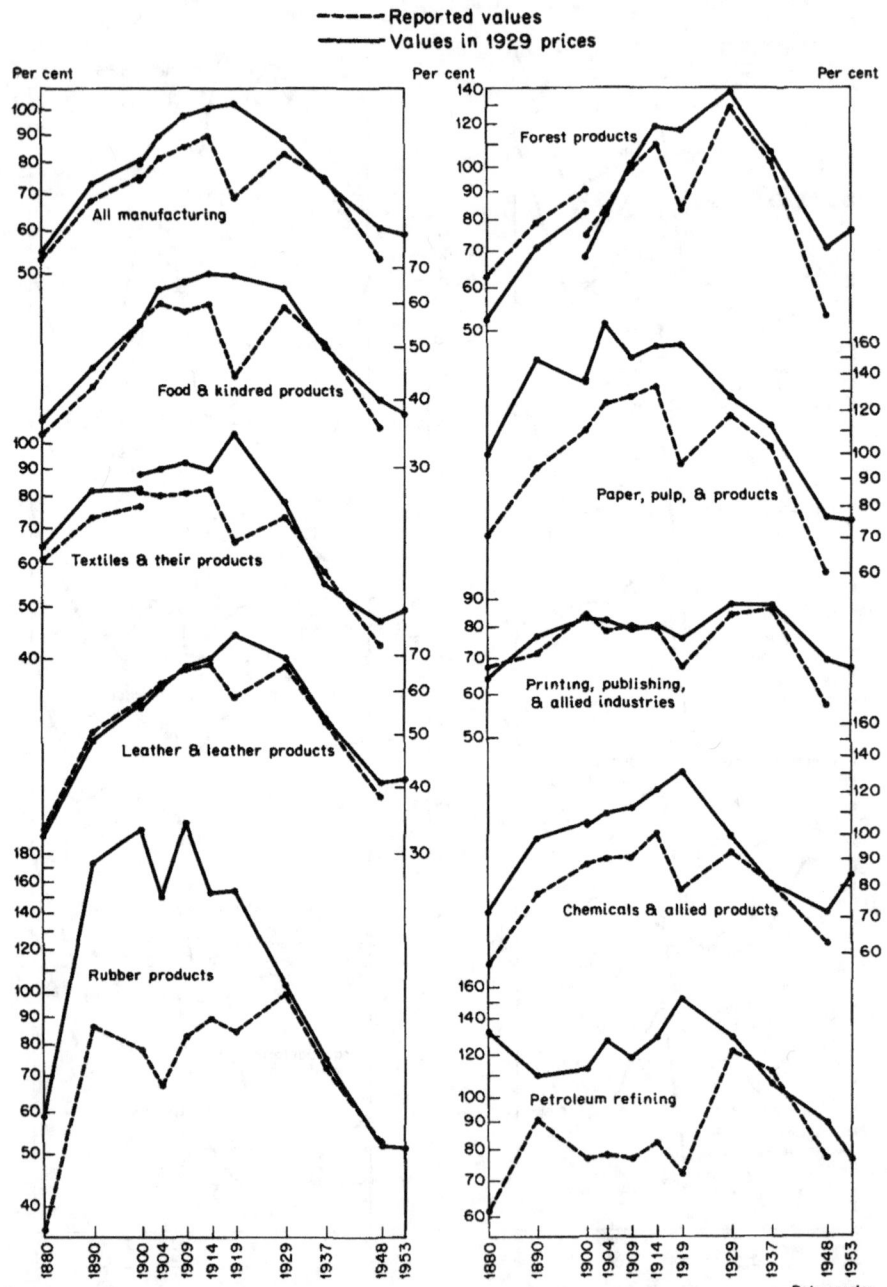

CHART 9 (concluded)

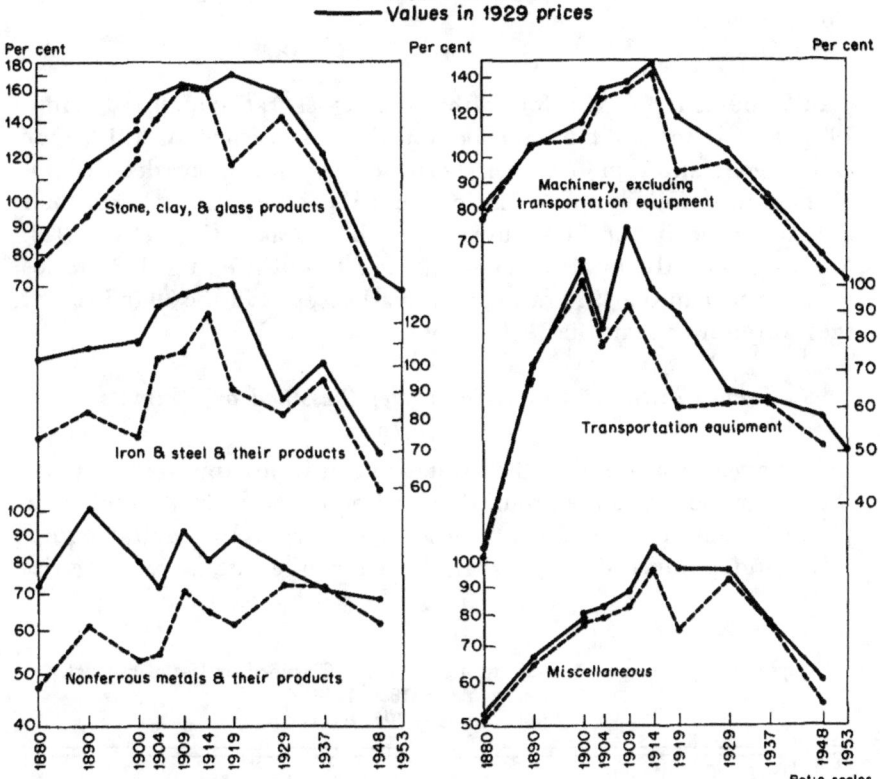

Source: 1880–1948: for ratios based on values in 1929 prices, see Appendix Table A-13; ratios based on reported prices are derived from data in Appendix Tables A-8 and A-10; 1953: based on Appendix Table A-15.

Note: Data for iron and steel and their products and nonferrous metals and their products are not available separately in 1953.

Ratios in Constant Prices, by Minor Industries, 1880–1948

The ratios for the major industry groupings are, in effect, averages of the ratios of the minor industries comprising the major groupings. In Appendix Table A-13, we present the capital-output ratios based on values in 1929 prices for 39 minor industries for all benchmark years.[11] At this point, we merely indicate the distribution of the peak ratios according to the year of occurrence, disregarding peak ratios that occurred in 1904 and 1914, years of business contraction.

[11] Capital-output ratios for 1953 were computed only for major industry groups, since data were not available for the minor groups at the time of writing.

51

Year in Which Peak Capital-Output Ratio Occurred

	1880	1890	1900	1909	1919	1929	1937	1948
No. of minor industries	0	3	4	6	18	7	1	0

In 31 industries (about four-fifths), the highest ratios occurred before 1929, and in nearly half, the peak ratio was reached in 1919. Our earlier generalization has been borne out by the more detailed information. It follows, by definition, that the 1929 ratio is lower than the 1919 ratio in the 31 industries that had peak ratios before 1929. More significantly, in all except 3 of the 39 industries, the 1937 ratios were lower than the 1929 ratios, and in all except 4 of the 39 industries, they were lower than the 1919 ratios.

Trends in the Ratios of Industries Classified by Ultimate Use of Output

The reversal in trend of the capital-output ratios appears also when the minor industries are grouped according to the ultimate use of the product—consumption goods, construction materials, capital equipment, and producers' supplies. Industries in the last three categories

TABLE 13

Capital-Output Ratios: Manufacturing Industries Classified by Use of Product, Selected Years, 1880–1948
(*based on values in 1929 prices*)

Benchmark Years	Capital-Output Ratios in Industries Producing—			
	Consumption Goods	Construction Materials	Capital Equipment	Producers' Supplies
1880	0.467	0.570	0.868	1.357
1890	0.619	0.773	1.059	1.655
1900				
Comparable with preceding years	0.681	0.944	1.052	1.691
Comparable with following years	0.692	0.801	1.055	1.695
1909	0.794	1.198	1.267	1.607
1919	0.860	1.329	1.218	1.695
1929	0.775	1.410	0.921	1.282
1937	0.614	1.109	0.929	1.071
1948	0.522	0.739	0.653	0.796

Source: Based on data in Appendix Tables A-8 and A-10. The computation was not extended to 1953 because data for minor industries were not available when this record was prepared.

produce commodities that enter into the stock of manufacturing capital.[12]

The peak ratio for industries producing capital equipment was reached in 1909, and in 1919 for industries turning out producers' supplies which form part of unfinished inventories (Table 13). The ratios for production of construction materials reached the peak in 1929, as did those for lumber and basic timber products, an industry with heavy weight in construction materials output. Thus, in all the industries contributing to the stock of reproducible wealth of the producer goods industries, the "real" capital cost per unit of output first increased up to 1909 or 1929 and then decreased. The same trends appear in the consumption goods industries. The capital-output ratio increased until 1919 and then began to decline.

A Measure of the Effect of Changing Composition

The following computations measure the effects of the changing composition of manufacturing on the capital-output ratio for aggregate manufacturing (Table 14). They, too, suggest the general pattern of a rising capital-output ratio followed by a declining one. The effects can be indicated both for the rising and the declining phases. For the rising phase, we compare the average capital-output ratio in 1880 with the average of the 1880 ratios for each of thirty-eight minor industries weighted by 1919 outputs, the year in which peak ratios occurred in roughly half of the industries. The actual average ratio for 1880 is 0.547; the hypothetical average ratio of the 1880 ratios weighted by 1919 outputs is 0.629; and the actual average ratio in 1919 is 1.022. Thus, the ratio for all manufacturing increased by 87 per cent between 1880 and 1919, whereas the hypothetical average for 1919, which allows only for the changed importance of industries, increased by 15 per cent over the 1880 ratio. Thus, about one-sixth of the rise between 1880 and 1919 can be attributed to the altered composition of the manufacturing total. In other words, throughout the structure of manufacturing industries, basic changes occurred in the relationship of capital to output during 1880–1919.

However, output and, to a lesser extent, capital investment in 1919 were distorted by the war and postwar inflation. The inflation also causes additional difficulties in obtaining values in constant prices. The use of 1919 output weights, therefore, might yield fortuitous results. Accordingly, we weight the 1880 ratio by 1909 output, instead

[12] The grouping of industries is based on the classifications prepared by Charles A. Bliss, *The Structure of Manufacturing Production* (National Bureau of Economic Research, 1939, Appendix I, pp. 141–166).

TABLE 14

Capital-Output Ratios: Effect of Changes in Internal Composition of Industries, All Manufacturing, Selected Years, 1880–1937
(*based on values in 1929 prices*)

A

Capital-output ratios:[a]	
Actual[a]	
a. 1880	0.547
b. 1909	0.967
c. 1919	1.022
d. 1937	0.755
Hypothetical[a]	
e. 1880 ratios weighted by 1909 outputs (38 minor industries)	0.608
f. 1880 ratios weighted by 1919 outputs (38 minor industries)	0.629
g. 1909 ratios weighted by 1937 outputs (39 minor industries)	1.098
h. 1919 ratios weighted by 1937 outputs (41 minor industries)	1.096

B

Change between:	$100 \times$ line	Per cent
i. 1880 actual ratio and 1880 weighted by 1909 outputs	$\frac{e-a}{a}$	+11.2
j. 1880 actual ratio and 1909 actual ratio	$\frac{b-a}{a}$	+76.8
k. Relative importance of change in internal composition	$i \div j$	+14.6
l. 1880 actual ratio and 1880 weighted by 1919 outputs	$\frac{f-a}{a}$	+15.0
m. 1880 actual ratio and 1919 actual ratio	$\frac{c-a}{a}$	+86.8
n. Relative importance of change in internal composition	$l \div m$	+17.3
o. 1909 actual ratio and 1909 weighted by 1937 outputs	$\frac{g-b}{b}$	+13.0
p. 1909 actual ratio and 1937 actual ratio	$\frac{d-b}{b}$	−22.3
q. 1919 actual ratio and 1919 weighted by 1937 outputs	$\frac{h-c}{c}$	+7.2
r. 1919 actual ratio and 1937 actual ratio	$\frac{d-c}{c}$	−26.1

[a] Output figures for 1937 were not adjusted for net physical change in inventories.

Source: Based on Appendix Tables A-10 and A-13. The computation was not extended to 1953 because data for minor industries were not available when these estimates were prepared.

of 1919 output. The hypothetical average ratio for 1909 is 0.608, compared with the actual average ratios of 0.967 in 1909 and 0.547 in 1880. That is, of the 77 per cent rise in ratios between 1880 and 1909, only about a seventh is explained by the changing composition of manufacturing industries. Thus, whether the comparison is with 1909 or with 1919, the inference is the same. *Throughout* manufacturing industries, important alterations took place in the relation between capital and output.

Similar computations were made for the years after 1909 and 1919, when the capital-output ratio for all manufacturing industries was declining. We weight ratios in 1909 and those in 1919 by 1937 output.[13] We then compare the respective hypothetical averages with the actual averages in 1909, 1919, and 1937. The actual ratio for all manufacturing industries fell by 26 per cent between 1919 and 1937. If, however, we assume that individual industry ratios in 1937 were identical with those in 1919, but accept whatever shifts have occurred in the relative importance of the individual industries, the ratio for aggregate manufacturing for 1937 would have increased by 7 per cent over the 1919 ratio. In other words, the decline in the actual ratios occurred *despite* the changing composition of industry. When 1909 ratios are used in place of those for 1919, similar results are obtained. Again, the inference is clear for the period of declining ratios: it is a trend that has characterized most minor industry groups.

Effect of Changes in the Composition of Mining Industries

The rates of growth of individual mining industries differ (Tables 10 and 15). It follows that changes in the capital-output ratio of all mining are not determined solely by changes in capital-output ratios within individual industries. As in manufacturing, we must investigate the effects of shifts in the relative importance of the individual industries on the movement of the aggregate capital-output ratio. Before doing so, however, we must examine the changing importance, since 1870, of the various mining industries as producers and as fields of investment. We must also know about the stability of interindustry differences in the amount of capital used per unit of output.

In 1870, the beginning of the period studied, anthracite and bituminous coal mining were the most important industries. Together they accounted for about 50 per cent of total capital and total output of all mining industries (Table 15). During the next decade, however, the precious metals industry, particularly gold mining, began to displace coal as the principal capital user.[14] In both 1880 and 1890, precious metals mining accounted for more than 40 per cent of all mining capital. (However, its share of output was considerably less. Throughout the entire period, its share of capital was larger than its

---

[13] We use 1937 output in place of 1948 for the same reasons that prompted us to substitute 1909 output for 1919.

[14] The census data for precious metals mining are seriously understated in 1870. Precious metals mining may have been the leading field of investment in this year.

CAPITAL AND OUTPUT TRENDS

TABLE 15
Share of Major and Minor Mining Industries in Total Mining, Selected Years, 1870–1947
(per cent)

	1870	1880	1890	1909	1919a	1919b	1929	1940	1947
All metals:									
Output in current prices	31.0	43.9	34.5	29.9	17.5	17.0	16.0	17.6	10.6
Total capital in book values	37.7	55.5	55.8	36.1	27.0	26.4	20.4	16.0c	10.2
Capital (excluding land) in 1929 prices	29.6	42.5	38.8	31.4	17.9	17.7	12.7	11.9	8.8
Iron:									
Output in current prices	8.7	9.2	8.0	9.3	7.0	6.8	5.0	5.0	3.5
Total capital in book values	8.4	8.2	7.0	9.2	7.2	7.1	n.a.	3.1	2.7
Capital (excluding land) in 1929 prices	5.0	5.6	6.4	8.7	5.7	n.a.	n.a.	n.a.	n.a.
Copper:									
Output in current prices	3.4	3.9	4.5	10.4	5.8	5.6	7.1	5.6	4.1
Total capital in book values	3.7	5.5	5.7	9.2	12.3	12.0	n.a.	6.2	3.8
Capital (excluding land) in 1929 prices	2.1	3.2	2.7	7.1	7.4	n.a.	n.a.	n.a.	n.a.
Lead and zinc:									
Output in current prices	1.0	1.5	1.1	2.5	2.4	2.3	2.0	2.2	1.8
Total capital in book values	1.4	1.1	0.8	1.9	2.8	2.7	n.a.	1.0	0.9
Capital (excluding land) in 1929 prices	1.5	1.2	0.8	1.7	1.8	n.a.	n.a.	n.a.	n.a.
Precious metals:									
Output in current prices	17.4	29.3	20.5	7.4	2.0	2.0	0.8	3.9	0.8
Total capital in book values	23.6	40.5	41.9	15.3	4.4	4.3	n.a.	4.1	2.0
Capital (excluding land) in 1929 prices	20.4	32.4	28.6	13.4	2.8	n.a.	n.a.	n.a.	n.a.
Other metals									
Output in current prices	0.5	n.a.	0.4	0.3	0.3	0.3	0.3	0.8	0.4
Total capital in book values	0.6	0.2	0.4	0.5	0.3	0.3	n.a.	1.1	0.8
Capital (excluding land) in 1929 prices	0.6	0.1	0.3	0.5	0.2	n.a.	n.a.	n.a.	n.a.

(continued)

TABLE 15 (*concluded*)

	1870	1880	1890	1909	1919[a]	1919[b]	1929	1940	1947
Anthracite coal:									
Output in current prices	25.2	16.7	17.2	12.6	11.6	11.4	9.7	5.8	4.9
Total capital in book values	24.2	18.0	9.8	7.5	6.2	6.1	5.1	3.7	3.1
Capital (excluding land) in 1929 prices	29.5	22.6	12.7	6.1	4.3	4.2	3.7	2.2	1.9
Bituminous coal:									
Output in current prices	23.0	21.2	22.5	33.8	36.7	35.7	24.3	24.6	30.9
Total capital in book values	27.9	14.1	13.7	29.3	27.4	26.8	18.5	16.3	15.3
Capital (excluding land) in 1929 prices	24.7	13.1	12.8	20.5	18.5	18.2	12.0	10.9	12.3
Petroleum and natural gas:									
Output in current prices	12.6	9.7	11.5	14.8	28.9	28.2	39.2	42.8	46.3
Total capital in book values	4.7	7.7	12.2	20.8	34.8	34.0	48.0	57.2	65.6
Capital (excluding land) in 1929 prices	10.1	16.6	26.7	36.4	56.0	55.1	65.7	69.2	72.5
Other nonmetals:									
Output in current prices	8.2	8.5	14.3	8.9	5.3	7.7	10.8	9.2	7.7
Total capital in book values	5.5	4.7	8.5	6.3	4.6	6.7	8.0	6.8	5.8
Capital (excluding land) in 1929 prices	6.1	5.2	9.0	5.6	3.3	4.8	5.9	5.8	4.5

n.a. = not available.
[a] Comparable with earlier years.
[b] Comparable with later years.
[c] Includes some capital which could not be allocated by minor industries.
Source: Based on Appendix Tables B-7, B-9, and B-11.

share of output.) The "gold period" came to an end in the 1890's. Thereafter, its relative decline was so pronounced that precious metals mining, once the largest, became one of the smaller mining industries. In 1919, it accounted for only 4 per cent of total mining capital and only 2 per cent of total mining output.

The period of relative decline in the precious metals industry coincides with that of relative increase in oil and gas production. The share of the oil and gas industry in total capital rose gradually from about 12 per cent in 1890 to about 21 per cent in 1909. Thereafter, the increase averaged more than 1 percentage point per year. The rise of its share in mining output was equally impressive. By 1948, the oil and gas industry accounted for about 68 per cent of the total capital in-

TABLE 16

Capital-Output Ratios in Mining: Major and Minor Industries, Averages for Selected Groups of Years, 1870–1947

	1870, 1880 and 1890	1909 and 1919	1937 and 1947
	BASED ON REPORTED VALUES (*including land*)		
All mining	2.05	2.50	1.55
Metals	2.87	3.40	1.79
Iron	1.86	2.52	1.03[a]
Copper	2.63	3.59	1.12[a]
Lead and zinc	1.79	2.38	0.58[a]
Precious metals	3.39	5.26	3.09[a]
Anthracite coal	1.72	1.43	1.28
Bituminous coal	1.56	2.03	1.15
Petroleum and natural gas	1.66	3.29	1.79
Other nonmetals	1.23	1.94	1.32
	BASED ON VALUES IN 1929 PRICES (*excluding land*)		
All mining	1.08	2.05	1.33
Metals	2.11	2.33	1.17
Iron	1.15	2.08	n.a.
Copper	1.11	1.97	n.a.
Lead and zinc	0.75	1.38	n.a.
Precious metals	3.70	4.40	n.a.
Anthracite coal	0.51	0.52	0.56
Bituminous coal	0.77	1.15	0.87
Petroleum and natural gas	2.53	5.46	1.90
Other nonmetals	n.a.	1.24	0.78

n.a. = not available.
[a] 1947 only.
Source: Based on Appendix Tables B-7 through B-11, and worksheets.

CAPITAL-OUTPUT RATIOS

vested in mining and for about 53 per cent of its production. The percentage of total capital is significantly understated because it does not include the value of leased land; the overwhelming majority of mineral lands in operation are leased.[15] Like precious metals mining, oil and gas production accounted for a greater share of capital than of output throughout most of the period.

Other industries use considerably less capital per unit of output (Table 16). The relative importance of coal output was much greater than that of capital during the whole period (except in 1870, when

TABLE 17
Capital-Output Ratios in Mining: Actual and Hypothetical, and Ratio of Actual to Hypothetical Capital, Selected Years, 1870–1948
(based on values in 1929 prices)

	1870	1880	1890	1909	1919	1929	1937	1948
Capital-output ratios:								
Actual	0.72	1.16	1.36	1.80	2.30	2.14	1.36	1.34
Hypothetical — assuming industry ratios as in:								
1890	1.09	1.36	1.36	1.55	1.75	2.26	2.53	2.65
1919	1.22	1.57	1.61	1.89	2.30	3.13	3.58	3.83
1948	0.68	0.78	0.80	0.90	1.00	1.18	1.28	1.34
Ratio of actual to hypothetical								
1890	0.66	0.85	1.00	1.16	1.31	0.95	0.54	0.51
1919	0.59	0.74	0.85	0.95	1.00	0.69	0.38	0.35
1948	1.05	1.47	1.70	1.99	2.30	1.82	1.06	1.00

Source: Based on Appendix Tables B-8 and B-11, and worksheets.

coal was the leading field for mining investment). From 1880 to 1919, the coal mining industry was the most important contributor to the value of total mining production; its share was about 47 per cent in 1919, while its share of capital in that year was only about 33 per cent. (During the twenties, the petroleum and gas industry became the leader in share of output.) The other nonmetals group also uses less capital per unit of output. The iron, copper, and lead and zinc industries are intermediate.

What has been the impact of these shifts on aggregate capital used in mining? Has the observed increase and subsequent decline in the aggregate capital-output ratio occurred despite the interindustry shifts?

[15] This explains why the percentages excluding land run considerably higher than those including land.

To provide an answer (Table 17), we use the same procedure as in manufacturing. We assume, first, that the capital-output ratios of the major industries remain at the 1890 level in all years. To estimate the hypothetical capital for each of these industries in all other years, we multiply this constant ratio by actual output in the year. The sum of these hypothetical capital figures for the major industries, divided by the sum of their actual value of output in the given year, gives a hypothetical aggregate ratio. This hypothetical ratio is then compared with the actual aggregate ratio. The hypothetical capital figure represents the amount of capital that would have been invested in all mining industries in the benchmark years if the capital-output ratios within the industries had remained at the 1890 level. Since the interindustry differences in the ratios have changed, we repeat the computations using the industry ratios for 1919 and for 1948.

Had industry shifts been the only influence, the aggregate mining ratio would have increased continuously during the whole period. The increase would have occurred whether the interindustry differences in the capital-output ratios had been as they were in 1890, in 1919, or in 1948, and despite the shrinkage of precious metals mining, with its high capital-output ratio. Thus, the actual increase in the aggregate ratio between 1870 and 1919 was, in part, a result of the shifts in industry weights. However, the ratio has declined since 1919 *despite* these shifts. Indeed, if the 1919 ratios for each industry had prevailed in 1948, almost 3 times as much capital would have been used in mining as actually was used in that year. This means that capital would have risen to about 3.9 times the 1919 level during those twenty-nine years compared with a rise in output to more than 2.3 times the level in 1919. Actually, capital used in 1948 was only 1.4 times that used in 1919. Even if the relatively low industry ratios of 1890 had been maintained through 1948, the volume of capital in that year would have been twice as high as it really was. And, *per contra*, if the industry's utilization of capital in the other years had been as low as it was in 1948, capital in 1919 would have been only about 43 per cent of the actual amount used in that year and, in 1890, about 57 per cent of the actual amount.

Size of Firm and the Capital-Output Ratio

The impact of changes in the size structure of industry upon the capital-output ratio cannot be measured with any reasonable degree of precision because the data are fragmentary and too crude for this purpose. However, particularly for manufacturing, we can infer the probable direction of the impact for 1880–1919.

CAPITAL-OUTPUT RATIOS

To show the relationship between asset size and the capital-output ratio, we use unpublished material, by Stanley S. Schor,[16] based on data from the "Source Book" of *Statistics of Income* for 1947. Using these data, we can compute ratios by major and minor industries by ten asset-size classifications, separately for net-income and no-net-income corporations. Our analysis is restricted to net-income corporations; in 1947, the vast majority of corporations in all industries was in this category. To reduce the detail to manageable proportions, we work with twenty-two major industry groups and with unweighted average ratios for the following four size groups (in thousands of dollars): under $100, $100 and under $1,000, $1,000 and under $10,000, $10,000 and over.

The evidence is unmistakable (Table 18). In 19 of the 22 industry groups (the exceptions are food and kindred products, beverages, and tobacco products), the ratio for the largest group is substantially higher than the ratio for the smallest group. For all manufacturing industries, the ratio for the largest corporations exceeds the ratio for the smallest corporations by 126 per cent. In the three nonconforming industries, inventories constitute a relatively important element in the total capital structure. If, for these, the total capital-output ratio is used in place of the fixed capital-output ratio, the average ratio for the largest corporations exceeds the average ratio for the smallest corporations.[17] In a very real sense, then, the capital-output ratio for all the major industry groups tends to increase with increasing asset size. As additional evidence we note that in 18 of the 22 industry groups the highest ratios occurred in the largest corporations. In 13 groups the lowest ratios were found in corporations with less than $100,000 of assets; in 18 groups, in corporations with less than $1 million.

These empirical findings agree with a priori inferences. Scitovsky argues that "the scope for using labor-saving machinery increases with size; [that] large firms are likely to be in a better bargaining position

[16] "The Capital-Product Ratio and Size of Establishment for Manufacturing Industries" (Ph.D. dissertation, University of Pennsylvania, 1952). Schor computed the ratio of fixed capital to gross sales. Gross sales closely approximates our definition of output. The following are the ten asset-size groups (in thousands of dollars) for which ratios are calculated: Under $50, $50 and under $100, $100 and under $250, $250 and under $500, $500 and under $1,000, $1,000 and under $5,000, $5,000 and under $10,000, $10,000 and under $50,000, $50,000 and under $100,000, and $100,000 and over.

[17] Total capital-output ratios by asset size (in thousands of dollars) are:

	Under $100	$100 and under $1,000	$1,000 and under $10,000	$10,000 and over
Food and kindred products	0.246	0.262	0.294	0.304
Liquor and beverages	0.446	0.498	0.463	0.489
Tobacco products	0.566	0.364	0.719	0.768

TABLE 18

Fixed Capital-Output Ratios of Net Income Corporations, by Manufacturing Industries: by Asset Size, 1947
(based on reported values)

	Fixed Capital-Ouput Ratio of Firms with Assets of ('000 omitted):			
	Under $100	$100 but under $1,000	$1,000 but under $10,000	$10,000 and over
All manufacturing	.098†	.116	.154	.221*
Food and kindred products	.112*	.111	.108	.101†
Liquors and beverages	.228	.258*	.204	.130†
Tobacco products	.118	.066†	.172*	.077
Cotton textile products	.076†	.111	.139	.151*
Other textile mill products	.098†	.124	.162	.236*
Apparel	.035	.028†	.044	.090*
Leather and leather products	.047	.046	.066	.073*
Rubber products	.133	.130†	.180*	.153
Lumber and basic timber products	.117†	.160	.310	.633*
Furniture and finished wood products	.088†	.116	.168	.180*
Pulp, paper, and products	.096†	.131	.224	.368*
Printing, publishing, and allied industries	.129†	.169	.250	.456*
Petroleum refining	.140	.121†	.158	.405*
Chemicals and allied products	.104†	.122	.168	.286*
Stone, clay, and glass products	.170†	.225	.348	.366*
Iron and steel and their products	.132†	.144	.160	.249*
Nonferrous metals and their products	.094†	.105	.112	.286*
Electrical machinery and equipment	.077†	.100	.114	.136*
Other machinery and equipment	.160	.152	.147†	.203*
Motor vehicles, complete or parts	.090†	.092	.120	.156*
Other transportation equipment	.130	.146	.121†	.219*
Miscellaneous	.090†	.121	.168	.210*

* Highest ratio.
† Lowest ratio.

Source: Stanley S. Schor, "The Capital-Product Ratio and Size of Establishment for Manufacturing Industries," unpublished Ph.D. dissertation, University of Pennsylvania, 1952.

vis-a-vis the producers of equipment and therefore obtain the latter at more favorable prices than do small firms; [and that] the factor limiting size of small firms is usually their limited access to capital, whereas the size of large firms is limited by various other considerations. Capital theory suggests that this difference in the limit to size makes for the

CAPITAL-OUTPUT RATIOS

use of more capital-intensive methods of production in the large firm."[18]

These reasons appear so cogent as to suggest that, throughout the period analyzed in this paper, a rising capital-output ratio would have been associated with increasing asset size of an enterprise. Unfortunately, there are no reliable statistics by asset size over a long-term period and, therefore, this generalization cannot be empirically tested.[19] It is possible, however, to compare the interindustry changes in the capital-output ratio by asset size in 1937 and 1947 (Table 19). Once again we draw on Schor's computations of ratios of fixed capital to sales for net-income corporations by major industry groups and use the four asset-size classes. In each year, we express the ratios of each of the three larger classes as a percentage of the ratio of the smallest class. The difference between the ratio of the smallest firms and of the largest firms was appreciably reduced in 1947 compared with 1937. This was true not only in aggregate manufacturing, but also in each of the 15 industry groups.

Another way of expressing the change is to say that the fixed capital-output ratio for large firms declined more rapidly between 1937 and 1947 than did the ratio for small firms. This suggests that the more capital per unit of output, the greater are the possibilities for capital-saving innovations.[20]

If we knew the relationship between size of firm and the fixed capital-output ratio and could measure the changes in the size

---

[18] Tibor Scitovsky, "Economic Theory and the Measurement of Concentration," *Business Concentration and Price Policy, Special Conference Series*, Universities—National Bureau Committee for Economic Research (Princeton University Press, 1955, p. 111).

[19] Schor has analyzed the capital-output ratios for 1904 by size of establishment, with size measured in terms of output. In 22 of 40 industries that Schor surveys, he finds that the ratio of the smallest establishments is larger than the ratio for the largest establishments. It is difficult to know how much weight to place on these results for 1904. There are several reasons for skepticism. The computations are based on no-net-income companies as well as net-income companies; and in a depression year such as 1904, small companies may not have fared as well as the larger companies. We have reason to believe that the number of establishments in many of the larger size classes was small, and the ratios, therefore, may not be stable. It seems likely, although proof is lacking, that in 1904 the practice of depreciation accounting was largely restricted to the larger corporations. If this was true, it would operate in the direction of a declining ratio with increasing size.

[20] We find a similar relationship in Chapter V, where we discuss the change in capital-output ratios by industries between 1919 and 1948. Some part of this larger differential rate of decline in capital-output ratios among the larger firms may be caused by the higher price level (for which no adjustment has been made) implicit in the book value of assets in 1947. For example, because of the price rise, a firm with assets of $100,000 in 1947 would be a smaller firm measured in "real" capital than a firm with $100,000 assets in 1937. And the smaller the firm is, the lower the capital-output ratio.

structure of manufacturing industries between 1880 and 1948, we could evaluate the effect of a change in the size of a firm on over-all or industry ratios. Unfortunately, precise measures cannot be made with the available data. However, the average size of establishment undoubtedly increased between 1880 and 1919. For example, the un-

TABLE 19

Fixed Capital-Output Ratios of Net Income Corporations, by Manufacturing Industries: Largest Firms Compared to Smallest Firms, 1937 and 1947
(based on reported values)

	Index of Fixed Capital-Output Ratio in Firms with Assets ('000 omitted) of:—					
	$100 but under $1,000		$1,000 but under $10,000		$10,000 and over	
	1937	1947	1937	1947	1937	1947
	(ratio in firms with assets less than $100 thous. = 100)					
All manufacturing	162	118	260	157	360	226
Food and kindred products	136	99	157	96	175	90
Liquors and beverages	127	113	149	90	n.a.	57
Tobacco products	154	56	136	146	201	65
Textile mill products	249	127	455	160	n.a.	214
Apparel	165	80	535	126	492	257
Leather and leather products	159	98	274	140	n.a.	155
Rubber products	161	98	221	135	245	115
Forest products	181	137	415	253	n.a.	616
Paper, pulp, and products	176	136	406	233	612	383
Printing, publishing, and allied industries	147	131	187	194	191	354
Petroleum refining	101	86	222	113	414	289
Chemicals and allied products	167	117	272	162	390	275
Stone, clay, and glass products	152	132	310	205	302	215
Metals and metal products except motor vehicles	153	109	206	113	418	175
Motor vehicles, complete or parts	218	102	260	133	288	173

n.a. = not available.
Source: Same as Table 18.

weighted average capital (in 1929 prices) per establishment for a sample of 34 industries comprising about two-thirds of all manufacturing was $94,000 in 1880, $415,000 in 1900, and $860,000 in 1919.[21] On our assumption of a rising ratio with increasing size, the rising

[21] To minimize the lack of comparability among censuses because of differences in the total number of establishments covered, we adjust the number of establishments in 1880 to eliminate custom and repair shops, and factory establishments with value of product less than $500. By using an unweighted average, we eliminate the effect on the average of the shifting relative importance of the individual industries.

capital-output ratio that characterized these decades could be partly explained on the statistical level by the trend toward larger establishments. On the level of economic analysis, however, change in size cannot be considered as an independent variable, for many of the technological innovations of the period that caused a rising capital-output ratio also resulted in larger establishments.

To judge by aggregative data, the size of structure changed little between 1919 and 1929. The trend toward larger establishments resumed between 1929 and 1937. The average number of wage earners per establishment was 40.1 in 1919, 40.5 in 1929, and 51.4 in 1937.[22] Thus, size structure was a neutral factor in the decline of the ratio between 1919 and 1929. However, the decline between 1929 and 1937 occurred *despite* the indicated trend toward larger establishments. The number of employees per establishment in 1937 and 1947 (58.7 and 59.3, respectively)[23] suggests that the change in size structure between those years was virtually nil. On this basis, we tentatively conclude that the change in size was again a neutral factor in the continued decline of the ratio between 1937 and 1948.

Summary of Findings

1. Up to 1919, an increasing fraction of a dollar of manufacturing capital was used to produce a dollar of output; since 1919, a decreasing fraction of a dollar of capital has been sufficient to produce a dollar of output. These trends were observed whether the capital-output ratio was based on reported or deflated values. This is consistent with the interpretation that, in the earlier decades, capital innovations on balance probably served more to replace other factor inputs than to increase output. Since World War I, capital innovations serve more to increase the efficiency of capital, hence to increase output, than to replace other factor inputs.

2. Trend movements in the capital-output ratio were much the same in mining as in manufacturing. The general configuration of the trend movements is similar whether the ratios are based on reported values or on values in 1929 prices. The ratio based on 1929 prices reached a peak around 1919. It has continued downward through 1953, the final year of our estimates.

3. A review of the data deficiencies does not disclose any weakness of a magnitude that shakes our confidence in the validity of the trend

---

[22] Temporary National Economic Committee Monograph No. 27, "The Structure of Industry" (1941), p. 4.

[23] *Census of Manufactures, 1947*, Volume I, Table 1. We use "all employees" because of the shift from "wage earners" to "production workers" between 1937 and 1947.

in the capital-output ratios, particularly when our interest is centered on the broad pattern of movement.

4. This reversal in the direction of movement of the capital-output ratio for manufacturing is found in all 39 branches, the number that can be distinguished on a reasonably comparable basis over these decades. In 31 branches, about four-fifths, the highest ratio occurred before 1929, and in nearly half, the peak ratio was reached in 1919.

5. The changing importance of particular industries accounted for about one-sixth of the total increase in the capital-output ratio for all manufacturing between 1880 and 1919. Between 1919 and 1937, the decline in the capital-output ratio occurred despite the changing composition of industry. That is, if the only change was the change in industry composition, the ratio would have risen by 7 per cent. The inference is clear: whether in the period of rising or falling capital-output ratio, the trend characterized most minor industry groups.

6. In mining also, if the only influence had been that of industry shifts, the aggregate mining ratio would have increased continuously during the whole period. Here, too, the actual increase in the aggregate ratio between 1870 and 1919 was, in part, a result of the shifts in industry weights. And the decline in this ratio since 1919 has taken place despite these shifts.

7. According to the evidence of the "Source Book" of *Statistics of Income for 1947*, the capital-output ratio in the major manufacturing groups tends to increase with increasing asset size. The highest ratios, for example, occurred in the largest corporations in 18 of the 22 industry groups. In 13 groups, the lowest ratios were found in corporations with less than $100,000 of assets; in 18 groups, in corporations with less than $1 million. The trend toward larger establishments, in the first decades of this period, would also help to explain the rising capital-output ratio of those decades. However, change in size is not an independent variable, for many of the technological innovations of the period that caused a rising capital-output ratio also resulted in larger establishments. Between 1919 and 1929 and between 1937 and 1948, the size structure appears to have been a neutral factor in the decline of the ratio. Between 1929 and 1937, the decline occurred despite the indicated trend toward larger establishments.

CHAPTER IV

Trends in Ratios of Fixed and Working Capital to Output

AGGREGATE capital data can also be broken down by type of asset. For some of the benchmark years, data are separately available for fixed capital (land, buildings, and equipment) and for working capital (cash, notes and accounts receivable, inventories, and miscellaneous assets). For these years, we can relate each component in 1929 prices to output in 1929 prices.

Manufacturing, 1890–1948

The subdivision between fixed and working capital can be made for seven benchmark years (Table 20). Aside from 1904 (1904 is a year of

TABLE 20

Ratios of Fixed and Working Capital to Output:
All Manufacturing, Selected Years, 1890–1953
(*based on values in 1929 prices*)

Benchmark Years	Ratio to Output of—	
	Working Capital	Fixed Capital
1890	.366	.364
1900	.387	.416
1904	.420	.471
1929	.452	.433
1937	.395	.346
1948	.324	.285
1953	.320	.270

Source: Based on data in Appendix Tables A-8, A-9, A-10, and A-15.

business contraction; this tends to raise capital-output ratios), for all manufacturing, the ratios of both fixed and working capital to output have risen, presumably to 1919 and most certainly not beyond 1929. This has been followed by a downward movement in both ratios that seems to have continued to 1948.

The percentage rise from 1890 to 1929 was somewhat sharper for the working capital-output ratio than for the fixed capital-output ratio (23 and 19, respectively). This may be due, in whole or in part, to reporting-errors in the earlier years when the capital data were derived from census sources. The census authorities believed that the breakdown of total capital by type of asset was reported with large errors.

For this reason, they discontinued the inquiry after 1904. Too much may have been reported as fixed capital and too little as working capital. Even so, only the rate, not the fact, of an upward trend can be questioned.

Beginning with 1929 we are on firmer statistical ground. The downward drift of both ratios between 1929 and 1948 is unmistakable—a 34 per cent drop in the fixed capital-output ratio and a 28 per cent fall in the working capital-output ratio. This is conclusive evidence that the decline in the *total* capital-output ratio between 1929 and

TABLE 21

Ratios of Fixed and Working Capital to Output: by Minor Manufacturing Industries, 1929, 1937, and 1948

(based on values in 1929 prices)

Ratio to Output of Capital as Specified:	1929	1937	1948	Per cent Change 1929–1948
All manufacturing				
Working	.452	.395	.324	−28.3
Fixed	.433	.346	.285	−34.2
Food and kindred products				
Working	.337	.294	.233	−30.9
Fixed	.302	.206	.167	−44.7
Bakery and confectionery				
Working	.322	.274	.156	−51.6
Fixed	.458	.344	.212	−53.7
Canned products				
Working	.590	.450	.333	−43.6
Fixed	.377	.226	.241	−36.1
Flour mill products				
Working	.183	.249	.170	−7.1
Fixed	.144	.160	.123	−14.6
Packing house products				
Working	.158	.149	.130	−17.7
Fixed	.119	.097	.082	−31.1
Sugar refining				
Working	.567	.501	.296	−47.8
Fixed	.885	.526	.367	−58.5
Liquors and beverages				
Working	.772	.337	.303	−60.8
Fixed	.707	.275	.268	−62.1
Other food products				
Working	.305	.284	.184	−39.7
Fixed	.476	.257	.205	−56.9
Tobacco products				
Working	.861	.665	.513	−40.4
Fixed	.106	.072	.056	−47.2

(continued)

RATIOS OF FIXED AND WORKING CAPITAL TO OUTPUT

TABLE 21 (continued)

Ratio to Output of Capital as Specified:	1929	1937	1948	Per cent Change 1929–1948
Textiles and their products				
Working	.461	.341	.306	−33.6
Fixed	.317	.207	.162	−48.9
Basic textiles				
Working	.504	.352	.374	−25.8
Fixed	.461	.283	.221	−52.1
Carpets and floor coverings				
Working	.606	.725	.319	−47.4
Fixed	.602	.474	.292	−51.5
Knit goods				
Working	.481	.301	.220	−54.3
Fixed	.373	.206	.170	−54.4
Clothing				
Working	.395	.339	.288	−27.1
Fixed	.090	.062	.051	−43.3
Leather and products				
Working	.518	.416	.314	−39.4
Fixed	.176	.119	.093	−47.2
Boots and shoes				
Working	.466	.408	.330	−29.2
Fixed	.154	.112	.084	−45.5
Other leather products				
Working	.604	.436	.300	−50.3
Fixed	.213	.132	.111	−47.9
Rubber products				
Working	.586	.503	.343	−41.5
Fixed	.440	.246	.175	−60.2
Tires and tubes				
Working	.631	.588	.345	−45.3
Fixed	.468	.216	.147	−68.6
Other rubber products				
Working	.490	.382	.370	−24.5
Fixed	.395	.372	.266	−32.7
Forest products				
Working	.612	.449	.311	−49.2
Fixed	.760	.614	.394	−48.2
Sawmill and planing				
Working	.712	.500	.423	−40.6
Fixed	1.074	.949	.761	−29.1
Other wood products				
Working	.498	.401	.248	−50.2
Fixed	.404	.310	.172	−57.4
Paper, pulp, and products				
Working	.507	.460	.293	−42.2
Fixed	.764	.664	.471	−38.4

(continued)

CAPITAL AND OUTPUT TRENDS

TABLE 21 (*continued*)

Ratio to Output of Capital as Specified:	1929	1937	1948	Per cent Change 1929–1948
Printing, publishing, and allied industries				
Working	.543	.572	.386	−28.9
Fixed	.334	.301	.305	−8.7
Petroleum refining				
Working	.438	.379	.317	−27.6
Fixed	.848	.678	.576	−32.1
Chemicals and allied substances				
Working	.588	.455	.351	−40.3
Fixed	.404	.352	.365	−9.7
Fertilizers				
Working	.782	.453	.259	−66.9
Fixed	.588	.385	.252	−57.1
Chemicals proper				
Working	.583	.489	.246	−57.8
Fixed	.739	.634	.453	−38.7
Allied chemical substances				
Working	.600	.468	.388	−35.3
Fixed	.321	.274	.323	+0.6
Stone, clay, and glass				
Working	.548	.455	.336	−38.7
Fixed	1.018	.763	.401	−60.6
Iron and steel products				
Working	.343	.426	.325	−5.2
Fixed	.506	.587	.372	−26.5
Blast furnaces and rolling mills				
Working	.225	.402	.290	+28.9
Fixed	.619	.738	.368	−40.5
Metal building materials and supplies				
Working	.519	.463	.432	−16.8
Fixed	.362	.354	.202	−44.2
Hardware, tools, etc.				
Working	.580	.487	.404	−30.3
Fixed	.487	.359	.309	−36.6
Nonferrous metals				
Working	.402	.397	.354	−11.9
Fixed	.382	.319	.331	−13.4
Precious metal products and processes				
Working	.605	.602	.437	−27.8
Fixed	.214	.212	.130	−39.3
Other nonferrous metal products and processes				
Working	.373	.384	.323	−13.4
Fixed	.420	.342	.311	−26.0

(*continued*)

RATIOS OF FIXED AND WORKING CAPITAL TO OUTPUT

TABLE 21 (concluded)

Ratio to Output of Capital as Specified:	1929	1937	1948	Per cent Change 1929–1948
Machinery				
Working	.669	.565	.437	−34.7
Fixed	.361	.288	.226	−37.4
Electrical				
Working	.619	.444	.397	−35.9
Fixed	.303	.216	.186	−38.6
Agricultural				
Working	.926	.760	.405	−56.3
Fixed	.428	.303	.226	−47.2
Office and store				
Working	.862	.732	.502	−41.8
Fixed	.308	.358	.386	+25.3
Factory, household, and miscellaneous				
Working	.641	.587	.463	−27.8
Fixed	.395	.327	.220	−44.3
Transportation equipment				
Working	.305	.344	.339	+11.1
Fixed	.343	.279	.240	−30.0
Motor vehicles				
Working	.277	.308	.284	+2.5
Fixed	.298	.223	.209	−29.9
Locomotives and railroads				
Working	.572	.629	.480	−16.1
Fixed	.773	.882	.305	−60.5
Aircraft				
Working	.371	.831	.650	+75.2
Fixed	.523	.474	.167	−68.1
Miscellaneous				
Working	.654	.508	.386	−41.0
Fixed	.313	.265	.223	−28.8

Source: Based on data in Appendix Tables 1-8 to A-10.

1948 was not caused by any change in the relative importance of fixed and working capital. Moreover, any full explanation of the factors that have made capital more efficient must relate to working capital as well as to fixed capital.

How pervasive has the downward movement been in these ratios? Ratios can be computed for 39 minor industry groups for the benchmark years 1929, 1937, and 1948 (Table 21). In only 2 industries (allied chemical substances, and office and store machinery and equipment) did the fixed capital-output ratio fail to decline between 1929 and 1948. Among the other 37 industries, the decline exceeds 25 per cent in all except 4 industries. The record for the working capital-output ratio is similar. In only 3 industries (blast furnaces and rolling mills, motor vehicles, and aircraft) were the ratios higher in 1948 than in 1929, and in only 5 of the industries with declining ratios was the relative drop less than 20 per cent. The downward trend in the ratio of these two components of capital to output was widespread, and the results for aggregate manufacturing would not have been significantly affected by any shift in the relative importance of the various industries.

It does not necessarily follow that all components of the working capital-output ratio followed the same downward course. In fact, the deflated ratio of inventories to output (based on a sample of large corporations) seems to have risen from 1919 to 1929 and again from 1929 to 1937 (Table 22). This ratio declined only between 1937 and

TABLE 22

Ratios of Inventories to Output, by Major Manufacturing Industries, Selected Years, 1919–1948
(based on values in 1929 prices)

	Ratio of Inventories[a] to Output			
	1919	1929	1937	1948
All manufacturing	.184	.194	.196	.168
Food, beverages, and tobacco	.128	.143	.149	.132
Textiles and textile products	.187	.222	.241	.196
Leather and leather products	.266	.265	.286	.198
Rubber and related products	.113	.306	.279	.215
Lumber and wood products	.248	.284	.216	.103
Paper, printing, etc.	.099	.122	.130	.109
Chemicals and allied	.288	.425	.434	.376
Stone, clay, and glass	.221	.222	.214	.141
Metals and metal products	.164	.193	.207	.196
Miscellaneous	.995	.284	.287	.310

[a] Inventories are averages of end-of-year inventories of given year and preceding year.
Source: Inventories in 1929 prices: for 1919, 1929, and 1937, from Moses Abramovitz, *Inventories and Business Cycles*, National Bureau of Economic Research, 1950, Table 108, p. 564; for 1948, extrapolated from the 1937 estimate using the percentage change in inventories in 1947 prices, estimated by Department of Commerce and taken from unpublished worksheet.
The output figures are the ones developed for this study (see Appendix Table A-10).

1948. The ratios of most of the 10 industry groups that can be distinguished for this computation trace the same pattern as the aggregate. It follows from this that the decline in the working capital-output ratio before 1948 must have been due to the increasingly efficient use of the other components of working capital—cash, notes and accounts receivable, and other assets.

RATIOS OF FIXED AND WORKING CAPITAL TO OUTPUT

TABLE 23
Capital[a]-Output Ratios in Mining: Major Industries, Selected Years, 1870–1953

Ratios to Output	1870	1880	1890	1909	1919	1929	1940	1948	1953
All mining									
Based on 1929 prices:									
Capital	0.72	1.16	1.36	1.80	2.30	2.14	1.59	1.34	1.26
Plant	0.61	1.02	1.19	1.52	2.00	1.57	1.10	0.92	0.84
Working capital	0.11	0.14	0.17	0.28	0.30	0.57	0.49	0.42	0.42
Based on reported values:									
Total capital	1.39	2.21	2.55	2.77	2.23	2.88	2.18	1.08	1.16
Land	0.83	1.34	1.46	1.22	0.84	0.89	0.50	0.12	0.10
Capital	0.56	0.87	1.09	1.55	1.39	1.99	1.68	0.96	1.06
Plant	0.43	0.74	0.92	1.22	1.05	1.41	1.20	0.59	0.69
Working capital	0.13	0.13	0.17	0.33	0.34	0.58	0.48	0.37	0.37
Metals									
Based on 1929 prices:									
Capital	1.29	2.30	2.73	2.50	2.16	1.71	1.24	1.00	1.39
Plant	1.14	2.11	2.37	1.84	1.49	1.10	0.59	0.54	0.77
Working capital	0.15	0.19	0.36	0.66	0.67	0.61	0.65	0.46	0.62
Based on reported values:									
Total capital	1.69	2.78	4.13	3.34	3.45	3.68	1.98	1.10	1.24
Land	1.20	1.98	2.90	1.63	1.78	2.09	0.87	0.20	0.18
Capital	0.49	0.80	1.23	1.71	1.67	1.59	1.11	0.90	1.06
Plant	0.40	0.71	1.03	1.12	0.84	0.99	0.55	0.42	0.56
Working capital	0.09	0.09	0.20	0.59	0.83	0.60	0.56	0.48	0.50
Anthracite									
Based on 1929 prices:									
Capital	0.41	0.63	0.50	0.51	0.53	0.83	0.55	0.43	0.64
Plant	0.35	0.54	0.45	0.43	0.45	0.45	0.34	0.25	0.32
Working capital	0.06	0.09	0.05	0.08	0.08	0.38	0.21	0.18	0.32
Based on reported values:									
Total capital	1.33	2.38	1.46	1.66	1.19	1.52	1.39	0.68	0.80
Land	0.70	1.21	0.66	0.91	0.68	0.75	0.76	0.30	0.23
Capital	0.63	1.17	0.80	0.75	0.51	0.77	0.63	0.38	0.57
Plant	0.50	0.98	0.71	0.60	0.37	0.40	0.40	0.19	0.27
Working capital	0.13	0.19	0.09	0.15	0.14	0.37	0.23	0.19	0.30
Bituminous coal									
Based on 1929 prices:									
Capital	0.91	0.70	0.69	1.06	1.25	1.06	0.88	0.88	1.17
Plant	0.66	0.52	0.59	0.90	1.07	0.72	0.53	0.48	0.72
Working capital	0.25	0.18	0.10	0.16	0.18	0.34	0.35	0.40	0.45
Based on reported values:									
Total capital	1.68	1.47	1.54	2.39	1.66	2.22	1.45	0.59	0.82
Land	1.02	0.90	0.92	1.46	0.95	1.23	0.72	0.14	0.11
Capital	0.66	0.57	0.62	0.93	0.71	0.99	0.73	0.45	0.71
Plant	0.42	0.41	0.51	0.75	0.52	0.65	0.46	0.21	0.42
Working capital	0.24	0.16	0.11	0.18	0.19	0.34	0.27	0.24	0.29

(*continued*)

CAPITAL AND OUTPUT TRENDS

TABLE 23 (*concluded*)

Ratios to Output	1870	1880	1890	1909	1919	1929	1940	1948	1953
Petroleum and natural gas									
Based on 1929 prices:									
Capital	1.75	2.06	3.78	5.05	5.86	3.58	2.25	1.79	1.41
Plant	1.64	1.95	3.45	4.75	5.51	2.79	1.73	1.32	1.01
Working capital	0.11	0.11	0.33	0.30	0.35	0.79	0.53	0.47	0.40
Based on reported values:									
Total capital	0.52	1.75	2.71	3.89	2.68	3.51	2.91	1.40	1.32
Land	0.06	0.20	0.22	0.24	0.17	0.20	0.17	0.07	0.07
Capital	0.46	1.55	2.49	3.65	2.51	3.31	2.74	1.33	1.25
Plant	0.42	1.45	2.23	3.34	2.21	2.52	2.15	0.89	0.87
Working capital	0.04	0.10	0.26	0.31	0.30	0.79	0.59	0.44	0.38
Other Nonmetals									
Based on 1929 prices:									
Capital	n.c.	1.04	1.16	1.28	1.19	1.17	0.94	0.56	0.61
Plant	n.c.	0.78	0.88	1.02	0.95	0.69	0.43	0.32	0.33
Working capital	n.c.	0.26	0.28	0.26	0.24	0.48	0.51	0.24	0.28
Based on reported values:									
Total capital	0.94	1.23	1.51	1.96	1.92	2.14	1.62	0.86	0.81
Land	0.49	0.64	0.81	0.97	0.99	1.04	0.60	0.23	0.11
Capital	0.45	0.58	0.70	0.99	0.93	1.10	1.02	0.63	0.70
Plant	0.34	0.42	0.50	0.72	0.60	0.63	0.50	0.30	0.36
Working capital	0.11	0.16	0.20	0.27	0.33	0.47	0.52	0.33	0.34

n.c. = not comparable.
[a] For definition of terms relating to capital see Chapter 2, p. 14.
Source: see notes to Appendix Tables B-7 to B-11.

Mining, 1870–1948

During the early decades, both the plant[1]-output ratio and the working capital-output ratio rose (Tables 23 and 24). In some of the industries, the increase was steeper in the plant-output ratios and, in the others, in the working capital-output ratios. These differences, however, might be due to reporting errors or to errors introduced by our estimates of the breakdown of total capital by type of asset for the years for which no breakdown was reported. For aggregate mining, the increase in the plant-output ratio appears to have been steeper than that in the working capital-output ratio. Here, the impact of errors in measurement is certainly smaller than in the case of the individual industries. On the other hand, the significance of the difference is reduced by the changes that occurred in the relative weights of the individual industries.

In the following decades, 1919–1948, the statistical data are more reliable, and the differences in the pattern of change in the ratio of plant and of working capital to output can be seen more clearly. In

[1] Net value of structures and equipment.

TABLE 24

Capital[a]-Output Ratios in Mining: Minor Industries, Selected Years, 1870–1947

Ratios to Output:	1870	1880	1890	1909	1919	1940	1947
Iron							
Based on 1929 prices:							
Capital	0.71	1.22	1.53	2.21	1.95	n.a.	n.a.
Plant	0.47	0.83	0.85	1.58	1.41	n.a.	n.a.
Working capital	0.24	0.39	0.68	0.63	0.54	0.25	0.37
Based on reported values:							
Total capital	1.35	1.98	2.24	2.74	2.30	1.36	1.03
Land	0.98	1.40	1.30	1.21	1.00	n.a.	n.a.
Capital	0.37	0.58	0.94	1.53	1.30	n.a.	n.a.
Plant	0.21	0.37	0.47	0.98	0.71	n.a.	n.a.
Working capital	0.16	0.21	0.47	0.55	0.59	0.22	0.44
Copper							
Based on 1929 prices:							
Capital	0.76	1.74	0.82	1.47	2.46	n.a.	n.a.
Plant	0.63	1.46	0.64	0.88	1.48	n.a.	n.a.
Working capital	0.13	0.28	0.18	0.59	0.98	0.72	0.49
Based on reported values:							
Total capital	1.50	3.14	3.24	2.43	4.75	2.42	1.12
Land	1.15	2.40	2.57	1.27	2.49	n.a.	n.a.
Capital	0.35	0.74	0.67	1.16	2.26	n.a.	n.a.
Plant	0.27	0.60	0.49	0.59	0.92	n.a.	n.a.
Working capital	0.08	0.14	0.18	0.57	1.34	0.78	0.57
Lead and zinc							
Based on 1929 prices:							
Capital	0.77	0.74	0.75	1.49	1.27	n.a.	n.a.
Plant	0.58	0.57	0.59	1.11	0.95	n.a.	n.a.
Working capital	0.19	0.17	0.16	0.38	0.32	0.51	0.39
Based on reported values:							
Total capital	1.99	1.66	1.71	2.13	2.62	1.00	0.58
Land	1.09	0.91	0.93	1.02	1.47	n.a.	n.a.
Capital	0.90	0.75	0.78	1.11	1.15	n.a.	n.a.
Plant	0.62	0.56	0.58	0.75	0.68	n.a.	n.a.
Working capital	0.28	0.19	0.20	0.36	0.47	0.44	0.30
Precious metals							
Based on 1929 prices:							
Capital	2.55	3.15	5.41	5.44	3.35	n.a.	n.a.
Plant	2.48	3.08	5.13	4.44	2.72	n.a.	n.a.
Working capital	0.07	0.07	0.28	1.00	0.63	0.95	0.77
Based on reported values:							
Total capital	1.89	3.05	5.22	5.71	4.80	2.26	3.09
Land	1.35	2.18	3.73	2.85	2.88	n.a.	n.a.
Capital	0.54	0.87	1.49	2.86	1.92	n.a.	n.a.
Plant	0.51	0.84	1.40	2.16	1.26	n.a.	n.a.
Working capital	0.03	0.03	0.09	0.70	0.66	0.46	0.68
Other metals							
Based on reported values:							
Total capital	n.c.	n.c.	n.c.	n.c.	2.51	3.01	1.99

n.a. = not available.
n.c. = not comparable.

[a] For definition of terms relating to capital see Chapter II, p. 14.
Source: See notes to Appendix Tables B-7 through B-11.

most industries, the ratios of working capital to output began to decline much later than the ratios of plant to output and the decline was much smaller. Thus, for aggregate mining, the ratio of working capital to output, whether based on reported values or values in 1929 prices, increased until 1929. On the other hand, the ratio of plant to output based on values in 1929 prices began to decline in 1919, and much more markedly than did the ratio of working capital to output. In the petroleum and natural gas industry, the ratio of working capital to output, whether based on 1929 or on reported values, continued to increase until 1929, while the plant-output ratio based on 1929 prices began to decline in 1919. Very nearly the same pattern is found in the metal mining industry: the decline in the working capital-output ratio began in 1919; the plant-output ratio in reported values declined in 1909, the deflated ratio in 1890. In bituminous coal mining, the ratio of working capital to output, based on 1929 prices, continued to increase up to 1948, and that based on reported values, until 1929. However, the plant-output ratio based on 1929 prices rose only until 1919. For the other nonmetals group, the ratio of working capital to output increased until 1940, but the ratio of plant to output began to decline after 1909. Anthracite mining appears to be the only industry where the reversal of trend in the plant- and working capital-output ratios occurred at the same time and where both ratios show an equally abrupt decline.

How can the difference in movement between the plant- and working capital-output ratios be explained? High tax liabilities might have been considered responsible for the slower decline in the working capital-output ratio, especially since 1940.[2] However, another factor, whose importance is difficult to assess, has had the opposite effect, at least on the working capital-output ratios based on reported values. This is the wide application of last-in, first-out (LIFO) accounting since 1940. (It was legalized in 1938.) This method has tended to understate working capital, because the inventory account is evaluated at the prices of inventory initially acquired or of inventory held when LIFO was introduced. These prices have lagged substantially behind current market values.

[2] A survey (taken from *Moody's*) of the balance sheets as of December 1948 of eighty large corporations engaged primarily in mining activities discloses a high share of tax liabilities. Thus, the sum of the items "accrued taxes" and "reserves for taxes" (reported under current liabilities) accounted for 7 per cent of total liabilities and 48 per cent of current liabilities. Using a 1 to 1 ratio between tax liabilities and tax funds, this sum would account for around 20 per cent of working capital. (This figure is rather exaggerated, first, because tax liabilities are presumably lower in smaller corporations than in those studied and, second, because there is no good reason to assume a 1 to 1 relationship between tax liabilities and funds available for taxes.)

RATIOS OF FIXED AND WORKING CAPITAL TO OUTPUT

At least two factors affect the behavior of the plant-output and working capital-output ratios differently in mining than in manufacturing. First, the composition of working capital in the two sectors is different. Cash is a substantially greater proportion of working capital in mining than in manufacturing. (For example, in the great majority of mining industries in 1948, cash was more than 40 per cent of total working capital, compared with less than 20 per cent in all manufacturing.) This may result in part from the relatively greater importance of leased properties in mining than in manufacturing. This, in turn, entails a greater need for cash to meet the payments for rentals and royalties.

TABLE 25

Capital-Output Ratios in Mining: Working Capital and Components, Major Industries, Selected Years, 1929–1948
(based on book values)

	1929[a]	1930[b]	1940	1948
Metals:				
Cash		.14	.26	.19
Notes and accounts receivable		.40	.13	.16
Inventories		.36	.17	.13
Total working capital[c]	.60	.90	.56	.48
Anthracite coal:				
Cash		.04	.08	.08
Notes and accounts receivable		.31	.11	.07
Inventories		.04	.04	.04
Total working capital[c]	.37	.39	.23	.19
Bituminous coal:				
Cash		.08	.08	.10
Notes and accounts receivable		.25	.15	.11
Inventories		.05	.04	.04
Total working capital[c]	.34	.39	.27	.24
Petroleum and natural gas:				
Cash		.17	.17	.19
Notes and accounts receivable		.56	.33	.16
Inventories		.16	.08	.10
Total working capital[c]	.79	.89	.59	.44
Other nonmetals:				
Cash		.11	.18	.12
Notes and accounts receivable		.23	.17	.13
Inventories		.19	.17	.08
Total working capital[c]	.47	.53	.52	.33

[a] From Table 23.
[b] Underlying data adjusted for consolidated returns.
[c] Because of rounding details may not add to total.

Source: *Statistics of Income*, Part 2, Bureau of Internal Revenue (now Internal Revenue Service) related years.

The ratio of cash to output has not only failed to decline but has even increased in all mining industries during the last decades (Table 25).[3]

The second factor is the relatively higher ratio of depreciable and depletable assets to output and the relatively greater retardation in growth of output and capital in mining than in manufacturing. Other conditions being equal, a declining rate of growth of capital means a rising ratio of accumulated depreciation and depletion reserves to net capital. Thus, "self-generating" liquidity becomes relatively more important the higher the total capital-output ratio, the greater the decline in this ratio, or the greater the slackening of the rate of growth. For this reason, the range of substitutability between fixed and working capital via depreciation and depletion charges may have been particularly wide in the mining industries. The combination of these factors may have reduced the incentive for more intensive use of working capital in mining. On the other hand, the greater retardation in growth of the mining industries during the period also implies a relatively higher increase in the ratio of replacements to the net value of plant. In turn, plant efficiency should rise and, consequently, the plant-output ratio should fall.

A declining rate of growth in an industry's capital formation coincident with a rising ratio of depreciation charges to capital (gross or net) raises a different problem. Are not accounting practices responsible, at least in part, for the observed decline in the plant-output ratio? Assume that depreciation charges exceed the real functional deterioration (owing to age, obsolescence, and undermaintenance) of structures and equipment. Then, in periods of sharp retardation in the rate of growth of capital, would not the accumulated depreciation reserves increasingly overstate and, therefore, net capital value increasingly understate, the "true" operational value of the capital assets?

The premise of the preceding question is that depreciation charges exceed the real functional deterioration of the capital units. Therefore, a precise answer is not possible. Indeed, if one considers the accelerated obsolescence of equipment, in recent decades, resulting from rapid technological advances, as much ground exists for believing that the prevailing rates are too low as for assuming that they are too

---

[3] Our record begins with 1930, the first year of the Great Depression, when the cash-output ratios are certainly overstated. Nevertheless, the ratios have risen between 1930 and 1948. We have, unfortunately, no data by which to trace these ratios in earlier years.

Note that the ratios of notes and accounts receivable to output dropped sharply during 1930–1948. The decline was so substantial that, taken as a sum, the ratios of cash and receivables to output also declined. The failure of the cash-output ratios to decline could thus be partly explained by substitutions between cash and receivables.

high.[4] This aspect of functional deterioration is usually neglected when the length of life assumed for estimating depreciation rates is compared with the actual operational length of life of a capital asset. Newer capital units are more efficient than the relatively older ones bought for the same values in constant prices, and the newer units should be more profitable to use than the older ones. One might argue that the older equipment will be used at a rate corresponding to its obsolescence, rather than to its operational capacity. How completely this relationship is realized depends on the extent of the divisibility of capital units, the necessity of coordinating a variety of machine operations, and the interest of the owner in amortizing the capital value of the old equipment. For industry as a whole, older equipment is used in proportion to its value adjusted for obsolescence, although its operational value may be considerably higher, i.e., rapidly growing plants have newer equipment and run nearer to operational capacity than do older plants. The same is true within a single plant, although the limiting conditions mentioned above would play a much greater role.[5]

Total Capital-Output Ratios, by Industries

The ratios of capital to output bear closely on changes in the demand for savings by the mining industries and serve to highlight technological and other changes. Such ratios, however, do not reflect the actual amount of wealth per unit of output used in the mining industries, because natural wealth, i.e., the mineral resources themselves, is not included. The discrepancy between the stock of reproducible wealth ("past labor") used in production and the actual amount of wealth used for the same purpose is unique in the mining industries.[6] The reason is that the nonreproducible assets—the mineral resources—constitute a large share of the value of total capital used in mining. Conversely, past labor constitutes only a small share of the total value of those assets.

This unique characteristic of mineral lands makes it difficult to analyze the movement of the land-output ratio and, hence, the total

[4] We are not considering here the accelerated depreciation of emergency defense facilities in the war and postwar period. This development affects a short time span only. Moreover, as stated in Appendix Table B-9, accelerated amortization is relatively unimportant in mining. At its peak in 1943, it amounted to only 5 per cent of normal depreciation.

[5] For a more extended discussion of some of these points, see Simon Kuznets' "Comment" in *Studies in Income and Wealth*, Volume 14 (National Bureau of Economic Research, 1951, pp. 62–68).

[6] To a lesser degree, the same situation exists in agriculture. There, however, the share of past labor in the total value of land is much higher, so that the difference between the value of past labor and the total value of land is neglected by certain authors.

capital-output ratio, in a manner similar to that for the other capital aggregates. The ratios of land to output based on reported values are subject to the restrictions imposed by the different valuation bases of numerator and denominator. Moreover, neither for practical nor conceptual reasons is an adjustment for the different valuation bases warranted.[7]

The social-accounting approach is probably the most useful for the purpose of this study. We assume that the value of mineral lands is equal to the value of their reproduction costs (the input factors provided for their discovery and development). However, except for the petroleum and natural gas industry, costs of discovery and development per unit of output are low, and the estimation of such a series does not seem to warrant the time and effort required. Therefore, the ratio of total capital (which includes land) to output is given only for reported values in Tables 23 and 24. These ratios increased during the earlier decades and declined during the later in much the same way as the ratios of capital (defined as plant and working capital only) to output. However, the former ratios rose less and declined more than the ratios of capital to output. The same is true, of course, to an even larger extent, of the ratios of land to output.

In general, these findings are what we might expect. Buying of mineral land to ensure supply for a growing market, an amount beyond that necessary merely to ensure production at current rates for a reasonably long period of time, should have been more frequent before 1900, when land prices were low, than in the later years. Also, the entrepreneur's early optimism about future developments would have expressed itself, at the outset, in relatively high land evaluation. For these reasons, the land-output ratios can be expected to begin at a relatively higher level than the capital-output ratios. On the other hand, the more pessimistic outlook during the time of slackened growth should have affected land values seriously, because they were not supported by the value of input of past labor. The market value of land per unit of output and, consequently, the book value, should have declined more than the value of capital.[8]

---

[7] For conceptual difficulties, see Appendix B, section E.

[8] The last consideration is not valid for the petroleum and natural gas industry. The rate of growth of output in this industry was accelerating rather than decelerating in 1919–1929. Moreover, because the number of transfers in this industry is high, one would expect high valuations of the book value of land (see p. 82). Indeed, our figures indicate no significant decline in the ratio of book value of land to output, except for 1948. The exception is probably entirely due to the postwar inflation of prices for petroleum and natural gas. The land-output ratio for this industry (Table 24) is low because the vast majority of oil lands are held under lease and, therefore, do not appear in our land estimates. For an estimate of the market value of oil leases at different benchmarks, see note 9.

RATIOS OF FIXED AND WORKING CAPITAL TO OUTPUT

The precise validity of the above considerations, however, is obscured by several factors other than the difference in the valuation bases of the numerator and denominator. First, the land figures do not include the value of leased land. Changes in the form of land tenure may have contributed to the observed differences in the movement of the ratios. Unfortunately, after 1919, we have no data to use as a check on such a possibility. The tendencies for the period before 1919, however, may be indicated by the following percentages (based on census data) of the total number of acres operated that were held under lease:

	1890	1902	1909	1919
Anthracite coal	49.8	n.a.	33.1	25.6
Bituminous coal	25.3	n.a.	30.1	29.9
Petroleum and natural gas	81.0	n.a.	94.6	90.4
Iron	n.a.	n.a.	68.4[a]	n.a.
Copper	n.a.	3.8	3.2	3.6
Lead and zinc	n.a.	n.a.	21.4	26.6
Precious metals	n.a.	5.6	15.4	20.0
All other	n.a.	n.a.	16.5	27.1

[a] Percentage of value of total output that was mined from leased land. The corresponding figure for 1880 was 33.0. Figures for 1880 for the other industry groups are not available.

It appears that, except in anthracite mining, for which the reverse has been true, there has been a tendency toward more extensive use of leased land. It is doubtful, however, whether this tendency has been strong enough to account for much of the change in the land-output ratios over time.[9]

[9] We are concerned with the book value of land primarily because of its importance in determining the capital dimensions of a mining enterprise, e.g., its asset structure as compared with its liability structure. No such importance can be ascribed to the value of leases. Moreover, the only way to approximate the value of leases is to capitalize royalties. The value of royalties strictly depends upon the value of output in a given year. Thus, the value of leases is directly related to the output value. However, we have calculated lease values for total mining by industries for those benchmark years prior to 1919 for which statistics could be found, and for oil and gas for the whole period. The estimates for the latter industry are of greater interest because of the magnitudes involved. In the following table, we show the estimated market value of oil and natural gas leases, exclusive of value added by drilling and equipping of wells.

	Lease Value (billions of dollars)	Average Life of Reserves (years)	Discount Rate (per cent)
1890	$0.04	–	–
1909	0.3	20	4.0
1919	1.1	15	4.5
1929	1.9	14	4.0
1940	2.0	15	3.5
1948	8.0	16	3.0

The figure for 1890 is given in *Report on Mineral Industries in the United States:*

Second, the book value of land is much affected by the extent of market turnover. As long as the mineral lands are not sold, their value may be kept on the books at levels approximating their reproducible costs, i.e., their cost of discovery and development. Thus, reported land values represent a mixture of different valuation bases, not only with respect to the time the transactions were made, but also with respect to the methods of valuation. Since the market value of land exceeds by far its development costs, the total of reported book values will depend, to a large extent, on the number of transactions made during the period preceding the year in which the reports were made. Transfers of mineral wealth were more frequent in earlier than in recent years. Hence, this factor should have worked for higher book values of land in the earlier years.

As depletion deductions received wider recognition (the tendency was strengthened by the inception of the corporation income tax in 1909), land values in book values tended to decline. However, later revenue acts counteracted this decline.

The Revenue Act of 1918 allowed depletion charges to be based on the market value as of March 1, 1913. The Act of 1921 allowed a further deduction, in determining taxable income from the operation of oil and mining properties, based on the appreciation of value resulting from the fresh discovery of minerals. As a result of the balancing of these two tendencies, book values of land in 1919 are comparable with those in 1909.[10]

The picture for 1929 and after is different. Relatively high depletion allowances continued, and were stepped up during the forties. However, upward revaluations of land became less frequent in 1925–1929; in the thirties, downward revaluations were predominant. The combination of these two developments is mainly responsible for the sharp decline in the land-output ratio after 1929. We hope our method of breaking down total capital into land and capital yields figures that

---

1890. For all other years, we used the current annuity value of royalties paid to the owners of oil lands, assuming that the latter remain unchanged during the lifetime of the mineral reserves. For the years 1909 and 1919, the amount paid for royalties was reported in the *Census of Mines and Quarries.* For the later years, the landowners' share of petroleum output was assumed to be 12.5 per cent and that of natural gas to be 10 per cent. [See H. Foster Bain, "Subsoil Wealth," in *Studies in Income and Wealth,* Volume Twelve (National Bureau of Economic Research, 1950, p. 266); it was also assumed that 90 per cent of petroleum and natural gas in these years was produced from leaseholds.]

[10] See, for instance, data on the surplus arising from the revaluation of property assets and on depletion and depreciation reserves in *Investments and Profits of Bituminous Coal Operators,* submitted by David L. Wing and James E. Black to the U.S. Coal Commission, and published in its *Report of the U.S. Coal Commission,* Part IV (1923), p. 2541.

account fully for the shrinkage in the book value of land since 1929.[11] Indeed, we have good reason to think that if any bias resulted, it is in an understatement of these land values.

The Record in Manufacturing, from 1948 to 1953

Between the postwar business cycle peak of 1948 and the succeeding peak of 1953, net fixed capital in manufacturing (measured in 1929 prices) increased by nearly one-fourth and total capital by slightly more. These represent substantial growth rates. In these circumstances, the movement of the capital-output ratios is of special interest.

As we noted at an early point, the total capital-output ratio (based on 1929 prices) for all manufacturing decreased by 3.1 per cent between 1948 and 1953. This decline occurred in 12 of the 19 groups for which we can compute the ratios to output of fixed and working capital (Table 26). In only 1 group (chemicals) did the total capital-output ratio exceed the 1937 ratio.

For all manufacturing, the fixed capital-output ratios decreased by 5 per cent between 1948 and 1953, and those for working capital decreased by 1 per cent. Perhaps of more significance is the predominant direction and magnitude of movement of the ratios for individual industry groups. In 15 of the 19 groups, the ratio of fixed capital to output declined between 1948 and 1953. In 11 groups, the decline was 10 per cent or more (Table 27). On the other hand, of the 4 industry groups with a rising ratio, the relative increase was nominal in paper and allied products and modest in textile mill products. It was substantial in iron, steel and nonferrous metals (15 per cent), and in chemicals and allied products (34 per cent),[12] both of which include government-owned but privately operated plants. Three of these industries (the exception is textile mill products) had a better-than-average percentage expansion of fixed capital between 1948 and 1953. On the other hand, 3 other industry groups, with an equally high relative expansion of fixed capital, continued to have declining fixed capital-output ratios.

Among the 15 industries with a declining ratio of fixed capital to output, 6 operated with less capital (in 1929 prices) in 1953 than in 1948. Leather excepted, the smaller amount of capital in 1953 produced a larger volume of output than did the larger amount of capital in 1948. In the other 9 industry groups, capital expanded, but production increased at a still more rapid rate.

In summary, nearly three-fourths of the major industry groups,

---

[11] For a description of our method, see Appendix B, note 33, and the notes to Appendix Table B-11.
[12] See Table 26, note a.

TABLE 26

Major Manufacturing Industries: Ratios to Output of Selected Capital Components, 1948 and 1953
(based on values in 1929 prices)

	\multicolumn{6}{c}{Ratio to Output of:}					
	Total Capital		Fixed Capital		Working Capital	
	1948	1953	1948	1953	1948	1953
All manufacturing	.609	.590	.285	.270[a]	.324	.320
Beverages	.571	.413	.268	.123	.303	.290
Food and kindred products	.347	.328	.164	.134	.183	.194
Tobacco products	.569	.658	.056	.039	.513	.619
Textile-mill products	.555	.631	.237	.249	.318	.382
Apparel	.338	.342	.051	.043	.287	.299
Forest products	.705	.760	.394	.383	.311	.377
Paper and allied products	.764	.753	.471	.472	.293	.281
Printing and publishing	.690	.669	.305	.303	.385	.366
Chemicals and allied products	.716	.840	.365	.488[a]	.351	.352
Petroleum and coal products	.893	.763	.576	.483	.317	.280
Rubber products	.518	.510	.175	.144	.343	.366
Leather and leather products	.407	.414	.093	.076	.314	.338
Stone, clay, and glass products	.738	.686	.401	.354	.337	.332
Iron, steel, and nonferrous metals and products	.695	.721	.363	.416[a]	.332	.305
Machinery excluding electrical	.712	.657	.250	.228	.462	.429
Electrical machinery	.583	.527	.186	.139	.397	.388
Transportation equipment excluding motor vehicles	.967	.666	.382	.247[a]	.585	.419
Motor vehicles and equipment	.493	.425	.209	.185	.284	.240
Miscellaneous[b]	.609	.577	.223	.170	.386	.407

[a] Except for the management fee, privately operated, government-owned facilities are excluded from the 1953 output estimates, but they are included in the capital estimates. A more realistic ratio, therefore, is obtained by excluding such facilities from fixed capital. With this exclusion from industries where this item is quantitatively important, the fixed capital-output ratios are:

    All groups   .250
    Chemicals and allied products   .371
    Iron and steel and nonferrous metals   .367
    Transportation equipment except motor vehicles   .107

Comparable absolute changes would appear in the total capital-output ratios.

[b] Includes instruments and miscellaneous industries; ordnance included with iron, steel, and nonferrous metals and products in both years.

Source: Based on Appendix Table A-15 and worksheets.

owning almost 60 per cent of all fixed capital (in 1929 prices) devoted to manufacturing in 1953, continue to operate with fixed capital of increasing efficiency. This suggests that the downward movement of the fixed capital-output ratio initiated after World War I had not yet spent itself, at least through 1953.

RATIOS OF FIXED AND WORKING CAPITAL TO OUTPUT

Beween 1948 and 1953, the ratio of working capital to output for all manufacturing declined in 10 of the 19 industry groups. The working capital in these 10 groups also equaled 60 per cent of all working capital used in manufacturing. However, since the decline occurred only in a bare majority of the industry groups, this indicates a departure from the previous pattern of decline in the working capital-

TABLE 27

Major Manufacturing Industries: Fixed Capital and Selected Capital-Output Ratios, Per Cent Change between 1948 and 1953
(based on values in 1929 prices)

	Per Cent Change Between 1948 and 1953 in—		
		Ratio to Output of—	
	Fixed Capital	Fixed Capital	Working Capital
All manufacturing	+23.4	−5.3	−1.2
Beverages	−0.8	−54.1	−4.3
Food and kindred products	−3.5	−18.3	+6.0
Tobacco products	−23.5	−30.4	+20.7
Textile-mill products	−1.6	+5.1	+20.1
Apparel	+9.9	−15.7	+4.2
Forest Products	−0.1	−2.8	+21.2
Paper and allied products	+26.1	+0.2	−4.1
Printing and publishing	+4.0	−0.7	−4.9
Chemicals and allied products	+69.7	+33.7	+0.3
Petroleum and coal products	+8.5	−16.1	−11.7
Rubber products	−2.9	−17.7	+6.7
Leather and leather products	−18.8	−18.3	+7.6
Stone, clay, and glass products	+16.6	−11.7	−1.5
Iron, steel, and nonferrous metals and products	+38.1	+14.6	−8.1
Machinery excluding electrical	+17.6	−8.8	−6.7
Electrical machinery	+32.2	−25.3	−2.3
Transportation equipment excluding motor vehicles	+86.9	−35.3	−28.4
Motor vehicles and equipment	+37.1	−11.5	−15.5
Miscellaneous	+14.2	−23.8	+5.4

Source: See Appendix Table A-15.

output ratio that characterized most branches of manufacturing. And this deserves further exploration.

In Table 28, each major component of working capital—cash, notes and accounts receivable, and inventories—is related to output (all in 1929 prices) for 1948 and 1953. Each component of working capital is an average of year-end book values in the given and preceding year.

CAPITAL AND OUTPUT TRENDS

In aggregate manufacturing, the ratio of cash to output declined by 13 per cent between 1948 and 1953, the inventory-output ratio increased by 3 per cent, and the ratio of notes and accounts receivable to output rose substantially (13 per cent). It was the rise in the latter

TABLE 28

Major Manufacturing Industries: Ratios of Selected Short-Term Assets to Output, 1948 and 1953
(based on values in 1929 prices)

	\multicolumn{6}{c}{Ratios to Output of—}					
	Cash		Notes and Accounts Receivable		Inventories	
	1948	1953	1948	1953	1948	1953
All manufacturing[a]	.061	.053	.085	.096	.148	.153
Beverages	.052	.047	.066	.064	.173	.165
Food and kindred products	.032	.032	.044	.051	.090	.095
Tobacco products	.031	.030	.135	.127	.461	.448
Textile-mill products	.062	.063	.072	.111	.151	.208
Apparel	.052	.045	.090	.100	.146	.145
Forest products	.058	.062	.087	.114	.146	.178
Paper and allied products	.063	.069	.078	.082	.124	.120
Printing	.082	.081	.122	.121	.083	.083
Chemical and allied products	.076	.074	.090	.101	.156	.163
Petroleum and coal	.061	.055	.106	.108	.101	.101
Rubber products	.055	.047	.111	.140	.170	.170
Leather and products	.051	.048	.093	.114	.158	.175
Stone, clay, and glass	.073	.072	.095	.098	.129	.127
Iron, steel, and nonferrous metals	.066	.060	.078	.080	.138	.150
Machinery excluding electrical	.074	.068	.109	.123	.223	.222
Electrical machinery	.073	.046	.127	.128	.220	.197
Transportation excluding motor vehicles[a]	.122	.047	.204	.145	.366	.208
Motor vehicles and equipment	.069	.040	.056	.072	.138	.118
Miscellaneous	.066	.055	.111	.129	.194	.195

[a] Shipbuilding excluded from numerator and denominator in all 1948 ratios but included in all 1953 ratios.
Source: Based on *Statistics of Income*, Part 2, Bureau of Internal Revenue (now Internal Revenue Service), for 1948 and 1953. For conversion to 1929 prices, see Appendix A, section B, part 1C.

two components that restricted the decline in the capital-output ratio to slightly more than 1 per cent. However, the inventories-output ratio rose in only 7 of the 19 industries; in 3 industries, this ratio was unchanged. On the other hand, the receivables-output ratio rose in all except 4 of the industry groups.

The inventory-output ratio in 1948 probably was unduly low owing to the shortages of the immediate postwar years.[13] Probably the same set of circumstances also depressed the 1948 ratio of notes and accounts receivable to output. That is, in a strong sellers' market, manufacturers had less need to finance their customers. With the subsequent rapid expansion of capital stock and capacity, there was a gradual shift from the sellers' market to one in which the buyer was no longer at a disadvantage. To expand sales in this situation, manufacturers financed a larger proportion of their sales.[14]

These special circumstances of 1948 suggest that the rise in the working capital-output ratio between 1948 and 1953 may well prove to be a temporary interruption to the downward trend, rather than a trend reversal. This determination must wait upon data for years following 1953.

The Record in Mining, 1948–1953

The downward trend in the capital-output ratio (in 1929 prices) for total mining has continued to 1953 (Table 29). The ratio in the latter

TABLE 29

Selected Capital-Output Ratios, by Major Mining Industries, 1948 and 1953
(based on values in 1929 prices)

	Ratios to Output of—					
	Capital		Plant		Working Capital	
	1948	1953	1948	1953	1948	1953
All mining	1.34	1.26	0.92	0.84	0.42	0.42
Metals	1.00	1.39	0.54	0.77	0.46	0.62
Anthracite coal	0.43	0.64	0.25	0.32	0.18	0.32
Bituminous coal	0.88	1.17	0.48	0.72	0.40	0.45
Petroleum and natural gas	1.79	1.41	1.32	1.01	0.47	0.40
Other nonmetals	0.56	0.61	0.32	0.33	0.24	0.28

Source: Based on data in Appendix Tables B-8 and B-11, and worksheets.

[13] The inventories-output ratio in 1948 was 14 per cent below that of 1937 (Table 22). The ratio for 1953 is 3.4 per cent higher than the 1948 ratio, making for a lower ratio in 1953 than in 1937. The ratios for 1948 differ because of differences in the method of expressing inventories in 1929 prices. The method used in preparing Table 22 is the preferred one. Data for this method were not readily at hand for 1953.

[14] The four industries with declining ratios of notes and accounts receivable to output serve to confirm this generalization. In two (beverages, and tobacco manufacturing) fixed capital declined; in printing and publishing, fixed capital rose a modest 4 per cent. In the fourth industry, transportation equipment except motor vehicles, military airplanes were the principal component to rise rapidly during this period of the Korean War. Since the Federal government was the buyer, the manufacturers had no pressing need to finance their sales with book credit.

year was 6 per cent below the ratio for 1948. If the numerator of the ratio is restricted to plant (structures and equipment) the decline is even larger, nearly 9 per cent. On the other hand, the ratio of working capital to output was unchanged in 1948 and 1953. On closer inspection, it appears that the continued decline of the ratio for all mining is due to developments in the petroleum and natural gas industry which, in 1953, used 68 per cent of all capital (in 1929 prices) devoted to mining. In the other 4 major mining groups, all ratios (capital, plant, and working capital to output) were higher in 1953 than in 1948. Indeed, the 1953 ratios for metals, anthracite, and bituminous coal even exceeded the 1940 ratios; but, except in bituminous coal, the 1953 ratios were less than the 1929 ratios. The conclusion seems inescapable: the downward trend in the capital-output ratios in mining (except in the petroleum and natural gas industry), evident since 1909 or 1919, reversed in the five-year period 1948–1953. In manufacturing, the evidence of any reversal of trend, except for working capital, was much less definitive.[15]

Changes between 1953 and 1957 in Capital-Output Ratios for Manufacturing

Since the preparation of this manuscript, preliminary estimates of capital for 1957 (another peak year in business activity) were prepared by major manufacturing industry groups for the National Industrial Conference Board.[16] These can be used to extend the estimates that form the core of Part I of this monograph and, thereby, to provide a view of developments in this area over the first post-World War II decade.

The fixed-capital estimates based on data from *Statistics of Income* were prepared for 1956 and extended to 1957 using a sample (the *Quarterly Financial Report, United States Manufacturing Corporations*) taken by the Federal Trade Commission and the Securities and Exchange Commission. The 1957 estimate, therefore, is probably less firmly based than are the estimates for 1948 and 1953. At best, it must be considered preliminary.

Another caution relates to the change, after 1953, in the depreciation regulations for acquisitions of depreciable assets. They introduce an

---

[15] The reversal in trend of the capital-output ratios provides an unusual opportunity to analyze the changes in technology and other factors that made first for a declining ratio of capital to output and then for a rising ratio. This would require a series of detailed industry case studies that cannot be undertaken for this monograph.

[16] For a description of the estimates, see Daniel Creamer, *Technical Paper*, National Industrial Conference Board (forthcoming).

element of incomparability into the balance-sheet data because the new regulations permit a faster recovery of new investment than was possible under the straight-line depreciation previously prescribed. Thus, estimates of net fixed capital derived from book values would be relatively more net of depreciation after 1953 than in 1953 and earlier years. The elimination of this element of incomparability raised the 1956 estimate of net fixed assets for all manufactures in 1929 prices by 1.6 per cent and, therefore, the fixed capital-output ratio by the same amount.[17] This adjustment could not be made by industry subgroups. Departure from the average adjustment of all subgroups would depend on the rate of expansion of fixed-capital assets since 1953 and on the portion subject to accelerated amortization as an emergency facility. We fall back on an arbitrary arrangement: We treat a decline in the fixed capital-output ratio of 2 per cent or less between 1953 and 1957 as equivalent to no change.[18]

Although fixed capital in manufacturing expanded at an average annual rate of 4.3 per cent between 1948 and 1953—perhaps the highest rate since World War I—it achieved a still higher rate, 4.7, over the 1953–1957 business cycle (Table 30). In the former period, 9 of the 21 industry groups had average or better-than-average rates of growth. With the exception of chemicals and allied products, and paper and allied products, all these industries were engaged in the manufacture of consumers' and producers' metal products. These, apparently, were the industries in which technical innovations and the long suppression of demand created the strongest pressures for expansion. These, then, were the industries that would outbid all others for the limited resources available for expansion. In the next cycle, although the urgency for expansion was less, these industries continued to grow at a relatively high rate. That is, in 6 of the 9 groups, the average annual rate of increase was less in the 1953–1957 cycle than in the preceding cycle; but, also in 6 groups, the rate equaled or exceeded the annual growth rate for all manufacturing.

Half of the 12 industry groups with less than the average rate of growth between 1948 and 1953 actually sustained a contraction in fixed capital measured in constant prices. In each case, however, the contraction was either nominal or of modest proportions. In the next period, 9 of the 12 had a higher rate of expansion (or a lower rate of contraction), and 5 groups actually expanded at a higher annual rate than all manufacturing. Once the chemical and metal working

[17] This adjustment will be described in Creamer, *op. cit.*

[18] Estimates for both 1957 and 1953 include fixed capital owned by government but operated by private industry. The output estimate is the annual rate of output of the peak quarterly output in 1957, as indicated by the Federal Reserve Board's index of manufacturing production.

TABLE 30

Change in Fixed Capital and in Its Ratio to Output, by Major Manufacturing Industries, 1948–1953 and 1953–1957
(based on values in 1929 prices)

	Rate of Change per year in Fixed Capital		Per Cent Change in Fixed Capital-Output Ratio	
	1948–1953	*1953–1957*	*1948–1953*	*1953–1957*
All manufacturing	+4.3	+4.7	−5.3	+8.1
Miscellaneous including ordnance	+18.5	+0.3	+71.5	−11.8
Transportation equipment excluding autos	+13.3	+5.9	−35.3	+13.4
Chemicals and allied products	+11.2	+7.9	+33.7	+5.3
Instruments and professional apparatus	+10.4	+7.6	−17.8	+12.1
Motor vehicles	+6.5	+8.6	−11.5	+48.1
Electrical machinery	+5.8	+3.7	−25.3	+18.7
Paper and allied products	+4.8	+6.6	+0.2	+5.9
Fabricated metal products	+4.3	+3.6	−7.7	+5.4
Primary metals	+4.3	+4.7	+10.4	+19.6
Machinery other than electrical	+3.3	+5.5	−8.8	+12.3
Stone, clay, and glass products	+3.1	+8.7	−11.7	+26.0
Apparel	+1.9	0.0	−15.7	−7.0
Petroleum and coal products	+1.7	+7.0	−16.1	+2.3
Printing and publishing	+0.8	+3.7	−0.7	−5.0
Lumber and products	+0.6	+6.9	−4.0	+16.0
Textile-mill products	−0.3	−1.8	+5.1	−16.1
Rubber products	−0.6	+3.7	−17.7	+5.6
Food and kindred products[a]	−0.6	−0.8	−27.2	−6.9
Furniture and fixtures	−2.4	+2.7	−10.7	−6.7
Leather and leather products	−4.1	−1.5	−18.3	−21.1
Tobacco products	−5.2	+7.2	−30.4	+35.9

[a] Includes beverages.

Note: The industry groups are arranged by order of the rate of change between 1948 and 1953, starting with the highest.

Source: Daniel Creamer, *Technical Paper*, National Industrial Conference Board (forthcoming).

industries had satisfied their more pressing needs for capital, other branches of manufacturing were able to grow at a faster rate.

We have already noted that in most branches (16 out of 21), the fixed capital-output ratio declined between 1948 and 1953, thus continuing the general pattern that had persisted since about 1919. Over the course of the 1953–1957 cycle, the continuance of the relatively high rates of expansion caused the stock of fixed capital to grow more rapidly than output, resulting in a significant rise in the fixed capital-output ratio. This occurred in two-thirds of the 21 industry groups.

With one exception, the rise in the ratio amounted to 5 per cent or more and to 10 per cent or more in 9 industries. Thus, for the first time in about four decades, manufacturing industries typically used more fixed capital in constant prices, *not less*, to produce a unit of output. This was the predominant trend from 1880 to 1919. Perhaps it is no coincidence that the condition reappeared in 1957, when the annual rate of capital expansion was approaching that of some of these earlier decades. The latter supposition is consistent with the low rates of growth of the 7 industries with declining fixed capital-output ratios between 1953 and 1957. Five of these industries had either stood still or declined, and the remaining 2 rose less than 4 per cent.

The ratio of working capital to output in 1956 (the last year for which the computation can be made) was 5 per cent above the ratio for 1953 and 3.7 per cent above the 1948 ratio. The reversal in the direction of the trend initiated in half of the industry groups in the 1948–1953 period became more pervasive, having occurred in all but 5 of the 22 subgroups. Once again, to judge by a limited examination of the evidence, the need to hold an ever larger volume of accounts and notes receivable per unit of output has been mainly responsible for the rising ratio of working capital to output. Thus, to utilize the rapidly expanded capacity, producers have been obliged to finance an increasing proportion of their sales.

Summary of Findings

1. For manufacturing, the subdivision between fixed and working capital can be made for seven benchmark years beginning 1890. The ratios of both fixed and working capital to output, have risen up to 1919 or, at the latest, 1929. Both ratios declined thereafter up to 1948. The rise from 1890 to 1929 was somewhat sharper for the working capital-output ratio than for the fixed capital-output ratio (23 and 19 per cent, respectively). The decline from 1929 to 1948 was greater for the fixed capital-output ratio than for the working capital-output ratio (34 and 29 per cent, respectively). This is conclusive evidence that the changes in the total capital-output ratio were not caused by any change in the relative importance of fixed and working capital.

2. In mining industries, also, during the earlier decades, the ratios of plant (net value of structures and equipment) to output and of working capital to output rose. The increase in the former was steeper. Between 1919 and 1948, in most mining industries, the ratios of working capital to output began to decline later (1929 rather than 1919) than the ratios of plant to output, and the decline was much smaller.

3. The discrepancy between the stock of reproducible wealth ("past labor") used in production and the actual amount of wealth used for

the same purpose is unique for mining industries in that nonreproducible assets—the mineral resources—constitute a large share of the value of total capital used in mining. Conversely, past labor constitutes only a small share of the total value of these assets. Because of conceptual difficulties, the ratio of total capital (which includes land) to output is given only for reported values. These ratios increased during the earlier decades and declined during the later ones in much the same way as the ratios of capital (defined as plant and working capital only) to output. The rise in the former ratios, however, was less pronounced and the decline more marked than in the ratios of capital to output. The same is true, of course, to an even larger extent, of the ratios of land to output.

4. After 1948, nearly three-fourths of the major industry groups, owning almost 60 per cent of all fixed capital (in 1929 prices) devoted to manufacturing in 1953, continued to operate with fixed capital of increasing efficiency. That is, the fixed capital-output ratio continued to decline despite the relatively rapid rate of annual expansion in fixed capital between 1948 and 1953. The working capital-output ratio also declined for all manufacturing and for about half of the 19 industry groups. This nonconformity of nearly half of the industry groups represents a departure from the pattern that had persisted since about the end of World War I.

5. The downward trend in the capital-output ratio in mining, evident since 1919, was reversed in 1948–1953, except in the petroleum and natural gas industries. This was true for mining industries that expanded their capital (in 1929 prices), such as metals and other nonmetals, as well as for those that contracted their capital stock, such as anthracite, or maintained a constant stock, such as bituminous coal.

6. The continuance in the 1953–1957 cycle of the relatively high growth rates initiated in the 1948–1953 business cycle caused the stock of fixed capital to increase more rapidly than output, resulting in a significant rise in the fixed capital-output ratio. This occurred in two-thirds of the 21 industry groups. Thus, for the first time in about four decades, manufacturing industries typically used more fixed capital in constant prices, *not less*, to produce a unit of output. The working capital-output ratio also increased in this period (by 5 per cent) and this increase occurred in all except 5 of the industry groups.

CHAPTER V

Some Relationships Bearing on Changes in the Capital-Output Ratios

Pattern of Change in Capital-Output Ratios in Individual Manufacturing Industries

Is there any pattern underlying the change in the capital-output ratios of individual industries that helps to explain the reversal of trend in the ratio for total manufacturing?

One pattern is clear: Between 1880 and 1919, when the capital-output ratio for all manufacturing was rising, the dispersion of the minor-industry ratios about the all-manufacturing ratio, measured by the coefficient of variation, declined by nearly two-fifths (Table 31).

TABLE 31

Coefficient of Variation of the Capital-Output Ratios in Thirty-seven Manufacturing Industries, Selected Years, 1880–1948
(*based on values in 1929 prices*)

Benchmark Years	Coefficient of Variation (Percentage)
1880	63.1
1890	70.3
1900	
Comparable with preceding years	65.5
Comparable with following years	66.9
1904	58.5
1909	49.3
1914	50.5
1919	38.3
1929	33.0
1937	35.6
1948	31.3

Source: Based on data in Appendix Table A-13.

All of the decline occurred after 1900. This must mean that the rate of increase in the capital-output ratio of industries with relatively low ratios in 1880 was typically higher than for industries with relatively high ratios. The continued narrowing of the dispersion of the minor industry ratios after 1919, when the capital-output ratio of all manufacturing was declining, is consistent with only one inference: The ratios of industries with relatively high ratios in 1919 generally declined more rapidly than the ratios of industries with relatively low ratios in 1919. This trend toward less dispersion of the capital-output ratios suggests a hypothesis which, however, cannot be tested. During the earlier period, the smaller the importance of capital in 1880, i.e., the lower the capital-output ratio, the greater the scope for additional mechanization of processes; during the later period, the greater the importance of capital in 1919, i.e., the higher the capital-output ratio, the larger the scope for improving the efficiency of capital.[1]

The relationship between changes in the capital-output ratios and changes in the rate of growth measured by output in constant prices is not particularly helpful. True, the percentage changes in output and in capital (both in 1929 prices) are highly correlated (the coefficient of correlation between relative changes in output and capital for the 50 or more industries is $+0.85$ for 1880–1919 and $+0.68$ for 1919–1948). However, the correlation is high only because, over the long term, output and plant capacity must change in much the same way. Thus, a lower degree of association is expected in the second period when capital-saving innovations have predominated. However, the association between the relative changes in output and in the capital-output ratio is negative and of a low order in both periods (-0.39 for 1880–1919 and -0.37 for 1919–1948).[2]

Relation between Labor and Capital per Unit of Output and Capital per Man-hour

MANUFACTURING. The reversal in the trend in the capital-output ratios suggests that technological innovations before World War I tended to replace other factor inputs with capital rather than to increase the efficiency of capital, while, more recently, the reverse has been true. This generalization is consistent with the trends in capital (in 1929 prices) per man-hour worked and in man-hours per unit of output.

Man-hours per unit of output (the reciprocal of "labor productivity") are reduced whenever labor is replaced by other factor inputs or whenever other factor inputs operate more efficiently if the efficiency of labor itself remains unchanged. One or the other or both factors have been in continuous operation since 1900, and the index of man-hours per unit of output (in 1929 prices) has declined by substantial amounts from decade to decade during this period (Table 32). Additional

[1] For an analysis of interindustry differences in capital-output ratios as of 1929, see Charles A. Bliss, *The Structure of Manufacturing Production* (National Bureau of Economic Research, 1939, pp. 88–119).

[2] All coefficients are statistically significant.

CHANGES IN CAPITAL-OUTPUT RATIOS

TABLE 32

Indexes of Selected Ratios: Man-hours, Capital, and Output,
All Manufacturing, Selected Years, 1880–1957
(1929 = 100)

Benchmark Years	Ratios of—				
	Man-hours Worked to Output	Total Capital to Man-hours Worked	Fixed Capital to Man-hours Worked	Total Capital to Output	Fixed Capital to Output
1900[a]	191.7	46.4	48.0	90.7	96.1
1900[b]	186.4	48.1	n.a.	89.7	n.a.
1909	172.5	63.8	n.a.	109.8	n.a.
1919	151.7	76.1	n.a.	115.5	n.a.
1929	100.0	100.0	100.0	100.0	100.0
1937	84.2	99.4	94.9	83.7	79.9
1948	73.7	93.4	89.3	68.8	65.8
1953	65.0	103.1	96.3	66.7	62.4
1957	55.7	n.a.	121.0	n.a.	67.4

n.a. = not available.
Note: Capital and output dollar values are in 1929 prices.
[a] Including custom and neighborhood shops.
[b] Excluding custom and neighborhood shops.
Source: Output and capital estimates from Appendix Tables A-8 to A-10 and A-15. Man-hours worked is the product of (a) average hours worked per week from *Historical Statistics of the United States, 1789–1945*, p. 67. Table 123, for 1900 and 1909; Bureau of Labor Statistics *Handbook of Labor Statistics*, 1950 Edition, pp. 58–59, Table C-1, for 1919–1948; and the *Economic Report of the President, January 1959*, Table D-26, p. 169, for 1953 and 1957; and (b) total employment (active proprietors, salaried personnel and wage earners) from *Census of Manufactures* for 1900–1919; *National Income, 1954 Edition, A Supplement to the Survey of Current Business*, Table 28, pp. 202–203, for 1929–1953; for 1957, from Office of Business Economics, *U.S. Income and Output: A Supplement to the Survey of Current Business* (1959), Table VI-16.

factors have been—to mention a few—the probable increase in the efficiency of labor itself owing to wider public education, the aging of the labor force, and the shorter work-week. During 1900–1929, the reduction in man-hours per unit of output was principally associated with the continuous increase in the amount of capital per man-hour worked. The extraordinary reduction in man-hours per unit of output between 1919 and 1929 was associated with an unusually large increase in capital per man-hour, as well as with a modest increase in capital efficiency (the capital-output ratios declined between 1919 and 1929). Between 1929 and 1948, increased capital efficiency was primarily responsible for the more moderate reductions in man-hours per unit of output, since the amount of capital (total or fixed) per man-hour worked decreased substantially.[3] That is, in "real" terms, labor was

---

[3] This discussion assumes that the improved efficiency of labor input *per se* has been a minor factor in the reduction of man-hour requirements.

equipped with less capital in 1937 and 1948 than in 1929; but because the capital was more efficient, man-hours per unit of output declined by 16 per cent between 1929 and 1937, and by 12.5 per cent between 1937 and 1948. These were matched by increases in capital efficiency, i.e., the capital-output ratio fell by 16 and 18 per cent, respectively.

Over 1948–1953, the reduction in man-hours worked per unit of output was 12 per cent, and between 1953 and 1957, 14 per cent. In contrast to the developments in the preceding two decades, the ratio of fixed capital to labor (man-hours) increased (by 8 and 26 per cent in 1948–1953 and 1953–1957, respectively), and the ratio of fixed capital to output decreased by 5 per cent in the 1948–1953 business cycle but increased by 8 per cent over the 1953–1957 cycle. That is, on balance, capital was moderately more efficient in 1953 than in 1948 but somewhat less efficient in 1957. However, in each year, each man-hour of work was carried out with the use of more capital, both fixed and working.

The relationship between labor per unit of output, capital per employee, and capital per unit of output is more clearly revealed by examining the movements of these ratios by manufacturing industry groups (Table 33).[4] For each of 20 industry groups, we can prepare the following ratios for selected benchmark years: (1) number employed to output in 1929 prices; (2) capital in 1929 prices to number employed; and (3) capital to output, both in 1929 prices. Each ratio is expressed as an index, with the 1929 ratio taken as 100. We use these data to answer two questions: (1) Is the decrease in the index of labor per unit of output between 1900 and 1929 related to the increase in the index of capital per employee during the same period? (2) Is the decrease in the index of labor per unit of output between 1929 and 1948 related to the decrease in the index of capital per unit of output (i.e., the increase in capital efficiency) during that period?

To answer the first question, we rank the 20 industries by the absolute amount of decline in the index of labor per unit of output between 1900 and 1929, starting with the largest decrease. This ranking is compared with the ranking of the same industries according to the size of the increase in the index of capital to number employed. For the 20 industries, the coefficient of rank correlation, which varies from $+1$ to -1, is $+0.67$. If, however, two industries are omitted—motor

[4] Since we do not have separate indexes of man-hours worked for each industry group, we make no effort to convert number employed to a man-hour basis. Labor per unit of output is measured by the ratio of number employed to output, and we substitute number employed for man-hours to relate labor to capital. Number employed is the total of active proprietors, salaried personnel, and wage earners (monthly average).

TABLE 33
Indexes of Selected Ratios: Number Employed, Capital, and Output, by Major Manufacturing Industries, Selected Years, 1900–1953
$(1929=100)$[b]

Ratio of:	Index of Ratios						
	1900	1909	1919	1929	1937	1948	1953
Food and kindred products							
1. Labor[a] to output	100.0	111.4	125.3	100.0	94.9	84.3	64.1
2. Capital to labor[a]	91.1	96.3	86.7	100.0	83.4	74.3	89.5
3. Capital to output	91.0	107.7	109.2	100.0	78.9	62.7	57.4
Tobacco products							
1. Labor[a] to output	292.1	259.6	178.1	100.0	65.8	32.9	31.5
2. Capital to labor[a]	19.3	27.6	47.1	100.0	115.5	179.9	216.9
3. Capital to output	56.0	71.6	83.6	100.0	76.2	58.8	68.0
Textile mill products							
1. Labor[a] to output	184.7	167.4	149.5	100.0	92.1	81.6	76.1
2. Capital to labor[a]	64.1	73.5	87.8	100.0	69.8	71.3	87.3
3. Capital to output	118.5	123.4	131.3	100.0	64.3	58.3	66.5
Apparel							
1. Labor[a] to output	154.1	150.7	132.2	100.0	136.6	99.5	79.9
2. Capital to labor[a]	60.3	71.6	103.6	100.0	60.6	70.6	88.3
3. Capital to output	92.8	108.0	136.7	100.0	82.7	70.1	70.5
Leather and leather products							
1. Labor[a] to output	96.7	78.9	100.9	100.0	117.4	94.8	92.1
2. Capital to labor[a]	83.8	121.2	108.4	100.0	65.7	61.9	64.7
3. Capital to output	81.3	95.8	109.7	100.0	77.1	58.6	59.7
Rubber products							
1. Labor[a] to output	658.8	515.0	280.6	100.0	88.1	59.0	53.8
2. Capital to labor[a]	29.5	38.6	53.2	100.0	82.5	85.4	92.1
3. Capital to output	194.9	199.2	149.5	100.0	73.0	50.5	49.7
Lumber and basic timber products							
1. Labor[a] to output	68.4	90.8	104.6	100.0	104.3		
2. Capital to labor[a]	54.1	67.0	68.1	100.0	77.7		
3. Capital to output	37.0	61.0	71.2	100.0	81.1	1. 84.0	76.6
Furniture and finished lumber products						2. 61.1	72.3
						3. 51.4	55.4
1. Labor[a] to output	84.3	89.9	106.3	100.0	100.6		
2. Capital to labor[a]	93.6	110.3	105.7	100.0	78.1		
3. Capital to output	79.0	99.4	112.6	100.0	78.8		
Paper and allied products							
1. Labor[a] to output	189.5	147.5	150.0	100.0	109.9	89.5	80.4
2. Capital to labor[a]	56.5	80.2	82.5	100.0	80.5	66.9	73.5
3. Capital to output	107.3	118.4	124.2	100.0	88.4	60.1	59.2
Printing, publishing, and allied industries							
1. Labor[a] to output	140.1	125.7	114.4	100.0	106.9	98.5	103.4
2. Capital to labor[a]	67.5	71.7	75.4	100.0	93.2	79.8	73.7
3. Capital to output	94.6	90.3	86.4	100.0	99.5	78.7	76.3
Petroleum refining							
1. Labor[a] to output	277.8	225.9	300.0	100.0	77.8	69.6	58.5
2. Capital to labor[a]	31.5	40.4	39.2	100.0	103.5	100.0	101.5
3. Capital to output	87.6	91.8	117.9	100.0	82.2	69.4	59.3
Chemicals and allied products							
1. Labor[a] to output	178.7	159.6	185.1	100.0	93.6	85.2	74.5
2. Capital to labor[a]	59.4	70.9	71.3	100.0	86.8	84.8	113.3
3. Capital to output	105.6	113.1	131.6	100.0	81.4	72.2	84.7

(continued)

CAPITAL AND OUTPUT TRENDS

TABLE 33 (concluded)

Ratio of:	Index of Ratios						
	1900	1909	1919	1929	1937	1948	1953
Stone, clay, and glass products							
1. Labor[a] to output	210.3	149.0	144.9	100.0	90.9	75.7	59.9
2. Capital to labor[a]	42.6	70.3	75.1	100.0	85.3	62.2	73.1
3. Capital to output	89.7	104.9	109.0	100.0	77.8	47.1	43.8
Iron and steel and their products							
1. Labor[a] to output	181.2	136.9	138.1	100.0	124.4		
2. Capital to labor[a]	69.5	113.8	117.2	100.0	93.2		
3. Capital to output	126.0	155.6	162.4	100.0	115.9	1. 92.5	80.1
Nonferrous metals and their products						2. 88.4	105.0
1. Labor[a] to output	206.4	145.0	145.9	100.0	89.0	3. 81.9	84.2
2. Capital to labor[a]	50.1	80.9	78.1	100.0	103.3		
3. Capital to output	102.8	117.0	113.6	100.0	91.3		
Machinery except electrical							
1. Labor[a] to output	171.8	147.0	146.4	100.0	100.0	90.1	76.6
2. Capital to labor[a]	64.1	89.1	77.9	100.0	86.8	73.7	79.7
3. Capital to output	110.1	131.1	114.2	100.0	86.9	66.3	61.2
Electrical machinery							
1. Labor[a] to output	86.3	81.6	93.0	100.0	85.6	50.5	39.1
2. Capital to labor[a]	119.1	160.4	121.5	100.0	83.7	125.3	146.1
3. Capital to output	102.7	130.9	112.8	100.0	71.6	63.2	57.2
Transportation equipment except motor vehicles							
1. Labor[a] to output	130.9	144.7	111.2	100.0	103.3	139.5	111.6
2. Capital to labor[a]	59.0	54.7	71.0	100.0	109.1	59.8	48.6
3. Capital to output	77.3	79.1	79.1	100.0	113.3	83.6	54.5
Motor vehicles							
1. Labor[a] to output	964.9	598.2	162.3	100.0	96.5	82.5	63.9
2. Capital to labor[a]	65.5	58.5	93.6	100.0	95.0	103.3	114.9
3. Capital to output	634.8	351.8	152 3.	100.0	92.3	85.7	73.9
Miscellaneous							
1. Labor[a] to output	262.9	233.1	291.9	100.0	137.9	108.1	182.2
2. Capital to labor[a]	31.7	39.3	34.5	100.0	58.2	58.3	30.1
3. Capital to output	83.1	91.3	100.5	100.0	79.9	63.0	54.8

Note: In 1948, we can calculate the following additional indexes:

	Ratios of:		
	Labor[a] to Output	Capital to Labor[b]	Capital to Output
Lumber and basic timber products	143.4	46.2	66.5
Furniture and finished lumber products	42.8	108.9	46.7
Iron and steel and their products	90.6	87.8	79.7
Nonferrous metals and their products	128.4	68.3	87.4

[a] "Number employed" or "labor" refers to the total of active proprietors, salaried personnel, and wage earners (monthly average).
[b] Capital and output dollar values are in 1929 prices.
Source: Estimates of output and capital from Appendix I, Table A-8, A-10, and A-15. For employment data, see Appendix Table A-16.

CHANGES IN CAPITAL-OUTPUT RATIOS

vehicles, with a phenomenal reduction in the index of labor per unit of output (from 965 in 1900 to 100 in 1929), and lumber and basic timber products, with an actual increase in labor per unit of output—the coefficient is +0.91. Thus, for most industries, the reduction in labor per unit of output between 1900 and 1929 is closely associated with the extent of additional capital provided all employed personnel.

We use a similar procedure to answer the second question. The 20 industries are arrayed by order of the decrease in the index of labor per unit of output between 1929 and 1948, and this ranking of industries is compared with their ranking according to the decrease in the index of capital per unit of output. The coefficient of rank correlation is +0.56. That is, the continued decline in labor per unit of output after 1929 was associated, but only to a moderate degree, with the extent of the decline in capital per unit of output (increased efficiency of capital). Omission of the 4 industries with increasing labor per unit of output between 1929 and 1948 does not improve the degree of association. To demonstrate that these correlated movements are important links in a causal chain requires an entirely different set of data and analyses.[5]

MINING. Much the same set of relationships is found in mining as in manufacturing. The increase in the capital-output ratios in all mining industries during the early decades was accompanied by an increase in capital per wage earner and man-hour and a decrease in man-hours to output; the relative increase in capital per unit of labor was greater than the relative decline in the ratio of man-hours to output (Table 34). The downturn in the capital-output ratios was also accompanied by an increase in capital per unit of labor and a decrease in labor per unit of output. But after 1929, capital per unit of labor rose only moderately in some industries and leveled off or declined in others.[6] Labor per unit of output, however, continued to decrease vigorously throughout the period.

These findings are compatible with the hypothesis that replacement of labor by capital was more common before World War I than after. With one exception, increases in output per unit of labor after World War I resulted primarily from the increased efficiency of equipment, better organizational methods, and greater skill. The decade 1919-1929 was an exception because capital per worker continued to grow at a

---

[5] Some of these aspects of productivity are discussed by George J. Stigler, *Trends in Output and Employment* (National Bureau of Economic Research, 1947), and by Frederick C. Mills, *Productivity and Economic Progress*, Occasional Paper 38 (National Bureau of Economic Research, 1952). Other aspects will be discussed by John Kendrick in his monograph now being prepared for the National Bureau.

[6] See also Chapter II, note 11.

CAPITAL AND OUTPUT TRENDS

TABLE 34

Indexes of Selected Ratios: Wage Earners, Man-hours, Capital, and Output, by Major Mining Industries, Selected Years, 1880–1953

(1929 = 100)

Ratio of	1880	1890	1909	1919	1929	1939	1948	1953
All mining								
Wage earners to output	387	314	204	168	100	81	58	41
Man-hours to output	393	350	n.a.	165	100	63	53	39
Capital to wage earners	14	20	41	64	100	98	108	142
Capital to man-hours	14	18	n.a.	65	100	125	119	152
Capital to output	54	64	84	107	100	79	62	59
Metals								
Wage earners to output	745	499	198	163	100	99	80	69
Man-hours to output	631	431	n.a.	165	100	84	70	62
Capital to wage earners	18	32	74	78	100	83	73	119
Capital to man-hours	21	37	n.a.	76	100	98	84	131
Capital to output	134	160	146	126	100	82	59	81
Anthracite coal								
Wage earners to output	127	140	109	87	100	83	68	84
Man-hours to output	136	143	108	102	100	65	70	69
Capital to wage earners	60	43	56	73	100	83	77	92
Capital to man-hours	56	42	57	63	100	107	75	112
Capital to output	76	60	61	64	100	69	52	77
Bituminous coal								
Wage earners to output	297	207	153	139	100	109	80	68
Man-hours to output	282	260	157	128	100	83	74	65
Capital to wage earners	22	31	65	85	100	82	105	162
Capital to man-hours	23	25	63	92	100	109	113	169
Capital to output	66	65	99	118	100	90	83	110
Petroleum and natural gas								
Wage earners to output	267	213	161	192	100	65	43	36
Man-hours to output	404	331	211	205	100	52	36	30
Capital to wage earners	22	50	87	85	100	101	115	108
Capital to man-hours	14	32	67	80	100	128	140	128
Capital to output	58	105	141	163	100	66	50	39
Other nonmetals								
Wage earners to output	934	545	282	179	100	89	74	58
Man-hours to output	1,058	608	n.a.	193	100	69	64	51
Capital to wage earners	10	18	39	57	100	97	65	90
Capital to man-hours	8	17	n.a.	53	100	127	75	100
Capital to output	89	99	110	102	100	87	48	52

n.a. = not available.

Note: Capital and output dollar values are in 1929 prices.

Source: Based on data in Appendix Tables B-8, B-11, and B-15. Capital-output ratios for 1939 from worksheets.

rate generally comparable with that prevailing during the early period.[7]

Mining: Factors Contributing to Interindustry Differences in the Rate of Change of the Capital-Output Ratios

In our search for factors responsible for interindustry differences in the rate of change of capital-output ratios during any given period, we related these changes with (1) the rate of growth of output of the industry and (2) the rate of decrease in workers or man-hours per unit of output.

From 1880 to 1919, increases in the capital-output ratios were

TABLE 35

Total Change in the Capital-Output Ratio, Output, and Wage Earners per Unit of Output, by Major Mining Industries, 1880–1919 and 1919–1953
(*per cent based on values in 1929 prices*)

	Metals	Coal		Petroleum and Natural Gas	Other Nonmetals
		Anthracite	Bituminous		
1880–1919:					
Capital-output ratio	−6	−16	+79	+184	+14
Output	+510	+210	+980	+1,520	+660
Wage earners per unit of output	−78	−32	−53	−28	−81
1919–1953:					
Capital-output ratio	−36	+21	−6	−76	−49
Output	+57	−65	0	+636	+259
Wage earners per unit of output	−58	−3	−51	−81	−68

Source: Table 34, and Appendix Table B-8.

[7] The coexistence, in recent decades, of the above relationships—declining ratio of capital to output and of supplies to output, only slight increases in capital per worker, and continuous and substantial increases in output per worker—is interesting from another aspect. It has been pointed out by several investigators that technological innovations have, so far, successfully struggled against the mounting difficulties of extraction resulting from the depletion of high-grade resources. The net effect of the struggle has been not diminishing returns, but a continuous increase in output extracted per man-hour [see in particular Harold Barger and Sam H. Schurr, *The Mining Industries, 1899–1939: A Study of Output, Employment and Productivity* (National Bureau of Economic Research, 1944)]. Our findings indicate that this struggle has been successful not only in terms of direct labor used in the process of extraction, but also in terms of effort incorporated in the other input factors of plant, equipment, and supplies. That is, improvements in technology have been so considerable that, in spite of increasing difficulties of extraction, output per labor unit has increased during the last two decades without necessitating an increase in the physical volume of capital per worker.

positively correlated with relatively higher rates of growth of production. The relative increase in the capital-output ratio or rate of growth of output and the decrease in labor per output unit seem to be uncorrelated. Thus, we find the relatively highest increase in the capital-output ratio between 1880 and 1919 to be in the petroleum and natural gas industry, followed, in the order of the size of the percentage change in the capital-output ratio, by the bituminous coal, other nonmetals, metal, and anthracite mining industries (Table 35). The same order holds when one compares the percentage growth in output in these industries between 1880 and 1919.[8] However, the decrease in wage earners per unit of output was sharpest during that period in other nonmetals mining, followed by metal, bituminous coal, oil, and anthracite mining.

After 1919, other relationships emerge. Industries having the highest relative rates of growth or the lowest relative declines in output, as the case may be, are those in which the worker-output ratio and the capital-output ratio declined the most. In other words, intensive use of capital and of labor is positively correlated with higher rates of growth in production. However, rates of growth during this period were moderate compared with those for earlier decades. Thus, the oil industry had the highest percentage increase in output, followed, in order of percentage increase, by other nonmetals, metal, bituminous coal, and anthracite mining (which actually declined). The same order is found in the percentage decline in wage earners per unit of output and in the percentage decline in the capital-output ratio.[9]

This suggests that the relatively high rates of growth prevailing in the earlier period had a different impact on the declining labor-output ratio and the efficient use of capital (capital-output ratio) than had the relatively lower rates of growth prevailing during the later period. Exceedingly high and exceedingly low rates of growth seem to have

[8] A similar, although somewhat less pronounced, association with the change in capital-output ratios for the period is found if growth is measured by the change in the number of wage earners employed or man-hours worked. Some might argue that a correlation between the percentage change in the capital-output ratio and that in output is bound to yield spurious results because of the algebraic factor common to the two variables. This objection is overcome if changes in employment are taken as the measure of an industry's growth. On the other hand, changes in employment are bound to be an inferior indicator of an industry's relative growth because of variations in the rate of change of output per labor unit, as well as for other considerations.

[9] Similar relationships are found when the comparisons are based on shorter time intervals than those used in Table 35. Because of the greater danger of errors in measurement, short time intervals are not well suited to these comparisons. Nonetheless, it is noteworthy that the most pronounced association between growth and an increase in the capital-output ratio occurred during 1890–1909, and the most pronounced association between growth and a decline in the ratio, during the period 1919–1929.

been associated with less efficient use of the input factors, while more moderate rates of growth have been associated with higher technical efficiency in the use of the input factors. This suggested relationship is reasonable only if the border line between excessively high or low rates of growth and optimal rates is flexible and varies with the given stage of economic and technological development.

Comparison with Manufacturing

We can get some help in forecasting the future growth of capital and output in the mining industry by comparing its past pattern with that in manufacturing. This comparison also permits us to present parameters of changes in some of the raw materials used for a given manufacturing volume. It may also help us determine whether any marked difference in the use of capital per unit of output exists between the two basically different technological processes of manufacturing and mining. Finally, since we assume that the same factors may have contributed to the increase and the subsequent decline in the capital-output ratio in both mining and manufacturing, a comparison of the shape of the curve traced by the two sets of ratios is of some importance.

Though the average value of mining output is only about 5 per cent of that in manufacturing, the capital used in mining averages about 10 per cent of the amount invested in manufacturing (Table 36). The latter percentage would be considerably higher if the value of the mineral resources were included (see note to Table 36). The ratio of mining to manufacturing output, based on values in current prices, varied only slightly during the entire period. Its average for the seven benchmark years is 5.3 per cent; the highest percentage was 6.1 in 1909, and the lowest was 4.3 per cent in 1953. When the ratios are based on values in constant prices, the range is somewhat greater—from 6.2 in 1909 to 3.8 in 1953. Both series show a rise to 1909 and a decline thereafter. Similarly, the ratio of mining to manufacturing capital did not change a great deal. After 1919, the relative importance of mining as a field of investment declined, as indicated by the ratios based on both reported and constant price values. Since, as shown in Chapter I, the factors working for a decline in material requirements are still active, the 1953 ratio of mining to manufacturing output in constant prices (3.8 per cent) could be used, *ceteris paribus*, to project an upper limit for future mining output, and the ratio of mining to manufacturing capital in 1953 (9.3 per cent) could be used as a guide in forecasting future capital investment in mining.

The petroleum industry is largely responsible for the presence of a higher capital-output ratio in mining than in manufacturing. This

CAPITAL AND OUTPUT TRENDS

TABLE 36
Comparison of Manufacturing and Mining: Output and Capital, Selected Years, 1880–1953
(*per cent*)

	1880	1890	1909	1919	1937	1948	1953
Mining output as a percentage of manufacturing output:							
Based on reported values	5.3	5.4	6.1	5.5	5.5	5.2	4.3
Based on values in 1929 prices	4.3	4.8	6.2	5.6	5.3	4.5	3.8
Mining capital as a percentage of manufacturing capital:							
Based on reported values	8.7	8.6	11.0	10.9	9.8	9.8	9.0
Based on values in 1929 prices	9.2	8.9	11.1	12.3	9.8	10.5	9.3

Note: The capital figures for manufacturing include land; those for mining exclude it. Since land is a negligible proportion of manufacturing capital, the figures may be considered comparable. For 1890, 1937, and 1948, when the data permit us to exclude land from both numerator and denominator, the percentages are 9.5, 10.3, and 10.0, respectively, in terms of reported values, and 9.9, 10.3, and 10.7, respectively, in terms of 1929 price values. For the same years, the inclusion of land in both numerator and denominator increases the series of percentages based on reported values to 20.2, 14.1, and 11.1, respectively.

Source: Manufacturing data from Appendix Tables A-8 and A-10 with adjustments for duplication (Appendix Table B-16); mining data from Appendix Tables B-7 to B-11. Figures for years before 1919 adjusted for comparability. Manufacturing data include shipbuilding in 1953 but not in earlier years.

industry not only uses more capital per unit of output than any other mining industry except precious metals, but also more than any of the major manufacturing industries. Other mining industries are also characterized by relatively high capital-output ratios. This, however, is due to the higher proportion of value added to total value in mining than in manufacturing. Indeed, if we substitute value added for the total value of output (Table 37), the resulting ratios vary considerably from those implicit in the percentages in Table 36.

In 1890, 1909, and 1948, the ratio of capital to value added in total mining did not differ significantly in level from the ratio in total manufacturing. The shape of the curve traced by the two sets of ratios is fairly similar, except that the amplitude of the curve representing the mining ratios is greater. Further examination, however, shows that this difference in amplitude was due entirely to the rapid expansion and subsequent decline in the ratio for the petroleum industry. When we exclude this industry from total mining, the ratio of capital to value added for all remaining mining industries appears to have varied less than that for total manufacturing. Furthermore, the ratio of capital (excluding land) to value added in all mining industries except

CHANGES IN CAPITAL-OUTPUT RATIOS

TABLE 37
Comparison of Manufacturing and Mining: Capital and Value Added,
Selected Years, 1880–1948
(based on values in 1929 prices)

Ratio of capital to value added in—	1880	1890	1909	1919	1937	1948
1. Manufacturing[a]	1.51	1.65	2.31	2.56	1.81	1.55
2. Mining[b]	1.24	1.66	2.20	2.89	1.59	1.56
3. Mining excluding petroleum and natural gas[c]	1.12	1.27	1.53	1.60	1.25	0.96
4. (3) as percentage of (1)	73.7%	77.0%	66.2%	62.5%	69.1%	61.9%

Note: The capital figures for manufacturing include land; those for mining exclude land. Since land is a negligible proportion of manufacturing capital, the figures may be considered comparable.

[a] From Table 11, above.

[b] Value added (in 1929 prices) was estimated by applying to the value of output (in 1929 prices) the ratio of value added to value of output (from census reports). The ratio for 1937 was obtained by interpolation between 1929 and 1939. For 1948, the 1939 ratio was used.

[c] Value added (in 1929 prices) was estimated as in note b. For 1937 and 1948, the 1939 ratio was used.

petroleum is lower than the ratio for total manufacturing; capital used per dollar of value added in mining varied from about three-fifths to about three-fourths of that in manufacturing.

Summary of Findings

1. Between 1880 and 1919, when the capital-output ratio for all manufacturing was rising, the dispersion of the minor-industry ratios about the all-manufacturing ratio, as measured by the coefficient of variation, declined by nearly two-fifths; and the dispersion continued to decline by nearly one-fifth between 1919 and 1948, when the capital-output ratio was falling. This trend toward less dispersion suggests a hypothesis: During the earlier period, the smaller the importance of capital in 1880, i.e., the lower the capital-output ratio, the greater the scope for additional mechanization of processes; during the later period, the greater the importance of capital in 1919, i.e., the higher the capital-output ratio, the greater the scope for improving the efficiency of capital.

2. During 1900–1929, the reduction in man-hours per unit of output (i.e., the increase in "labor productivity") was principally associated with the continuous increase in the amount of capital per man-hour worked. The more moderate reductions from 1929 to 1948 in man-hours per unit of output are primarily correlated with the increased

efficiency of capital, since the amount of capital (in 1929 prices) per man-hour worked decreased substantially. Over the next five years, 1948–1953, the reduction per unit of output was 12 per cent and between 1953 and 1957, 14 per cent. In contrast to the developments in the preceding decades, the ratio of total and fixed capital to labor increased—by about 8 per cent and 26 per cent in 1948–1953 and 1953–1957, respectively; the capital-output ratio first declined modestly and then increased modestly. That is, once again, increased labor productivity was associated with the use of more capital per worker.

3. Much the same set of relationships is found in mining as in manufacturing. Increases in the capital-output ratios of individual industries, 1880–1919, were positively correlated with relatively higher rates of growth. However, neither the relative increase in the capital-output ratio nor the rate of growth in output appear to be correlated with the decrease in labor per unit of output. After 1919, other relationships emerge. Industries having the highest relative rates of growth or the lowest relative declines in output, as the case may be, are those in which worker-output and capital-output ratios declined the most. In other words, intensive use of capital and of labor is positively correlated with higher rates of growth in production.

4. A comparison of output and capital in mining and manufacturing reveals that the average value of mining output is only about 5 per cent of that in manufacturing, but the capital used in mining (excluding land) averages about 10 per cent of the amount invested in manufacturing. Although these percentages did not change a great deal over the various benchmark years, the relative importance of mining as a field of investment declined after 1919. The relative constancy of the percentages could be used however, as a guide in forecasting future capital investment in mining, *ceteris paribus*.

PART II

Long-Term Trends in Capital Financing

BY

SERGEI DOBROVOLSKY
ASSISTED BY MARTIN BERNSTEIN

CHAPTER VI

Internal and External Financing

IN this part of the report, financial trends in manufacturing and in mining over the past half-century are reviewed. Attention is focused primarily on two aspects of the financial growth of these industries. In this chapter, long-run tendencies in internal and external financing are examined and compared. In the following chapter, the various debt and equity components of external financing are analyzed, and the trends in total debt and total equity (both from internal and external sources) are compared. At the outset, however, the basic concepts should be discussed and some technical terms defined.

Concepts and Definitions

It has become customary to refer to funds obtained through income retention as "internal financing." The amounts so designated will differ depending on the degree of netness or grossness desired. Here, "net income retention" (or net internal financing) will designate the undistributed net profit remaining in the business after dividend payments. "Gross income retention" (or gross internal financing) will denote the amount of undistributed net profit plus depreciation and depletion allowances.[1] "External financing," will refer to funds obtained through new capital stock issues (external equity financing) and through various types of loans, e.g., bond issues, mortgages, bank loans, trade credit, etc.[2]

The sum of internal and external funds from all sources represents the total new financing available for investment in business assets—both physical (land, buildings, equipment, and inventories) and financial (claims in the form of cash, government and corporate

[1] Funds obtained internally are sometimes called "corporate saving." Here again, one must distinguish between the net and gross amounts of corporate saving, depending on whether depreciation and depletion are excluded or included with the amount of net income retained.

[2] Current liabilities of corporations reporting net income include accrued income taxes. Since tax accruals represent a form of debt financing (the companies in question temporarily retain the money owed to the government), they are usually included in external financing (see, for example, *Economic Report of the President*, January 1956, Table D-55, p. 227). We shall, generally, adhere to this classification. However, since accrued taxes represent a part of the income stream, it is sometimes appropriate to include them in retained gross income. To avoid possible misunderstanding, specific indication will be given in the text when this, or any other, reclassification is made.

securities, and loans and advances to other firms and individuals). Although, in a closed economic system considered as a whole, financial claims and liabilities will necessarily cancel out, clearly, this is not true of an individual firm or industry. Therefore, to analyze changes in the invested capital of a firm (industry), changes in financial claims on other sectors of the economy must be studied along with changes in physical assets.

However, investment in different types of assets does not have the same effect on the balance of claims between the investing firm (industry) and the rest of the economy. Assume, for example, that a corporation obtains new funds, from various sources, totaling $100 million, and that $60 million is spent on physical-plant expansion, and the remaining $40 million is used to expand financial assets (accounts receivable, and loans to and investments in other firms). The liabilities of the company to its investors (including both the creditors and the stockholders) will then rise by $100 million, but the change will be partially offset by the $40 million increase in the claims of the company on other economic units. The net balance of claims between the firm and the rest of the economy will change by $60 million. However, if the expenditures on physical plant were $80 million and those on financial assets only $20 million, the change in total assets and total liabilities would still be $100 million; but the change in the net balance $80 million instead of $60 million.

Changes in the net balance of claims between a given sector and the rest of the economy have sometimes been called by economists "net inflow" or "net absorption" of capital funds by the sector in question.[3] Such a "net inflow" does not represent an accumulation of cash within the sector, because outpayments are involved in acquiring both physical and financial assets. But when physical assets are expanded, outpayments represent payments to factors used to produce new plant, equipment, inventories, etc.[4] In other words, to the recipients, such outpayments represent income, rather than capital funds. On the other hand, when financial assets are expanded, capital funds are transferred to other sectors as capital funds, not as payments for current productive services.

Net inflow of capital funds represents, then, the amount of new

---

[3] See, for example, George Terborgh, *The Bogey of Economic Maturity*, Machinery and Allied Products Institute, 1945, p. 141.

[4] Of course, if the physical-asset expansion does not involve new production but is merely a transfer of assets previously held by another sector, then the expenditures do not represent payments for current productive services. However, the expansion of physical assets owned by the entire manufacturing and mining sector over the period reviewed has been due mainly to new production, rather than to transfers from other sectors.

financing used for real capital formation within the sector. It is net of funds transferred to other sectors and used by them for real capital formation.

In addition to the net balance of all financial transactions for a given sector, one may wish to compute the net balance of claims and liabilities arising from a particular type of transaction. Thus, the amount of new security issues sold by the sector, less the amount of securities purchased by it, will represent the net balance of security transactions; the change in accounts payable, less the change in accounts receivable, the net balance of trade credits; and the change in bank loans, less the change in cash balances held in the banks, the net balance of bank financing.

Or, one may wish to analyze changes in the net balance of claims between the sector and the government by comparing the change in tax accruals with the change in government securities held by the sector. And changes in the net balance of claims between the firms concerned and their stockholders over a given period will be indicated by the amount of new stock issues plus the amount of retained profits, less the change, if any, in loans or advances by the firms to their stockholders.

The sum of changes in all the liabilities, representing various forms of external financing, adjusted for the sum of changes in the various claims represented by financial assets, can be called the net balance of external financing. This measure is useful because it indicates the total amount of funds obtained, on balance, from the money and capital markets. It has been developed and used by Terborgh in his analysis of financial trends in the United States.[5]

All major types of financial assets (cash, receivables, and government and corporate securities) represent logical counterparts of one or another type of external financing. Does this mean that our concept of net balance is applicable only to external financing? Actually, net internal financing, as defined above, already represents the net balance between the revenue and expenditure flows. But the expenditures involved do not usually result in any accumulation of financial assets that should be taken as an offset to the accumulation of earned surplus. In some statements of sources and uses of funds, the entire net profit is shown as a source of funds and dividends paid, as a use of funds. In such a statement, net internal financing is equal to the difference between a fund inflow (profit) and a fund outflow (dividends). However, this outflow represents an income payment, not a transfer of capital funds, and does not result in an expansion of any financial asset on the

[5] *Ibid.*, pp. 139–148.

balance sheet of the firm—the change in the earned surplus of the firm already represents the net balance between the two flows.

Admittedly, the type of analysis of capital fund flows outlined above has certain limitations. The available corporate financial statements do not, as a rule, show the exact items for which the funds obtained from a given source were spent. If a corporation raised $50 million in a given year through a new stock flotation and spent $30 million during the same year in expanding its holdings of the securities of other companies, we may conclude that the company, has, on balance, drawn $20 million from the security market. But the funds used to purchase securities do not necessarily represent part of the funds received through the stock flotation unless the latter was the only source of new financing during that year. If the firm retained $40 million from operations during the same year, the funds obtained from the stock sale may have been used to expand plant and equipment and the internal funds, to purchase securities.

Even more caution is required, of course, in drawing conclusions from aggregate data for groups of corporations (e.g., the entire manufacturing industry). If all companies combined show a negligible net balance of security financing in a given year, clearly, it does not mean that this type of financing was unimportant for each and every individual firm. Some may have relied heavily on the security market as a source of new funds while others may have been returning funds to the market through security purchases and retirements.

Internal funds of some corporations may be invested in new security issues of other companies, and the money may be used by the latter to expand their physical assets. The consolidated balance sheet for both groups of companies will show no external financing. Yet, the firms which expanded their physical assets clearly could not have done so if they had not received external financial help from the other companies. A study of such intercompany financial flows within an industry would be of considerable importance; unfortunately, our data are inadequate for this purpose.

Sources of Data

Our analysis of financial trends in manufacturing and in mining is confined to corporations, since almost no data are available for noncorporate establishments. However, in recent years, corporations have accounted for over 90 per cent of the total value of output. Even at the beginning of the century, when the relative share of corporations was somewhat smaller, it exceeded two-thirds of the total. Thus, in discussing the financing of corporations, we shall be dealing with a major portion of the two industries in the early years and with practically the entire industry in the latter part of the period reviewed.

Even for corporations, our data on sources and uses of funds are far from complete. Annual series on corporate retained profits, depreciation and depletion allowances, and security issues are available for the entire 1900–1953 period.[6] We also have annual series on plant and equipment expenditures since 1900. But statistical information on external financing obtained from sources other than security issues is rather limited. Some sample data have been assembled for large manufacturing corporations, from which statements of sources and uses of funds have been prepared. These sample materials cover the entire period, although the samples are of different size and the data prior to 1914 are not sufficiently detailed to permit a complete flow-of-funds analysis.

The Department of Commerce has prepared statements of sources and uses of funds for all manufacturing corporations, but only for post-World War II, 1946–1953. However, the balance sheet and income data published in the *Statistics of Income* permit one to make rough estimates of the various types of financing used by all manufacturing and mining corporations over a considerably longer period, 1926–1953.

A rough indication of the relative importance of internal and external financing over the past half-century may be obtained by comparing corporate retained profits with corporate asset expansion. This is done in the next section. Later, we examine the various components of corporate financing in more detail, using such data as are available for different subperiods.

Asset Growth and Profit Retentions

During the first half of this century, the manufacturing and mining industries taken together were one of the fastest growing sectors of our economy. The combined output (in current prices) of manufacturing and mining rose from $11.7 billion in 1900 to $224 billion in 1948. Around 1900, slightly more than one-fifth of national income originated in these industries; in the twenties, their share rose to roughly one-quarter of the total; in recent years, it has been nearly one-third.

The growth in output obviously required a rapid expansion of capital facilities. As Table 38 indicates, the book value of corporate assets in manufacturing and mining rose from $6.8 billion in 1900 to

---

[6] These series are based on the data compiled by Raymond Goldsmith and W. Braddock Hickman. See Appendix C, section A for a more detailed description of these and other statistical materials used.

TABLE 38

Growth of Corporate Assets and the Relative Importance of External and Net Internal Financing, All Manufacturing and Mining Corporations, Selected Years, 1900–1953

(dollars in millions)

	Assets		Retained Net Profit	New Security Issues	Annual Rate of Asset Growth	Retained Net Profit	Security Issues
	Total[a]	Change from Prior Year				As Percentage of Asset Change	
						(Col. 3) ÷ (Col. 2)	(Col. 4) ÷ (Col. 2)
	(1)	(2)	(3)	(4)	(5)	(6)	(7)
1900	$6,769						
1909	16,446	$+9,677	$+3,992	$+3,029	+9.7%	41.3%	31.3%
1914	21,078	+4,632	+2,382	+1,410	+5.1	51.4	30.4
1919	41,990	+20,912	+10,978	+2,927	+14.8	52.5	14.0
1929	63,292	+21,302	+5,565	+9,175	+4.2	26.1	43.1
1937	52,322	−10,970	−10,646	−401	−2.4	n.c.	n.c.
1948	109,888[b]	+57,566	+30,809	+7,087	+7.0	53.5	12.3
1948	110,403[c]						
1953	155,530	+45,127	+22,191	+10,188	+7.1	49.2	22.6

n.c. = not computed; both numerator and denominator are negative.
[a] Book value. Total assets excluding investments in securities. Fixed assets are net of depreciation reserves.
[b] Excludes shipbuilding.
[c] Includes shipbuilding.

Column   Source
1   Appendix Table B-16, adjusted to exclude noncorporate enterprises on the basis of census ratios.
2   Appendix Table C-2, column 1.
3   Appendix Table C-1, column 3.

$155.5 billion in 1953.[7] The rate of change varied widely from decade to decade. A declining tendency can be observed over 1900–1937 (except during the World War I years, 1914–1919), but a reversal is evident during 1937–1953. The expansion rate for 1948–1953 was 1.7 times as high as that for 1919–1929, although still below the rate for 1900–1909.

Since the asset values given in Table 38 do not include investments in securities and no adjustments were made for revaluations, the net asset changes shown in column 2 do not measure accurately the total funds (internal plus external) used for expansion. Yet, by comparing the changes with net profits retained over corresponding periods, one can obtain a rough indication of the relative importance of net internal financing. Substantial profit retentions were made in every period except 1929–1937. The ratio of retained profit to asset change showed a rising tendency over 1900–1919. In 1919–1929, however, the ratio was relatively low,[8] while in 1929–1937 income retention gave place to net dissaving. The ratio reached a new high in 1937–1948, but declined once more in 1948–1953. Although the postwar figure is much higher than that for the twenties, it does not appear high when compared with the earlier ratios.

In general, then, the data presented in Table 38 reveal no definite trend in the relative importance of retained profit over the entire period, although, owing to their obvious limitations, they do not prove conclusively that there was no long-term trend. If more observations over a longer period were available, a significant trend might appear, although it could hardly be more than a mild one. But imperfect as they are, the figures can show the historical processes in broad outline. They indicate the existence of long swings, lasting more than one

[7] The data in Table 38 represent the book value of total assets *excluding* investments in government and corporate securities. The figures on total assets *including* investments in securities are available in *Statistics of Income* only since 1926. They are presented below for several selected years. Net profit data shown below are from Appendix Table C-1, column 3. Dollar amounts are in millions; the ratio was not computed for 1937 because both numerator and denominator were negative.

	Assets			Retained Net Profit	
	Total	Change from Prior Year	Rate of Change per year (*per cent*)	Total since Prior Year	Ratio to Asset Change (*per cent*)
1926	$ 68,272				
1929	72,903	$+4,631	+2.2%	$2,012	43.4%
1937	64,869	−8,034	−1.4	−10,646	–
1948	130,750	+65,881	+6.6	30,809	46.7
1953	188,966	+58,216	+7.6	22,191	38.1

[8] The low figure obtained for 1919–1929 is mainly the result of low profit retentions in the early part of the decade. For 1926–1929, the ratio of retained profit to asset change was 40 per cent—moderately below the figure for 1948–1953.

decade, in both the asset expansion rate and the ratio of retained profit to asset expansion. A downswing (or an upswing) that continues for two or three decades may look like a secular trend, and one may be tempted to take it as a basis for long-run projections. However, it may be just one phase of a long wave.

Table 38 also includes figures on new security issues. In general, security sales were much less important as a source of new financing than was net profit retention, especially during 1914–1919 and 1937–1948. The ratio of security issues to asset change have varied inversely with the ratio of retained profits to asset change: the security ratio was relatively low in 1914–1919 and 1937–1948 when the profit ratio was relatively high, and the security ratio rose in 1919–1929, while the profit ratio declined. However, although the security ratio for 1948–1953 is much lower than it was for 1900–1909 and 1909–1914, the profit ratio shows no counterbalancing upward shift in the postwar period. Other sources of funds must have gained in relative importance, and corporate income tax reserves are clearly a case in point. Income tax reserves are conventionally considered to be a part of short-term external financing. However, since they represent a portion of sales revenue earmarked for a specific purpose, they may also be considered as a kind of short-term income retention. Thus, changes in the relative importance of the combined long-term and short-term income retentions (i.e., retained profits plus additions to income tax reserves) may be relevant. The ratios to net asset changes of the sum of retained net profits plus net additions to tax reserves are as follows:

Period	Ratio of Retained Net Profit plus Tax Accruals to Asset Change[a] (per cent)
1900–09	41.3
1909–14	51.4
1914–19	59.1
1919–29	22.0
1929–37	–
1937–48	64.8
1948–53	51.9

[a] Retained net profits are from Appendix Table C-2, column 1; tax accruals are based on data in *Statistics of Income*; assets are from Appendix Table C-1, column 3. Since income tax reserves are not given as a separate item in the corporate balance sheets published in *Statistics of Income*, they had to be estimated on the basis of tax liability for different years. Considering how large corporate tax liability has been in recent years, the change in the ratios resulting from the inclusion of this item may appear to be surprisingly small. However, while the total annual amount of tax liability has often been much larger than the annual amount of retained profit, the *increase* in tax reserves from one year to the following has generally been much smaller than the increase in earned surplus.

Federal income tax, at the modest rate of 1 per cent of net income, was first imposed on corporations in 1909. The first substantial rise in the tax liability—and, consequently, in the reserves made to meet it—occurred during World War I. In the interwar period, the tax liability declined, but it rose again during World War II. After a brief reversal in the immediate postwar period, the upward trend was resumed as a result of the outbreak of the Korean hostilities in 1951. Accordingly, adding net changes in the income tax reserves to the total amount retained considerably increases the ratio of retentions to asset changes in 1914–1919, 1937–1948, and 1948–1953. As a result, the total retention ratio shows something of an upward trend over the entire 1900–1953 period.

Accumulation of tax reserves has not been the only expanding source

TABLE 39

Growth of Corporate Assets and the Relative Importance of External and Net Internal Financing, Large Manufacturing Corporations, 1900–1954
(*per cent*)

Period	Rate of Change per Year in:		External Financing	Retained Net Profit
	Total Assets	Physical[a] Assets	As Percentage of Total New Financing	
1900–1910	+2.6	n.a.	43.1	56.9
		POSITIVE BUSINESS CYCLES[b]		
1914–1919	+12.8	+9.1	48.0	52.0
1919–1921	+1.4	+3.1	1.8	98.2
1921–1924	+4.9	+6.0	37.0	63.0
1924–1927	+4.3	+3.4	15.6	84.4
1927–1932	+1.1	+1.3	c	c
1932–1938	+0.6	+1.0	62.6	37.4
1938–1946	+5.4	+2.7	40.8	59.2
1946–1949	+10.8	+15.1	43.0	57.0
1949–1954[d]	+9.8	+10.3	49.4	50.6
		INVERTED BUSINESS CYCLES[b]		
1913–1918	+14.1	+9.2	49.7	50.3
1918–1920	+6.3	+7.1	28.3	71.7
1920–1923	−1.8	+0.3	c	c
1923–1926	+4.4	+3.6	23.9	76.1
1926–1929	+4.1	+3.5	6.0	94.0
1929–1937	−0.2	+0.6	33.8	66.2
1937–1944[e]	+8.5	+3.4	57.4	42.6
1944–1948	+4.5	+9.2	21.4	78.6
1948–1954[d]	+9.9	+10.2	46.9	53.1

n.a. = not available.
[a] Plant and equipment plus inventories.
[b] Based on National Bureau of Economic Research business cycle chronology.
[c] Ratios are not computed when numerator, denominator, or both, are negative.
[d] Underlying data cover 1949–1953.
[e] Underlying data cover 1938–1944.
Source: 1900–1938: National Bureau of Economic Research samples; 1938–1953: Federal Reserve Board sample of large manufacturing corporations.

LONG-TERM TRENDS IN CAPITAL FINANCING

of funds available to corporations. Another characteristic of the post-World War II period has been the substantial expansion of short-term notes and accounts payable to commercial banks and other creditors. Also, a new type of medium- and long-term credit (the "term" loan) has been developed. (These new developments are discussed in some detail in Chapter VII.)

The data for all manufacturing and mining corporations combined, presented in Table 38, are supplemented in Table 39 by the available sample data for large manufacturing companies. The sample materials include balance sheets and statements of sources and uses of funds, from which the rate of expansion of both total assets (including investment in securities) and physical assets (plant and equipment plus inventories) could be computed and the relative importance of total external, as well as internal financing measured. Annual data are available from 1914 on, although the sample does not remain identical over the entire period. Since we are interested in the long-run tendencies, rather than in short-run cyclical fluctuations, the figures in Table 39 are presented in the form of averages for both the positive (trough-to-trough) and inverted (peak-to-peak) business cycles.

Broadly speaking, the ratios for large corporations reveal a picture similar to that portrayed by the figures for all corporations. Tables 38 and 39 indicate that both external and internal funds were important in financing asset expansion during most of the period reviewed. The ratio of retained net profit to total new financing (Table 39) fluctuates widely from one business cycle to another, but here again, no clear and persistent trend may be discerned.

However, some important differences between the two sets of data do appear. The figures for large corporations show the clear predominance of internal funds during the twenties. In the 1923–1926 and the 1926–1929 peak-to-peak cycles, and also in the 1924–1927 trough-to-trough cycle, the ratio of retained net profit to total new financing rose sharply, while external financing became relatively insignificant. In contrast, the data on all corporations indicate a relatively heavy dependence on external financing during the twenties. In the postwar period, however, large corporations again used external funds on a substantial scale, and their ratios were not essentially different from those for all corporations.[9]

The ratios for large companies indicate that the relative importance of external funds varied with the rate of asset expansion. When assets

---

[9] Since the data for large corporations were not derived by the same method and are not, therefore, strictly comparable with the data for all corporations, one should be cautious in attaching significance to relatively minor differences between the ratios in Tables 38 and 39.

expanded at moderate rates, internal funds were generally sufficient to cover most capital requirements; external financing was little needed, even though retained profits were not especially high. When assets expanded more rapidly, profits were generally higher; but the rise in profits was less pronounced than the rise in capital requirements and, therefore, the need for external financing increased.

As Table 39 indicates, the rates of total asset growth and physical asset growth of large manufacturing corporations were much higher in the postwar cycles (1946–1949 and 1949–1954) than they had been during any of the interwar cycles. The ratio of external financing to total new financing was also higher after the war. The World War I cycle (1914–1919) was characterized by a more pronounced asset expansion than the World War II cycle (1938–1946). Accordingly, the ratio of external to total financing was higher during the first war.

Obviously, the relative importance of external financing was determined by a number of factors. The ratio of external to total financing was considerably lower in 1926–1929 than in the other cycles with comparable asset expansion rates because of the relatively high profitability and high retention ratios of the late twenties compared with the other parts of the interwar period. Also, the ratio of external to total financing was relatively high in 1932–1938, even though the asset expansion rate was very low during that cycle. However, the dollar value of external financing was quite small in 1932–1938, and its ratio to the total was high only because the amount of net internal financing was exceedingly small. Thus, the significance of the ratio is greatly reduced. In addition, corporate finance in 1936 and 1937 was affected by the undistributed profits tax. which markedly reduced the proportion of net profit retained.

The data on all corporations (Table 38) do not indicate any clear relation between the ratio of external funds to total financing and the rate of asset growth, partly, perhaps, because of imperfect data. The ratios for all companies could be computed only for relatively long periods. Thus, the effect of the expansion rate may have been obscured by the interference of other factors. However, it is probably also true that, large firms, which have generally had an easier access to the capital market, could increase the use of external funds more rapidly, when fast asset expansion was warranted by business conditions, than could smaller firms.[10]

[10] In Dobrovolsky's earlier study, *Corporate Income Retention, 1915–1943*, National Bureau of Economic Research, 1951, the following regression equations were obtained for 1921–1941:
  Large companies: $R = +1.71 + .50G - .12t$
  Small companies: $R = -1.01 + .65G + .02t$
where R is the annual rate of retained profit, G is the annual rate of total asset

Gross Internal Financing and Security Issues

As already mentioned, annual series on internal financing and security issues are available beginning 1900 (see Appendix Tables C-1 and C-2). But, since both series are characterized by strong cyclical fluctuations, the data are presented as cycle averages in Table 40. The average annual values are given for both trough-to-trough (positive) and peak-to-peak (inverted) business cycles.

The average amount of gross internal financing increased fifteen times in the half-century between the 1900–1904 and the 1949–1954 cycles.[11] The average amount of new plant and equipment expenditures showed a thirteenfold rise over the same period. In contrast, the average amount of new security issues showed only a fivefold rise.[12] However, although the three series differ widely from one another in the extent of growth, they show similar major swings. As Chart 10 and Table 40 indicate, cycle averages rose only moderately in 1900–1911. Pronounced upswings occurred during and after World War I. The averages remained high in the twenties, but substantial downswings took place in the thirties. Finally, all three series display exceedingly high upswings in the forties—both during and after World War II.

A closer look at the data reveals that major movements in the securities series tended to lag behind those in the gross internal financing series. Thus, while the gross internal financing cycle average rose sharply in the 1914–1919 trough-to-trough (or 1913–1918 peak-to-peak) cycle, the securities average advanced only moderately in the war cycle but much more sharply in the following cycle (1919–1921 or 1918–1920). Again, while the gross internal financing average showed a pronounced rise in the 1938–1946 (1937–1944) cycle and a further pronounced increase in the 1946–1949 (1944–1948) cycle, the securities series displayed a relatively small advance in the former, but a much larger one in the latter cycle.

Specific conditions created by the two major wars account for these lags. Each time, the wartime expansion in output was accompanied by a rise both in corporate profits (even after taxes) and in depreciation and depletion allowances. On the other hand, the market for corporate

---

expansion and t represents time (both R and G are expressed as percentages of total assets at the beginning of the year).

The equation for large companies indicates that while R varied directly with G, the ratio of R to G decreased as G increased. The data for small companies, on the other hand, show a direct relationship not only between R and G, but also between R/G and G.

[11] Averages for the 1949–1954 positive cycle cover 1949–1953.

[12] These rates of change are obtained by comparing the first and the last trough-to-trough cycles. Almost identical rates are obtained when the first and the last peak-to-peak cycles (1899–1903 and 1948–1953) are compared with each other.

INTERNAL AND EXTERNAL FINANCING

TABLE 40
All Manufacturing and Mining Corporations: Gross Internal Financing, New Security Issues, and Plant and Equipment Expenditures, 1900–1953

Period	Gross Internal Financing	New Security Issues	Plant and Equipment Expenditures	Gross Internal Financing	New Security Issues	Gross Internal Financing and New Security Issues
	Average Annual Amount[a] in Millions			As Percentage of Plant and Equipment Expenditures		
	(1)	(2)	(3)	(4)	(5)	(6)
POSITIVE BUSINESS CYCLES[b]						
1900–1904	$ 719	$ 412	$ 803	89.5%	51.3%	140.8%
1904–1908	781	256	1,002	77.9	25.5	103.5
1908–1911	962	317	1,066	90.2	29.7	120.0
1911–1914	1,101	271	1,187	92.8	22.8	115.6
1914–1919	3,138	488	2,041	153.7	23.9	177.7
1919–1921	2,230	1,242	2,706	82.4	45.9	128.3
1921–1924	2,281	668	2,097	108.8	31.9	140.6
1924–1927	3,024	873	2,557	118.3	34.1	152.4
1927–1932	1,318	587	2,285	57.7	25.7	83.4
1932–1938	1,206	−75	1,763	68.4	n.c.	64.2
1938–1946	4,765	206	3,171	150.3	6.5	156.8
1946–1949	9,770	1,935	8,382	116.6	23.1	139.6
1949–1954[c]	11,078	2,128	10,308	107.5	20.6	128.1
INVERTED BUSINESS CYCLES[b]						
1899–1903[d]	705	416	791	89.1	52.6	141.7
1903–1907	756	256	951	79.5	26.9	106.4
1907–1910	893	288	774	115.4	37.2	152.6
1910–1913	1,074	328	875	122.7	37.5	160.2
1913–1918	2,659	365	1,722	154.4	21.1	175.6
1918–1920	3,435	1,060	2,861	120.1	37.0	157.1
1920–1923	1,695	848	2,169	78.1	39.1	117.2
1923–1926	3,012	753	2,400	125.5	31.4	156.9
1926–1929	2,995	1,008	2,813	106.5	35.8	142.3
1929–1937	754	10	1,736	43.4	0.6	44.0
1937–1944	4,051	107	2,695	150.3	4.0	154.3
1944–1948	7,637	1,346	6,434	118.7	20.9	139.7
1948–1953	10,869	2,101	9,703	112.0	21.7	133.7
SELECTED PERIODS						
1900–1914	865	307	993	87.1	30.9	118.0
1919–1929	2,755	939	2,555	107.8	36.8	144.6
1936–1940	2,243	156	2,433	92.2	6.4	98.6
1946–1953	10,300	2,054	9,370	109.9	21.9	131.8

n.c. = not computed because numerator is negative.

[a] In computing averages for business cycle periods, values for terminal years are weighted by one-half for complete cycles. For incomplete cycles, only values at peak or trough terminal years are weighted by one-half.
[b] Based on National Bureau of Economic Research business cycle chronology.
[c] Averages cover 1949–1953.
[d] Averages cover 1900–1903.

Source: Column 1, Appendix Table C-3; Column 2, Appendix Table C-1; Column 3, Appendix Table C-3.

securities remained relatively inactive during the war years but became very buoyant after the end of hostilities.

CHART 10

Internal Financing, New Security Issues, and Plant and Equipment Expenditures, All Manufacturing and Mining Corporations, 1900–1953

(*averages during positive business cycles*)

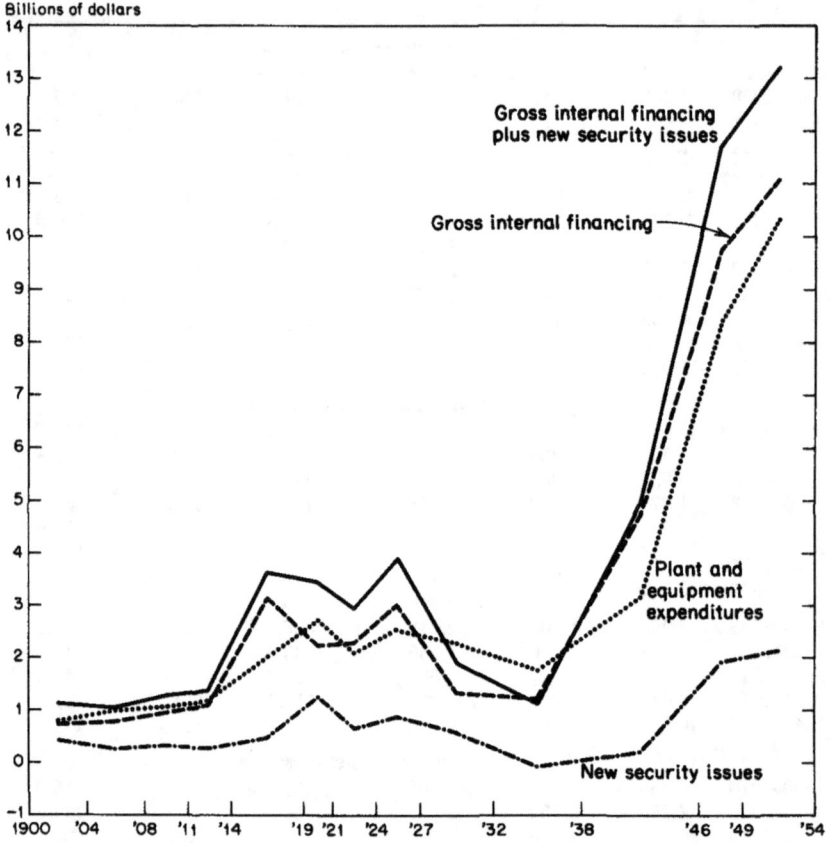

Source: Table 40.

The securities series also lags the major downswings of the thirties. The gross internal financing average shows a pronounced drop in the 1927–1932 trough-to-trough cycle, followed by a further moderate decline in the 1932–1938 cycle. The securities average, on the other hand, shows a relatively small contraction in 1927–1932 but a much

INTERNAL AND EXTERNAL FINANCING

sharper one in 1932–1938. The data on the peak-to-peak cycles reveal this lag even more clearly. Gross internal financing has a mild contraction in 1926–1929 followed by a more pronounced drop in 1929–1937. But, in the securities series, the upswing of the twenties includes 1926–1929, and the sharp reversal does not occur until 1929–1937. Several factors accounted for the lag in the thirties. Corporate net profits had already declined substantially in the early years of the depression. Corporate retained profits declined even more sharply because many companies maintained dividends in excess of current earnings. On the other hand, the most pronounced decline in net security issues (new issues less retirements) occurred in the later stages of the depression, when large accumulations of inactive cash allowed substantial bond retirements (again, see Appendix Tables C-1 and C-2).

Generally similar trends and major swings are evident in the ratios of new security issues to gross internal financing for all manufacturing and for the samples of large manufacturing concerns (Chart 11). However, there are some significant differences. Thus, in

CHART 11

Ratios of New Security Issues to Gross Internal Financing, All Manufacturing and Mining Corporations and Sample, 1900–1953

(*averages during positive business cycles*)

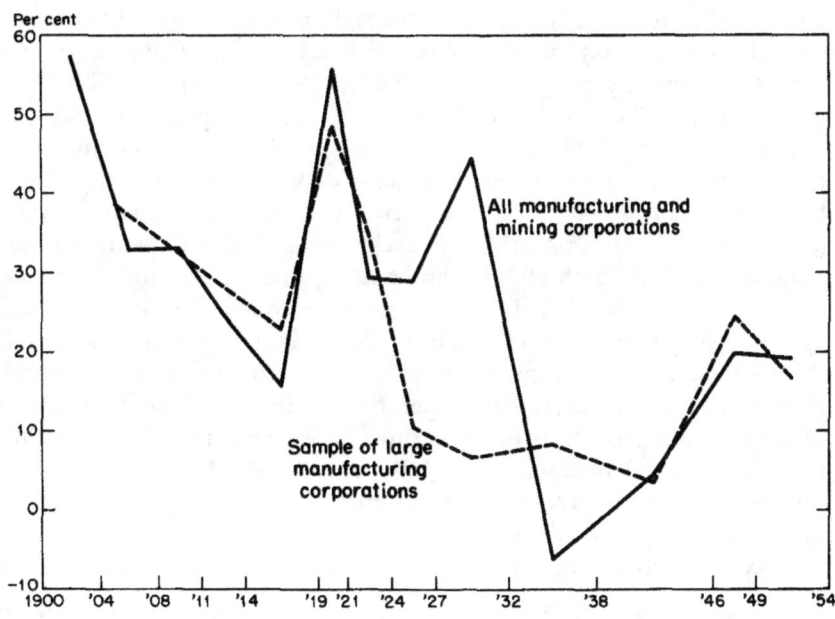

Source: Tables 40 and 44.

the twenties, when the security market was, in general, very active, security issues (net of retirement) of large manufacturing corporations were surprisingly low in relation to their internal financing (12 and 6 per cent for 1923–1926 and 1926–1929, respectively; the corresponding figures for all manufacturing and mining were 25 and 33 per cent; see Table 40). Apparently, the high profitability of large corporations during that period allowed them to meet most of their capital outlay requirements with funds obtained internally. Indeed, some large companies, notably the U.S. Steel Corporation, were able, in the late twenties, to retire large amounts of previously issued securities.[13]

The ratio of security issues to gross internal financing for all manufacturing and mining corporations dropped sharply from 1926–1929 to 1929–1937 (from 1927–1932 to 1932–1938, trough-to-trough) but the corresponding ratio for large corporations showed little change. In the World War II cycle (1938–1946 or 1937–1944) security issues were relatively unimportant both for the large corporations and for all corporations combined. In the first postwar cycle (1946–1949), the ratio of security issues to gross internal financing rose to 24 per cent for large companies and to 20 per cent for all companies combined.

Gross Internal Financing and Expenditures on Plant and Equipment

A comparison of gross internal financing with gross expenditures on plant and equipment is made in Charts 12 and 13. Internal funds are not, of course, always used exclusively for financing fixed assets, nor are fixed assets always financed internally. Yet, throughout 1900–1953, gross retained funds differed from plant and equipment outlays by only a small margin (total gross retentions were $180 billion, and total expenditures amounted to $163 billion—or 91 per cent of retentions). However, the differences are considerably larger for individual cycles (for example, in both world war cycles, gross internal financing was roughly 1.5 times as high as plant and equipment expenditures; see Chart 12 and Table 39). In all the nonwar cycles, the ratio was considerably lower. In the cycles before World War I, internal funds fell short of plant and equipment expenditures. In the interwar period, internal financing exceeded expenditures in cycles that included relatively mild recessions but fell short of expenditures in cycles that included major depressions (especially in the early thirties). Finally, in the cycles following World War II, internal funds were greater than expenditures by a considerable margin.

In contrast to the behavior of gross internal financing, the ratio of

---

[13] Cf. Albert R. Koch, *The Financing of Large Corporations, 1920–1939*, National Bureau of Economic Research, 1943, pp. 94–95. See also Table 42, below.

security issues to capital expenditures, measured either trough-to-trough or peak-to-peak, has declined. Security issues amounted to slightly more than 50 per cent of plant and equipment expenditures in the 1900–1904 (1899–1903) cycle. In 1926–1929, the ratio was only 35 per cent; in the two most recent cycles, only slightly over 20 per cent.

Charts 12 and 13 show that, in the pre-World War II cycles, the ratio

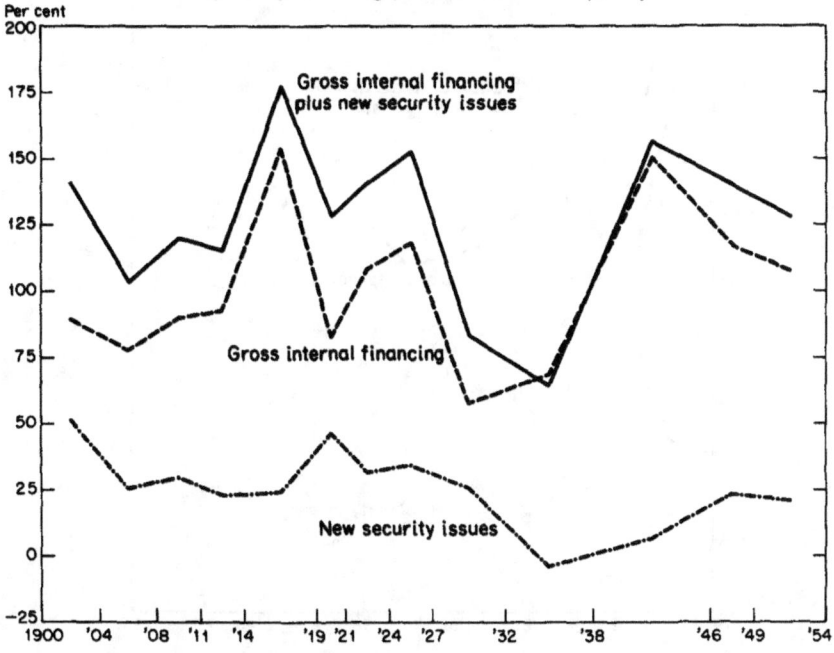

CHART 12

Gross Internal Financing and New Security Issues as Percentages of Plant and Equipment Expenditures, All Manufacturing and Mining Corporations, 1900–1953

(averages during positive business cycles)

Source: Table 40.

of gross internal financing to expenditures was much higher for large corporations than for all corporations. Gross internal financing of large corporations exceeded their plant and equipment expenditures by a considerable margin even during the thirties, when for all corporations, gross internal financing dropped to practically one-half of such expenditures. In the World War II cycle, the ratio for large corporations was approximately the same as that for all corporations; but in the postwar period, the ratio was lower for large ones.

LONG-TERM TRENDS IN CAPITAL FINANCING

New security issues of large corporations were higher in relation to their plant and equipment expenditures in the 1914–1919 and 1919–1921 cycles than were security issues of all manufacturing and mining,

CHART 13

Gross Internal Financing and New Security Issues as Percentages of Plant and Equipment Expenditures, Large Manufacturing Corporations, 1914–1953

(*averages during positive business cycles*)

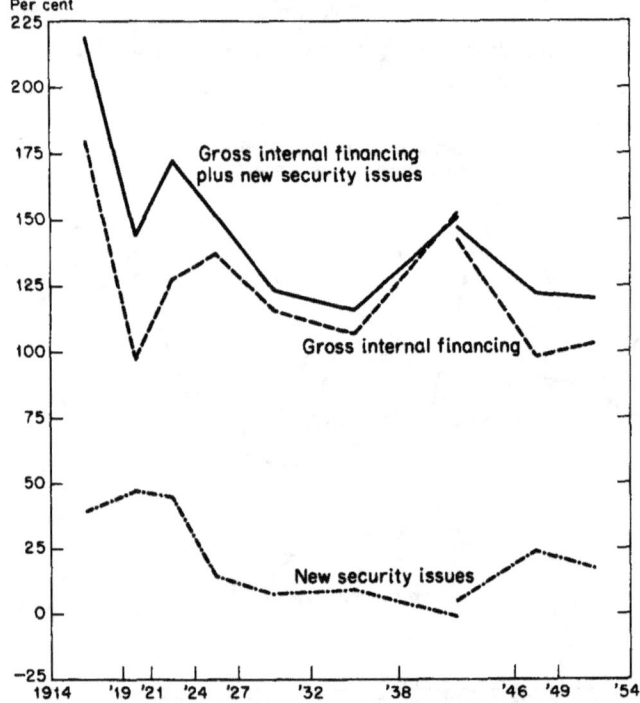

Source: Table 44 for gross internal and security financing; for plant and equipment expenditures, see the source note to Table 43.

but the reverse was true in most of the later cycles. As already mentioned above, the relatively low level of security issues of large corporations in the late twenties is especially noteworthy. In the postwar periods, the ratio of security issues to plant and equipment expenditures was slightly lower for large firms than for the entire industry.

Since plant and equipment expenditures represent the main use of long-term funds, one would expect the demand for long-term external financing to depend largely on how high such expenditures are in relation to the available internal financing. When the ratio of internal funds to plant and equipment outlays is high, the demand for long-term external funds should be low; when the ratio is low, the demand for long-term external funds should be stronger.

Our data confirm this expectation: the relation between the ratio of gross internal financing to plant and equipment expenditures and that of new security issues to total long-term financing (internal funds plus security issues) is clearly inverse (see Chart 14, panel A). The ratio of internal financing to expenditures was especially high in the two war cycles; the ratio of security issues to total financing was then lower than in any other cycle except that of 1932–1938. On the other hand, the ratio of security issues to the total was highest in the 1900–1904 and 1919–1921 cycles, both characterized by relatively low plant and equipment expenditures.

The cycle of the Great Depression (1932–1938) is the only one not conforming to the general pattern of relationship. Then, as Chart 14 shows, there was an *outflow* of external funds (retirements exceeding new issues), although gross internal financing fell far short of plant and equipment expenditures. This is accounted for by the substantial contraction and partial conversion into cash of such current assets as marketable securities, receivables, and inventories, which took place in that period. The cash enabled many companies with sharply diminished retained earnings to maintain a minimum of required plant and equipment expenditures without recourse to the securities market.

The regression line, fitted by the least squares method to all the cycles except 1932–1938, indicates that, on the average, security issues amounted to 30 per cent of the total long-term financing when internal funds were equal to three-fourths of plant and equipment expenditures; 23 per cent of the total, when internal funds were equal to the full amount of the expenditures; and only 10 per cent of the total, when internal funds were one and one-half times as large as the expenditures. Thus, new security issues represented an appreciable share of total new financing even when gross internal funds exceeded plant and equipment expenditures. Many individual companies had low retained income and had to rely largely on external financing even during cycles in which the ratio of retained income to expenditures was high for the industry as a whole. Furthermore, some companies with a high ratio of retained earnings to plant expenditures still needed substantial external financing to strengthen their working capital position or to make new investment in subsidiaries. For example, in the twenties, large corporations considerably expanded their financial interests (by

CHART 14

All Manufacturing and Mining Corporations: Relation between New Security Issues as a Percentage of Total Long-Term Financing and Gross Internal Financing as a Percentage of Plant and Equipment Expenditures, 1900–1953

(based on averages during positive business cycles)

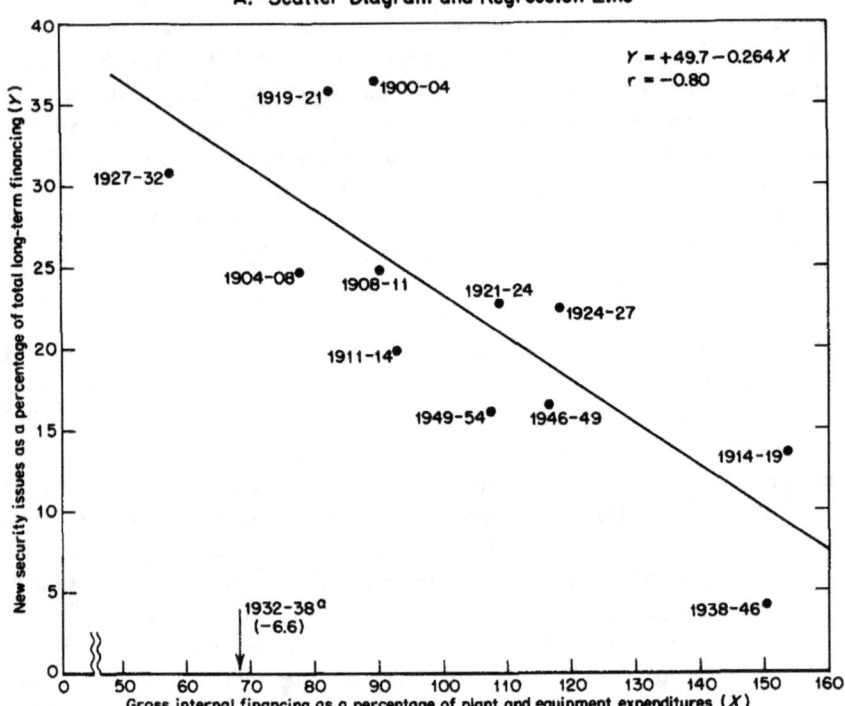

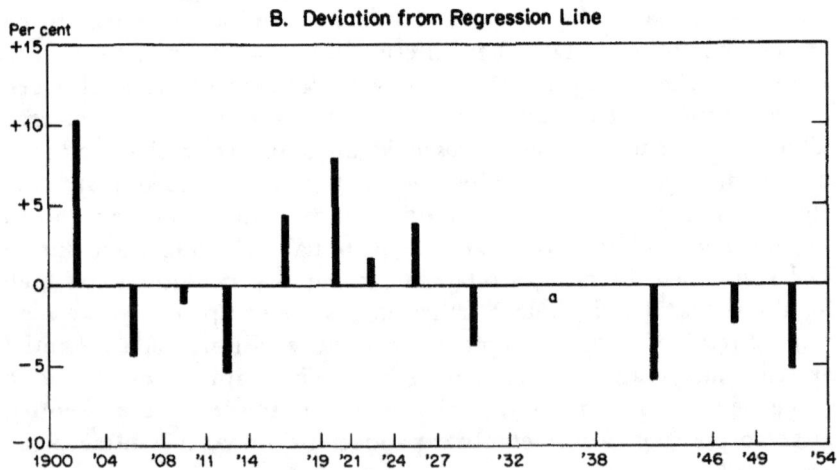

investment and loan) in subsidiary companies; the relatively high ratios of security issues to internal financing reflect this activity.

Deviations from the regression line of the security issues-total long-term financing ratio show no persistent trend over 1900–1953 (see Chart 14, panel B). The deviations were negative from the 1927–1932 cycle on. However, there is a cluster of positive deviations during 1914–1924. The ratio of gross internal financing to plant and equipment expenditures was approximately the same for both war cycles, but the ratio of security issues to total long-term financing was much lower in the second. In the 1946–1949 and 1949–1953 cycles, the ratio of internal financing to expenditures was approximately the same as in the 1921–1924 and 1924–1927 cycles. But again, the ratio of security issues to the total was substantially lower in the recent cycles.

Since gross internal financing was high in relation to plant and equipment expenditures in the postwar cycles, security issues would be expected to represent a relatively small fraction of total financing. The actual ratio of security issues to the total was, however, even lower than the "normal" computed from the regression line fitted to the whole period, 1900–1953.

We conclude this section with a brief examination of changes in total long-term financing (the sum of gross internal financing and new security issues) over the whole period.[14]

As Charts 12 and 13 indicate, long-term financing exceeded plant and equipment expenditures by a substantial margin in almost all the cycles. The data for all manufacturing and mining corporations indicate that only in the thirties (the 1927–1932 and 1932–1938 cycles) did the inflow of long-term funds decline to a level far below that of the expenditures. For large manufacturing corporations, on the other hand, total long-term financing exceeded plant and equipment expenditures throughout 1914–1953.

For all manufacturing and mining corporations, no trend in the ratio of long-term financing to plant and equipment expenditures can be discerned for the entire period, 1900–1953, either in trough-to-trough or peak-to-peak cycle data. The ratio was highest in the World War I cycle (1914–1919 or 1913–1918) (long-term financing was 1.8 times as high as expenditures—see Table 40). During the World War II cycles (1938–1946 or 1937–1944), the ratio was approximately 1.5—about the same as the highest ratio attained during the interwar period.

[14] In recent years, the sum of internal financing and new security issues falls short of total noncurrent financing of corporations, because it does not include term loans (see Chapter VII for a discussion of term loans). Commercial banks began making long-term loans to industry on a significant scale in the middle thirties. However, the data on such loans are rather scant. The available estimates indicate that the amount has been small in relation to security issues in the postwar period.

In the two postwar cycles, the ratio declined moderately. However, the figure obtained for 1946–1953 (132 per cent) exceeded that found for 1900–1914 (118 per cent) although far short of that for 1919–1929 (145 per cent).

In general, total long-term financing showed no clear trend in relation to plant and equipment expenditures. But the relative importance of the internal and the external components shifted appreciably. Internal funds became relatively more important, while funds raised through security issues declined in relation to both total financing and plant expenditures.[15]

Although the ratio of new security issues to gross internal financing in the postwar period was lower than those for 1900–1914 and 1919–1929, it was much higher than the ratio for 1936–1940. Does the rise observed after World War II represent the beginning of a new long swing? Since the general institutional framework of our economy seems to foreshadow a continued heavy reliance by corporations on internal financing, a prolonged upward movement in the ratio of external to internal funds could hardly be expected. However, if the national economy continues to expand at a relatively high rate, the demand for new external funds will probably remain substantial. Only if further economic growth were retarded could a drop in the relative importance of new external financing be expected.

Components of Gross Internal Financing

Gross internal financing, as considered above, represents the sum of: (1) depreciation and depletion allowances and (2) undistributed net profit. We now turn to a separate examination of each.

DEPRECIATION AND DEPLETION. In a simple conceptual framework, depreciation and depletion allowances, if earned, represent funds retained from the gross revenue stream to make up for the loss incurred through capital consumption. But, of course, the allowances computed by conventional accounting methods may differ significantly from the actual loss of value through use. This occurs especially during periods of wide price fluctuations, when replacement costs deviate substantially from the original expenditures on durable capital goods.

In studies of real capital formation, depreciation data must be adjusted so as to represent, as accurately as possible, real capital consumption. On the other hand, these adjustments are unnecessary in an examination of the financial aspects of investment; the actual

[15] The figures on security issues considered in this section represent the gross inflow of funds through security transactions. Net inflow of external funds (adjusted for changes in financial assets) is discussed in the last section of this chapter.

TABLE 41
All Manufacturing and Mining Corporations: Depreciation and Depletion Allowances and Retained Net Profit, 1900–1953

	Depreciation and Depletion		Retained Net Profit		Depreciation as Percentage of Depreciation Plus Retained Net Profit	
	Un-adjusted	Adjusted	Un-adjusted	Adjusted	(Col.1) ÷ [(Col. 1) + (Col. 3)] Unadjusted	(Col. 2) ÷ [(Col. 2) + (Col. 4)] Adjusted
Period	(1)	(2)	(3)	(4)	(5)	(6)
	(average annual amount[a] in millions)					

POSITIVE BUSINESS CYCLES[b]

Period	(1)	(2)	(3)	(4)	(5)	(6)
1900–1904	$ 260	$ 300	$ 459	$ 439	36.2%	40.6%
1904–1908	364	436	417	357	46.7	55.0
1908–1911	488	569	474	415	50.7	57.8
1911–1914	616	633	485	506	55.9	55.6
1914–1919	1,170	1,366	1,968	1,038	37.3	56.8
1919–1921	1,612	2,270	618	1,475	72.3	60.6
1921–1924	1,907	2,168	374	544	83.6	79.9
1924–1927	2,161	2,308	863	1,091	71.5	67.9
1927–1932	2,306	2,310	−988	−14	175.0	100.6
1932–1938	1,889	1,729	−683	−824	156.6	191.0
1938–1946	2,763	2,769	2,002	1,447	58.0	65.7
1946–1949	4,083	4,526	5,687	3,347	41.8	57.5
1949–1954[c]	6,581	7,206	4,497	3,220	59.4	69.1

INVERTED BUSINESS CYCLES[b]

Period	(1)	(2)	(3)	(4)	(5)	(6)
1899–1903[d]	244	284	461	434	34.6	39.6
1903–1907	335	396	421	379	44.3	51.1
1907–1910	449	531	444	340	50.3	61.0
1910–1913	574	630	500	492	53.4	56.1
1913–1918	988	1,067	1,671	1,019	37.2	51.2
1918–1920	1,568	2,181	1,867	1,226	45.6	64.0
1920–1923	1,782	2,189	−87	691	105.1	76.0
1923–1926	2,079	2,255	933	969	69.0	69.9
1926–1929	2,333	2,430	662	851	77.9	74.1
1929–1937	2,018	1,890	−1,264	−824	267.6	177.3
1937–1944	2,437	2,412	1,614	1,301	60.2	65.0
1944–1948	3,629	3,876	4,008	1,894	47.5	67.2
1948–1953	6,052	6,627	4,817	3,739	55.7	63.9

SELECTED PERIODS

Period	(1)	(2)	(3)	(4)	(5)	(6)
1900–1914	417	466	448	427	48.2	52.2
1919–1929	2,011	2,290	744	906	73.0	71.7
1936–1940	2,002	1,892	241	350	89.3	84.4
1946–1953	5,411	5,941	4,889	3,091	52.5	65.8

[a] In computing averages for business cycle periods, values for terminal years are weighted by one-half for complete cycles. For incomplete cycles, only values at peak or trough terminal years are weighted by one-half.
[b] Based on National Bureau of Economic Research business cycle chronology.

(continued)

allowances, irrespective of whether they adequately cover replacement requirements, are the object of study. Of course, one may also wish to compare the actual allowances with the theoretically adequate ones.

The data for both reported and adjusted depreciation, 1900–1953, are presented in Table 41 and Chart 15. Reported depreciation[16] was lower than the adjusted amount in all the cycles except that of 1932–1938 (or 1929–1937, peak-to-peak), that is, the allowances were, generally, too low to cover actual capital consumption. However, the differences are not pronounced. Both exhibit an almost uninterrupted growth throughout 1900–1953. In contrast, retained net profit fluctuated markedly.

The unadjusted depreciation allowances were smaller than unadjusted retained net profit in 1900–1904 and 1904–1908 (prior to 1909, when the federal income tax on corporations was introduced, depreciation accounting was very imperfect), in the World War I cycle, and, once again, in 1946–1949. In all the other cycles, depreciation exceeded net profit retention. Throughout 1900–1953, the amount of depreciation was 1.7 times as great as the amount of net profit retained. This large difference is mainly due to the large amount of net corporate dissaving in 1921 and during the thirties. However, even when the years of net dissaving are omitted, depreciation for all the remaining years exceeds retained net profit by 19 per cent.

Adjusted depreciation is greater than net profit retention in all the cycles except those of 1900–1904 (trough-to-trough) and 1899–1903

---

c Average covers 1949–1953.
d Averages cover 1900–1903.

Column	Source
1 and 3	Appendix Table C-2.
2 and 4	Depreciation and depletion adjustments in column (2) include conversion from the original to a replacement cost basis and, in 1940–1947, elimination of excess depreciation resulting from accelerated write-offs of war facilities.

Retained net profit adjustments in column (4) include the depreciation and depletion adjustments plus adjustments for inventory gains and losses, excess development cost in mining, excess capital expenditures charged to current expenses, and capital gains and losses.

The adjustments are based on data in Raymond W. Goldsmith, *A Study of Savings in the United States*, Princeton University Press, 1955, Vol. I; *Statistics of Income*, Bureau of Internal Revenue (now Internal Revenue Service), Part 2; and *National Income, 1954 Edition, A Supplement to the Survey of Current Business*, Department of Commerce.

[16] "Depreciation" will designate the total of depreciation and depletion. Depletion allowances are a major component of internal financing in mining but are of lesser importance in manufacturing. For both industries combined, depletion has, in recent years, amounted to approximately 29 per cent of the total amount of depreciation and depletion accruals and approximately 15 per cent of gross internal financing.

CHART 15

All Manufacturing and Mining Corporations: Depreciation and Depletion Allowances, and Retained Net Profit, 1900–1953

(averages during positive business cycles)

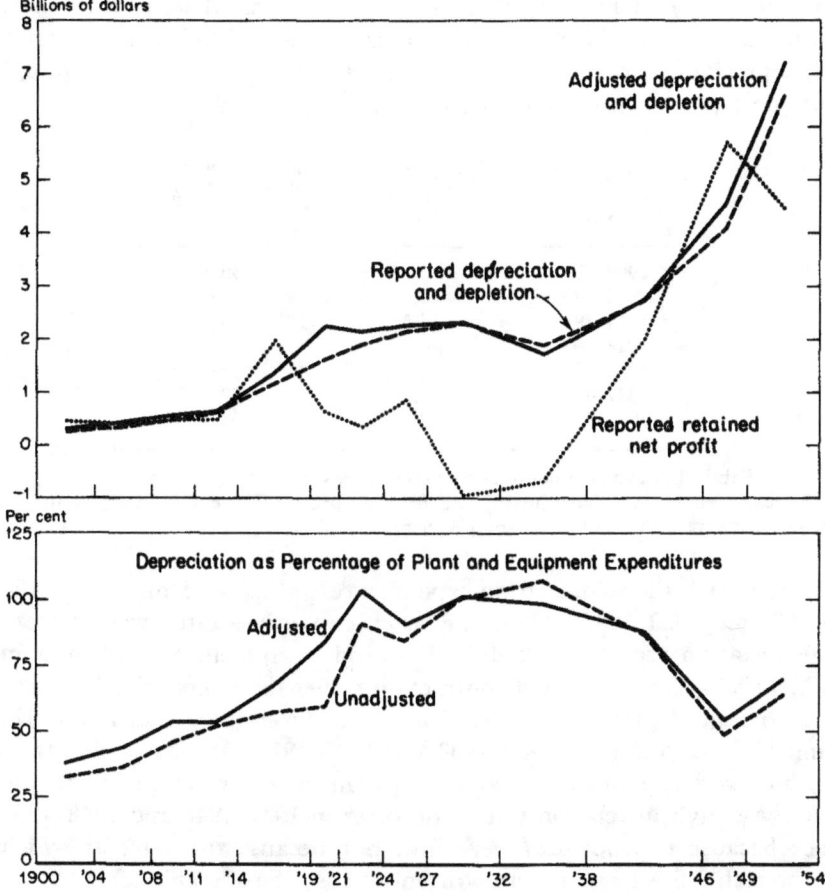

Source: Depreciation and retained net profit (reported and adjusted) from Table 41; plant and equipment expenditures from Table 40.

(peak-to-peak). Throughout 1900–1953, adjusted depreciation was 2.4 times as great as the adjusted retained net profit.

The ratios of depreciation to plant and equipment expenditures show wide fluctuations. As Chart 15 reveals, the ratio rose substantially during the first two decades, but the reverse tendency set in during the thirties. Other things being equal, a rise in the ratios indicates that a greater proportion of total expenditures represents replacement, and correspondingly less represents net expansion, of fixed assets (on the assumption that depreciation is a rough measure of actual capital consumption). Conversely, a decline indicates the reverse tendency.

Owing to lack of data, we could not compute the rates of growth of fixed assets for successive business cycles, or even successive decades. However, we do have average rates of expansion of all assets other than securities for several consecutive periods (in Table 38). When the ratios of depreciation to plant and equipment expenditures are computed for these periods, the following results are obtained:

Period	Rate of Asset Change per Year[a]	Ratio of Depreciation to Plant and Equipment Expenditure[b]
1900–09	+9.7%	36.7%
1909–14	+5.1	51.0
1914–19	+14.8	56.6
1919–29	+4.2	81.5
1929–37	−2.4	115.4
1937–48	+7.0	69.0
1948–53	+7.1	64.0

[a] See Table 38. Assets are net of depreciation reserves.

[b] Depreciation data (unadjusted) are from Appendix Table C-2, and plant and equipment expenditures data are from Appendix Table C-3.

As expected, the depreciation-expenditures ratios were highest (1919–1929 and 1929–1937) when the asset expansion rates were lowest. Depreciation accruals exceeded plant and equipment expenditures in 1929–1937—a period of net contraction rather than expansion of assets.

Although depreciation-expenditures ratios were higher in 1937–1948 and 1948–1953 than in 1900–1909 and 1909–1914, asset expansion rates in both recent periods were above those in the early periods. Depreciation was high in relation to expenditures in 1937–1948 and 1948–1953 not because expenditures were low, but because the rates at which depreciable fixed assets were written off rose considerably after World War I. In fact, the expenditures on new assets have been so large in recent years that, even with faster write-offs, the net amount of assets increased at relatively high rates.

NET PROFIT RETENTION. Conceptually, the retained part of net profit represents funds available for *net* asset expansion, i.e., expansion after replacement requirements have been taken care of. But an accurate computation of net asset expansion is difficult. Any inaccuracy in computing depreciation results in a corresponding inaccuracy in the amount of net profit. For example, if the depreciation allowance in a given year were lower than actual replacement requirements by

INTERNAL AND EXTERNAL FINANCING

$1 billion, then net profit and retained profit in that year would be overstated by $1 billion.[17]

Furthermore, the question arises whether net profit and retained profit should include such items as capital gains (or losses) and inventory profits (or losses) resulting from price changes. In any analysis of real investment and saving, it is appropriate to eliminate these gains. From the financial standpoint, on the other hand, capital gains represent a real source of funds to the business firms concerned, and sales from inventories at higher prices also provide additional funds—though not necessarily additional physical stocks if the costs are also rising. For the sake of comparison, both the adjusted and the unadjusted data are presented here.

In contrast to depreciation, retained net profit (both reported and adjusted) exhibits very wide intercycle variation over the period

CHART 16

All Manufacturing and Mining Corporations: Retained Net Profits and New Security Issues, 1900–1953

(*averages during positive business cycles*)

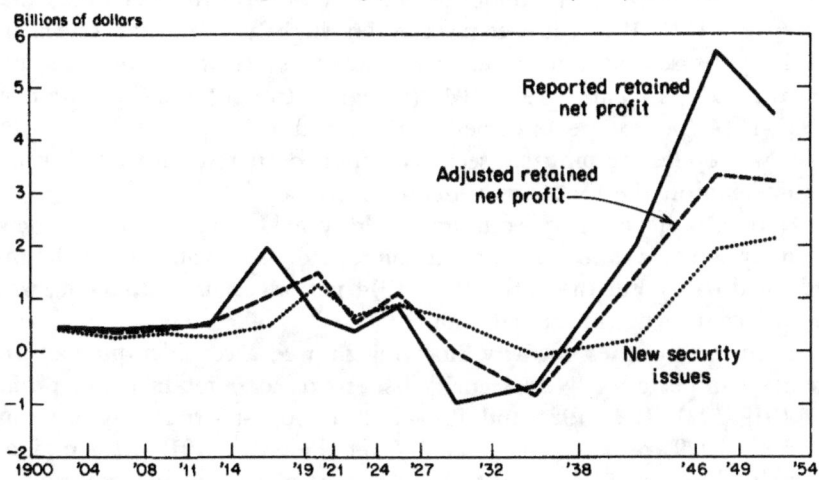

Source: Retained net profit, reported and adjusted from Table 41; new security issued from Table 40.

[17] Of course, if the depreciation had been increased by $1 billion in that year, and if the higher amount had been accepted by the government for tax purposes, net profit after taxes would have been reduced by less than $1 billion because the tax liability would have been lowered. But when depreciation data, reported by corporations, are later adjusted by economists, the amount of the tax payment remains unchanged. Therefore, any such adjustment of depreciation calls for an adjustment of net profit by the same amount but in the opposite direction.

(Table 41).[18] The cycle averages were relatively stable before World War I, rose steeply in 1914–1919, and declined in the interwar period (Chart 16). In the twenties, retentions were substantial. On the other hand, net corporate dissaving characterized the 1927–1932 and 1932–1938 cycles. The upswing that unadjusted net retentions registered in the World War II and the postwar cycles was less pronounced, but still substantial, in the adjusted profit data.

Net retentions (both adjusted and unadjusted) have a far greater amplitude of fluctuation than new security issues. However, most of the movements from one cycle to the following were in the same direction in both series: a rise in net profit retention was associated with a rise in new security issues, and vice versa. The conformity between the two series is closer when adjusted profit data are used.

Even though changes in the dollar amounts were generally in the same direction, the relative importance of internal and external funds showed wide variation owing to differences in the degree of change from one cycle to the next. The ratio of new security issues to unadjusted profit retention was especially low in the World War I and World War II cycles (see Table 42): in 1914–1919 (trough-to-trough cycle) security financing amounted to only one-fourth of retained net profit; in 1913–1918 (peak-to-peak cycle), slightly more than one-fifth. During the second war cycle, new security issues were even less important: 10 per cent in 1938–1946 (trough-to-trough) and 7 per cent in 1937–1944 (peak-to-peak) of net profit retention.

If war cycles are omitted, security issues compared with unadjusted profits exhibit the following general tendencies:

1. In all the cycles preceding World War I, the amount of new security issues was lower than the amount of net profit retained (unadjusted data). For the entire 1900–1914 period, security financing was 68 per cent of net profit retention.

2. In the twenties, security financing showed a considerable gain in relative importance. New security issues exceeded retained net profit in 1919–1921, 1921–1924 and 1924–1927 (trough-to-trough cycles) and in 1926–1929 (peak-to-peak cycle).[19] Over the entire 1919–1929 period, security financing amounted to 126 per cent of net profit retention.

3. In the thirties, net corporate profit retention gave place to corporate dissaving (net profit after taxes and dividends were

---

[18] The year-to-year variation is even wider. We use cycle averages and thereby eliminate the differences between the expansion and the contraction years within the business cycles.

[19] In 1923–1926 (peak-to-peak cycle) the amount of new issues was lower than the amount of retained net profit, but the ratio of security financing to net profit retention was higher than the corresponding ratio in all prewar cycles except that of 1899–1903.

TABLE 42
Ratio to Net Plant and Equipment Expansion[a] of Retained Net Profit and of New Security Issues, and Ratio of New Security Issues to Retained Net Profit, All Manufacturing and Mining Corporations, 1900–1953
(per cent)

Period	Unadjusted Retained Net Profit As per Cent of Unadjusted Net Plant and Equipment Expansion (1)	New Security Issues As per Cent of Unadjusted Net Plant and Equipment Expansion (2)	New Security Issues as per Cent of Unadjusted Retained Net Profit (3)	Adjusted Retained Net Profit As per Cent of Adjusted Net Plant and Equipment Expansion (4)	New Security Issues As per Cent of Adjusted Net Plant and Equipment Expansion (5)	New Security Issues as per Cent of Adjusted Retained Net Profit (6)
			POSITIVE BUSINESS CYCLES[b]			
1900–1904	84.5	75.9	89.8	87.3	81.9	93.8
1904–1908	65.4	40.1	61.4	63.1	45.2	71.7
1908–1911	82.0	54.8	66.9	83.5	63.8	76.4
1911–1914	84.9	47.5	55.9	91.3	48.9	53.6
1914–1919	225.9	56.0	24.8	153.8	72.3	47.0
1919–1921	56.5	113.5	201.0	338.3	284.9	84.2
1921–1924	196.8	351.6	178.6	n.c.	n.c.	122.8
1924–1927	217.9	220.5	101.2	438.2	350.6	80.0
1927–1932	n.c.	n.c.	n.c.	n.c.	n.c.	n.c.
1932–1938	n.c.	n.c.	n.c.	n.c.	n.c.	n.c.
1938–1946	490.7	50.5	10.3	360.0	51.2	14.2
1946–1949	132.3	45.0	34.0	86.8	50.2	57.8
1949–1954[c]	120.7	57.1	47.3	103.8	68.6	66.1
			INVERTED BUSINESS CYCLES[b]			
1899–1903[d]	84.3	76.1	90.2	85.6	82.1	95.9
1903–1907	68.3	41.6	60.8	68.3	46.1	67.5
1907–1910	136.6	88.6	64.9	139.9	118.5	84.7
1910–1913	166.1	109.0	65.6	200.8	133.9	66.7
1913–1918	227.7	49.7	21.8	155.6	55.7	35.8
1918–1920	144.4	82.0	56.8	180.3	155.9	86.5
1920–1923	n.c.	219.1	n.c.	n.c.	n.c.	122.7
1923–1926	290.7	234.6	80.7	668.3	519.3	77.7
1926–1929	137.9	210.0	152.3	222.2	362.2	118.4
1929–1937	n.c.	n.c.	n.c.	n.c.	n.c.	n.c.
1937–1944	625.6	41.5	6.6	459.7	37.8	8.2
1944–1948	142.9	48.0	33.6	74.0	52.6	71.1
1948–1953	131.9	57.5	43.6	121.6	68.3	56.2
			SELECTED PERIODS			
1900–1914	77.6	53.2	68.5	81.0	58.3	71.9
1919–1929	136.8	172.6	126.2	341.9	354.3	103.6
1936–1940	55.9	36.2	64.7	64.7	28.8	44.6
1946–1953	123.5	51.9	42.0	90.1	59.9	66.5

n.c. = not computed when numerator, denominator, or both, are negative.
[a] Net plant and equipment expansion equals plant and equipment expenditures less adjusted or unadjusted depreciation.
[b] Based on National Bureau of Economic Research business cycle chronology.
[c] Underlying data cover 1949–1953.
[d] Underlying data cover 1900–1903.
Source: Tables 40 and 41.

negative). New security financing showed a small negative balance (retirements being larger than new issues) in 1932–1938 (trough-to-trough cycle) but a small positive balance in 1929–1937 (peak-to-peak cycle).

4. In the cycles following World War II, new security issues were much lower in relation to net profit retention than in any previous nonwar cycle. For 1946–1953 (one full and one incomplete cycle), security financing was only 42 per cent of net profit retained.

The relative behavior of external and internal funds was substantially different in years when the excess profit tax was in effect compared to years when it was not. During 1946–1950, when the tax was not in effect, security issues were only 28 per cent of retained net profit. During 1951–1953, when the tax was again imposed, retentions contracted sharply; and the ratio of security issues to retentions rose to 72 per cent. Clearly, changes in the corporate tax load have been—and doubtless will be in the future—a significant factor in the determination of the relative importance of internal and external corporate financing.

The trend in the ratio of security issues to retained net profit for large manufacturing corporations is generally similar to that for all corporations (Table 43). However, there are some significant differences between the two series. For large corporations, the ratio was very high in the early twenties (1920–1923) and relatively low in the late twenties. In contrast, the ratio for all corporations reached an all-time high in the 1926–1929 cycle. In the thirties, net profits of large corporations dropped substantially but remained positive, and this enabled them to continue net profit retention; however, all corporations showed net dissaving. New security issues of the large concerns also remained positive in the 1932–1938 cycle, but all corporations combined had a negative balance. In the postwar period, the ratio of security issues to retained net profit was somewhat lower for large corporations than for all corporations.

When adjusted profit figures are substituted for the unadjusted ones, the relative importance of internal and external funds changes (see Table 42). In both war cycles, the ratio of new security issues to retained net profits rose substantially because of our downward profit adjustments. However, it was still much lower than the ratios for all the nonwar cycles.

On the nonwar cycles, the following general observations may be made:

1. Before World War I, small downward profit adjustments were made, and the ratio of new security issues to retained net profit is, therefore, slightly increased. For the entire 1900–1914 period, the value

TABLE 43

Ratio to Net Plant and Equipment Expansion[a] of Retained Net Profit and of New Security Issues, and Ratio of New Security Issues to Retained Net Profit, Large Manufacturing Corporations, 1900–1954
(per cent)

Period	Retained Net Profit	New Security Issues	New Security Issues as per Cent of Retained Net Profit
	As per Cent of New Plant and Equipment Expansion		
	SELECTED PERIOD		
1900–1910	330.1	229.4	69.5
	POSITIVE BUSINESS CYCLES[b]		
1914–1919[c]	259.4	79.1	30.5
1919–1921	94.7	79.7	84.1
1921–1924[d]	209.8	159.8	76.2
1924–1927	210.4	41.8	19.9
1927–1932	182.9	39.9	21.8
1932–1938	176.3	94.2	53.5
1938–1946[e]	284.2	5.8	2.0
1946–1949	96.8	33.8	34.9
1949–1954[f]	105.5	31.6	29.9
	INVERTED BUSINESS CYCLES[b]		
1913–1918[g]	286.5	68.1	23.8
1918–1920	147.5	93.9	63.7
1920–1923[h]	78.2	100.6	128.7
1923–1926	269.9	62.9	23.3
1926–1929	218.4	24.9	11.4
1929–1937	157.5	71.7	45.5
1937–1944[i]	323.2	33.2	10.3
1944–1948	100.9	34.9	34.6
1948–1953	109.8	30.4	27.7

[a] Net plant and equipment expansion equals plant and equipment expenditures less depreciation.
[b] Based on National Bureau of Economic Research business cycle chronology.
[c] Underlying data cover 1915–1919.
[d] Underlying data cover 1922–1924.
[e] Underlying data cover 1939–1946, Federal Reserve Board sample.
[f] Underlying data cover 1949–1953.
[g] Underlying data cover 1915–1918.
[h] Underlying data cover 1920–1922.
[i] Underlying data cover 1937–1943, National Bureau of Economic Research sample.

Source: 1900–1910: Sample of 14 large manufacturing corporations; 1915–1922: Data Book of Financial Research Program, National Bureau of Economic Research, Section A, Table 87, p. 154; 1922–1943: *ibid.*, Section A, Table 120, pp. 278–279; 1939–1953: *Federal Reserve Bulletin*, July 1953 and August 1954.

of security financing is 72 per cent of the adjusted amount of retained net profit.

2. In 1919–1929, our adjustments raise both net profit and retained profit. Consequently, the relative importance of security financing compared with adjusted retentions declines. (But security issues over this period still exceed—by 4 per cent—retained net profit.)

3. The amount of net corporate dissaving during the thirties is reduced by profit adjustments. However, the adjusted data still show a substantial negative balance of net internal financing and a small positive balance of security financing.

4. In the postwar period, retained net profit is substantially lower because of profit adjustments. Yet the ratio of new security issues to adjusted profit retention is considerably lower for the postwar cycles than for most other nonwar cycles. For the entire 1946–1953 period, security financing was 66 per cent of retained net profit—much less than for 1900–1914 and 1919–1929.

In conclusion, examination of the relations between retained net profit and new security issues, on the one hand, and net expansion of plant and equipment (total expenditure less depreciation), on the other, shows that the adjusted ratios differ significantly from the unadjusted ones in some of the cycles. However, both series have generally similar long-run tendencies (Table 42). Before World War I, the ratios of retained net profit (unadjusted and adjusted) to plant expansion and of new security issues to plant expansion were relatively low. Both ratios rose substantially during the war and the twenties .The thirties were characterized by net corporate dissaving as well as net contraction of plant and equipment. In the World War II cycle, the profit retention ratio was again very high (the security ratio was relatively low) and then dropped sharply in the postwar period. The postwar ratios were much lower than those for the twenties, although higher than those for cycles before the first war.

The difference between the recent cycles and those before 1914 is considerably larger in the unadjusted than in the adjusted series, although the change is in the same direction. The ratio of security issues to plant and equipment expansion showed a slight increase in the postwar period, although the level remained well below that reached in the twenties and was no higher than in the cycles preceding World War I.

Most of the variables considered in this section display exceedingly wide fluctuations from one cycle to another. Major long-term changes in their relationships show more clearly when averages are computed for periods containing several business cycles (see Table 42). The relative magnitudes of retained net profit, security issues, and plant

INTERNAL AND EXTERNAL FINANCING

expansion for 1946–1953 were closer to those for 1900–1914 than to those for either 1919–1929 or 1936–1940, especially if the ratios based on adjusted profit data are compared. The ratio of retained net profit to plant and equipment expansion was higher in 1946–1953 than in 1900–1914, although not nearly so high as in 1919–1929. The ratio of new security issues to retained net profit was lower in 1946–1953 than in 1900–1919. It was relatively high in 1919–1929 owing to an unusually large volume of new security flotations.

Total Short-Term and Long-Term External Financing

We now turn to the available data on total external financing, which includes funds obtained through security sales plus several other important components. Balance sheets and profit and loss statements are available for samples of large manufacturing corporations for the entire period, 1900–1953. However, the size and composition of the samples differ substantially in different periods: 1900–1910 includes only 14 large corporations; 1915–1922, 50; and 1922–1943, 44. (These three samples were compiled at the National Bureau.) For 1939–1953, a sample of about 200 corporations, compiled by the Federal Reserve Board, is used.

The statements of sources and uses of funds prepared for the samples permit an analysis of new financing absorbed by large manufacturing corporations. Although the samples are not identical, some conclusions about major financial trends can be reached by inspecting changes in the *ratios* of different types of funds to total financing.

Gross External Financing

In their usual form, statements of sources and uses of funds indicate the inflow (or outflow) of funds from various sources (gross of changes in the financial assets). For example, a statement for a given company shows an inflow of $100 million through stock and bond issues. This means that new issues exceeded retirements (and purchases of own stock to be held in the treasury) by this amount over the period concerned. If, during the same period, the company purchased $50 million worth of securities of other corporations, the amount will be shown as a use of funds on the other side of the statement. The net inflow of funds through security transactions (funds received from the capital market through security sales less the amount released to the capital market through security purchases) is the remainder after the $50 million on the "uses" side is subtracted from the $100 million on the "sources" side.

LONG-TERM TRENDS IN CAPITAL FINANCING

We consider, first, the relation between internal and external financing, without an adjustment for financial asset acquisitions. No clear trend is evident in the relative importance of internal and external financing of large corporations during the period (Table 44). In

TABLE 44
Internal and External Sources of Funds, Large Manufacturing
Corporations, 1900–1954
(dollars in millions)

		Internal Financing			External Financing		
Period	Total Financing (1)	Total (2)	Undistributed Net Profit (3)	Depreciation (4)	Total (5)	Short-Term (6)	Long-Term (7)
			SELECTED PERIOD				
1900–1910	$1,207.0	$850.0	$472.0	$378.0	$357.0	$ 29.0	$328.0
			PER CENT OF TOTAL FINANCING				
1900–1910	100.0%	70.4%	39.1%	31.3%	29.6%	2.4%	27.2%
			POSITIVE BUSINESS CYCLE AVERAGES[a]				
1914–1919[b]	$ 743.5	$447.1	$322.4	$124.6	$296.5	$194.7	$101.8
1919–1921	371.8	367.8	212.5	155.2	4.0	−174.3	178.2
1921–1924[c]	502.4	395.2	182.3	212.9	107.2	−30.0	137.2
1924–1927	705.8	644.2	332.9	311.5	61.4	−5.8	67.2
1927–1932	507.1	574.4	170.5	403.9	−67.3	−104.9	37.7
1932–1938	623.4	495.6	76.5	419.1	127.8	86.9	40.9
1938–1946[d]	3,093.0	2,348.0	1,083.0	1,265.0	745.0	664.0	81.0
1946–1949	6,066.0	4,145.0	2,550.0	1,595.0	1,920.0	908.0	1,012.0
1949–1954[e]	8,635.0	5,675.0	3,036.0	2,639.0	2,959.0	2,013.0	947.0
			PER CENT OF TOTAL FINANCING				
1914–1919[b]	100.0%	60.1%	43.4%	16.8%	39.9%	26.2%	13.7%
1919–1921	100.0	98.9	57.2	41.7	1.1	−46.9	47.9
1921–1924[c]	100.0	78.7	36.3	42.4	21.3	−6.0	27.3
1924–1927	100.0	91.3	47.2	44.1	8.7	−0.8	9.5
1927–1932	100.0	113.3	33.6	79.7	−13.3	−20.7	7.4
1932–1938	100.0	79.5	12.3	67.2	20.5	13.9	6.6
1938–1946[d]	100.0	75.9	35.0	40.9	24.1	21.5	2.6
1946–1949	100.0	68.3	42.0	26.3	31.7	15.0	16.7
1949–1954[e]	100.0	65.7	35.2	30.5	34.3	23.3	11.0
			INVERTED BUSINESS CYCLE AVERAGES[a]				
1913–1918[f]	$ 782.3	$450.7	$336.1	$114.6	$331.6	$246.6	$ 85.0
1918–1920	557.9	444.7	286.7	158.0	113.2	−67.6	180.8
1920–1923[g]	174.1	240.8	86.3	154.5	−66.7	−177.7	111.0
1923–1926	672.3	576.0	305.8	270.2	96.3	25.1	71.2
1926–1929	804.4	779.2	395.3	383.9	25.2	−22.9	48.1
1929–1937	464.1	445.4	36.7	408.7	18.7	2.2	16.5
1937–1944[h]	1,412.2	897.5	381.7	515.9	514.6	465.9	48.7
1944–1948	3,625.0	3,171.0	1,663.0	1,508.0	454.0	−252.0	706.0
1948–1953	8,110.0	5,433.0	3,027.0	2,406.0	2,676.0	1,785.0	892.0

(continued)

TABLE 44 (concluded)

Period	Total Financing (1)	Internal Financing			External Financing		
		Total (2)	Undistributed Net Profit (3)	Depreciation (4)	Total (5)	Short-Term (6)	Long-Term (7)
		PER CENT OF TOTAL FINANCING					
1913–1918	100.0%	57.6%	43.0%	14.6%	42.4%	31.5%	10.9%
1918–1920	100.0	79.7	51.4	28.3	20.3	−12.1	32.4
1920–1923	100.0	138.3	49.6	88.7	−38.3	−102.1	63.8
1923–1926	100.0	85.7	45.5	40.2	14.3	3.7	10.6
1926–1929	100.0	96.9	49.1	47.7	3.1	−2.8	6.0
1929–1937	100.0	96.0	7.9	88.1	4.0	0.5	3.6
1937–1944	100.0	63.6	27.0	36.5	36.4	33.0	3.4
1944–1948	100.0	87.5	45.9	41.6	12.5	−7.0	19.5
1948–1953	100.0	67.0	37.3	29.7	33.0	22.0	11.0

[a] Based on National Bureau of Economic Research business cycle chronology. In computing averages, values for terminal years are weighted by one-half for complete cycles. For incomplete cycles, only values at peak or trough terminal years are weighted by one-half.
[b] Underlying data cover 1915–1919.
[c] Underlying data cover 1922–1924.
[d] Underlying data cover 1939–1946, Federal Reserve Board sample.
[e] Underlying data cover 1949–1953.
[f] Underlying data cover 1915–1918.
[g] Underlying data cover 1920–1922.
[h] Underlying data cover 1937–1943, National Bureau of Economic Research sample.
Source: Same as Table 43.

fact, the ratio of gross internal to total new financing during 1948–1953 (67 per cent) was close to the corresponding ratio during 1900–1910 (70 per cent). However, considerably higher ratios are obtained for the interwar period. In the 1920–1923 cycle, gross internal financing amounted to 138 per cent of the total, indicating that the inflow of internal funds was accompanied by a substantial outflow of external funds through repayment of loans, retirement of securities, etc. In 1926–1929 and 1929–1937, gross internal financing represented almost 100 per cent of the total (external financing was of negligible relative importance). The ratio of gross internal to total financing declined in the World War II cycle, and the postwar ratios compared with the interwar ratios remained relatively low. However, the ratio for the World War II cycle was higher than that for the World War I cycle.

The ratio of retained net profit to total new financing likewise lacks a definite trend. During the twenties, net profit retention was especially high relative to the other components but dropped to a very low level in the thirties. The ratio for the World War II cycle was substantially lower than that for the World War I cycle. The ratios for 1946–1949 and 1949–1953 were considerably below the highest ratios for the twenties but fairly close to the figure for 1901–1910.

The significance of the changes that took place over the half-century can be seen more clearly if the short-term and long-term components of external financing are examined separately. The short-term component represents the sum of changes in current liabilities: mainly, short-term bank loans, accounts payable, and accrued items. The long-term component is equal to the sum of changes in long-term loans and securities outstanding (both stocks and bonds).

Short-term external financing was substantial only in the two war cycles (1914–1919 and 1938–1946) and the two cycles following World War II (1946–1949 and 1949–1954). In contrast, during 1901–1910, the inflow of short-term funds was relatively unimportant, and in the interwar period, most cycles were characterized by negative balances (net decreases in current liabilities).

As the following table indicates, the rise in the relative importance of short-term funds in the war and postwar cycles was largely accounted for by increased accruals for income tax purposes:

Positive Business Cycle Averages
(dollars in millions)

Period	Total Short-Term Financing[a] (1)	Increase in Tax Liability[b] (2)	(Col. 2) as per Cent of (Col. 1) (3)
1914–1919	$ 195	$ 90	46
1938–1946	664	220	33
1946–1949	908	396	44
1949–1954[c]	2,013	1,084	54

[a] Average from Table 44, column 6.
[b] Sources same as those in Table 44.
[c] Underlying data cover 1949–1953.

The rise in tax accruals during the two war cycles was due partly to higher taxable income and partly to higher tax rates. Corporate profits before taxes expanded along with the general volume of production. At the same time, the corporate income tax rates were raised and special wartime excess profit taxes were imposed in both periods. The increase in tax liability in the 1946–1949 cycle, on the other hand, was due entirely to profit expansion. The wartime excess profit tax was repealed at the end of 1945, and the income tax rate for corporations remained unchanged (at 38 per cent, including the surtax) during 1946–1949. Finally, in the 1949–1954 cycle, which included the years of the Korean conflict, both factors were at work again: profits expanded and the tax rates were increased once more. A new excess profit tax was imposed in 1950, and the income tax and surtax rate were raised to 42 per cent in 1950 and to 52 per cent in 1951.

Although changes in the tax liability were important, other components of short-term financing (mainly bank and trade credit) also showed substantial increases in all four cycles. In fact, even if the tax accruals are excluded from short-term financing, the ratio of the remaining short-term components to total financing is higher for these cycles than is the ratio of all short-term components (including tax accruals) to total financing for most of the remaining cycles.

The ratio of long-term external financing to total new financing has a downward trend throughout 1900–1953. Although the relative importance of long-term external financing rose substantially after World War II, the ratio remained well below the peak levels reached in 1919–1924.

The data on long-term external financing include new stock issues, bond issues, and other types of long-term loans (see Table 44). Until the mid-thirties, corporate long-term debt consisted almost entirely of bond issues. Since then, however, types of long-term loans other than bond issues have become significant components of total new financing.[20] Substantial amounts of such loans have been made to industry by commercial banks and other lending institutions and, also, by life insurance companies.

Unfortunately, the sample data for large manufacturing corporations do not permit the separation of the bond issues from all the other types of long-term lending. Separate figures on long-term loans received from commercial banks are available since 1939. The amounts and the relative importance of these loans as a component of long-term external financing are indicated below:

Positive Business Cycle Averages
(dollars in millions)

Period	Total Long-Term Financing[a] (1)	Increase in Long-Term Bank Loans[b] (2)	(Col. 2) as per Cent of (Col. 1) (3)
1938–1946	$ 81	$ 59	73
1946–1949	1,012	123	12
1949–1954[c]	947	36	4

[a] Averages from Table 44, column 7.
[b] Sources same as in Table 44.
[c] Underlying data cover 1949–1953.

Bank long-term lending was only moderately important as a source of new funds for large manufacturing corporations in the war and postwar cycles. The percentage figure shown above for 1938–1946 is

[20] See the section on term-lending in Chapter VII.

misleading, because all long-term external financing was then only 2.6 per cent of total new financing (external plus internal). In the 1946–1949 and 1949–1954 cycles, long-term financing in the form of new security issues greatly expanded. In contrast, long-term bank lending increased only moderately.

Data on the sources and uses of funds for all manufacturing corporations are available only for 1946–1953 (Table 45). The behavior of the

TABLE 45

Internal and External Sources of Funds, All Manufacturing Corporations, 1946–1953
(dollars in billions)

Period	Total Financing	Internal Financing			External Financing		
		Total	Retained Net Profit	Depre- ciation	Total	Short- Term	Long- Term
		POSITIVE BUSINESS CYCLE AVERAGES[a]					
1946–1949	$12.1	$8.7	$6.1	$2.6	$3.4	$1.3	$2.1
1949–1954[b]	16.3	9.8	5.6	4.2	6.5	4.2	2.3
		PER CENT OF TOTAL FINANCING					
1946–1949	100%	72%	50%	22%	28%	11%	17%
1949–1954[b]	100	60	34	26	40	26	14

[a] Based on National Bureau of Economic Research business cycle chronology. In computing averages, values for terminal years are weighted by one-half.
[b] Underlying data cover 1949–1953.
Source: *Survey of Current Business*, Department of Commerce, December 1954, p. 14.

ratios based on these data is not materially different from that of the ratios for large corporations. In 1946–1949, gross internal financing relative to total new financing was slightly more important for all companies; in 1949–1953, it was a little more important for large corporations. In 1946–1949, the ratio of short-term external financing to total financing was considerably smaller for all corporations than it was for large firms; but in 1949–1954, the ratios for all corporations were higher. Finally, the ratio of long-term external financing to total financing was slightly higher for all corporations than for large ones in both the 1946–1949 and 1949–1954 cycles.

Net Balance of External Financing

The *net* balance of external financing is the inflow of external funds adjusted for changes in financial assets. The data on large manufacturing corporations indicate a net release, rather than absorption, of external funds in four out of nine positive cycles and in five out of

CHART 17

Ratios of Gross Internal Financing to Capital Expenditures on Physical Assets, All Manufacturing and Mining Corporations and Sample, 1913–1954

(averages during business cycles)

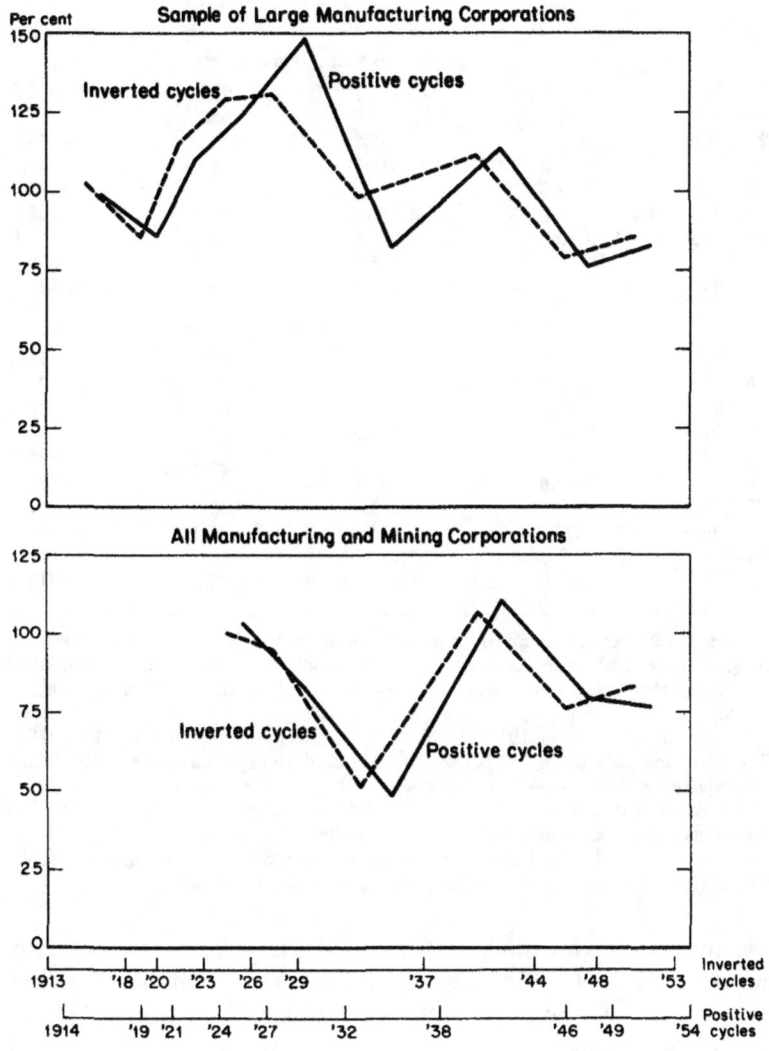

Source: Tables 46 and 47.

TABLE 46

Capital Expenditures on Physical Assets, Gross Internal Financing, and Net Balance of External Financing, Large Manufacturing Corporations, 1913–1953

(dollar amounts are annual averages in millions)

Period	Capital Expenditures on Physical Assets (1)	Gross Internal Financing (2)	Ratio of (Col. 2) to (Col. 1) (per Cent) (3)	Net Balance of External Financing (Col. 1) minus (Col. 2) (4)
		POSITIVE BUSINESS CYCLES[a]		
1914–1919[b]	$ 450.6	$ 447.1	99.2%	$ 3.5
1919–1921	428.5	367.8	85.8	60.7
1921–1924[c]	359.6	395.2	109.9	−35.6
1924–1927	520.0	644.2	123.9	−124.2
1927–1932	388.0	574.4	148.0	−186.4
1932–1938	603.9	495.6	82.1	108.3
1938–1946[d]	2,070.0	2,348.0	113.4	−278.0
1946–1949	5,453.0	4,145.0	76.0	1,308.0
1949–1954[e]	6,860.0	5,675.0	82.7	1,185.0
		INVERTED BUSINESS CYCLES[a]		
1913–1918[f]	438.8	450.7	102.7	−11.9
1918–1920	518.1	444.7	85.8	73.4
1918–1920	518.1	444.7	85.8	73.4
1920–1923[g]	208.6	240.8	115.4	−32.2
1923–1926	445.5	576.0	129.3	−130.5
1926–1929	596.0	779.2	130.7	−183.2
1929–1937	452.5	445.4	98.4	7.1
1937–1944[h]	807.5	897.5	111.1	−90.0
1944–1948	4,022.0	3,171.0	78.8	851.0
1948–1953	6,345.0	5,433.0	85.6	912.0

[a] Based on National Bureau of Economic Research business cycle chronology. In computing averages, values for terminal years are weighted by one-half for complete cycles. For incomplete cycles, only values at peak or trough terminal years are weighted by one-half.
[b] Underlying data cover 1915–1919.
[c] Underlying data cover 1922–1924.
[d] Underlying data cover 1939–1946, Federal Reserve Board sample.
[e] Underlying data cover 1949–1953.
[f] Underlying data cover 1915–1918.
[g] Underlying data cover 1920–1922.
[h] Underlying data cover 1937–1943, National Bureau of Economic Research sample.

Source: 1915–1943, National Bureau of Economic Research samples; 1938–1953, Federal Reserve Board sample of large manufacturing corporations.

nine inverted cycles during 1913–1953 (Chart 17 and Table 46).[21] In the World War I cycle, the amount of gross internal financing was close to that of physical asset expenditures (the sum of plant and equipment expenditures and inventory changes), and the net balance

[21] The sample data for 1900–1910 are incomplete and do not permit computation of the net balance of external financing.

of external financing was relatively insignificant. In the first postwar cycle—1919–1921 (trough-to-trough) or 1918–1920 (peak-to-peak)—the net inflow of external funds was considerable, but a substantial net outflow was characteristic of the cycles following in the twenties. The balance was positive in the 1932–1938 cycles, negative in the World War II cycle, and positive again (substantially so) in the two postwar cycles. Over the entire period, the ratio of gross internal financing to physical asset expenditures shows a slight downward trend, while the ratio of net external financing to such expenditures shows an upward tendency.

The net balance of short-term external financing for large manufacturing corporations was negative in most cycles from 1913 through 1946. In 1946–1949 and 1949–1953, however, substantial positive balances were registered, mainly as a result of large tax accruals. The net balance of long-term external financing was positive in the World War I cycle and the two immediate postwar cycles. But the remaining part of the interwar period was characterized by a net outflow of long-term external funds. The negative balance was especially large in the 1926–1929 cycle when large corporations made substantial investments in securities of other companies. In the second war, we find a small net inflow of long-term external funds. Much larger positive balances are found in the two postwar cycles.

From the balance sheet and profit and loss data published in *Statistics of Income* since 1923, together with the available estimates of plant and equipment expenditures, we derived the net balance of external financing for all manufacturing and mining corporations combined. In making the derivations, we followed the method developed by Terborgh[22] which may be summarized as follows:

1. Net inflow of all (short- and long-term) external funds is obtained by subtracting the amount of gross internal financing from the amount of expenditures on new physical assets (plant and equipment outlays plus inventory changes). A negative balance shows a net outflow of external funds.[23]

The net inflow (or outflow) thus obtained is equivalent, in terms of balance sheet items, to the algebraic sum of all changes in current liabilities, noncurrent debt, and capital stock (adjusted for book transfers, such as stock dividends) less the algebraic sum of all changes in nonphysical, or financial, assets (cash, accounts and notes receivable, and government and corporate security holdings).

[22] Terborgh, *op. cit.*, p. 45.
[23] In his own derivations, Terborgh includes changes in cash with capital expenditures. He indicates, however, that one may wish to consider cash (mainly bank deposits) as a form of credit extended by corporations to banks. The latter approach seems preferable to us and is used in this study.

TABLE 47

Capital Expenditures on Physical Assets, Gross Internal Financing, and Net Balance of External Financing, All Manufacturing and Mining Corporations, 1923–1953
(dollar amounts are annual averages in millions)

Period	Capital Expenditures on Physical Assets (1)	Gross Internal Financing (2)	Ratio of (Col. 2) to (Col. 1) (per cent) (3)	Net Balance of External Financing (Col. 1) minus (Col. 2) (4)
	POSITIVE BUSINESS CYCLES[a]			
1924–1927	$2,607	$2,692	103.3%	$ −85
1927–1932	2,190	1,806	82.5	384
1932–1938	1,985	960	48.4	1,025
1938–1946	3,626	4,008	110.5	−382
1946–1949	9,209	7,273	79.0	1,936
1949–1954[b]	12,607	9,665	76.7	2,942
	INVERTED BUSINESS CYCLES[a]			
1923–1926	2,554	2,559	100.2	−5
1926–1929	3,067	2,915	95.0	152
1929–1937	1,724	883	51.2	841
1937–1944	3,365	3,597	106.9	+232
1944–1948	6,907	5,258	76.1	1,649
1948–1953[c]	11,631	9,657	83.0	1,974
	SELECTED PERIODS			
1923–1929	2,975	2,806	94.3	169
1936–1940	2,996	2,120	70.8	876
1946–1952	10,941	8,175	74.7	2,766

[a] Based on National Bureau of Economic Research business cycle chronology. In computing averages, values for terminal years are weighted by one-half for complete cycles. For incomplete cycles, only values at peak or trough terminal years are weighted by one-half.

[b] Underlying data cover 1949–1952.

[c] Underlying data cover 1948–1952.

Column	Source
1	Plant and equipment expenditures (from Appendix Table C-3) reduced to balance sheet levels *plus* inventory valuation adjustment (from *National Income Supplement, 1954, Survey of Current Business*, Department of Commerce, Table 23 for 1935–1952, and extrapolated by data from George Terborgh's worksheets for 1923–1934) *plus* change in inventories of balance sheet corporations (from *Statistics of Income* for 1935–1952 and extrapolated by data from Terborgh's worksheets for 1923–1934).
2	Net retained profits for balance sheet corporations (from *Statistics of Income* for 1935–1952 and extrapolated by data from Terborgh's worksheets for 1923–1934) *plus* inventory valuation adjustment (described above) *less* net capital gains for all corporations (from *Statistics of Income* for 1935–1952 and extrapolated by data from Terborgh's worksheets for 1923–1934) *plus* unadjusted depreciation, depletion, and amortization for corporations with balance sheets (from *Statistics of Income* for 1935–1952 and extrapolated by data from Terborgh's worksheets for 1923–1934).

INTERNAL AND EXTERNAL FINANCING

2. The total inflow of external funds is then broken down into short-term and long-term components. In our derivations, the net balance of short-term financing equals the sum of changes in current liabilities less the sum of changes in cash, marketable securities, and accounts receivable. The net balance of long-term financing equals the sum of changes in long-term debt and capital stock (adjusted) less the sum of changes in long-term investments in financial assets. Since long-term debt includes loans that do not involve security issues (mortgage loans made by a single creditor, and term loans by banks), the net balance of long-term financing obtained by this method is not equivalent to the net balance of corporate security transactions alone.

Since the available data for all companies combined are far from exact, they must be interpreted broadly. In most cycles, 1923–1953, the ratio of gross internal financing to capital expenditures on physical assets (plant and equipment expenditures plus inventory changes) for all manufacturing and mining companies was lower than the ratio for large manufacturing concerns (Chart 17 and Tables 46 and 47). However, both series exhibit generally similar intercycle fluctuations.

In 1923–1926 (or 1924–1927), the ratio for all manufacturing and mining was close to 100 per cent, i.e., the net balance of external financing was negligible. However, the relative importance of net external funds increased substantially in the following two cycles. In 1929–1937, gross internal financing amounted to only 51 per cent (net external financing being 49 per cent) of the total amount spent on physical assets. During the World War II cycle, external funds were, on balance, released to other sectors. But after the war, there was again a considerable net inflow of external financing.

Ratios computed for periods longer than a single business cycle show that the net inflow of external funds was larger in relation to internal financing in 1946–1952 than in 1923–1929 but smaller in 1946–1952 than in 1936–1940 (Table 47). This is true whether net external financing is related to net profit retentions or to gross retentions and whether adjusted or unadjusted profit data are used.[24]

The net balance of short-term external financing was negative in all three periods. In Table 48, short-term financing of all manufacturing and mining corporations is broken down into two parts. One part represents the change in income tax liability less the change in government security holdings, i.e., the change in the net balance of claims between the corporations and the government. As the table

---

[24] The adjusted profit figures discussed in this section differ from the unadjusted ones by the sum of the depreciation, inventory valuation, and capital gain adjustments.

TABLE 48

All Manufacturing and Mining Corporations: Components of Net External Financing Related to Gross and Net Internal Financing, Selected Periods, 1923–1952
(per cent)

	Type of External Financing								
	As Percentage of Gross Internal Financing				As Percentage of Net Internal Financing				
	Short-Term				Short-Term				
Period	Private	Government	Total	Long-Term	Total	Private	Government	Total	Long-Term	Total
	UNADJUSTED DATA								
1923–1929	−10.0	−2.1	−12.0	14.0	2.0	−37.5	−7.8	−45.3	52.7	7.4
1936–1940	−30.4	+13.6	−16.8	55.5	38.7	−243.3	+109.0	−134.2	443.4	309.2
1946–1952	−8.1	+6.3	−1.8	25.0	23.1	−15.9	+12.3	−3.6	49.1	45.5
	ADJUSTED DATA								
1923–1929	−10.0	−2.1	−12.0	18.1	6.0	−45.1	−9.4	−54.5	81.9	27.4
1936–1940	−32.0	+14.4	−17.7	58.9	41.3	−245.7	+110.1	−135.6	452.3	316.7
1946–1952	−10.0	+7.7	−2.3	36.1	33.8	−29.8	+23.1	−6.7	107.7	101.0

Source: External financing data for corporations are from *Statistics of Income*, Part 2 (returns with balance sheets) and are extrapolated by data taken from George Terborgh's worksheets. Adjusted gross internal financing and retained net profit data (described in source note to Table 41) are reduced to the level of corporate returns with balance sheets.

Note: Detail may not add to totals because of rounding.

shows, the net amount owed to the government decreased in 1923–1929. In 1936–1940 and 1946–1952, on the other hand, the net liability to the government rose.

The other part of short-term financing represents the net change in the balance of short-term claims between the companies in question and other private sectors of the economy (the change in notes and accounts payable less the change in cash and accounts receivable). As the table indicates, the net liability to private short-term creditors declined throughout 1923–1952.

In contrast, the net balance of long-term external financing was positive during all three periods. New funds obtained through security issues and long-term loans exceeded the funds invested in corporate securities and long-term advances to other business units. However, the relative importance of long-term external financing varied widely. Its ratio to gross internal financing was highest in 1936–1940. The ratio for 1946–1952, while considerably lower than that for 1936–1940, was much higher than the ratio for 1923–1929. Its ratio to retained net profit was also exceedingly high in 1936–1940. The unadjusted ratio for 1946–1952 is slightly lower than the ratio for 1923–1929; but when the adjusted profit data are used, the 1946–1952 ratio exceeds the one obtained for 1923–1929.[25]

In general, then, our data do not indicate any clear trend in the relative importance of the net external and the internal components of total new financing. Net external funds were relatively less important in the postwar period than they had been in the late thirties. On the other hand, net external funds were of greater relative importance in the postwar years than they had been in the twenties.

Since there are no data on inventory changes prior to 1923, we could not compare gross internal financing with total capital expenditures and thus determine the net inflow of external funds in the earlier periods. However, the ratio of gross internal financing to plant and equipment expenditures (Table 40) was somewhat lower in 1946–1953 than in 1923–1929, but much higher in 1946–1953 than in 1900–1914. Probably, the ratio of gross internal financing to total capital expenditures on physical assets was also higher (and the relative importance of net external financing correspondingly lower) in 1946–1953 than in 1900–1914.[26]

[25] The ratio to internal financing of new security issues less retirements was substantially higher in 1923–1929 than in 1946–1952 (see Table 40 and Chart 11). However, the inflow of funds from the security markets was largely offset by the pronounced expansion of financial assets in the twenties. This is why the *net* balance of long-term external financing was relatively low in 1923–1929.

[26] Sample data for large manufacturing corporations indicate substantial increases in inventories in 1900–1910.

LONG-TERM TRENDS IN CAPITAL FINANCING

Summary of Findings

1. In manufacturing and mining, internal funds represented a much greater proportion of total new financing than did external funds. Net profit retained by all corporations in these industries was roughly twice as large as their new security issues, net of retirements, during 1900–1953. Their gross internal financing (the sum of retained profit and depreciation and depletion allowances) was more than five times as large as their new security issues. Sample data for large manufacturing corporations indicate that gross internal funds represented around 70 per cent and total external funds (both long- and short-term) only around 30 per cent of total new financing during the same period.

2. The relative importance of internal and external funds varied considerably from one part of the period to another. The relative share of internal financing tended to be smaller, and the relative share of external financing correspondingly greater, in periods of rapid asset expansion than in those of moderate asset-growth.

3. While the data do not permit the exact determination of relative trends in internal and external financing over the entire period, some broad tendencies emerge when the available figures are examined. The ratio of internal funds to funds obtained through new security issues rose considerably. However, owing to a rapid rise in short-term external financing in the latter part of the period, the ratio of internal to total external financing shows no upward trend. Thus, for all companies, the approximate relative share of net profit retentions in financing the expansion of assets was (in percentages): 1900–1909, 41; 1909–1919, 52; 1919–1929, 26; 1937–1948, 54; 1948–1953, 45. For large manufacturing companies the comparable figures are: 1900–1910, 39; 1913–1918, 43; 1923–1929, 47; 1944–1953, 42. The ratios of gross internal financing to total new financing of the large companies are (in percentages): 1900–1919, 70; 1913–1918, 58; 1923–1929, 91; 1944–1953, 73.

Income tax accruals represented the fastest growing component of short-term financing. If these accruals were treated as a kind of short-term retention and included in internal financing, the ratio of internal to total financing would show a moderate upward trend over the period.

4. In most parts of the period reviewed, depreciation and depletion allowances provided a considerably greater amount of internal funds than did net profit retention. The ratio of depreciation and depletion allowances to gross internal financing was (in percentages): 1900–1914, 48; 1919–1929, 73; 1936–1940, 89; 1946–1953, 53. When valuation adjustments are made, the figures become 52, 72, 84, and 66, respectively.

INTERNAL AND EXTERNAL FINANCING

Over the entire period, gross internal financing provided approximately a tenth more funds than the amount required to finance total plant and equipment expenditures (gross of depreciation). The ratio of gross internal financing to such expenditures, 1900–1953, shows an upward trend.

5. External financing adjusted for changes in financial assets, so as to obtain net inflow of capital funds from other sectors of the economy, is considerably smaller than the gross (unadjusted) amount in most parts of the period reviewed.

Only a rough estimate of net external financing can be made for the years before World War I. Apparently, the net inflow of external funds was then considerable. The data available for the interwar period indicate that the net balance of external financing was very small in relation to total financing during the twenties, but assumed greater relative importance during the thirties. (In the depression years, the net inflow of external funds resulted mainly from liquidation of financial assets.) During World War II, the net balance of external financing was negative: funds were released to other sectors through large accumulations of financial assets. Finally, in the postwar period, the net inflow is again substantial.

CHAPTER VII
Debt and Equity Financing

SINCE most manufacturing and mining industries have been subject to wide cyclical fluctuations, it has, traditionally, been considered unwise for them to rely heavily on debt financing, especially if it is long-term. Some corporations, even in the largest size class, have never issued bonds. Some have also not used bank credit, confining their debt financing to an unavoidable minimum of accounts payable, accrued taxes, and a few other minor items. However, for all manufacturing and mining corporations combined, borrowed funds, both short-term and long-term, have been an important addition to equity capital.

Definitions

Before we examine debt-equity relationships in detail, some basic terms must be defined. Short-term liabilities include short-term bank loans (notes payable), trade credit (accounts payable), accrued items (mainly tax accruals), and other short-term liabilities (e.g., the portion of long-term debt payable within a year). Long-term liabilities consist of bonds, mortgages, and long-term bank credit (term loans). Total debt is the sum of all short-term and long-term liabilities. Equity (or net worth) includes capital stock, surplus, and capital reserves (but not reserves for depreciation and other valuation reserves).

Equity funds are obtained by corporations from external sources (through capital stock flotations) and from internal sources (through income retention). All debt funds, except for accrued liabilities, are obtained from external sources. Accrued liabilities are similar to retained earnings in that they represent funds derived from the revenue stream. But they are usually treated as short-term financing extended to the company by the payee (the government, in the case of tax accruals) and are included, along with other short-term liabilities, in external financing. We are following this procedure, except when our analysis requires a summing up of all the funds (short- and long-term) retained from the revenue stream.

Total Debt

For manufacturing, our data on total interest-bearing debt extend from 1890 through 1952, though the earliest figures are only rough estimates (Table 49).[1] The 1890 ratio of total interest-bearing debt to

[1] The 1890 census gives interest payments in manufacturing. The interest-bearing debt outstanding in 1890 was estimated by capitalizing interest payments at 5 per cent. The census also gives total operating assets in manufacturing. (The census definition of capital includes all operating assets but excludes investments in securities.)

TABLE 49

All Manufacturing and Mining Corporations: Ratios of Debt to Assets, Selected Years, 1890–1952
(dollars in millions)

	Interest-Bearing Debt (1)	Total Debt (2)	Operating Assets[a]		Total Assets (book value) (5)	Interest-Bearing Debt as Per Cent of			Total Debt as Per Cent of		
						Operating Assets		Total Assets (book value) (Col. 1) ÷ (Col. 5) (8)	Operating Assets		Total Assets (book value) (Col. 2) ÷ (Col. 5) (11)
			(book value) (3)	(current value) (4)		(book value) (Col. 1) ÷ (Col. 3) (6)	(current value) (Col. 1) ÷ (Col. 4) (7)		(book value) (Col. 2) ÷ (Col. 3) (9)	(current value) (Col. 2) ÷ (Col. 4) (10)	
MANUFACTURING											
1890[b]	$ 824	n.a.	$ 5,697	$ 5,627	n.a.	14.5%	14.6%				
1919	n.a.	$13,568	38,225	48,488	$42,472				35.5%	28.0%	31.9%
1923[c]	6,193	n.a.	43,644	n.a.	n.a.	14.2					
1929[c]	n.a.	13,964[d]	54,188	56,674	60,237				25.8	24.6	23.2
1937	7,497	14,484	46,198	48,860	55,723	16.2	15.3	13.5	31.4	29.6	26.0
1948	15,608	37,624	103,023	119,781	121,708	15.2	13.0	12.8	36.5	31.4	30.9
1952	25,945	60,786	144,361	167,144	170,282	18.0	15.5	15.2	42.1	36.4	35.7
MINING											
1923[c]	$ 2,736	n.a.	$13,941	n.a.	n.a.	19.6%					
1929[c]	n.a.	$ 3,119[c]	11,204[e]	12,017	$12,666				27.8%	26.0%	24.6%
1937	1,511	2,523	7,409	8,119	9,146	20.4	18.6%	16.5%	34.1	31.1	27.6
1948[e]	1,425	2,840	7,243	9,087	9,394	19.7	15.7	15.2	39.2	31.3	30.2
1948[f]	1,449	2,864	7,019	8,755	9,042	20.6	16.6	16.0	40.8	32.7	31.7
1952	2,186	4,102	9,685	12,135	12,034	22.6	18.0	18.2	42.4	33.8	34.1

n.a. = not available.
[a] Total assets minus investments in government and corporate securities.
[b] 1890: all establishments; other years: corporations with balance sheets.
[c] Adjusted for deconsolidation.
[d] Includes "surplus reserves."
[e] Comparable with 1937.
[f] Comparable with 1952.

Source: Columns 1, 2, 3, and 5: 1890: *Report on Manufacturing Industries in the United States at the Eleventh Census; 1890*, Part 1; 1919: Column 3 from Appendix A, section A1a and Table A-3. Column 5 estimated from sample data in a manner similar to that described in Appendix A, section A1a. Column 2 is the difference between total assets and net worth; the latter is given in Appendix A, section A1a and Table A-3. 1923: *Statistics of Income for 1924*. The figures for operating assets include an estimate of "other assets."
1929, 1937, 1948, and 1952: *Statistics of Income*.
Column 4: Data in column 3 deflated by an index of replacement cost computed by the National Bureau of Economic Research.

LONG-TERM TRENDS IN CAPITAL FINANCING

total operating assets is nearly the same as the ratio for 1923 (around 14 per cent). But a moderate rise occurred in later years, and the ratio reached 18 per cent in 1952.

The data on total debt, including the non-interest-bearing items (accounts payable and accrued tax liabilities), are available since 1919. (Again, the figure for 1919 is only a rough estimate.) The ratios of total debt to operating assets and of total debt to total assets declined from 1919 to 1929, but they increased significantly thereafter. By 1952, total debt amounted to more than one-third of total assets and more than two-fifths of operating assets.

Generally similar tendencies are revealed by sample data on large manufacturing corporations. The ratio of total debt to total assets was 21 per cent in 1901 (see Chart 20 below). The ratio rose during World War I; but in the twenties, it dropped back to nearly the 1901 level and continued downward in the thirties. It rose substantially during and after World War II. In 1952, the ratio was 38 per cent.

While total debt before World War II was less important for large corporations than for all corporations, the reverse became true in the postwar period. For mining, the ratios of total debt to operating assets and of total debt to total assets, available only for 1923–1952, are closely similar to those obtained for manufacturing.

The above measures relate debt to assets as they are valued on the books. Somewhat different results are obtained when debt is related to assets in current (i.e., replacement) prices. When prices are rising, current values tend to exceed the original cost of durable assets. Since the amount of debt is not affected by price changes, net worth is increased by the entire amount of asset appreciation. As a result, the relative importance of the debt declines.[2] The reverse tendency develops, of course, during periods of falling prices.

As Table 49 shows, the postwar ratios of debt to operating assets are higher than the prewar ones, even when the assets are expressed in replacement values, but the change is less.[3] The ratio of interest-bearing debt to adjusted operating assets has changed only slightly (14.6 per cent in 1890, 15.5 per cent in 1952). The ratio of total debt to adjusted operating assets has changed somewhat more (28.0 per cent in 1919, 29.6 per cent in 1937, and 36.4 per cent in 1952).

Although, for total manufacturing, the ratio of debt to book value of capital declined between 1919 and 1929, the debt ratios rose in seven

---

[2] On the one hand, the creditors lose, because the real value of the capital they have lent falls. On the other hand, they gain greater security for their loans: the greater the asset appreciation, the smaller the burden of the debt and the smaller the chance of default.

[3] The indexes, prepared at the National Bureau, permit us to convert the book values of operating assets, but not total assets, into current values.

DEBT AND EQUITY FINANCING

of the ten industry groupings we can distinguish for this purpose (Table 50). The three industry groups in which the debt ratio declined

TABLE 50

Ratios of Total Debt to Operating Assets and Relative Change in Operating Assets, by Manufacturing Industries, Selected Years, 1919–1948

(per cent)

	Percentage Ratio of Total Debt to Operating Assets			Percentage Change in Operating Assets	
	1919	1929	1948	1919–1929	1929–1948
Food and kindred products	33.6	26.2	32.5	+50	+64
Textiles and products	26.7	22.9	22.7	+36	+43
Leather and leather products	28.8	21.5	25.6	−3	+10
Rubber products	25.3	34.0	35.1	+34	+36
Forest products	21.1	24.8	24.7	+49	+7
Paper, pulp, and products	21.7	25.7	23.2	+115	+66
Printing and publishing	10.5	27.9	27.5	+204	+44
Chemicals and allied products[a]	14.4	18.4	27.6	+234	+96
Stone, clay, and glass products	9.3	18.6	21.3	+143	+24
Metals and their products	25.3	17.2	24.2	+36	+88

[a] Includes petroleum refining.

Source: Underlying data for 1919 based on data in Appendix A, section A1a and Table A-3; for 1929 and 1948, *Statistics of Income*, Bureau of Internal Revenue (now Internal Revenue Service).

—food and kindred products, leather and leather products, and textiles and their products—had the three highest debt ratios in 1919. Furthermore, the rate of growth of operating assets of these groups between 1919 and 1929 was relatively low.

By 1948, the debt ratio in six of the ten industry groups exceeded, by a considerable margin, the ratios for 1929. In the other four, the 1948 figures were slightly below the 1929 ones. In most of the ten, the percentage change in the debt ratio between 1929 and 1948 is directly associated with the percentage increase in operating assets (the higher the relative expansion in operating assets, the higher the relative change in the debt ratio). This is, of course, consistent with the general trend of increased reliance upon debt to finance the acquisition of new assets.

The relative importance of debt and equity financing for different asset size classes in 1937 and 1948 can be seen in Chart 18.[4] In both

[4] The data underlying Chart 18 are presented in Appendix C, section D, and Appendix Table C-4. Statistics for different asset size classes of corporations have been published by the Internal Revenue Service since 1931. The years selected for our analysis, 1937 and 1948, are the last prewar, and the first postwar, cyclical peak years, respectively.

CHART 18
Ratios of Debt to Total Assets, All Manufacturing and Mining Corporations with Balance Sheets, by Total-Asset Classes, 1937 and 1948

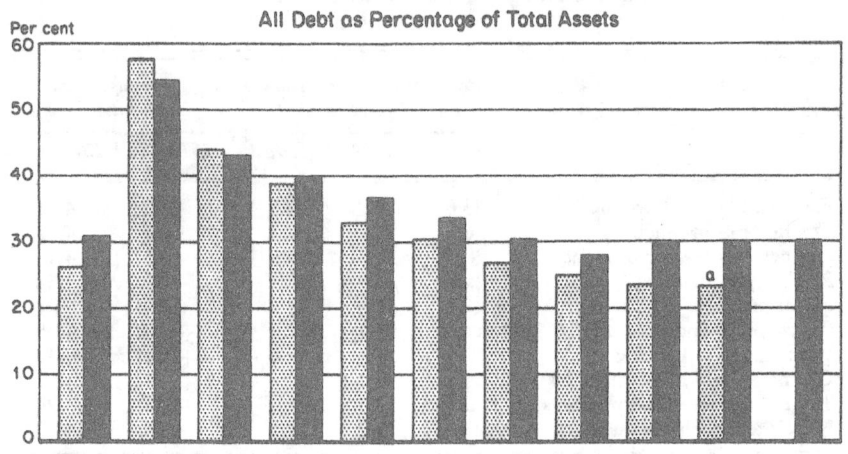
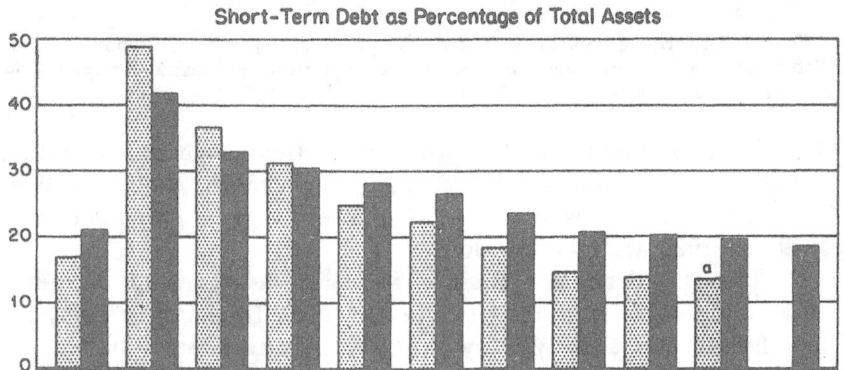
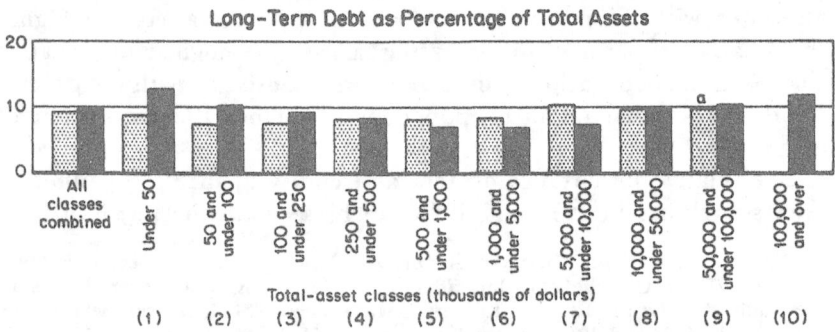

a Last two classes combined. Source: Appendix Table C-4.

DEBT AND EQUITY FINANCING

years the ratio of total debt to total assets was lower for large corporations than for small ones. In 1937, the ratio decreased consistently as the asset size increased. (It was 57 per cent for corporations in Class 1 but only 23 per cent for those in Class 9.[5] In 1948, the ratio decreased from 54 per cent for Class 1 corporations to 28 per cent for Class 7. The ratio was slightly higher for Classes 8, 9, and 10 than for Class 7 but much lower than for all the lowest asset-classes.

Total debt was of greater relative importance in 1948 than in 1937 for all classes except the two lowest. The rise in the ratio was relatively small for medium-size corporations, but somewhat more pronounced for corporations with assets of $10 million and over. For all classes combined, the ratio rose from 26 per cent in 1937 to 31 per cent in 1948 (and to 35 per cent in 1952).

In both 1948 and 1937, total debt was considerably less important for corporations with net income than for corporations without net income. This was true of all asset-size classes in manufacturing and mining industries alike. Both income and no-income companies, however, show a similar relationship between the ratio of debt to assets and asset size. For most classes, the relation is inverse: the ratio diminishes as assets increase. Only the highest asset-size classes deviate from this pattern (especially companies without net income, where the ratios for Classes 9 and 10 are considerably higher than are those for Classes 7 and 8). But, even though the ratios for the largest corporations show some rise, they remain well below the level observed for most of the smallest.

The income and the no-income groups are also similar in that both show a significant rise in the ratio of debt to assets from 1937 to 1948. This rise is found in most classes, notable exceptions being the two lowest net-income classes in manufacturing.

For all classes combined, the debt-asset ratio for manufacturing corporations with net income rose from 23 per cent in 1937 to 30 per cent in 1948. For those without net income, the corresponding figures were 42 per cent and 51 per cent. In mining, the ratio increased from 19 per cent in 1937 to 28 per cent in 1948 for corporations with net income, and from 43 per cent to 51 per cent for those without net income.

Long-Term Debt: New Bond Issues

Data on new bond issues of all manufacturing and mining corporations for 1900–1953 are given in Table 51. A more detailed industrial

[5] This tendency was not confined to manufacturing and mining corporations (see Walter A. Chudson, *The Pattern of Corporate Financial Structure: A Cross-Section View of Manufacturing, Mining, Trade and Construction, 1937*, National Bureau of Economic Research, 1945).

TABLE 51

Security Issues, Retained Net Profit, and Net Plant and Equipment Expansion,[a] All Manufacturing and Mining Corporations, 1900-1953
(dollar amounts are annual averages in millions)

Period	New Security Issues			Retained Net Profit		Net Plant and Equipment Expansion		New Stock Issues as Percentage of:		Total New Security Issues (Col. 2) ÷ (Col. 3) (10)	New Bond Issues as Percentage of:			
	Stocks (1)	Bonds (2)	Total (3)	(unadjusted) (4)	(adjusted) (5)	(unadjusted) (6)	(adjusted) (7)	Retained Net Profit			Retained Net Profit		New Stock Issues Plus Retained Net Profit	
								(unadjusted) (Col. 1) ÷ (Col. 4) (8)	(adjusted) (Col. 1) ÷ (Col. 5) (9)		(unadjusted) (Col. 2) ÷ (Col. 4) (11)	(adjusted) (Col. 2) ÷ (Col. 5) (12)	(unadjusted) [(Col. 1) + (Col. 2)] ÷ [(Col. 1) + (Col. 4)] (13)	(adjusted) (Col. 2) ÷ [(Col. 1) + (Col. 5)] (14)
POSITIVE BUSINESS CYCLES[a]														
1900-1904	$158	$254	$412	$459	$439	$543	$503	34.4%	36.0%	61.7%	55.3%	57.9%	41.2%	42.5%
1904-1908	143	113	256	417	357	638	566	34.3	40.1	44.1	27.1	31.7	20.2	22.6
1908-1911	177	140	317	474	415	578	497	37.3	42.7	44.2	29.5	33.7	21.5	23.6
1911-1914	212	59	271	485	506	571	554	43.7	41.9	21.8	12.2	11.7	8.5	8.2
1914-1919	410	78	488	1,968	1,038	871	675	20.8	39.5	16.0	4.0	7.5	3.3	5.4
1919-1921	815	427	1,242	618	1,475	1,094	436	131.9	55.3	34.4	69.1	28.9	29.8	18.6
1921-1924	385	288	668	374	544	190	−71	102.9	70.8	42.4	75.7	52.0	37.3	30.5
1924-1927	569	304	873	863	1,091	369	249	65.9	52.2	34.8	35.2	27.9	21.2	18.3
1927-1932	733	587	1,320	−146	−988	−21	−25	n.c.	n.c.	n.c.	n.c.	n.c.	n.c.	n.c.
1932-1938	174	−249	−75	206	−824	−126	34	n.c.	n.c.	n.c.	n.c.	n.c.	n.c.	n.c.
1938-1946	234	−23	206	2,002	1,447	408	402	11.7	16.2	58.1	19.8	33.6	17.3	27.1
1946-1949	810	1,125	1,935	5,687	3,347	4,299	3,856	14.2	24.2	67.5	32.0	44.6	27.7	36.7
1949-1954[b]	691	1,437	2,128	4,497	3,220	3,727	3,102	15.4	21.5					
INVERTED BUSINESS CYCLES[a]														
1899-1903	167	249	416	461	434	547	507	36.2	38.5	59.9	54.0	57.4	39.6	41.4
1903-1907	132	124	256	421	379	616	555	31.4	34.8	48.4	29.5	32.7	22.4	24.3
1907-1910	164	124	288	444	340	325	243	36.9	48.2	43.1	27.9	36.5	20.4	24.6
1910-1913	224	104	328	500	492	301	245	44.8	45.5	31.7	20.8	21.1	14.4	14.5
1913-1918	295	70	365	1,671	1,019	734	655	17.6	28.9	19.2	4.2	6.9	3.6	5.3
1918-1920	878	182	1,060	1,867	1,226	1,293	680	47.0	71.6	17.2	9.7	14.8	6.6	8.7
1920-1923	442	406	848	−87	691	387	−20	n.c.	64.0	47.9	n.c.	58.8	114.4	35.8
1923-1926	529	224	753	933	969	321	145	56.7	54.6	29.7	24.0	23.1	15.3	15.0
1926-1929	953	55	1,008	662	851	480	383	144.0	112.0	5.5	8.3	6.5	3.4	3.0
1929-1937	259	−249	10	−1,264	−824	−282	−154	n.c.	n.c.	n.c.	n.c.	n.c.	n.c.	n.c.
1937-1944	133	−26	107	1,614	1,301	258	283	8.2	10.2	n.c.	n.c.	n.c.	n.c.	n.c.
1944-1948	798	548	1,346	4,008	1,894	2,805	2,558	19.9	42.1	40.7	13.7	28.9	11.4	20.4
1948-1953	707	1,394	2,101	4,817	3,739	3,651	3,076	14.7	18.9	66.3	28.9	37.3	25.2	31.4

(continued)

TABLE 51 (concluded)

	SELECTED PERIODS						
1900-1914	166	141	307	448	427	576	527
1919-1929	749	190	939	744	906	544	265
1936-1940	216	-60	156	241	350	431	541
1946-1953	1,282	772	2,054	4,889	3,091	3,959	3,429

n.c. = not computed when numerator, denominator, or both, are negative.
a Based on National Bureau of Economic Research business cycle chronology. In computing averages, values for terminal years are weighted by one-half for complete cycles. For incomplete cycles, only values at peak or trough terminal years are weighted by one-half.
b Averages cover 1949-1953.
Source: Columns 1, 2, and 3: Appendix Table C-1; columns 4 and 5: Table 41; columns 6 and 7: Plant and equipment expenditures in Table 40, column 3 minus depreciation in Table 41, column 1 (unadjusted) or column 2 (adjusted).

TABLE 52

Net Bond Issues during Cycles in Business Activity, All Manufacturing and Mining Corporations and Major Manufacturing Industries, 1900-1943

(annual averages in millions of dollars)

Positive Business Cycle Period[a]	Mining and Manu- fac- turing	All Mining	All Manu- fac- turing	Food and Kindred Products	Textiles and Products	Forest Products	Paper	Printing	Chemicals	Petroleum and Coal Products	Rubber	Leather	Stone, Clay and Glass	Iron and Steel	Non- ferrous Metals	Mach- inery	Trans- por- tation Equip- ment	Miscel- laneous
1900-1904	253.9	35.7	218.2	50.2	5.5	2.4	2.1	0.0	1.7	0.5	3.2	1.0	0.5	142.4	4.4	0.9	3.2	0.1
1904-1908	112.2	38.0	74.2	-1.4	-2.0	5.4	4.9	0.3	5.7	1.8	1.1	8.3	1.8	27.2	2.8	13.1	3.9	1.1
1908-1911	140.0	45.4	94.5	26.1	3.7	9.4	-3.0	4.3	3.2	6.7	0.8	0.2	1.9	18.4	0.7	8.5	14.4	-0.9
1911-1914	58.9	17.7	41.1	-11.0	1.4	10.4	5.9	0.0	7.2	11.6	-0.6	-2.0	8.7	17.8	-1.2	-4.3	-0.8	-2.0
1914-1919	78.9	1.4	77.5	43.7	-3.7	-8.0	-3.1	0.0	5.3	9.1	9.6	-1.6	2.0	15.7	7.0	-2.2	5.0	5.0
1919-1921	426.4	23.2	403.2	95.0	20.4	0.5	6.5	1.3	18.4	120.9	55.0	6.0	-7.5	2.9	22.5	50.0	9.5	1.8
1921-1924	282.2	76.4	205.8	-1.6	24.6	21.1	10.2	0.0	22.0	46.6	11.0	-1.0	-1.0	68.7	0.8	14.7	16.4	2.9
1924-1927	305.4	42.0	263.4	24.5	6.6	19.8	52.8	17.2	6.2	85.4	14.0	-6.0	23.9	-9.8	-3.0	-0.4	9.0	23.4
1927-1932	-146.6	-67.6	-79.0	-41.7	2.6	16.9	-3.8	9.4	-15.6	29.5	-7.7	-2.7	6.1	-63.9	11.0	-2.6	-9.7	-6.8
1932-1938	-248.3	-41.2	-207.1	-29.5	-27.3	-31.7	-10.7	-9.4	-5.2	-40.2	-6.4	-0.4	-10.1	8.4	-15.6	-6.8	-14.8	-7.2
1938-1946[b]	-18.9	-29.4	10.5	29.9	7.2	-8.5	-3.2	-5.8	6.6	23.7	-5.8	-0.7	-8.6	-26.1	14.8	-4.8	-3.0	-5.0

a Based on National Bureau of Economic Research business cycle chronology. In computing averages, values for terminal years are weighted by one-half for complete cycles. For incomplete cycles, only values at peak or trough terminal years are weighted by one-half.
b Averages cover 1938-1943.
Source: Based on unpublished tables of W. Braddock Hickman used for his study The Volume of Corporate Bond Financing since 1900, Princeton University Press for National Bureau of Economic Research, 1953.
Note: Detail may not add to totals because of rounding.

breakdown of new bond issues (available for 1900–1943 only) is presented in Table 52. Cycle averages for manufacturing do not have close conformity with those for mining. Nevertheless, both series show the following general characteristics:[6]

1. There was a large inflow of funds through bond transactions in 1900–1929. This was followed by an outflow of funds (retirements in excess of new issues) during the thirties and early forties;

2. The highest peak reached by new bond issues, 1900–1943, was in the early twenties (1919–1921 in manufacturing and 1921–1924 in mining).

Most major manufacturing industries show an inflow of bond funds during 1920–1927, an outflow during 1927–1943. However, the relative importance of individual industries as bond issuers changed substantially over the period reviewed.

The large amount of new bond financing in 1900–1904 was mainly accounted for by the iron and steel industry (the U.S. Steel Corporation was organized in 1901). Food and kindred products ranked second in importance during that cycle. The average value of new bond issues was much smaller in the three cycles following (1904–1908, 1908–1911, and 1911–1914); the main bond issuers were the iron and steel, forest products, machinery, and transportation equipment industries.

In the World War I cycle (1914–1919), the largest bond issues in manufacturing were in the food, iron and steel, petroleum, and rubber industries. During the twenties (the 1919–1921, 1921–1924, and 1924–1927 cycles), the petroleum industry became by far the most important bond issuer, although the food, paper, forest products, and textile industries each accounted for a considerable fraction of the total. Iron and steel issues were important only in the 1921–1924 cycle.

In the 1927–1932 and the 1932–1938 cycles, retirements generally exceeded new issues by manufacturing industries. In 1927–1932, only petroleum, forest products, and nonferrous metals showed substantial positive averages. In 1932–1938, retirements exceeded new issues in all industries except iron and steel. However, in 1938–1943, petroleum, chemicals, nonferrous metals, food, and textiles began again to absorb funds through bond transactions.

Stock and bond issues during 1900–1919 showed divergent trends (the stock average rose from $158 million in 1900–1904 to $410 million in 1914–1919; the bond average declined from $254 million to $78 million—see Chart 19 and Table 51). From 1919 to 1949, the

---

[6] Since the value of bond issues in manufacturing greatly exceeded that in mining, fluctuations in the data for both industries combined reflect mainly the movements shown by manufacturing.

DEBT AND EQUITY FINANCING

CHART 19

New Bond and New Stock Issues, All Manufacturing and Mining Corporations, 1900–1953

(*averages during positive business cycles*)

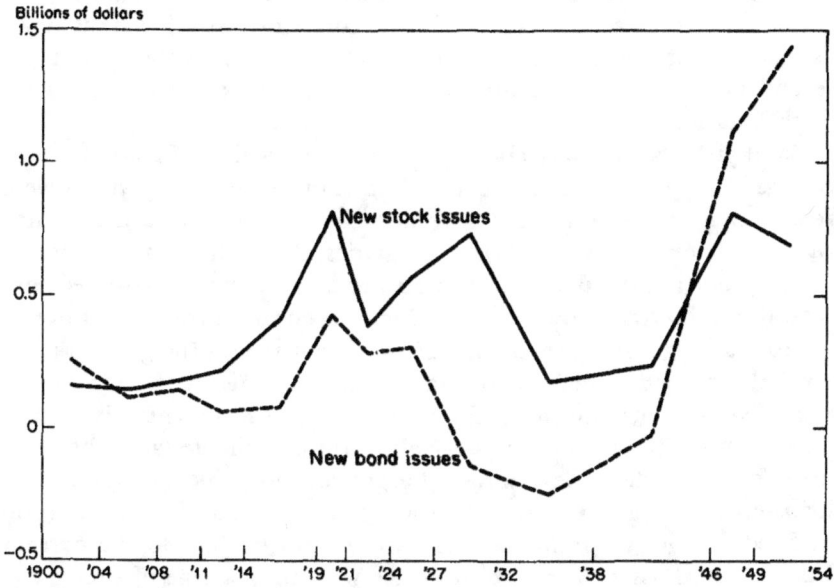

Source: Table 51.

stock and bond averages generally moved in the same direction, but the bond series fluctuated more widely.

In the 1919–1921, 1921–1924, and 1924–1927 cycles, both stock and bond issues were relatively high, but the stock average exceeded the bond average by a considerable margin. The stock average rose still higher in 1927–1932, but the bond average dropped sharply. In fact, bond financing showed a negative balance (retirements in excess of new issues).[7]

Bond financing remained negative in the 1932–1938 and 1938–1946 cycles. The stock average remained positive, although well below the high levels of the twenties. Finally, in 1946–1949 and 1949–1953, both stock and bond issues rose sharply. The bond average showed a much more pronounced rise and exceeded the stock average by a considerable margin in both cycles. Thus, the postwar cycles stand in sharp contrast

[7] The 1923–1926 and 1926–1929 peak-to-peak cycles also have this divergent movement. The bond average contracted sharply in 1926–1929, although it remained positive, unlike the average for the 1927–1932 trough-to-trough cycle.

to all the interwar cycles (and also to the cycles before World War I, except 1900–1904) in that bond financing provided much more funds than did stock financing.

There were a number of reasons for the heavier reliance on bond financing in the postwar years. Because the level of economic activity was high and relatively stable, corporate managements became more confident of the earning power of their companies and less hesitant to assume the risks associated with trading on equity. At the same time, several factors tended to reduce the cost of bond issues compared with stock flotations.

Bond yields were relatively low, mainly as a result of Treasury policy in regard to government obligations. In contrast, dividend yields were relatively high, reflecting the generally conservative and cautious attitude of investors towards "risk" securities. Also, the deductibility of interest, but not dividends, in computing taxable income assumed considerable importance owing to the high corporate income tax rates.

From a longer-run viewpoint, the persistent rise in the general price level also tended to make bonds (and loans in general) relatively more attractive to corporations. Although rising prices generally meant higher revenues and higher asset values (in current dollars), they had no effect on either the interest charges or the principal amount of loans outstanding. Consequently, for a given amount of debt, the ratio of fixed charges to profits as well as the ratio of debt to the current value of total assets tended to decrease with the passage of time.

Bond Issues and Equity Financing

However, a rise in bond financing relative to stock financing does not, necessarily, mean a shift from equity to debt capital, because equity funds are obtained internally as well as externally. It is important, therefore, to examine changes in bond financing relative not only to stock issues (external equity expansion), but also to income retention (internal equity accumulation).

The relevant data, 1900–1953, for all manufacturing and mining corporations show no clear trend in the ratio of bond issues to retained net profit (Table 51). This is true whether the ratios are computed from reported profit data or from adjusted profit data.[8]

The ratios of new stock issues to retained profit for the 1946–1949 and 1949–1954 cycles were considerably lower than any of the ratios prior to World War II. The three cycles preceding (1927–1932, 1932–1938, and 1938–1946) had shown an excess of retirements over new

[8] See the section on net profit retention in Chapter VI for an explanation of the difference between unadjusted and adjusted profit data.

DEBT AND EQUITY FINANCING

bond issues. However, in all of the earlier (pre-1927) cycles, new bond issues showed substantial positive balances (sometimes, the ratio of bond issues to retained profit was higher than in 1946–1949 or 1949–1953).

The ratios of new bond issues to total equity financing (new stock issues plus retained profits), also, do not show any definite trend (Table 51). However, although the postwar ratios are not the highest, they exceed most of the ratios for the cycles preceding World War II, especially when computed from adjusted profit figures. The adjusted figure for 1946–1953 exceeds the adjusted figure for 1900–1914 as well as that for 1919–1929.

We can use the available statements of sources and uses of funds for samples of large manufacturing companies to examine the importance of long-term debt financing (including bonds and other loans with maturity longer than one year) in relation to other types of financing and to the total flow of funds from all sources (Table 53).[9]

The inflow of long-term debt funds compared with new stock financing of large corporations, exhibits tendencies generally similar to those of new bond and stock issues of all manufacturing and mining companies combined, but with some significant differences.

In 1946–1949, the inflow of long-term debt funds into large corporations was 2.6 times as high as the inflow of funds through stock sales; in 1949–1953, even higher (4.6 to 1). Before World War II, new long-term debt financing was never more than a small fraction of new stock financing. In the thirties, there was a net outflow of long-term debt funds, while stock transactions showed a net inflow. In the twenties, the inflow of debt funds, even at its highest (in 1919–1921), was only 22 per cent of the inflow of equity funds. The relative importance of long-term debt financing was considerably higher in 1900–1910 than in the interwar period. Yet the ratio of such financing to stock financing (1.3) was not nearly so high as after World War II.

Long-term debt financing in the postwar period included substantial amounts of bank loans (term lending). If these loans are excluded, the remainder may be taken to represent, fairly closely, the amount of bond financing. For large corporations, the inflow of this remainder, new bond issues, was 2.6 times as large as the inflow of funds from stock sales in 1946–1949 and 4.6 times as large in 1949–1953. For all manufacturing and mining corporations, the ratio of new bond issues to new stock issues was less (1.4 in 1946–1949 and 2.1 in 1949–1953).

[9] Since the samples vary in size and composition, caution is required in using these data for an analysis of long-run trends. This must be borne in mind especially when comparing 1900–1910 with later periods, because the 1900–1910 sample is much smaller than the other samples, and the figures represent changes over a decade rather than over business cycle periods.

TABLE 53
Ratios of New Stock Issues and New Long-Term Debt Financing to Retained Net Profit, Large Manufacturing Corporations, 1900–1953
(*per cent*)

Period	New Stock Issues as Per Cent of Retained Net Profit	New Long-Term Debt Financing as Per Cent of—		
		New Long-Term Debt plus New Stock Issues	Retained Net Profit	New Stock Issues plus Retained Net Profit
1900–1910	30.1	56.7	39.4	30.3
		POSITIVE BUSINESS CYCLES[a]		
1914–1919	24.7	19.1	5.8	4.7
1919–1921	68.8	18.2	15.3	9.1
1921–1924	77.8	b	b	b
1924–1927	17.2	13.5	2.7	2.3
1927–1932	62.9	b	b	b
1932–1938	56.1	b	b	b
1938–1946	2.8	b	b	b
1946–1949	9.7	72.2	25.2	23.0
1949–1954[c]	5.3	82.2	24.6	23.3
		INVERTED BUSINESS CYCLES[a]		
1913–1918	17.6	25.8	6.1	5.2
1918–1920	57.6	9.6	6.1	3.9
1920–1923	88.1	31.6	40.7	21.6
1923–1926	27.6	b	b	b
1926–1929	20.3	b	b	b
1929–1937	171.9	b	b	b
1937–1944	b	b	0.2	0.2
1944–1948	12.6	63.4	21.9	19.5
1948–1953	5.5	80.2	22.2	21.0

[a] Based on National Bureau of Economic Research business cycle chronology.
[b] Percentage not shown when either numerator or denominator is negative.
[c] Underlying data cover 1949–1953.
Source: Same as Table 43.

In the interwar period, the reverse was true. For large corporations, the highest ratio was 22 per cent in 1919–1921; for all manufacturing and mining, the ratio was as high as 42 per cent in 1919–1921 and went up to 74 per cent in 1921–1924. Thus, it was the large-corporation sector that showed an especially pronounced change in the relative importance of new stock and bond financing since 1919.

However, when we examine the importance to large companies of long-term debt financing in relation to retained profits and to total financing from all sources, we see a substantially different picture. The ratio of long-term debt funds to retained net profit, 1900–1953, shows no clear trend in either direction. The ratios for 1946–1949 and 1949–

DEBT AND EQUITY FINANCING

1953 were lower than the figure for 1900–1910 but substantially higher than the other ratios.

Long-term financing in relation to total new financing (the sum of all external and internal funds including depreciation) likewise shows no clear trend over the half-century reviewed. Here, again, the ratio displays a long downswing in the first three decades followed by an upswing in the following twenty years. The ratios in the postwar period are considerably below the ratio for 1900–1910, but exceed those for the interwar cycles. (However, the ratio for 1919–1921 is only slightly lower than that for 1949–1953.)

The ratio of new stock financing to total financing is characterized by a strong downward trend from 1900 through 1953. It was this decline, rather than an increase in long-term debt financing, that was primarily responsible for the rising ratio of long-term debt funds to funds obtained through stock sales.

Total Bond Debt Outstanding

In manufacturing, total bond debt outstanding has never been large in relation to total invested capital. As Table 54 indicates, all manufacturing corporations had $208 million of bonds outstanding in 1900, i.e., only 3.9 per cent of their combined operating assets.[10]

Presumably, the continuing wave of mergers through 1909 is mainly responsible for the rise in bond debt to $1.5 billion (11.4 per cent of operating assets of all manufacturing corporations). By 1929, the amount outstanding had reached $4.1 billion, but this was only 7.7 per cent of operating assets.

Bond debt increased substantially between 1909 and 1919, and again between 1919 and 1929, but the debt-to-assets ratio declined from the 1909 peak. In 1937, the dollar amount as well as the ratio declined from the 1929 levels. Finally, in the postwar period, a pronounced rise occurred in the amount of bond debt, but the debt-to-assets ratio shows no definite trend. In 1948, the ratio was lower than in any previous year except 1900. In 1952, the ratio rose considerably but was still below the 1929 level and much below the 1909 level. No clear trend in the ratio may be discerned throughout 1900–1952.

---

[10] *Census of Manufactures, 1900*, Volume VII, p. lxxix. The Census reports that "combinations" in existence as of June 1, 1900 had issued bonds valued at $216 million. We may infer from this that almost all bonds issued by manufacturing firms at the beginning of this century had been issued by "combinations." When related to capital invested in "combinations" as defined in that census, bonds outstanding are found to have represented approximately 14 per cent of the total. But when taken in relation to operating assets of all manufacturing corporations, bonds outstanding amounted to only 3.9 per cent. Total invested capital as defined in the census is equal to the sum of all operating assets, i.e., total assets less investments.

TABLE 54
Operating Assets and Par Value of Bonded Debt Outstanding, All Manufacturing Corporations, Selected Years, 1900–1952
(dollars in millions)

	Par Value of Bonded Debt Outstanding (1)	Operating Assets of Manufacturing Corporations		Bonded Debt as a Per Cent of Operating Assets	
		Book Value (2)	Replacement Value (3)	Book Value (Col. 1) ÷ (Col. 2) (4)	Current Value (Col. 1) ÷ (Col. 3) (5)
1900	$ 208	$ 5,309ᵃ	$ 5,648	3.9%	3.7%
1909	1,531	13,380ᵃ	14,143	11.4	10.8
1919	2,188	38,225	48,488	5.7	4.5
1929	4,149	54,188ᵇ	56,674	7.7	7.3
1937	2,570	46,198	48,860	5.6	5.3
1948	5,460	103,023	119,781	5.3	4.6
1952	10,560	144,361	167,144	7.3	6.3

ᵃ Adjusted to corporate level.
ᵇ Adjusted to deconsolidated basis.

Column	Source
1	1900–1937: Unpublished tables of W. Braddock Hickman, *The Volume of Corporate Bond Financing since 1900*, Princeton University Press for the National Bureau of Economic Research, 1953; 1948: Estimated from data on par value of all industrial bonds given in Hickman, *ibid.*, p. 255; 1952: Estimated by adding annual net changes in par value of manufacturing bonds outstanding, given in an unpublished table of the Securities and Exchange Commission, to the 1948 figure.
2	1900–1919: Appendix Table A-8; 1929–1952: *Statistics of Income*, Part 2.
3	Data in Col. 2 deflated by an index of replacement cost computed by the National Bureau of Economic Research.

If bond debt is related to operating assets expressed in current values the postwar ratios become considerably lower. However, the major tendencies remain similar to those discussed in the preceding paragraph, and the ratio still does not show any definite trend.

Essentially similar tendencies are shown by sample data for large manufacturing corporations (Chart 20). The ratio of total long-term debt outstanding to total assets rose sharply from 7 per cent in 1900 (12 per cent in 1901) to 20 per cent in 1914, the highest point of the entire 1900–1954 period. The ratio declined in the years following and was down to 12 per cent in 1919. Thereafter, it remained remarkably stable during most of the interwar period. A further decline was registered during the World War II years (in 1945, the ratio was as low as 8 per cent), but the trend was reversed in 1946. In 1952–1954, the ratio was slightly more than 12 per cent—close to what it had been in the early twenties.

DEBT AND EQUITY FINANCING

CHART 20

Ratios of Selected Liabilities to Total Assets, Large
Manufacturing Corporations, 1900–1954

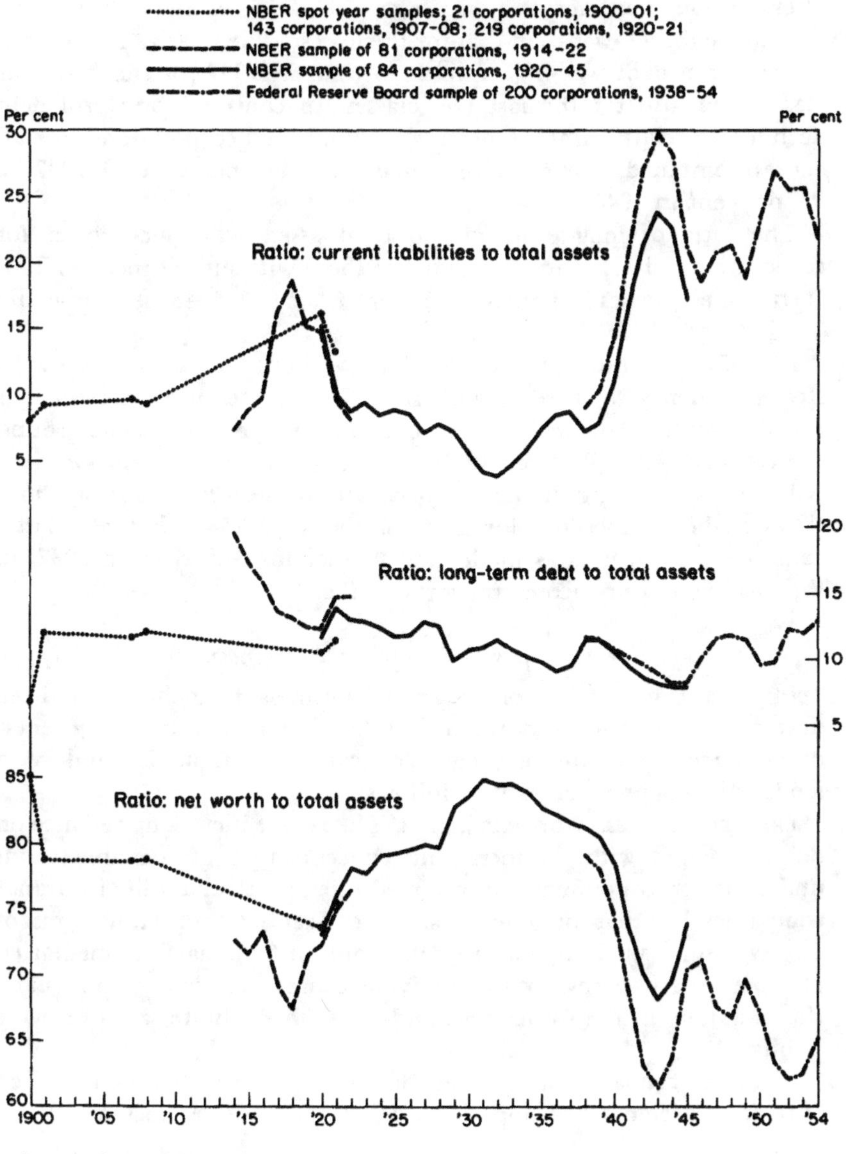

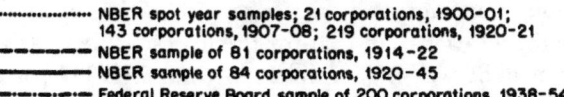

.... NBER spot year samples; 21 corporations, 1900–01;
143 corporations, 1907–08; 219 corporations, 1920–21
————— NBER sample of 81 corporations, 1914–22
———— NBER sample of 84 corporations, 1920–45
—·—·— Federal Reserve Board sample of 200 corporations, 1938–54

Source: Same as Table 43.

The 1937 and 1948 data for different asset size classes show no clear and consistent relation between the size of assets and the relative importance of long-term debt (Chart 18). In 1937, the ratio shows a slight tendency to increase with asset size. In 1948, the ratio decreases as the asset size increases up to the $1 million to $5 million asset class. Thereafter, although it increases with size, the ratio for the highest class remains slightly lower than that for the lowest. The relative importance of long-term debt was higher in 1948 than in 1937 for the first four classes and also for the last two classes. In contrast, long-term debt declined in relative importance for medium-sized corporations. For all classes combined, the ratio increased from 9.3 per cent in 1937 to 9.9 per cent in 1948.

The ratio of long-term debt to total assets was much lower for corporations with net income than for those without net income. This is true of all classes in both years except Class 9 in 1948 (see Appendix Table C-4).

In 1937, the ratio for corporations without net income shows a strong tendency to increase with size. No such tendency, however, is revealed by the data for 1948. In both income and no-income groups, the ratio rose sharply from 1937 to 1948 for the smaller corporations (Classes 1–5). Among the larger corporations, the 1948 ratio was sometimes higher, sometimes lower, than the 1937 ratio. For all classes combined, the ratio was moderately higher in 1948 than in 1937, in the income and no-income categories alike.

New Types of Long-Term Financing

Important new types of long-term business financing have been developed since the early thirties. A brief review of two major new developments—private placement of corporate securities and term lending by commercial banks—follows.

PRIVATE PLACEMENT OF SECURITIES. The recent increasing reliance on debt coincides with an increasing concentration of loanable funds under the control of financial intermediaries, particularly life insurance companies.[11] It has become possible to negotiate for large sums of money from a single one or a small group of financial intermediaries. No longer is it necessary to subdivide claims into many small parts (for example, in the form of a bond issue) to facilitate sale to a wide public.

Securing funds directly from financial intermediaries is called "private placement," as opposed to the public sale of stock and bond

[11] See Raymond W. Goldsmith, *The Share of Financial Intermediaries in National Wealth and National Assets*, National Bureau of Economic Research, Occasional Paper 42, 1954.

DEBT AND EQUITY FINANCING

issues after registration with the Securities and Exchange Commission. Owing to the growth of financial intermediaries, the added cost of floating public issues which results from the registration requirement, and for other reasons, private placements have come to be an important mechanism for channeling funds into manufacturing enterprises.

The growing importance of private placement of corporate securities is indicated by estimates prepared by the Securities and Exchange Commission (Table 55). Since World War II, about two-fifths of all

TABLE 55
All Corporate Securities, Total and Private Placements, 1934–1951
(dollars in millions)

	All Issues	Privately Placed	
		Value	As Per Cent of All Issues
1934	$ 397	$ 92	23.2%
1935	2,332	387	16.6
1936	4,572	373	8.2
1937	2,309	330	14.3
1938	2,155	692	32.1
1939	2,164	706	32.6
1940	2,677	765	28.6
1941	2,667	813	30.5
1942	1,062	420	39.5
1943	1,170	372	31.8
1944	3,202	787	24.6
1945	6,011	1,022	17.0
1946	6,900	1,917	27.8
1947	6,577	2,235	34.0
1948	7,078	3,087	43.6
1949	6,052	2,502	41.3
1950	6,362	2,680	42.1
1951	7,741	3,415	44.1

Source: *Privately Placed Securities—Cost of Flotation*, Securities and Exchange Commission, September 2, 1952, p. 3 (processed).

corporate securities issued for cash were privately placed. Between 1934 and 1951 nearly 98 per cent of all privately placed securities were debt issues; 2 per cent were stocks, mostly preferred. Of the publicly offered securities, 73 per cent were debt issues, and the remainder was stock, equally divided between common and preferred.[12]

The dominant role of the life insurance companies in the private

[12] *Hearings* before a Subcommittee of the Committee on Interstate and Foreign Commerce, House of Representatives, Eighty-second Congress, Second Session, part 2 (1952), Table 7, p. 957.

placement of securities is revealed by Table 56. In 1947, they absorbed 93 per cent of the total amount of corporate bonds and notes privately

TABLE 56

Distribution of Privately Placed Corporate Debt, by Type of Investor, 1947, 1949, and 1950

(*per cent*)

	1947	1949	1950
Life insurance companies	93.0	90.5	83.4
Other insurance companies	0.1	0.4	0.7
Banks	2.7	4.9	12.1
Other institutions	2.5	0.5	0.5
Individuals and corporations[a]	0.4	3.6	2.5
Unknown	1.3	0.1	0.8
Total	100.0	100.0	100.0

Note: Debt includes bonds, notes, and debentures.
[a] Includes purchases by private pension funds in 1949 and 1950.
Source: Based on data from Securities and Exchange Commission as taken from *Hearings* before a Subcommittee of the Committee on Interstate and Foreign Commerce, House of Representatives, 82nd Congress, 2nd Session, part 2 (1952), Table 5, p. 956.

negotiated. By 1950, their relative share declined somewhat, while the shares of pension funds and banks rose considerably. But the insurance companies still accounted for 83 per cent of the total.[13]

The importance to manufacturing and mining of this method of financing can be shown in another way. The Securities and Exchange Commission estimates that gross proceeds from cash sales of new corporate securities (debt and equity) by industrial corporations (including, in addition to manufacturing and mining, trade and services) for 1934–1949 amounted to $21.7 billion. Of this, an estimated $9.2 billion (42 per cent) was raised by private placements.[14] Private placement has been even more important for manufacturing during the postwar years. Between 1948 and 1951, for example, 65 per cent of

[13] Private sales were made mainly to a small group of large life insurance companies. According to E. Raymond Corey, direct placements acquired by the eighteen largest insurance companies (out of over 580 life insurance companies in the United States) represented almost 90 per cent of the dollar value of all directly negotiated securities. Case studies made by Corey lead him to the conclusion that "the large life insurance companies exercise an involuntary leadership in the direct placement market in two ways. First, they frequently are active in distributing to other institutional investors portions of the direct placements they have negotiated. Second, the decision on the part of a large insurance company to buy a part of a direct placement will almost invariably ensure its success. Similarly, rejection of an issue by a large company may seriously jeopardize the success of an issue." (E. Raymond Corey, *Direct Placement of Corporate Securities*, Harvard University Press, 1951, pp. 6, and 106–107).

[14] *Hearings, op. cit.*, p. 960.

TABLE 57

Distribution of Privately Placed Securities, by Major Manufacturing Industries, during 1951–1952

	Notes	Mortgages	Debentures	Preferred Stock	Common Stock	Not Specified	All Security Issues
Food and kindred products	5.2%	5.9%	3.4%	1.7%	n.i.	4.7%	4.9%
Textiles and products	6.2	0.5	0.6	14.5	55.9%	18.8	4.7
Leather and products	1.5	0.1	0.2	n.i.	n.i.	n.i.	1.1
Forest products	1.2	0.2	0.7	8.7	12.4	n.i.	1.1
Paper, pulp, and products	6.8	6.8	1.5	3.7	10.9	63.4	6.0
Printing and publishing	0.7	1.4	0.4	1.5	n.i.	1.4	0.7
Chemicals and allied products	17.7	4.8	10.0	31.7	20.8	n.i.	14.6
Petroleum refining	4.9	6.7	2.7	0.9	n.i.	n.i.	4.7
Rubber and products	5.7	n.i.	0.9	n.i.	n.i.	n.i.	3.9
Stone, clay, and glass products	3.5	0.3	1.4	1.7	n.i.	n.i.	2.6
Iron and steel and products	6.4	29.6	24.5	11.4	n.i.	8.6	13.0
Nonferrous metals and products	1.9	38.0	n.i.	n.i.	n.i.	n.i.	6.8
Machinery, excluding transportation	27.2	1.2	51.2	9.5	n.i.	3.1	27.1
Transportation equipment	9.7	4.4	1.7	14.7	n.i.	n.i.	7.5
Miscellaneous	1.5	0.3	1.0	n.i.	n.i.	n.i.	1.2
All manufacturing	100.0	100.0	100.0	100.0	100.0	100.0	100.0
Millions of Dollars	$1,411	$364	$510	$39	$20	$4	$2,348

n.i. = none issued.
Note: Detail may not add to totals because of rounding. The dollar amounts represent totals for 1951 and 1952.
Source: E. V. Hale, *1952 and 1953 Yearbooks of Private Placement Financing*, E. V. Hale and Company, Chicago, Ill.

all securities (as much as 82 per cent of debt) issued by corporate manufacturing was placed privately.[15]

Because of the prime importance of private placement to manufacturing firms and the likelihood of its continued importance, we prepared a cross-section analysis of private placements by manufacturing corporations during 1951 and 1952, using the listing of private placements compiled by E. V. Hale.[16] While his listing makes no claim to completeness, there can be no doubt that its coverage is comprehensive and accounts for more than 90 per cent of all private placements.

During 1951 and 1952, years of industrial mobilization for the Korean War, manufacturing firms raised $2.3 billion by private placement of securities. All major industry groups used this method of financing (Table 57). The largest amounts were obtained by the machinery group (excluding transportation equipment), chemicals and allied products, and iron and steel products (55 per cent of all private placements during 1951 and 1952—no other group accounted for even as much as 10 per cent). Printing and publishing, leather and its products, and forest products made the least use of private placement.

TABLE 58

Manufacturing Industries: Distribution of New Plant and Equipment Expenditures and of Privately Placed Loans, during 1951–1952

(per cent)

	Expenditures for New Plant and Equipment[a]	*Loans Privately Placed*[b]
All manufacturing	100.0	100.0
Food and kindred products	7.4	4.9
Paper, pulp, and products	3.4	6.0
Chemicals and allied products	11.8	14.6
Petroleum and coal products	20.6	4.7
Rubber products	1.3	3.9
Machinery, excluding transportation	9.6	27.1
Transportation equipment	9.7	7.5
Stone, clay, and glass products	3.1	2.6
Iron and steel and products plus nonferrous metals and products	19.4	19.8
All other manufacturing industries	13.7	8.9

[a] *Survey of Current Business*, Department of Commerce, September 1953, p. 4.
[b] See Table 57.

[15] *Privately Placed Securities—Cost of Flotation*, Securities and Exchange Commission, 1952, p. 6.
[16] The 1952 and 1953 *Yearbooks of Private Placement Financing*, E. V. Hale and Company, Chicago, Ill.

DEBT AND EQUITY FINANCING

The value of securities placed privately by industries can be compared only approximately to the interindustry distribution of new capital employed (Table 58). For a list of major industries shorter than Hale's, the table shows the percentage distribution of private placements including refunding issues and the Department of Commerce estimates of expenditures for new plant and equipment. If we take the latter to indicate the demand for total new capital, we can say that in eight of the ten groups the percentage shares of new capital and of private placements were similar. In petroleum and coal products, private placements were relatively small compared with capital expansion, and in machinery (excluding transportation equipment), relatively large.

For the two years, debt issues represented more than 98 per cent of all private placements (Table 59).[17] Notes accounted for about two-thirds of the debt and mortgages and debentures for about one-sixth each. The predominance of notes is found in each industry group except iron and steel and their products and nonferrous metals and their products. In the former, the distribution among notes, mortgages, and debentures was equal; and in the latter, mortgages were four-fifths of the total, notes one-fifth. Only in two groups—textiles and their products and forest products—did equities amount to more than 5 per cent of total placements.

The predominance of notes supports the contention that flexibility in the arrangement of terms is the chief advantage of private placement. That is, the debt claim can be tailored to fit the needs of the particular borrower. The note as a debt instrument is eminently suited to provide this flexibility.

On the length of the term between issue and maturity of debt, our tabulation of Hale's figures yields the following distributions:

Number of Debt Issues Placed Privately During 1951
and 1952, Classified by Years to Maturity

Years to Maturity	Number of Issues
5 or less	85
6 to 7	36
8 to 10	202
11 to 15	354
16 to 20	141
Over 20	42
Not specified	25
Total (excluding "not specified")	860
Median number of years	13

---

[17] This is something of an overstatement, since common stocks privately placed in 1952 were not completely listed by Hale "because of difficulties involved in obtaining accurate information." Other evidence suggests, however, that the inclusion of all privately placed common stocks would have little effect on the distribution.

TABLE 59

Manufacturing Industries: Distribution of Privately Placed Securities, by Type, during 1951–1952

(per cent)

Industry	Notes	Mortgages	Debentures	Preferred Stock	Common Stock	Not Specified	All Security Issues
All manufacturing	65.9	14.6	17.5	1.3	0.5	0.2	100.0
Food and kindred products	69.8	17.5	12.0	0.5	n.i.	0.2	100.0
Textiles and products	86.1	1.6	2.1	3.9	5.3	0.9	100.0
Leather and products	96.1	0.7	3.2				100.0
Forest products	71.3	3.1	10.7	9.9	5.0	n.i.	100.0
Paper, pulp, and products	75.0	16.5	4.4	0.8	0.8	2.5	100.0
Printing and publishing	61.1	26.7	9.2	2.6	n.i.	0.5	100.0
Chemicals and allied products	79.9	4.8	11.9	2.8	0.6	n.i.	100.0
Petroleum refining	68.6	21.0	10.2	0.2	n.i.	n.i.	100.0
Rubber and products	96.0	n.i.	4.0	n.i.	n.i.	n.i.	100.0
Stone, clay, and glass products	87.9	1.8	9.5	0.9	n.i.	n.i.	100.0
Iron and steel and products	32.5	33.4	32.9	1.1	n.i.	0.2	100.0
Nonferrous metals and products	18.3	81.7	n.i.	n.i.	n.i.	n.i.	100.0
Machinery, excluding transportation	66.0	0.6	32.9	0.4	n.i.	n.i.	100.0
Transportation equipment	85.0	8.6	3.9	2.5	n.i.	n.i.	100.0
Miscellaneous	81.6	3.8	14.6	n.i.	n.i.	n.i.	100.0

n.i. = none issued.
Source: See Table 57.

The median of thirteen years is practically equal to the term of 12.2 years for industrial bonds during 1930–1939. On the other hand, it is considerably lower than the 1900–1929 median.[18] Thus, while there has been a trend toward shortening the maturity term of bonds, the development of private placements does not appear to have further reduced the average duration of long-term credit.

BANK TERM LOANS. In recent decades, the demand of business enterprises for short-term credit failed to keep pace with increases in the general volume of business. Large corporations, having ample liquid resources, required little, if any, short-term bank credit. On the other hand, many firms—both large and small—developed a need for medium-term credit (i.e., loans with a maturity of more than one year but much less than the term of a typical bond issue). In response to this growing demand, commercial banks have changed their traditional policy of making only short-term "self-liquidating" loans and have developed a new type of financing called "term lending."

A term loan has a maturity of more than one year. It is usually redeemed by serial or installment repayments. It may be secured or unsecured, and may be obtained to expand the firm's current assets, fixed assets, or both.

Estimates of short-term and long-term bank loans to corporations (all industries combined) have been prepared for 1932–1952 by Irwin Friend (Table 60).[19] The volume of long-term loans outstanding has risen substantially (from $0.1 billion at the end of 1933, to $4.62 billion in 1952. Although the ratio of long-term loans to all bank loans was only 2 per cent in 1933, it rose to 36 per cent by 1948. In the years following, the ratio declined somewhat. However, long-term loans still accounted for 24 per cent of the total in 1952.

Friend's estimates cover loans to all industries. But, from the survey conducted by the Federal Reserve Board in 1947, we know that term loans by member banks to manufacturing and mining industries accounted for slightly more than one-half of the total amount of such loans outstanding near the end of 1946. The survey also showed that the ratio of term loans to all bank loans was higher in these two industries than in most of the others. In 1946, term loans were 42 per cent of the total in manufacturing and mining, while the figure for all industries was only 34 per cent.[20]

The ratio of long-term loans to total bank loans was higher for large manufacturing concerns (the FRB sample of 200 companies, 1938–1954),

[18] W. Braddock Hickman, *The Volume of Corporate Bond Financing since 1900*, Princeton University Press for National Bureau of Economic Research, 1953, p. 76.
[19] *Individuals' Saving, Volume and Composition*, Wiley, 1954, p. 37.
[20] Duncan Mc. C. Holthausen, "Term Lending to Business by Commercial Banks in 1946," *Federal Reserve Bulletin*, May 1947, pp. 498–517.

than for all corporations (Friend's estimates). For large concerns, term loans represented 65 per cent of all bank loans outstanding at the end of 1949. The relative importance of long-term credit, however, declined somewhat in the following years; indeed, by the end of 1954, long-term and short-term bank loans outstanding were almost equal.

TABLE 60

Corporate Short- and Long-Term Loans Outstanding held by Commerical Banks, All Corporations, 1932–1952
(dollars in billions as of end of year)

	Loans			Long-Term as Per Cent of Total
	Short-Term	Long-Term	Total	
1932	$ 4.68	$0.00	$4.68	0.0%
1933	4.04	0.10	4.14	2.4
1934	3.84	0.20	4.04	5.0
1935	3.65	0.37	4.02	9.2
1936	3.96	0.56	4.52	12.4
1937	4.68	0.68	5.36	12.7
1938	3.43	0.89	4.32	20.6
1939	3.64	1.32	4.96	26.6
1940	4.02	1.78	5.80	30.7
1941	5.21	2.22	7.43	29.9
1942	3.95	2.12	6.07	34.9
1943	4.36	1.86	6.22	29.9
1944	4.77	1.78	6.55	27.2
1945	5.03	2.24	7.27	30.8
1946	7.18	3.29	10.47	31.4
1947	8.62	4.47	13.09	34.1
1948	9.16	5.09	14.25	35.7
1949	7.51	3.84	11.35	33.8
1950	9.56	3.28	12.84	25.5
1951	13.44	3.85	17.29	22.3
1952	15.07	4.62	19.69	23.5

Source: Irwin Friend, *Individuals' Saving: Volume and Composition*, Wiley, 1954, p. 37.

The FRB survey revealed that, as of the end of 1946, 82 per cent of all term loans by member banks were made to corporations, 18 per cent to unincorporated businesses. In manufacturing and mining, corporations were even more important—91 per cent of the total.

Unsecured term loans accounted for 59 per cent, secured term loans for 41 per cent, of the total outstanding. The most important types of collateral used were plant or other real estate, chattel mortgages (particularly on equipment), and stocks and bonds including securities of affiliated companies. These three types were used for 72 per cent of the volume of secured loans.

A distribution of term loans according to the date of final payment is presented in Table 61. As of November 20, 1946, loans maturing

TABLE 61

Business Term Loans Outstanding Held by Member Banks, by Year of Final Payment, as of November 20, 1946

	Loans			
	Value[a] (millions of dollars)	Number (thousands)	Percentage Distribution	
			Value	Number
Loans past due	$ 13	0.8	0.3%	0.6%
Loans with final payment due in:				
1946	32	2.7	0.7	1.9
1947	437	39.0	9.6	27.0
1948	460	32.6	10.1	22.6
1949	326	19.1	7.2	13.2
1950	454	10.0	10.0	6.9
1951	577	14.4	12.7	9.9
1952	261	4.3	5.7	3.0
1953	327	3.1	7.2	2.1
1954	214	2.8	4.7	1.9
1955	691	4.3	15.2	2.9
1956	675	9.7	14.8	6.7
1957 or later	90	1.7	2.0	1.2
All term loans	4,558	144.4	100.0	100.0

Note: Detail may not add to totals because of rounding.

[a] Balance outstanding on November 20, 1946 on loans whose final payment falls due in the year indicated.

Source: Duncan McC. Holthausen, "Term Lending to Business by Commercial Banks in 1946," *Federal Reserve Bulletin*, May 1947, p. 499.

within five years accounted for four-fifths of the total number, and more than one-half of the total dollar amount, of loans outstanding. In contrast, only 1.2 per cent of the total number and 2 per cent of the total dollar amount had a term to maturity exceeding ten years. Most term loans, then, represented credit of much shorter duration than the prevalent type of corporate bonds. Small and medium-sized enterprises have needed this medium-term type of credit most, since, for many, the traditional sources of long-term credit have not been readily available. But large corporations, also, have made a significant use of term loans, along with the older types of long-term credit.

Short-Term External Financing

Except for recent years, our data on the flow of short-term funds are confined to samples of large manufacturing corporations. The statements of sources and uses of funds indicate that the relative importance of short-term financing, 1900–1953, fluctuated widely.

During 1900–1914, the inflow of short-term funds was only a small fraction of total new financing. But in 1914–1919, its relative importance rose sharply. The rise was largely due to a pronounced increase in accrued tax liabilities during the war; however, there was also a substantial rise in notes and accounts payable.

The inflow of all short-term funds was 26 per cent of total new financing (internal plus external) during the World War I cycle (see Table 44, above). In contrast, in the four cycles following, there was an outflow of short-term funds. In 1919–1921, tax accruals and accounts payable dropped sharply. The amount of notes payable (mainly short-term bank loans) was substantially reduced in the 1921–1924, 1924–1927, and 1927–1932 cycles. The contraction of short-term financing was especially significant in 1927–1932, when all major components—accruals, notes payable, and accounts payable—showed negative balances. The trend was again reversed in 1932–1938, when a considerable inflow of short-term financing was registered (all three components were positive).

In the 1938–1946 cycle, as in the 1914–1919 one, we find a pronounced rise in accrued tax liabilities. But the second war cycle differed from the first in that it showed no significant rise in short-term bank loans. Accounts payable, on the other hand, rose at a similar rate in both cycles. The inflow of all short-term funds amounted to 22 per cent of total new financing.

In the postwar cycles (1946–1949 and 1949–1954), large corporations continued to absorb short-term financing, mainly as accounts payable and income tax accruals. In this respect, the situation after World War II was essentially different from that observed after World War I, when the net outflow of short-term funds was substantial.

As a result of these fund flows, the balance sheet structure of large corporations changed significantly over the years from 1900 to 1953; the trend in the ratio of current liabilities to total assets is clearly upward (Chart 20).

Prior to 1914, current liabilities were about 10 per cent of total assets. The ratio increased sharply (to nearly 20 per cent) during World War I. It reversed during the twenties and the early thirties (in 1932, the ratio was as low as 4 per cent). The ratio began to increase again after 1932 and shot up to a new high during World War II (29 per cent in 1943). After the war, the ratio dropped to around 20 per cent—a level twice as high as that in the years following World War I.

A comparison between the 1937 and 1948 data for different asset-size classes shows that in both years the ratio of total current liabilities to total assets varied inversely with asset size (Chart 18). The range of variation in the ratio was, however, considerably greater in 1937 than in 1948. In every class except the two lowest the relative importance of short-term liabilities increased materially over the eleven years. For all classes combined, the ratio rose from 17 to 21 per cent.

As with long-term debt, the ratio is considerably lower for companies with net income than for companies without net income. This is true in both 1937 and 1948.

But there were certain differences in the behavior of the major components of short-term debt (Chart 21). The ratio of accounts payable to total assets shows a pattern of variation generally similar to that displayed by the ratio of total short-term debt to total assets. (Since accounts payable were roughly one-half of total current liabilities, variation in this component was largely responsible for variation in the total.)

Notes payable[21] differed from the other two components of short-term debt in that they rose more slowly beween 1937 and 1948 than did total assets. As a result, in every class, the ratio of notes payable to total assets was lower in 1948 than in 1937.

The ratio of other liabilities to total assets showed a pronounced rise from 1937 to 1948, especially in the highest classes. Although, in 1937, the ratio showed a strong tendency to decline as asset size increased, in 1948, it remained remarkably stable for most classes.

In 1948, "other liabilities," unlike the other components of short-term debt, were more important for corporations with net income than for those without net income. This was true of most classes in mining as well as in manufacturing. In manufacturing, for all classes combined, the ratio of other liabilities to total assets was 8.8 per cent for profitable concerns, 7.2 per cent for unprofitable concerns. (In mining, the corresponding figures were 8.5 and 8.3 per cent.) In 1937, on the other hand, "other liabilities" were less important for corporations with net income than for those without net income—a pattern similar to that found for the other components of short-term debt.

This difference between 1937 and 1948 is accounted for by a difference in the relative importance of income tax accruals included here under "other liabilities." In 1948, corporations with net income

[21] Primarily loans due to commercial banks. See Chudson, *op. cit.*, p. 46.

LONG-TERM TRENDS IN CAPITAL FINANCING

CHART 21

Ratios of Short-Term Debt to Total Assets, All Manufacturing and Mining Corporations with Balance Sheets, by Total-Asset Classes, 1937 and 1948

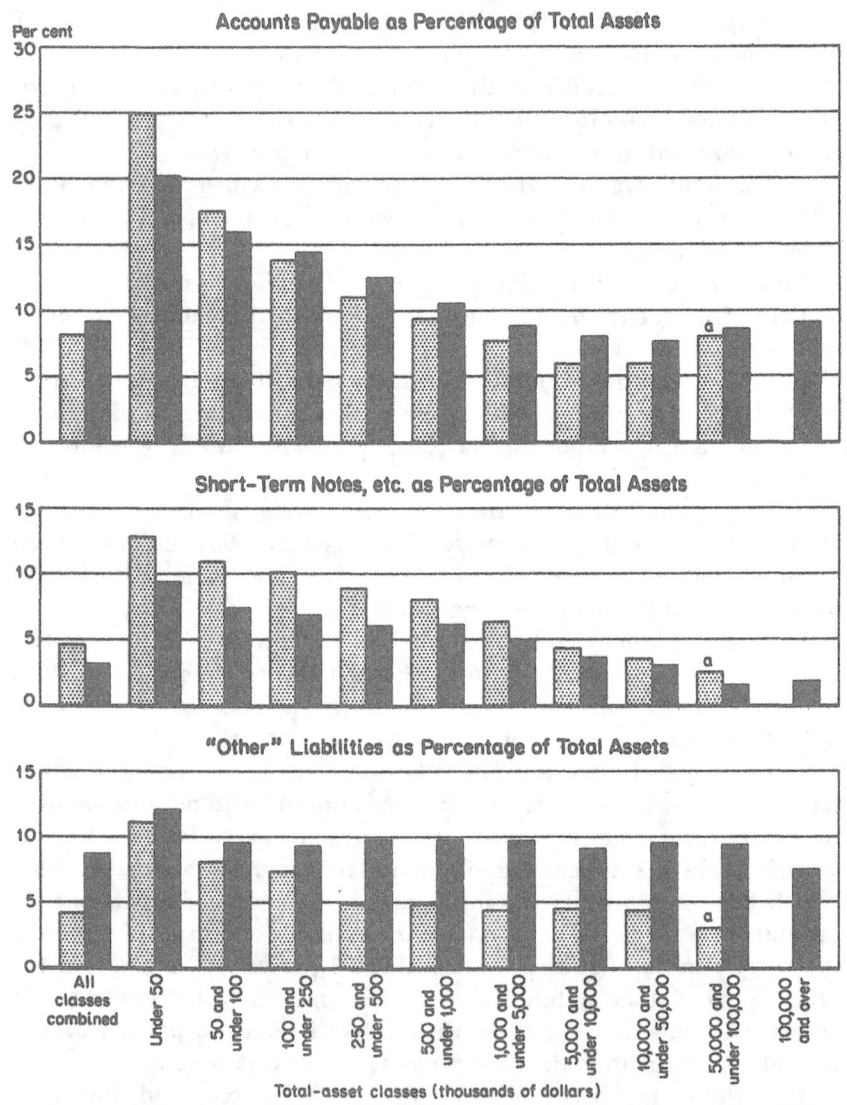

a Last two classes combined.
Source: Appendix Table C-4.

DEBT AND EQUITY FINANCING

CHART 22

Ratios of Selected Assets to Total Assets, Large Manufacturing Corporations, 1900–1954

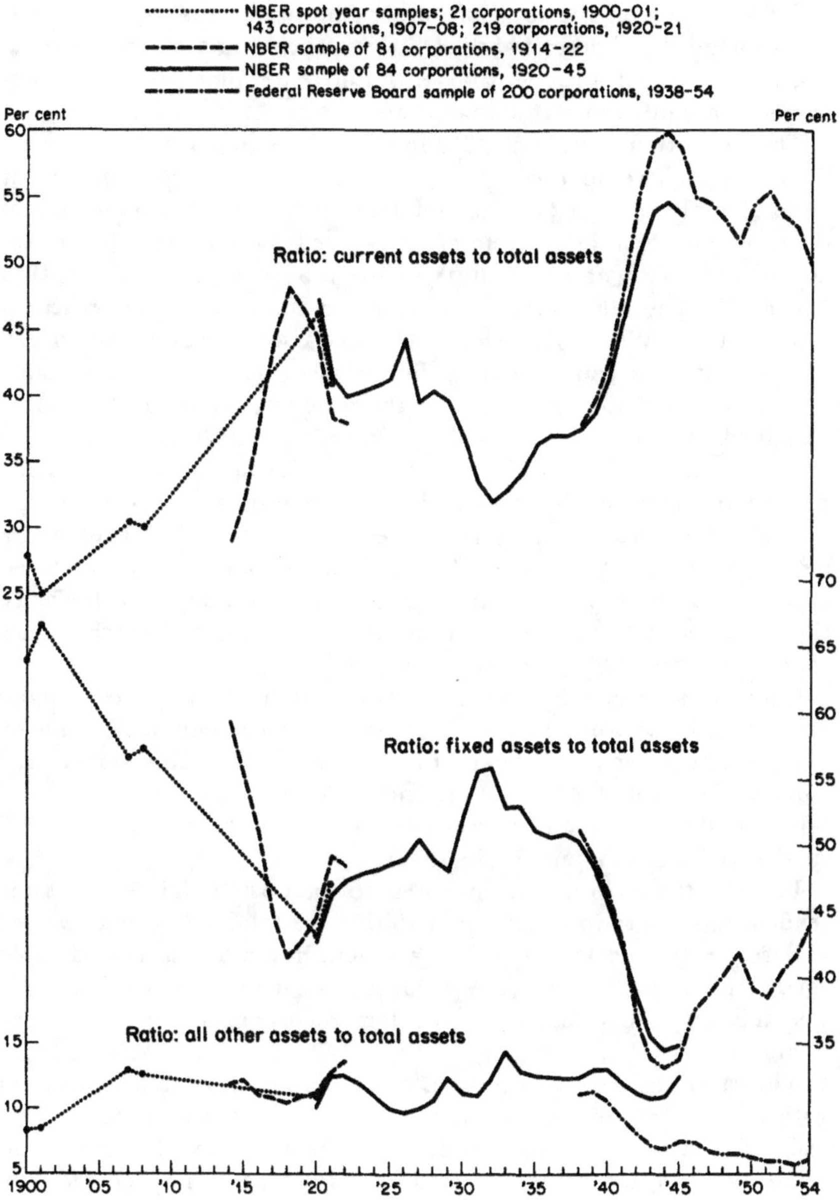

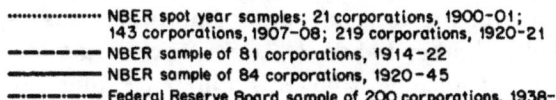

·············· NBER spot year samples; 21 corporations, 1900–01;
143 corporations, 1907–08; 219 corporations, 1920–21
– – – – NBER sample of 81 corporations, 1914–22
———— NBER sample of 84 corporations, 1920–45
–·–·–·– Federal Reserve Board sample of 200 corporations, 1938–54

Source: Same as Table 43.

had to accrue substantial amounts for tax purposes. These accruals were primarily responsible for the large total of "other liabilities" reported by such corporations. In 1937, tax accruals made by corporations with net income were smaller because of lower income tax rates, and their effect on the total of "other liabilities" was weaker. Other items included in "other liabilities" were much larger among corporations without net income, and this difference more than counterbalanced the difference in tax accruals.

The rise between 1900 and 1953 in the relative importance of current liabilities was accompanied by a similar tendency on the part of current assets. Sample data for large manufacturing corporations indicate that the ratio of current assets to total assets rose from less than 30 per cent at the beginning of the century to over 50 per cent around 1950 (Chart 22). The ratio increased during the first two decades, reaching a peak during World War I. The wartime rise was mainly accounted for by a large accumulation of liquid assets—cash and marketable securities. The ratio declined after the war, but the level at which it remained throughout most of the twenties was much higher than before the war. A further decline occurred during the early thirties, principally because of a contraction in inventories and accounts receivable. The ratio began to rise once more after 1932 and reached a new high during World War II, mainly on account of a pronounced expansion of liquid assets. After World War II (as after World War I), the ratio declined from its wartime peak but remained much higher than it had been before the war.

Current assets of large manufacturing corporations showed a more pronounced rise from 1900 to 1929 than did current liabilities (the current ratio—current assets divided by current liabilities—increased from 3.5 in 1900 to 4.0 in 1914, and to 5.4 in 1929). From 1930 on, however, the tendency was reversed (the current ratio declined to 4.2 in 1937, 2.5 in 1948, and 2.1 in 1952).

In 1937, the ratio of current assets to total assets showed the same tendency as the ratio of current liabilities to total assets: both varied inversely with size; the range of variation, however, was considerably smaller for current assets (Chart 23). Consequently, the current ratio was substantially stronger for the larger corporations than for the smaller ones.

The ratio of fixed assets to total assets did not show much variation with size in 1937. As expected, the ratio of all other assets to total assets was much higher for large corporations than for medium-sized and small ones, because "other assets" of the large concerns included substantial investments in subsidiaries.

In 1948, the ratios of current assets to total assets were generally

CHART 23

Ratios of Selected Assets to Total Assets, All Manufacturing and Mining Corporations with Balance Sheets, by Total-Asset Classes, 1937 and 1948

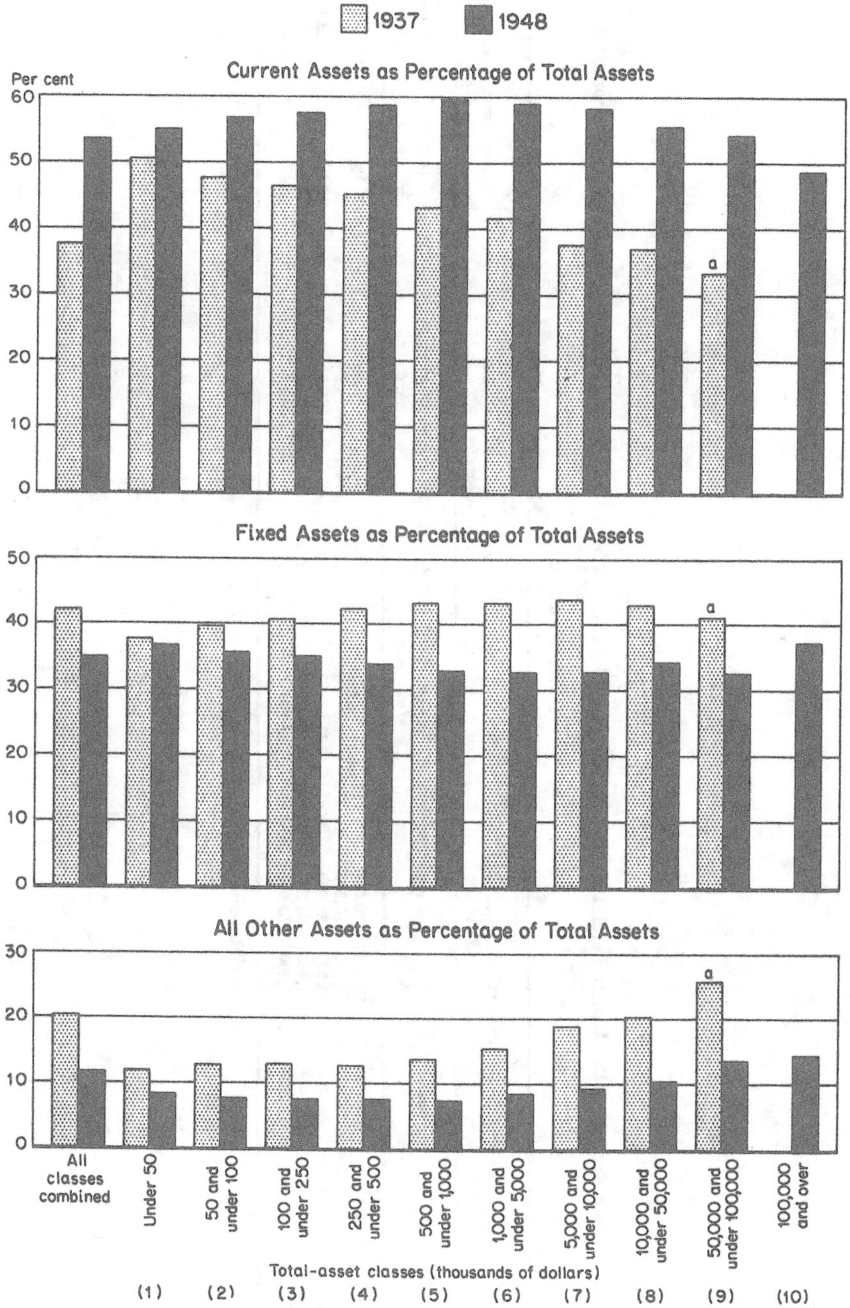

ᵃ Last two classes combined.   Source: Appendix Table C-4.

TABLE 62

Debt Excluding Tax Liability and Total Assets Excluding Government Securities, All Manufacturing and Mining Corporations
Selected Years, 1929–1952
(dollars in millions)

	Total Assets		Type of Debt				Debt Less Tax Liability as Percentage of Total Assets Less Government Securities		Debt as Percentage of Total Assets	
			Total		Current					
	(1)	Less Govt. Securities (2)	(3)	Less Tax Liability (4)	(5)	Less Tax Liability (6)	Total Debt (Col. 4) ÷ (Col. 2) (7)	Current Debt (Col. 6) ÷ (Col. 2) (8)	Total (Col. 3) ÷ (Col. 1) (9)	Current (Col. 5) ÷ (Col. 1) (10)
1929	$ 82,114	$79,876	$20,601	$20,013	$14,114	$13,526	25.1%	16.9%	25.1%	17.2%
1937	64,869	63,564	17,007	16,308	10,978	10,279	25.7	16.2	26.2	16.9
1943	100,201	90,674	35,623	25,025	28,472	17,874	27.6	19.7	35.6	28.4
1948	130,750	122,308	40,488	33,320	27,554	20,386	27.2	16.7	31.0	21.1
1952	182,316	169,535	64,888	53,037	43,684	31,833	31.3	18.8	35.6	24.0

Source: *Statistics of Income*, Bureau of Internal Revenue (now Internal Revenue Service), Part 2.

DEBT AND EQUITY FINANCING

higher than they had been in 1937, but the extent of inter-class variation was smaller. Only for the largest corporations (Class 10) was the ratio considerably below the general level. The ratios for small corporations were a little lower, rather than higher, than the ratios for the medium-sized ones (Classes 5 and 6).

As in 1937, the current ratio increased with size in 1948. However, the range of variation was narrower in the later year, owing to a considerable improvement in the ratios for the smaller corporations.

In all classes, fixed assets were less important in 1948 than in 1937. The postwar ratios, like the prewar ones, show no clear relation to size. The ratio of "other assets" to total assets, also, declined between 1937 and 1948 in all classes. In both years, this ratio has tended to increase with increasing asset size.

The growth in assets and liabilities that represents claims between corporations and the government has had an impact on the balance sheet structure. On the asset side, there was a pronounced rise in corporate holdings of government securities—both in relation to other balance sheet items and absolutely. On the liability side, there was an even more pronounced increase, both absolutely and relatively, in corporate income tax accruals. These changes were largely responsible for the shifts in the debt-to-assets ratio. If government items are omitted from the balance sheet, its structure appears much more stable. This is illustrated in Table 62 where two sets of debt-to-assets ratios are presented. For all manufacturing and mining, the ratio of total current liabilities to total capital (total assets) rose from 17 per cent in 1929 to 21 per cent in 1948 and to 24 per cent in 1952. But if current liabilities are adjusted to exclude tax accruals, and total assets, to exclude government securities, the ratio is practically the same in 1948 as in 1929 and 1937. The adjusted ratio for 1952 is higher than the prewar one, but by a much smaller margin than that shown by the unadjusted ratio. Also, the ratio of total debt to total assets was higher in 1948 than it was before the war or in 1952, whether the adjusted or the unadjusted data are used. Again, the exclusion of government items considerably reduces the differences.

Summary of Findings

1. In general, manufacturing and mining corporations have not relied heavily on debt financing—especially of the long-term type. However, total debt outstanding expanded considerably over the past half-century, not only in absolute volume, but also in relation to total capital invested. In manufacturing, the ratio of interest-bearing debt to total operating costs rose from approximately 14 per cent in 1890 to

18 per cent in 1952.[22] The ratio of total debt (long-term and current liabilities) to total assets increased from 23 per cent in 1923 to 36 per cent in 1952. Similar tendencies are revealed by the data for mining.

The debt-to-assets ratio rises even when the current values of assets are substituted for book values. However, the degree of change is much smaller when adjusted asset values are used.

The corporate asset-size data for 1937 and 1948 indicate that in both years the ratio for total debt to total assets was higher for large companies than for small ones. The data also show that in both years the relative importance of total debt was smaller for companies with net income than for companies without net income.

2. The ratio of bond debt outstanding to total capital invested in operating assets shows no clear trend over the period reviewed. In 1952, bond debt of all manufacturing corporations amounted to approximately 7 per cent of their combined operating assets. This figure is higher than the one for 1937, but lower than those for 1929 and some earlier years.

After World War II, the importance of new bond issues relative to new stock issues rose sharply. Low bond yields, the deductibility of interest charges in computing taxable income, and certain other factors were responsible for this change. On the other hand, new bond issues were not especially high in relation to the postwar accumulation of internal funds. In fact, the ratio of new bond issues to retained net profit, 1900–1953, shows a downward trend. The ratio of new bond issues to total inflow of equity funds (new stock issues plus net profit retention) also declined slightly in the same period.

3. Short-term debt rose substantially in relation to total assets over the period reviewed. Sample data for large corporations show that, before 1914, current liabilities represented approximately 10 per cent of total assets. The ratio increased sharply during World War I (up to nearly 20 per cent), but then declined in the twenties and the first half of the thirties (in 1932, it was as low as 4 per cent). It began to rise again in the second half of the thirties and reached a new high during World War II (29 per cent in 1943). After the war, the ratio dropped to around 20 per cent—still twice as high as the post-World War I figure.

The 1937 and 1948 data for different asset-size classes show that the ratio of current liabilities to total assets varies inversely with asset size. In both years, the ratio was lower for companies with net income than for companies without net income.

4. The rise, 1900–1953, in the relative importance of current liabilities was accompanied by a similar tendency on the part of current

[22] Operating assets are defined as total assets less investments in securities.

assets. The rise in current assets, however, was less pronounced. As a result, the current ratio (current assets divided by current liabilities) declined. For our samples of large manufacturing companies, the current ratio first rose (from 3.4 in 1900 and 1914, to 5.4 in 1929), but then declined (4.2 in 1937, 2.5 in 1948, and 2.1 in 1952).

5. Accrued tax liabilities represented the fastest growing component of total current liabilities. Accumulation of tax accruals on the liability side was accompanied by an expansion of corporate holdings of government securities on the asset side. If these items, representing transactions with the government sector, are omitted from the balance sheet, its structure shows considerable stability. Thus, the ratio of current liabilities, exclusive of tax accruals, to total assets, exclusive of government securities, is practically the same for 1948 as for 1937 or 1929. The ratio for 1952 is higher than the prewar ones, but the difference is much smaller when the above items are omitted than it is when they are included.

PART III
Appendixes A, B, and C

APPENDIX A

Notes on Estimates of Capital, Output and Employment in Manufacturing, 1880–1953

A. Sources and Adjustments of Reported Values

1. SOURCES

Censuses of Manufactures were the source of information on capital and output for the benchmark years between 1880 and 1919. For the benchmark years following 1919, the data were taken from the "Source Book" of *Statistics of Income*, Part II, the compilation of corporate income-tax returns prepared by the Internal Revenue Service (formerly Bureau of Internal Revenue) of the Treasury Department. The estimates of capital from these two sources can be considered as a continuous series only if the estimates from the two sources are comparable. The following paragraphs present the basis for our conviction that the two series are sufficiently comparable to be treated as continuous for our purposes. The comparability of concepts of capital used in the various censuses from 1880 to 1919 is discussed in Chapter I.

a. Value of Capital in Manufacturing and Mining: *Censuses of Manufactures* and *of Mines*, 1919[1] compared with *Statistics of Income for 1919*. After the census of 1870, Francis A. Walker, Superintendent of the Census, warned the public, in no uncertain terms, of the gross inadequacies of the census reports on the value of capital used in manufacturing industries. He asserted, "It is a pity, and may almost be said to be a shame, that statistical information, in many respects, of high authority and accuracy, should be discredited by association with statements [on capital] so flagrantly false, even to the least critical eye.... The aggregate amount of capital invested in manufactures in the United States is $2,118,208,769. It is doubtful whether this sum represents one-fourth of the capital actually contributing to the annual gross product of $4,232,325,442."[2]

At later canvasses by the Bureau of the Census, serious misgivings about the accuracy of the inquiry on capital continued to be expressed, although in somewhat more moderate terms. Even in 1919, the last census to include the query on capital, the authorities felt constrained to remark that "the data compiled in respect to capital ... [at this

---

[1] *Fourteenth Census of the United States, 1920*, Vol. VIII: *Manufactures, 1919* (hereafter, *Census of Manufactures, 1919*); Vol. IX: *Mines and Quarries, 1919*.

[2] *Ninth Census of the United Census, 1870*, Volume III, *The Statistics of Wealth and Industry of the United States, 1870*, p. 382.

195

APPENDIX A

census], as well as at all preceding censuses of manufactures, have been considered as being of limited value except as indicating very general conditions. While there are some establishments whose accounting systems are such that an accurate return for capital could be made, this is not true of the great majority...."[3]

Should these disclaimers be taken at face value? Should we disregard the census statistics on value of capital in manufacturing industries? There are strong a priori reasons for believing that the margin of error attached to statements on value of capital is wider than that which attaches to statements on value of product or number employed. Is the margin as gross as the authorities want us to believe? Certainly, the authorities have never demonstrated the validity of their claims.

Moreover, in view of the absence, prior to 1919, of other data on capital, the temptation to utilize these data is great indeed. Little wonder, then, that investigators who succumb to the temptation attempt to disprove the claim of the census authorities.

The attempt can be made only for 1919. We compare the value of capital as reported in the *Census of Manufactures, 1919* with the value of investment as reported to *Statistics of Income for 1919*. If the figures on capital derived from both sources are approximately the same, we may have confidence that the figure from either source is reasonably "true." If similar approximations can be shown to exist in manufacturing groups, our confidence in the data will be further strengthened.

Figures from each source must be adjusted to achieve comparability with respect to the following characteristics: (1) industrial coverage; (2) legal organization; and (3) definition of capital.

Industrial coverage. Statistics of Income for 1919 classifies investment in manufacturing corporations into 11 industry groups; no further industry detail is given. Capital in *Census of Manufactures, 1919*, however, is reported for minor industries classified into 14 major industry groups. In view of the inflexibility of the industry classification in *Statistics of Income*, comparability can be achieved only by rearranging the industry groups in the *Census of Manufactures* to conform with those in *Statistics of Income*.

This involves more than combining the 14 census groups into 11. Certain industries canvassed by the census are not included in the *Statistics of Income* classification of manufacturing and, accordingly, had to be eliminated from the census figures.[4] Other changes involved

---
[3] *Census of Manufactures, 1919*, p. 11.
[4] The most important of the eliminated industries are manufactured gas, shipbuilding, and railroad repair shops.

shifting various minor industries from one major classification to another. Undoubtedly, if complete knowledge of the industrial classification was available, additional shifts would be required for strict comparability, but the presumption is strong that such cases are not quantitatively important.

Legal organization. The tabulations from *Statistics of Income* useful for our purposes are those which relate only to corporations. Accordingly, it is necessary to eliminate capital used by unincorporated establishments from the census totals. This is accomplished by assuming that the ratio of capital used by unincorporated establishments to capital of all establishments is identical with the ratio of value of product in unincorporated establishments to the value of product in all establishments. Value of product by unincorporated and incorporated establishments is reported by minor industries in the *Census of Manufactures 1919*. The required ratios could, therefore, be computed for major classifications by aggregating the figures for the minor industries in a given major industrial classification.

Definition of capital. The census inquiry on capital asked each establishment to report the book value of:

1. Land, buildings, machinery, and tools
2. Materials, stocks in process, finished products, fuel, and miscellaneous supplies
3. Cash, bills receivable, and sundries.

The sum of these three entries equals the total capital of each establishment, and this total is equivalent to total assets excluding investments in other establishments.

Statistics of Income for 1919 reported invested capital—the sum of the par value of preferred and common stock and surplus. In other words, we are confronted with the problem of determining the relation between net worth (invested capital) and total assets excluding securities. For such a determination, balance sheet data are indispensable.

In practice, then, we are obliged to rely on balance sheets for 1919. These are in *Moody's Analyses of Investments, Industrial Securities, 1920* (*Moody's Manual of Industrials*). From this source, we compiled a sample of 619 manufacturing companies operating in the United States. The companies in the sample are classified into the 11 major industry groups used by *Statistics of Income*. For each subsample of companies we computed total net worth, total assets excluding securities, and the ratio of total assets to net worth. In this manner we obtain a ratio, for each major industry group, to raise the group total of invested capital reported (with adjustments) in *Statistics of Income*

APPENDIX A

to the census level. Invested capital inflated by these raising ratios is considered equivalent in concept to capital as reported in the *Census of Manufactures*.

How representative are raising ratios based on the large corporations which comprise the *Moody's* sample? Using *Statistics of Income for 1937*, Sidney S. Alexander has investigated the variation in the ratio of net worth to total assets of manufacturing corporations classified by asset size.

Net Worth as Per Cent of Total Assets, 1937

Total Assets (thousands of dollars)	
All combined	74.0
Under $50	43.5
$50 and under $100	56.5
$100 and under $250	61.7
$250 and under $500	68.5
$500 and under $1,000	70.8
$1,000 and under $5,000	73.8
$5,000 and under $10,000	76.3
$10,000 and under $50,000	76.7
$50,000 and under $100,000	73.3
$100,000 and over	77.0

Source: Sidney S. Alexander, "Financial Structure of American Corporations since 1900," manuscript, National Bureau of Economic Research, 1945, p. 100A.

These computations suggest that the net worth ratios for large manufacturing corporations are very similar to the average for all manufacturing corporations. Moreover, these ratios for the large corporations are more representative of all manufacturing than would be the net worth ratios for either the small or medium-sized corporations. These findings relate to 1937 and not to 1919. However, they may well hold for 1919 also, since Alexander finds "striking the long-run stability of the net worth ratio as indicated by data available from the various samples and aggregated materials for the years 1903–1939" (*ibid.*, p. 99).

In Table A-1 we present information on our corporate sample and the sample ratios of assets minus securities to invested capital (capital stock plus surplus).

Before we present the results of our comparison, it is necessary to describe adjustments made to the figures on invested capital reported in *Statistics of Income for 1919*. The reported figures relate only to net income corporations filing information on invested capital. To reach a total for all manufacturing corporations, we require estimates of invested capital in net income corporations that failed to submit such information and in deficit corporations. The estimating procedure and the results are set out in Table A-2 (parallel treatment was accorded

TABLE A-1

Assets as Percentage of Invested Capital, Sample Drawn from *Moody's* of Manufacturing and Mining Corporations, 1919

(dollars in thousands)

		Sample from Moody's			
	Corporations (number) (1)	Total Assets Minus Securities (2)	Total Invested Capital[a] (3)	Assets as Per cent of Invested Capital (Col. 2 ÷ Col. 3) (4)	Invested Capital as (Col. 3) Per cent of Universe[b] (5)
Mining	122	$3,127,206	$2,557,120	122.29%	50.06%
All manufacturing	619				
Food and kindred products	73	2,504,123	1,663,085	150.57	41.58
Textiles and their products	112	910,892	667,373	136.49	18.96
Leather and leather products	21	521,245	370,867	140.55	43.40
Rubber products	29	725,077	542,177	133.73	72.19
Forest products	13	177,673	140,126	126.80	7.44
Paper, pulp, and products	26	312,899	245,094	127.66	29.84
Printing, publishing, and allied products	8	48,065	43,062	111.62	5.73
Chemicals and allied products	52	1,729,612	1,480,012	116.86	46.29
Stone, clay, and glass products	15	145,810	132,140	110.35	15.32
Metals and metal products	256	8,058,931	6,020,088	133.87	52.47
Miscellaneous and unclassified	14	96,152	76,848	125.12	9.72

[a] Sum of par value of common and preferred stocks plus surplus.
[b] For manufacturing, the universe is from Table A-3, column 1, adjusted by distributing a part of unclassified invested capital in the "miscellaneous and unclassified" category among the other industries; for mining, from Table A-3, column 1.

Source: Sample drawn from *Moody's Manual of Industrials, 1920.*

APPENDIX A

TABLE A-2

Derivation of Total Invested Capital in All Manufacturing Corporations, by Major Industries, 1919

	Food and Kindred Products	Textiles and Their Products	Leather and Leather Products	Rubber Products	Forest Products	Paper, Pulp, and Products	Printing and Publishing	Chemicals and Allied Products	Stone, Clay and Glass Products	Metals and Metal Products	Miscellaneous	All Manufacturing
A. Net income of net income corps.	$ 619,825	$ 912,379	$ 241,384	$ 126,832	$ 284,224	$ 129,235	$ 128,968	$ 451,771	$ 107,048	$1,789,213	$ 428,467	$5,219,345
B. Net inc. of corps. reporting invested capital	618,403	911,336	240,559	126,281	283,952	128,634	127,183	450,349	106,789	1,788,471	427,827	5,209,784
C. Net inc. of corps. not reporting invest. cap. (A less B)	1,422	1,043	825	551	272	601	1,785	1,422	259	742	640	9,561
D. Invest. cap. of reporting net inc. corps.	2,550,966	3,269,687	794,375	671,118	1,675,613	741,567	642,853	2,807,053	748,114	10,126,361	2,163,959	26,191,665
E. Net inc. as % of invest. cap. for reporting corps., [(B/D) × 100]	24.24%	27.87%	30.28%	18.82%	16.95%	17.35%	19.78%	16.04%	14.27%	17.66%	19.77%	
F. Est. invest. cap. of net inc. corps. not reporting invest. cap., (C/E)	$ 5,866	$ 3,742	$ 2,725	$ 2,928	$ 1,605	$ 3,464	$ 9,024	$ 8,865	$ 1,815	$ 4,202	$ 3,237	$ 47,473
G. Total invest. cap. of net inc. corps., (D+F)	2,556,832	3,273,429	797,100	674,046	1,677,218	745,031	651,877	2,815,918	749,929	10,130,563	2,167,196	26,239,139
H. Gross income of all net inc. corps.	9,489,362	7,014,671	2,169,701	1,107,240	2,329,241	1,141,822	1,174,550	4,243,045	769,796	12,616,662	3,648,785	45,704,874
I. Gross inc. as % of invest. cap. of net inc. corps. [(H/G) × 100]	371.14%	214.29%	272.20%	164.27%	138.88%	153.26%	180.18%	150.69%	102.65%	124.54%	168.36%	
J. Gross inc. of deficit corps.	$4,550,450	$ 120,989	$ 29,295	$ 59,619	$ 143,523	$ 49,234	$ 106,795	$ 314,106	$ 67,820	$ 897,479	$ 245,393	$6,584,703
K. Est. invest. cap. of deficit corps. (J/I)	1,226,074	56,460	10,762	36,293	103,343	32,124	59,271	208,459	66,069	720,635	145,755	2,665,245
L. Total invest. cap., all corps. (G+K)	3,782,906	3,329,889	807,862	710,339	1,780,561	777,155	711,148	3,024,377	815,998	10,851,198	2,312,951	28,904,384

Source: Lines A, B, D, H, and J from *Statistics of Income for 1919*, Bureau of Internal Revenue (now Internal Revenue Service), pp. 9, 18, 18, 9, 10, respectively.

the published tabulations for mining corporations). The two estimates of capital, one based on tabulations in the *Census of Manufactures, 1919* and the other based on *Statistics for Income for 1919*, and the final steps in the estimating procedure are presented in Table A-3.

One element of incomparability in the two sources could not be eliminated. The Bureau of the Census collects reports on an establishment basis. This means that the capital of a multiindustry firm is unlikely to be classified as devoted to but one industry. On the other hand, the Internal Revenue Service, in 1919, permitted corporations to file a consolidated return. That is, a corporation engaged in multiindustry activity would file only one return, and the consolidated figures would be classified under the one industry that represented its single most important industrial activity. Thus, the capital devoted to coal mines operated by a steel mill would be classified under metals and their products (the appropriate classification for a steel mill) by the Internal Revenue Service. The Bureau of the Census, however, would classify under metals and their products only the capital used by the steel mill; the capital devoted to coal mining would be reported in the *Census of Mines*.

In view of the differences in reporting units, perfect agreement of the two estimates for a given industry group would not signify accuracy of the respective estimates. For all manufacturing industries, one would expect estimated capital derived from *Statistics of Income* to exceed the comparable estimate derived from the *Census of Manufactures*; for mining, the relationship should be reversed. For manufacturing and mining combined, one would expect, also, that an estimate based on consolidated returns would exceed an estimate based on establishment returns, since a consolidated return, in some instances, would include (in addition to capital used in mining) capital used in distribution and transportation ancillary to manufacturing activity.

A comparison of our estimates from the two sources (Table A-3, column 8) supports the above expectations. Thus, for all manufacturing, capital derived from *Statistics of Income* exceeds capital based on the *Census of Manufactures* by 6.4 per cent. In mining, however, capital from *Statistics of Income* is 6 per cent less than capital from the *Census of Mines*. On a combined basis, capital from *Statistics of Income* is 4.4 per cent higher than the comparable estimates from census reports. That is, the differences are small and in directions that seem reasonable. The allegations of gross inaccuracy made against the reports of capital in the *Census of Manufactures* appear to be without foundation for the aggregate in 1919.

For major industrial divisions, the differences between the two

APPENDIX A

TABLE A-3

Derivation of Estimates of Capital in Major Manufacturing Industries and in Mining, 1919
(dollars in thousands)

Manufacturing	Invested Capital (Stat. of Inc.) (1)	Assets as Per cent of Invested Capital (Sample from Moody's) (2)	Total Investment (col. 1 × col. 2) (3)	Capital of All Establishments (Census) (4)	Value of Output: Corporations as Per cent of All Establishments (5)	Capital of Corporations (col. 4 × col. 5) (6)	Total Investment after Allocation of Unclassified Investment[a] (7)	Investment (Stat. of Inc.) as Per cent of Capital (Census) (col. 7 ÷ col. 6) (8)
Food and kindred products	$3,782,906	150.57%	$5,695,922	$6,272,291	83.39%	$5,230,463	$5,966,925	114.08%
Textiles and their products	3,329,889	136.49	4,544,965	6,180,888	74.93	4,631,339	4,783,674	103.29
Leather and leather products	807,862	140.55	1,135,450	1,522,501	84.60	1,288,036	1,193,744	92.68
Rubber products	710,339	133.73	949,936	960,071	99.54	955,655	1,000,802	104.72
Forest products	1,780,561	126.80	2,257,751	2,731,251	79.29	2,165,609	2,385,402	110.15
Paper, pulp, and their products	777,155	127.66	992,116	1,194,579	93.92	1,121,949	1,047,554	93.37
Printing, publishing, and allied products	711,148	111.62	793,783	1,189,426	79.99	951,422	844,659	88.78
Chemicals and allied products	3,024,377	116.86	3,534,287	4,132,593	96.28	3,978,861	3,750,897	94.27
Stone, clay, and glass products	815,998	110.35	900,454	1,282,920	87.69	1,124,993	958,750	85.22
Metals and metal products	10,851,198	133.87	14,526,499	14,037,321	96.10	13,489,865	15,303,925	113.45
Miscellaneous and unclassified	2,312,951	125.12	2,893,964	1,189,681	83.12	988,863	988,863[a]	100.00[a]
All manufacturing	28,904,384		38,225,127	40,693,522		35,927,055	38,225,195	106.40
Mining	5,108,109	122.29	6,246,706	7,108,623		6,652,695[b]		93.90[c]
Total, manufacturing and mining	34,012,493		44,471,833	47,802,145		42,579,750		104.44[c]

(continued)

estimates are larger. However, in no case is the difference so large as to imply that the census estimate of capital is grossly understated. Indeed, in half of the industry groups, the census estimate is higher than the estimate from *Statistics of Income*. However, it is necessary to remember that an important link in the estimating procedure for *Statistics of Income* data is the adjustment of net worth by raising ratios derived from the *Moody's* sample. For some industries, the sample of corporations is small (Table A-1, column 5), and the ratio may not, therefore, be representative. For any one industrial group, the largest difference between the two estimates did not exceed 15 per cent; in 6 of the 10 groups (we exclude "miscellaneous"), the differences were 10 per cent or less.

The *Statistics of Income* estimate for metals and their products is some 13 per cent higher than the one derived from the census. The direction of the difference is, we believe, correct, since fabricating mills, included in this group, frequently operate mining properties. For the same reason, we would have expected the same direction of difference in stone, clay, and glass products, but, in this instance, our expectation was not fulfilled. However, our sample from *Moody's* for this particular group is small.

This reconciliation of estimates of capital based on reports submitted to two different federal agencies is reasonably close not only for all manufacturing, but also for the major subdivisions. We accept a reasonably close reconciliation as evidence of the approximate accuracy of the respective estimates.

It may be argued, however, that our reconciliation relates to 1919, eleven years after the enactment of the federal corporation income tax law which obliged most corporations to maintain a systematic set of accounting records. The census reports on capital prior to 1909, this

---

NOTES TO TABLE A-3

[a] The "miscellaneous" category of *Statistics of Income* includes, also, the investment of corporations that cannot be classified because of insufficient information. We have arbitrarily assumed that capital for "miscellaneous" industries as derived from *Census of Manufactures* is the "true" figure for this classification and that the excess of capital for this classification as derived from *Statistics of Income* represents capital of unclassified industries. This excess after reduction to invested capital as reported in *Statistics of Income* is then redistributed among the various industries, using invested capital in column 1 as weights. These additions of invested capital are raised by the appropriate ratios in column 2, and the resulting products added to the figures in column 3.

[b] Sum of mining industry components, estimated as for manufacturing.

[c] Column 3 divided by column 6.

Source: For manufacturing, column 1 from Table A-2, line 1; for mining, estimated as in Table A-2, based on *Statistics of Income, 1919*; column 2 from Table A-1, column 4; columns 4 and 5 from 1919 *Census of Manufactures and Census of Mines*.

APPENDIX A

argument contends, must involve larger errors which increase with each backward extension of the time period covered. We are able to make only an indirect assessment of this type of argument, and on this we must rely.

Since we have an approximately accurate measure of capital for our terminal year, 1919, we can examine the changes in this magnitude from one census year to another for "reasonableness"—the absence of any serious discrepancy between the movement of capital and that of output. The large majority of the minor industries pass this test of reasonableness.

We conclude this effort of appraising the accuracy of the census reports on capital by commenting on the findings of several other investigators. John R. Arnold (in "Manufacturing Capital and Output, 1839–1931; Main Factors in Their Changes," *Annalist*, July 7, 1933) presents a reconciliation of the two estimates of capital that has served as a prototype for our own reconciliation. Mr. Arnold finds that "the figure for corporate manufacturing capital at which we just arrived ($36,680,000,000) [based on *Statistics of Income*] represents 86.8 per cent of the capitalization [for corporate and noncorporate establishments] reported by the census, less 5 per cent for undeducted depreciation ($42,244,000,000). Corporations accounted in 1919 for 87.7 per cent of all manufacturing enterprises covered by the census." He concludes, "This correspondence is as close as could be expected from the data with which we are dealing. It cannot leave much doubt that the census figure for manufacturing capital in 1919 represents approximately the same thing as the income tax total which we have taken as corresponding to it."

Mr. Arnold has not attempted similar reconciliations by industry groups; nor, judging by his published description, has he made any adjustments for differences in industry coverage and for failure of certain corporations to report information on invested capital on the income tax return. Moreover, he reports, "Successive samples of balance sheets from the investment manuals show stock and surplus [invested capital] in 1919 as representing, with little variation, 84 or 85 per cent of the manufacturing capital indicated by the census figures." Using all domestic manufacturing corporations operating in continental United States that were included in *Moody's Manual* for 1920, we found that stock and surplus represented 76 per cent of capital (Table A-3, total of column 1 divided by total for column 3).

One other effort at verification of census capital figures has come to our attention—that of Paul Douglas (in *The Theory of Wages* [Macmillan, 1934], pp. 116–118). There, he compares the Bureau of the Census estimate of manufacturing capital for 1922 (presented in its monograph, *Wealth, Public Debt and Taxation*, 1922 [1924]) with S. H. Nerlove's estimate of corporate capital for the same year based on *Statistics of Income*. The Census used asset changes, 1919–1922, in 60 manufacturing corporations included in *Moody's* and *Poor's Manuals* to extrapolate capital as reported to the 1919 census (see *Wealth, Public Debt and Taxation*, p. 9). After reasonable adjustments for differences in coverage between the census and *Statistics of Income*, Douglas finds a discrepancy of 5 per cent: "Substantial agreement between the totals seems therefore to have been established. When two different estimates of such a large total agree within the range of 5 per cent, substantial verification can be claimed" (Douglas, *op. cit.*, p. 118). As with Arnold, the verification is restricted to aggregate manufacturing.

b. Reconciliation of Estimates of Fixed Capital Stock in Manufacturing Using Balance Sheet Data and Cumulative Annual Expenditures on Structures and Equipment. The next stage in gaining acceptance for our capital estimates is to demonstrate that the relative change between benchmark years in our estimates based on balance sheet data is reasonably close to the estimates based on cumulation of annual expenditures on plant and equipment. Because of differences in the scope and detail of the data over time, we must use one method of reconciliation for 1919–1929 and other methods for the subsequent benchmark comparisons.

The comparison of relative change between 1919 and 1929 was carried out in the following manner:

	1919	1929
	(dollars in millions)	
A. Total capital, from *Census of Manufactures*	41,433	
ESTIMATED FIXED CAPITAL:		
B. Including land (50% of A)	20,716	
C. Based on *Statistics of Income*		$27,410
D. 1929 as % of 1919 [(C÷B) × 100]		132.3%
E. Estimated Value of Buildings and Equipment	20,411	
1920–1929:		
F. Estimate of New Capital Expenditures		$21,327
G. Estimate of Depreciation		14,889
H. Net Capital Formation (F less G)		6,438
VALUE OF BUILDINGS AND EQUIPMENT:		
I. 1929 (E+H)		26,849
J. 1929 as % of 1919 [(I÷E) × 100]		131.5%

Line	Source
A.	National Bureau of Economic Research worksheets.
B.	Fixed capital as percentage of total capital excluding investment in securities equaled 49.1 per cent in 1904 and 49.8 per cent in 1930, both recession years; see Table 4.

APPENDIX A

Line	Source
C.	See Appendix Table A-9.
E.	Paul Douglas, *Theory of Wages* (Macmillan Co, 1934), p. 116.
F.	Lowell Chawner, "Capital Expenditures for Manufacturing, Plant and Equipment—1915 to 1940," *Survey of Current Business*, March 1941, p. 10.
G.	Solomon Fabricant, *Capital Consumption and Adjustment*, National Bureau of Economic Research, 1938, p. 32.

The relative changes on both bases are virtually identical. For 1929 and 1937, the comparison entailing the least number of adjustments is the one based on net fixed capital excluding land.

	Dollars in millions
A. Net Fixed Capital Excluding Land, 1929, *Statistics of Income*	$24,144
B. Expenditures for Structures and Equipment Minus Capital Outlays Charged to Current Expenses, 1930–1937	8,987
C. Cumulative Depreciation of Structures and Equipment	10,897
NET FIXED CAPITAL EXCLUDING LAND	
D. 1937 (A+B−C)	22,234
E. 1937, *Statistics of Income*	21,466
F. Based on Balance Sheet Data as % of Net Fixed Capital Based on Capital Expenditures [(E÷D) × 100]	96.5%

Line	Source
A. and E.	National Bureau of Economic Research worksheets.
B.	Donald G. Wooden and Robert C. Wasson, "Manufacturing Investment Since 1929," *Survey of Current Business* (November 1956), Table 1, p. 9. Estimate of capital outlays charged to current expenses supplied by letter by Mr. Wasson.
C.	Wooden and Wasson, *ibid.*, Table 2, p. 11, and letter.

	Dollars in millions
A. Gross Fixed Capital Including Intangible Assets but Excluding Land, 1937, *Statistics of Income*	$42,396
B. Expenditures for Structures and Equipment, 1938–1948	35,863
GROSS FIXED CAPITAL:	
C. Excluding Land, 1948 (A+B)	78,259
D. Including Intangible Assets but Excluding Land, 1948, *Statistics of Income*	77,094
E. Based on Balance Sheet Data as % of Gross Fixed Capital Based on Capital Expenditures [(D÷C) × 100]	98.5%
F. Expenditures for Structures and Equipment, 1949–1953	$35,271
GROSS FIXED CAPITAL:	
G. Excluding Land, 1953, Variant I (C+F)	113,530
H. Excluding Land, 1953, Variant II (D+F)	112,365
I. Including Intangible Assets but Excluding Land, 1953, *Statistics of Income*	113,794
BASED ON BALANCE SHEET DATA AS % OF GROSS FIXED CAPITAL BASED ON CAPITAL EXPENDITURES	
J. Variant I [(I÷G) × 100]	100.2%
K. Variant II [(I÷H) × 100]	101.3%

Line	Source
A., D. and I.	*Statistics of Income*, Part 2, raised to level of all firms.
B. and F.	Wooden and Wasson, *op. cit.*

NOTES ON ESTIMATES IN MANUFACTURING, 1880-1953

The reconciliation is reasonably close and the difference is in the expected direction, since one would look for a downward revaluation of balance sheet assets in a period of slow recovery from a deep depression. Gross fixed capital excluding land is the concept used for 1948 and 1953. Its use avoids many arbitrary assumptions which would be needed in estimating depreciation and accelerated amortization. For these periods, also, the two methods yield virtually identical estimates.

2. ADJUSTMENTS

Another essential for long-term comparisons is comparability of industry classifications. It was necessary to establish comparability among the various censuses and among the annual compilations of *Statistics of Income*, as well as between the census classifications and those of *Statistics of Income*. Establishing comparable industry groupings for intercensal years extends beyond the obvious exclusion of artisans and crafts from the earlier censuses. The task was greatly lightened by the previous researches of the late Daniel Carson carried out under the auspices of the National Research Project of the Works Progress Administration. (His effort to work out comparable industry groupings from the census data has not been published. However, a typed copy is in the files of the National Bureau of Economic Research.) Our own efforts were required to establish comparable groupings between the *Census of Manufactures* and *Statistics of Income*.

a. Establishment of Comparability between the Industrial Classifications of the *Census of Manufactures* and *Statistics of Income*. In transcribing the data for 1880-1919 on capital and value of product from the *Censuses of Manufactures*, we combined minor industries to achieve maximum comparability over this period. As mentioned above, we used, with slight modifications, the groupings established by the late Daniel Carson. Since we used *Statistics of Income* data for our capital and value of product estimates after 1919, we had to rearrange our groupings of the census data to make them comparable to the minor industry groupings in the "Source Book" of *Statistics of Income*.

The years we were concerned with after 1919 were 1929, 1937, and 1948.[5] Data on assets of minor industries are available in the "Source Book" only from 1930 on. (However, sales data for minor industries are available for 1929.) We computed the 1930 ratio of the capital (fixed and total) of the minor industries to the capital of the major groups to which they belonged. We then multiplied capital of the

---

[5] The estimates for 1953 represent an extension of the original estimates prepared for 1880-1948. The 1953 estimates are based on *Statistics of Income for 1953*, Part 2, which shows data for major groupings only.

APPENDIX A

major groups by these ratios to secure capital estimates for minor industries for 1929.

For 1929, 1930 and 1937, the "Source Book" distinguishes 45 identical manufacturing industries; but for 1948, data for 122 industries are available. In setting up comparable classifications over the seventy-year period, we are compelled to use the smallest number of classifications available in any one benchmark year. For 1880–1948, we have established 41 industries classified into 15 major industry groups. The decrease in the number of industries used (from 45 to 41) is due to our consolidation of certain industry groups: (1) factory, household, and miscellaneous machinery were combined into one industry; (2) bone, celluloid, and ivory products were combined with musical instruments, optical goods, etc., to form the miscellaneous group; and (3) radios and electrical machinery and equipment were combined into one industry (see Appendix Table A-4). We also combined the 122 *Statistics of Income* industries for 1948 and the census industries for 1880–1919 into 66 comparable industries.

TABLE A-4
Comparable Industrial Classifications, *Census of Manufactures, 1919* and *Statistics of Income, 1929* and *1930*

"Census of Manufactures, 1919"a	"Statistics of Income" Industrial Classification No.b	"Statistics of Income, 1929 and 1930"
All industries	27	Manufacturing, total
from Chem. and allied prods.		
— Coke, not incl. gas-house coke		
— Gas, illuminating and heating		
from Misc.:		
— Fuel, mfrd.		
— Shipbldg., steel		
— Shipbldg., wooden, including boat bldg.		
— Motion-picture projection films		
— R. R. repair shops		
— Automobile repairing (from Vehicles for land transpn.)		
Food and kindred prods.	28	Food prods., beverages, and tobacco
+ Liquors and bevs.		
+ Tobacco mfrs.		
+ Ice, mfrd. (from Misc.)		
Bread and other bakery prods.	31	Bakery and confectionery prods.
+ Chewing gum		

(*continued*)

NOTES ON ESTIMATES IN MANUFACTURING, 1880–1953

TABLE A-4 (continued)

"Census of Manufactures, 1919"[a]	"Statistics of Income" Industrial Classification No.[b]	"Statistics of Income, 1929 and 1930"
Food and kindred prods.	28	Food prods., beverages, and tobacco
+Chocolate and cocoa prods.		
+Confectionery and ice cream[c]		
Canning and preserving, fish	34	Canned prods.—Fish, fruit, veg., poultry, etc.
+Canning and preserving, oysters		
+Canning and preserving, fruits and veg.		
+Pickles, preserves, and sauces		
Slaughtering and meat packing	37	Packing-house prods.—Fresh meats, ham, lard, bacon, meat canning, by-prods., etc.
Flour-mill and gristmill prods.	40	Mill prods.—Bran, flour, feed etc.
Sugar, beet	44	Sugar—Cane, beet, maple, and prods.
+Sugar, cane		
+Sugar, refining, not incl. beet sugar		
Liquors and bevs.	51	Beverages—Soft drinks, cereal bevs., mineral water; wines; distilling
Tobacco mfrs.	64	Tobacco, cigarettes, cigars, snuff, etc.
Census industries comparable with 28	46	Other food prods.—artificial ice, butter substitutes, cereals, coffee, spices, dairy prods., etc.; food prods., n.e.c.
−Census industries comparable with 31, 34, 37, 40, 44, 51, and 64		
Textiles and their prods.	67	Textiles and their prods., incl. fur
−Hammocks (to Forest prods.)		
from Misc.:		
+Fur goods		
+Furs, dressed		
+Hats, straw		
Cotton goods	72	Cotton goods—Dress goods, plain cloth, etc.; napping, dyeing
+Cotton small wares		
+Cotton lace		
+Dyeing and finishing textiles, exclusive of that done in textile mills		
Woolen and worsted goods	76	Woolen and worsted goods—Wool yarn, dress goods, wool pulling, etc.
+Wool shoddy		
+Wool pulling		
+Wool scouring		

(continued)

APPENDIX A

TABLE A-4 (continued)

"Census of Manufactures, 1919"[a]	"Statistics of Income" Industrial Classification No.[b]	"Statistics of Income, 1929 and 1930"
Textiles and their prods.	67	*Textiles and their prods., inc. fur*
Silk goods	78	Silk and rayon goods—Silk fabrics, spinning, etc.
Knit goods	82	Knit goods—Sweaters, hosiery, etc.
Carpets and rugs, rag + Carpets and rugs, other than rag + Oil cloth and linoleum, floor + Mats and matting, from cocoa fiber, grass, and coir, etc.	85	Carpets, floor coverings, tapestries, etc.
Articles from textile fabrics for personal wear + Hats, wool-felt + Hats, fur-felt + Hat and cap materials + Hats, straw (from Misc.)	94	Clothing—Custom-made, factory-made, coats, underwear, millinery, and clothing, n.e.c.
Census industries comparable with 67 − Census industries comparable with 72, 76, 78, 82, 85, and 94	89	Textiles, n.e.c., cord, felt, fur, hospital and surgical supplies, linen, other textiles, etc.
Leather and its finished prods.	103	*Leather and its mfrs.*
Boots and shoes, not incl. rubber boots and shoes	104	Boots, shoes, slippers, etc.
Census group comparable with 103 − Census industry comparable with 104 from Misc.	107	Other leather prods.—Gloves, saddlery, harness, trunks; finishing and tanning leather, etc.
+ Belting and hose, rubber	112	or 113 *Rubber prods.*
+ Boots and shoes, rubber + Rubber tires, tubes, and rubber goods, n.e.c.	119	− Bone, celluloid, and ivory prods. (to Misc.)
Rubber tires and tubes (in Rubber tires, tubes, and rubber goods, n.e.c. industry)[d]	114	Tires and tubes
Census industries comparable with 112 or 113 minus 119 − Census industry comparable with 114	116	Other rubber goods—Boots, shoes, hose and artificial rubber
Lumber and its manufactures − Charcoal, not incl. prod'n. in the lumber and wood distillation industries (to Chem. and allied prod.)	120 or 121	*Forest prods.*

(continued)

NOTES ON ESTIMATES IN MANUFACTURING, 1880–1953

TABLE A-4 (continued)

"Census of Manufactures, 1919"[a]	"Statistics of Income" Industrial Classification No.[b]	"Statistics of Income, 1929 and 1930"
Lumber and its manufactures	120 or 121	Forest prods.
+Hammocks (from Textiles and their prods.)		
+Turpentine and rosin (from Chem. and allied prods.)		
from Vehicles for land transp. group:		
+Carriages and wagons, incl. repairs		
+Carriage and wagon materials		
+Carriages and sleds, children's		
+Wheelbarrows		
Lumber and timber prods.	123	Sawmill and planing-mill prods.
+Lumber, planing-mill prods., not incl. planing mills connected with sawmills		
+Window and door screens and weather strips		
Census industries comparable with 120 or 121	128	Other wood prods.—Carriages, wagons, furniture, baskets, etc.
−Census industries comparable with 123		
Paper and wood pulp (in Paper and printing)	136	Paper, pulp, and prods.
+Mfrs. of paper (in Paper and printing)		
−Paper patterns (from Mfrs. of paper industry to Printing and publishing and allied inds.)		
+Wall paper, not made in paper mills (in Paper and printing)		
+Pulp, from fiber other than wood (from Misc.)		
Printing and publishing (in Paper and printing)	142 or 143	Printing, publishing, and allied industries
+Industries relating to printing and publishing (in Paper and printing)		
+Paper patterns		
+Engravers' materials (from Misc.)		
Chemicals and allied prods.	151	*Chemicals and allied prods.*
−Coke, not incl. gas-house coke (elim. from All mfg.)	168	−Petroleum and other mineral refining
−Gas, illuminating and heating (elim. from All mfg.)		

(*continued*)

APPENDIX A

TABLE A-4 (continued)

"Census of Manufactures, 1919"[a]	"Statistics of Income" Industrial Classification No.[b]	"Statistics of Income for 1929 and 1930"
Chemicals and allied prods.	151	*Chemicals and allied prods.*
— Petroleum, refining		
— Turpentine and rosin (to Forest prods.)		
+ Charcoal, not incl. prod'n. in the lumber and wood distilling inds. (from Lumber and its remanufactures)		
+ Fireworks (from Misc.)		
+ Mucilage, paste, and other adhesives, n.e.c. (from Misc.)		
Chemicals and acids	153	Chemicals proper, acids, compounds, etc.
+ Explosives		
+ Dyestuffs and extracts, natural		
+ Bone, carbon, and lamp black		
+ Salt		
Fertilizers	163	Fertilizers
Census industries comparable with 151 minus 168	155	Allied chemical substances—Drugs, oils, paints, soaps, and other chem. substances, n.e.c.
— Census industries comparable with 153, 163, and 155		
Petroleum, refining (from Chem. and allied prods.)	168	*Petroleum and other mineral oil refining*
Stone, clay, and glass prods.	174	*Stone, clay, glass, and related prods.*
+ Graphite, ground and refined (from Misc.)		
Iron and steel and their prods. to Machinery:		*Iron and steel and their prods.* (186 + 188 + 192)
— Cast-iron pipe[e]		
— Steel barrels, drums, and tanks, portable[e]		
— Tempering and welding[e]		
— Cash registers and calculating machines		
— Engines, steam, gas, and water		
— Foundry and mach.-shop prods.		
— Gas machines and gas and water meters		
— Machine tools		
— Pens, steel		
— Pumps, steam and other power		
— Pumps, not incl. power pumps		
— Safes and vaults		
— Scales and balances		

(continued)

NOTES ON ESTIMATES IN MANUFACTURING, 1880–1953

TABLE A-4 (continued)

"Census of Manufactures, 1919"[a]	"Statistics of Income" Industrial Classification No.[b]	"Statistics of Income, 1929 and 1930"
Iron and steel and their prods. to Machinery: (*cont.*): — Sewing machines and attachments — Textile machinery and parts — Typewriters and supplies — Vault lights and ventilators — Locomotives, not made by R.R. cos. (to Transp. equipment) from Metals and metal prods., other than iron and steel: + Tinware, n.e.c. + Galvanizing and other coating processes + Stamped and enameled ware, n.e.c. from Misc.: + Enameling + Japanning + Ammunition		*Iron and steel and their prods.* (186 + 188 + 192)
Crude iron and steel and rolled prods. + Firearms + Forgings + Horseshoes + Ordnance and accessories + Springs, steel, car, and carriage + Tin plate and terneplate + Wire, not incl. wire depts. of rolling mills + Wirework, n.e.c., not incl. wire-drawing mills from Metals and metal prods., other than iron and steel: + Tinware, n.e.c. + Galvanizing and other coating processes + Stamped and enameled ware, n.e.c. from Misc.: + Enameling + Japanning + Ammunition	186	Iron and steel—Prods. of blast furnaces, rolling mills, foundries, etc.
Doors and shutters + Plumbers' supplies, n.e.c. + Steam fittings and steam and hot-water heating apparatus + Stoves and hot-air furnaces	188	Metal bldg. material and supplies

(*continued*)

APPENDIX A

TABLE A-4 (*continued*)

"Census of Manufactures, 1919"a	"Statistics of Income" Industrial Classification No.b	"Statistics of Income, 1929 and 1930"
Iron and steel and their prods.		*Iron and steel and their prods.* (186 + 188 + 192)
+Stoves, gas and oil		
+Structural ironwork		
+Wrought pipe		
Bolts, nuts, washers, and rivets	192	Hardware, tools, etc.
+Tools and cutlery		
+Hardware		
+Hardware, saddlery		
+Nails and spikes, cut and wrought, incl. wire nails		
+Screws, machine		
+Screws, wood		
Metals and metal prods., other than iron and steel		*Nonferrous metals and prods.* (203 + 207)
—Pens, gold (to Misc.)		
to Iron and steel prods.:		
—Tinware, n.e.c.		
—Galvanizing and other coating processes		
—Stamped and enameled ware, n.e.c.		
from Misc.:		
+Fire extinguishers, chem.		
+Lapidary work		
Gold and silver, reducing and refining, not from ore	203	Precious-metal prods. and processes; jewelry, etc.
+Gold and silver, leaf and foil		
+Clocks		
+Watches		
+Watch and watch materials		
+Watchcases		
+Electroplating		
+Jewelry		
from Iron and steel and their prods. group:		
+Cash registers and calculating machines	235	Office equip., etc.
+Plated ware		
+Silversmithing and silverware		
+Lapidary work (from Misc.)		
Census industries comparable with 203+207	207	Other metals, prods. and processes; combination of foundry and mach. shop
—Census industries comparable with 203		

(continued)

NOTES ON ESTIMATES IN MANUFACTURING, 1880-1953

TABLE A-4 (continued)

"Census of Manufactures, 1919"[a]	"Statistics of Income" Industrial Classification No.[b]	"Statistics of Income, 1929 and 1930"
from Iron and steel and their prods.:		Machinery, excl. transp. equip. ([212+215]+233+235+[224 +226+237])
+Cast-iron pipe[e]		
+Steel barrels, drums, and tanks, portable[e]		
+Tempering and welding[e]		
+Cash registers and calculating machines		
+Engines, steam, gas, and water		
+Foundry and mach.-shop prods.		
+Gas machines and gas and water meters		
+Machine tools		
+Pumps, not incl. power pumps		
+Pumps, steam and other power		
+Safes and vaults		
+Scales and balances		
+Sewing machines and attachments		
+Textile machinery and parts		
+Typewriters and supplies		
+Vault lights and ventilators		
from Misc.:		
+Agricul. implements		
+Electrical machy., apparatus, and supplies		
+Phonographs and graphophones		
+Washing machines and clothes wringers		
+Windmills		
from Misc.:		
+Electr. machy., apparatus, and supplies	212	Electr. machy. and equip.
+Phonographs and graphophones	215	+Radios, complete or parts (from Mfg. n.e.c.)
Agric. implements (from Misc.)	233	Agric. machy. and equip.
+Safes and vaults		
+Scales and balances		
+Typewriters and supplies		
Census industries comparable with (212+215), 233, 235, and (224+226+237)	224	Factory machy. — Food-prod'n. machy; leather, metal, paper, printing, textile, and woodworking machy.
−Census industries comparable with (212+215), 233, and 235		
	226	+Misc. machy.—Bldg. construction, gas, and mining machy. and equip.
	237	+Household machy. and equip., etc.

(continued)

APPENDIX A

TABLE A-4 (*continued*)

"*Census of Manufactures, 1919*"a	"*Statistics of Income*" Industrial Classification No.b	"*Statistics of Income, 1929 and 1930*"
Vehicles for land transp.		*Transp. equip.* (241+251+254)
—Automobile repairing (elim. from All mfg.)		
to Forest prods. group:		
—Carriages and wagons, incl. repairs		
—Carriage and wagon materials		
—Carriages and sleds, children's		
—Wheelbarrows		
Automobiles	241	Motor vehicles, complete or parts
+Automobile bodies and parts		
+Motorcycles, bicycles and parts		
Cars, steam—R.R., not incl. operations of R.R. cos.	251	Locomotives and R.R. equip.
+Cars, electric—R.R., not incl. operations of R.R. cos.		
+Locomotives, not made by R.R. cos. (from Iron and steel and their prods.)		
Aeroplanes, seaplanes, airships, and parts (from Misc.)	254	Airplanes, airships, seaplanes, etc. (from Mfg., n.e.c.)
Misc. industries	264	*Musical instruments, optical goods, canoes, etc.* (in Mfg., n.e.c. group)
elim. from All mfg.:		
—Fuel, mfrd.		
—Shipbldg., steel	119	+*Bone, celluloid, and ivory prods.* (from Rubber prods. group)
—Shipbldg., wooden, incl. boat bldg.		
—Motion-picture projection films		
—Ice, mfrd. (to Food and kindred prods.)		
to Textiles and their prods.:		
—Fur goods		
—Furs, dressed		
—Hats, straw		
to Rubber prods.:		
—Belting and hose, rubber		
—Belting and hose, rubber		
—Boots and shoes, rubber		
—Rubber tires, tubes, and rubber goods, n.e.c.		
—Pulp, from fiber other than wood (to Paper, pulp, and prods.)		
—Engravers' materials (to Printing, publ., and allied inds.)		
to Chem. and allied prods.:		
—Fireworks		

(*continued*)

NOTES ON ESTIMATES IN MANUFACTURING, 1880–1953

TABLE A-4 (concluded)

"Census of Manufactures, 1919"[a]	"Statistics of Income" Industrial Classification No.[b]	"Statistics of Income, 1929 and 1930"
Misc. industries		
— Mucilage, paste, and other adhesives, n.e.c.		
— Graphite, ground and refined (to Stone, clay, and glass prods.)		
to Iron and steel and their prods.:		
— Enameling		
— Japanning		
— Ammunition		
to Nonferrous metals and prods.:		
— Fire extinguishers, chem.		
— Lapidary work		
to Machinery:		
— Agric. implements		
— Electrical machy., apparatus, and supplies		
— Phonographs and graphophones		
— Washing machines and clothes wringers		
— Windmills		
— Aeroplanes, seaplanes, airships, and parts (to Transpn. equip.)		
+ Pens, steel (from Iron and steel and their prods.)		
+ Pens, gold (from Metals and metal prods. other than iron and steel)		

n.e.c. = not elsewhere classified.

[a] Classifications used are from *Fourteenth Census of the United States, 1920*, Vol. VIII, *Manufactures, 1919* (hereafter, *Census of Manufactures, 1919*), pp. 146–58, Tables 32–46.

[b] Industrial classification numbers are from *Statistics of Income for 1947* [Bureau of Internal Revenue (now Internal Revenue Service)], Part 2, pp. 64–68.

[c] Ice cream retained in confectionery products because the former was combined with confectionery in earlier censuses and could not be isolated.

[d] Only value of output data for tires and tubes are available for 1914 and 1919 in *Census of Manufactures, 1919* (Vol. X), p. 1001, Table 11. Capital for 1914 and 1919 was estimated by multiplying the ratio of the value of output for tires and tubes to that of the rubber products group by capital, 1914 and 1919, in the rubber products group. No census data are available for rubber tires and tubes before 1914.

[e] Transferred to machinery group because the industry was combined with foundry and machine-shop products in earlier censuses and could not be isolated.

Appendix Table A-4 lists the minor industries in the 1919 *Census of Manufactures* that are included in the 41 slightly modified 1929 or 1930 *Statistics of Income* minor industry classifications.

APPENDIX A

b. *Other Adjustments.* The data transcribed from *Statistics of Income* required five adjustments: (i) for the shift from consolidated to deconsolidated returns in 1934, which affects not only the totals for industry groups, but also the total for all manufacturing; (ii) for unincorporated firms; (iii) for accelerated depreciation in 1948 and 1953; (iv) for changes in inventory, to convert sales and receipts to output; and (v) for the exclusion of intangible assets from fixed capital in 1948 and 1953.

(i) *Adjustment for deconsolidation.* The Internal Revenue Service, in *Statistics of Income for 1934*, published tabulations of items from profit and loss statements on both a consolidated and deconsolidated basis. The ratio of gross sales on a deconsolidated basis to gross sales on a consolidated basis in 1934 was used to adjust both capital and output reported on a consolidated basis in 1929. Admittedly, this is a rough adjustment, particularly for capital. However, the adjustment for all manufacturing is slight, as it is for most industry groups except metals and metal products.

(ii) *Adjustment for unincorporated firms.* The data transcribed from *Statistics of Income* relate to corporations submitting balance sheets. Usually, only 1 to 2 per cent of all corporations in manufacturing do not submit balance sheets. Gross sales of all corporations and of corporations submitting balance sheets, classified by industry groups, are published annually in *Statistics of Income*. This relationship was used to raise totals for corporations submitting balance sheets to the level for all corporations.

There remains, then, the problem of estimating capital and output for unincorporated firms which, according to the tabulations in the *Censuses of Manufactures* for 1929 and 1947, accounted for about 8.5 per cent of value added in 1929–1947. The relationship of value of product of all establishments to that of corporate establishments was used to raise the corporate totals from *Statistics of Income* to the level of all firms. This relationship, derived from the 1929 *Census of Manufactures*, was applied to the data adapted from the 1929 *Statistics of Income*; the ratio from the 1937 *Census of Manufactures* was applied to the totals from the 1937 *Statistics of Income*; and the ratio from the 1947 *Census of Manufactures* was applied to the totals from the 1948 and 1953 *Statistics of Income*.

(iii) *Adjustment for accelerated depreciation.* In 1940–1945, corporations were permitted, for federal income tax purposes, to amortize capital assets acquired for national defense over an abnormally low period of 5 years. Since the data on net capital assets in the "Source Book" of *Statistics of Income for 1948* do not reflect the net value of this type of investment as it would be determined by the customary

TABLE A-5

Investment in Emergency Facilities; Amortization in Excess of Normal Depreciation, All Manufacturing, as of 1948

	Annual Amortization Charges, All Returns (1)	Year-to-Year Increase in Amortization Charges (col. 1: given year less prior year) (2) (thousands of dollars)	Investment in Emergency Facilities		Gross Capital Assets excluding Land			Annual Depreciation	
			New (col. 2 × 5.0) (3)	Cumulative (from col. 3) (4)	Amount (5)	Less Cumulative Investment in Emergency Facilities (col. 5 less col. 4) (6) (millions of dollars)	Annual Depreciation (7)	As Percentage of Adjusted Gross Capital Assets (col. 7 ÷ col. 6) (8)	Charge on Cumulative Investment in Emergency Facilities (col. 4 × col. 8) (9) (thousands of dollars)
1940	$ 5,980								
1941	88,599	$ 5,980	$ 29,900	$ 29,900	$40,772	$40,742	$1,511	3.71%	$ 1,109
1942	309,480	82,619	413,095	442,995	42,901	42,458	1,588	3.74	16,568
1943	533,663	220,881	1,104,405	1,547,400	47,236	45,689	1,722	3.77	58,337
1944	740,721	224,183	1,120,915	2,668,315	49,850	47,182	1,807	3.83	102,196
1945	a	207,058	1,035,290	3,703,605	50,243	46,539	1,802	3.87	143,330
1946								3.87[b]	143,330
1947								3.87[b]	143,330
1948								3.87[b]	143,330
								3.87[b]	
Total, 1940–1948				3,703,605					894,860
Amortization in excess of normal depreciation (sum of col. 3 less sum of col. 9)						$2,808,745			

[a] Amortization data for 1945 were not used because, with the ending of the emergency in 1945, corporations holding unexpired certificates were allowed to recompute their amortization deductions for each year involved on the basis of the shortened period instead of the five-year period originally stipulated.
[b] Depreciation rate for 1944 also used for 1945–1948.
Source: The data in columns 1, 5, and 7 are from *Statistics of Income*, Bureau of Internal Revenue (now Internal Revenue Service), *Part 2*, various issues.

APPENDIX A

depreciation-accounting procedure, we have attempted to add to the reported data estimates of undepreciated investment in emergency facilities. (A similar law was enacted after the start of the Korean War. This necessitated an adjustment of the reported book values of capital for 1953 and later years.)

The adjustment of the book values equals the difference between the amount charged off as accelerated amortization on the emergency facilities and the amount of depreciation that would have accrued had these facilities been subject to normal straightline depreciation. The estimating procedure is illustrated by showing how the adjustment was made for all manufacturing for 1948 (see Table A-5). The same procedure was used for the 21 major manufacturing industries in 1948, and for the derivation of a similar adjustment for the 1953 estimates. The data relate to corporations only. It is assumed that the amortization privilege affected a negligible number of business organizations other than corporations. Hence, no attempt was made to raise the adjustment to an all-establishment level.

(iv) *Adjustment of sales and of gross receipts from other operations for changes in inventory.* Sales in a given year may equal, exceed, or fall short of output over the same period. Only when sales equal output can sales without adjustment be used to represent the level of output. Since an excess of sales over output means that previously accumulated inventories have been drawn down, sales minus the amount of the decline in inventories equal output. Similarly, inventories rise when sales fall short of output, and sales plus the increase in inventories are a measure of output. The inventory change that is relevant is the change in physical inventories valued in current prices. The latter are estimated by the National Income Division of the Department of Commerce on the basis of data derived from *Statistics of Income*. This item can be estimated only for total manufacturing and for major industry groups. In none of the three years—1929, 1937, and 1948— did this item amount to as much as 3 per cent of output.

(v) *Adjustment of fixed capital for intangible assets.* Intangible assets (patents, copyrights, good will, etc.) were included with fixed capital in the 1948 and 1953 compilations of *Statistics of Income*. In other benchmark years, intangible assets were classified in other assets which were included with working capital. *Statistics of Income* reported intangible assets separately in 1954 after not listing them separately since 1939. Therefore, for each industry group, we interpolated along a straight line between the values in 1939 and 1954 to arrive at the value of intangibles in 1948 and 1953. These estimates of intangible assets were deducted from fixed capital as reported in 1948 and 1953.

These data from *Statistics of Income*, after the adjustments described, provide our estimates of capital and output in reported values with a workable degree of comparability in concept and in industry classification.

B. Capital and Output in 1929 Prices

1. DERIVATION OF THE BOOK VALUE OF NET FIXED AND TOTAL CAPITAL IN 1929 PRICES, MAJOR MANUFACTURING INDUSTRIES, SELECTED YEARS, 1879–1953

The method consists of deriving a series of composite indexes, one for each of fifteen major industry groups, from (1) an index of prices of machinery and equipment differently weighted in each major group according to the length of life typical of the industry; (2) an index of building costs based on a fifty-year life, which is identical for all industries; and (3) as a deflator of working capital, an index of wholesale prices of output of each major industry group. The composite index for a given major industry is applied to all minor industries classified under the given major industry.

a. Machinery and Equipment. In a given year, the book value of machinery and equipment with a specified average length of life equals the original cost of all machinery and equipment acquired during the immediately preceding period—the period measured by the specified average length of life—less the amount of the original cost depreciated over that period. To express the depreciated book values of a given year in constant prices, it is necessary to know (1) the average length of life of all machinery and equipment in each major industry group; (2) the value of machinery and equipment output in constant prices in each year of the period defined by the average length of life of the machinery and equipment; and (3) the price index of machinery and equipment. By reference to the average length of life, we estimate how much of the machinery and equipment represented in the depreciated book values of a given year was acquired in each year of the span composing the average length of life of machinery. These yearly values, which are in constant prices, are used to weight the price index of machinery covering the same span of years. The weighted average of these price indexes is the index used to convert depreciated book values in original cost prices to book values in constant prices.

The estimating procedure is illustrated by the computations, set out in Table A-6, by which we derive the 1937 index of the book value in 1929 prices of machinery and equipment in the food and kindred products group. We estimate the average length of life of machinery and equipment in this group to be fifteen years. The value of output in 1929 prices of machinery and equipment in all manufacturing, for

APPENDIX A

each year of the fifteen-year period, 1923–1937, is multiplied by the percentage of the output still in use in 1937. This product was then used to weight the price index (1929 = 100) of each year's machinery output. The sum of the fifteen final products was then divided by the sum of the weights to arrive at the index of book values for 1937. This

TABLE A-6

Derivation of 1937 Index for Expressing Book Values of Machinery and Equipment for Food and Kindred Products Group in 1929 Prices
(average life: 15 years; depreciation rate: 6.67 per cent)

	Output of Machy. and Equip., all Mfg. (millions of dollars in 1929 prices) (1)	Per Cent in Use in 1937 (2)	Weight (col. 1 × col. 2) (3)	Price Index of Machy. and Equip. all Mfg., (1929 = 100) (4)	Weighted Price Index (col. 3 × col. 4) (5)
1923	$1,498	6.7%	100	95.9	9,590
1924	1,299	13.3	173	97.0	16,781
1925	1,428	20.0	286	96.9	27,713
1926	1,586	26.7	423	96.8	40,946
1927	1,435	33.3	478	98.0	46,844
1928	1,470	40.0	588	99.0	58,212
1929	1,777	46.7	830	100.0	83,000
1930	1,407	53.4	751	91.8	68,942
1931	902	60.0	541	86.6	46,851
1932	560	66.7	374	81.4	30,444
1933	606	73.4	445	81.4	36,223
1934	768	80.0	614	92.8	56,979
1935	1,013	86.7	878	91.8	80,600
1936	1,277	93.3	1,191	91.8	109,334
1937	1,519	100.0	1,519	101.0	153,419
			9,191		865,878

1937 Index for Expressing Book Value in 1929 Prices $= \frac{\Sigma \text{ col. 5}}{\Sigma \text{ col. 3}} = 94.2$.

Source: See accompanying text.

procedure was repeated for each major group for each benchmark year.

The average length of life for a given major industry group is based on unweighted averages of depreciation rates, as published by the Internal Revenue Service,[6] for various types of machinery and equip-

[6] *Depreciation Studies-Preliminary Report* of the Bureau of Internal Revenue (now Internal Revenue Service), January 1932, and *Income Tax, Depreciation and Obsolescence, Estimated Useful Lives and Depreciation Rates* (Bulletin F, revised January 1942), Treasury Department, Internal Revenue Service.

ment used in the industry. This computation yields the following averages:

Average Length of Life of Machinery and Equipment, Selected Manufacturing Industries

	Average Length of Life (years)
Food and kindred products	15
Textiles and products	22
Leather and products	15
Rubber products	12
Forest products	20
Paper, pulp, and products	18
Printing, publishing, and allied industries	14
Chemicals and products	19
Petroleum refining	15
Stone, clay, and glass products	15
Iron and steel and products	17
Nonferrous metals and products	22
Machinery excluding transportation equipment	18
Transporation equipment	15
Miscellaneous	18

The output of machinery and equipment for 1889–1919 is first expressed in 1913 prices by dividing the value of output data estimated by William Howard Shaw in *Value of Commodity Output since 1869* (National Bureau of Economic Research, 1947) by the appropriate price indexes (1913 = 100) in the same study. Before 1899, the value of output data in Shaw's study, which are available only for 1869 and 1879, were used for interpolation purposes, and the price index data were taken from an unpublished worksheet of Simon Kuznets. Kuznets' index on an 1889 base was extrapolated back to 1859 and converted to the 1913 base.

For indexes of book value in 1929 prices for 1919, 1929, 1937, 1948, and 1953, we linked Shaw's data on output of industrial machinery and equipment in 1913 prices, 1898–1915, to Lowell J. Chawner's estimates, 1915–1939, of expenditures by manufacturing companies for capital equipment in 1939 prices converted to 1929 prices (Lowell J. Chawner, *op. cit.*, p. 11). Department of Commerce estimates, 1939–1953, of investment in producers' durable equipment in 1939 prices converted to 1929 prices were then linked to Chawner's data (see National Income Supplements to *Survey of Current Business*).

The price index on the 1929 base was calculated by linking Shaw's price index, 1898–1915, and the Department of Commerce implicit price index, 1939–1953, to Chawner's implicit price index on a 1929 base.

APPENDIX A

b. *Buildings and Land.* A method similar to that in (a) was used to estimate the index of book value of buildings and land. The computation of indexes of book value in 1913 prices for censal years, 1879–1919, was based on a fifty-year life of improvements in all major manufacturing industries. The data for the computations are from an unpublished worksheet of Simon Kuznets. The indexes of book value in 1929 prices used for 1919, 1929, and 1937 are those for nonresidential, nonfarm structures (available in an unpublished table prepared by Raymond W. Goldsmith for his "A Perpetual Inventory of National Wealth," in *Studies in Income and Wealth*, Volume 14, National Bureau of Economic Research, 1951). Goldsmith's computations were based on a useful life of forty to fifty years. For 1948 and 1953, we developed our own indexes using the price index of the Turner Construction Company weighted by the volume of construction in manufacturing based on a fifty-year life. Both the price index and the volume of construction are published in *Construction Volume and Costs, 1915–1954*, Statistical Supplement to *Construction Review*, issued jointly by the Departments of Commerce and Labor, Table 15, p. 36 (the initial estimate for volume of construction in manufacturing is for 1915). To cover a fifty-year period, this series was extended back by the relative changes in Goldsmith's series on nonresidential, nonfarm construction in his *A Study of Saving in the United States*, Volume I (Princeton University Press, 1955), Tables R-27 and R-28, pp. 619–620. Goldsmith's series was expressed in 1929 prices by applying to it his construction cost indexes, Table R-20, p. 609.

c. *Cash, Accounts Receivable, and Inventories.* The index of book value used in deflating cash, accounts receivable, and inventories was the wholesale price index (1929 = 100) for the output of each of the fifteen major industries. For the derivation of these indexes, see Appendix A, section 4.

d. *Total Capital.* To secure indexes of book value of total capital in 1929 prices for each major manufacturing group, we first linked the indexes in 1913 prices for each of the three components of total capital to those in 1929 prices. We then calculated a weighted harmonic mean of the three indexes. For benchmark years 1880–1937, the indexes were weighted by the average relative importance of the components in 1889, 1899, and 1904 as shown by census data. Limited evidence indicates that the relative importance of these three asset components changed little from 1880 to 1937. However, by 1948, their relative importance had changed significantly, and new weights were used, based on balance-sheet data reported in *Statistics of Income*, Part 2, 1948 and 1953. The index for the major group was also applied to the total capital of minor industries within the group.

e. Fixed Capital. Indexes of book value of fixed capital in 1929 prices were computed by taking a weighted arithmetic mean of the indexes of book value, for each major group, of (1) machinery and equipment and of (2) buildings and land and then linking the means in 1913 prices to those in 1929 prices. The index for the major group was also used to deflate fixed capital of minor industries in the group.

2. DERIVATION OF THE BOOK VALUE OF GROSS FIXED AND TOTAL CAPITAL IN 1929 PRICES, ALL MANUFACTURING, 1929–1948

In order to test whether the decline in the total and fixed capital-output ratios from 1929 to 1948 might be due to excessive depreciation, we recomputed total and fixed capital without making any allowance for depreciation of capital assets.

TABLE A-7

Computation of the Ratio of Net to Gross Fixed Capital, Corporations with Balance Sheets, All Manufacturing, 1937–1948
(*dollars in millions*)

	Fixed Capital		Estimated Cumulative Emergency Facilities after Normal Depreciation (3)	Adjusted Net Fixed Capital	
	Net (1)	Gross (2)		Amount (col. 1+col. 3) (4)	Ratio to Gross Fixed Capital (col. 4 ÷ col. 2) (per cent) (5)
1937	$23,303[a]	$40,590[a]		$23,303[a]	57.4%
1938	23,311[a]	41,188[a]		23,311[a]	56.6
1939	23,060	41,573		23,060	55.5
1940	23,605	42,750	$ 29	23,634	55.2
1941	24,726	44,898	426	25,152	56.0
1942	26,607	49,066	1,489	28,096	57.3
1943	27,038	51,614	2,566	29,604	57.4
1944	25,920	52,023	3,560	29,480	56.7
1945	25,143	53,868	3,417	28,560	53.0
1946	29,413	59,163	3,274	32,687	55.2
1947	35,380	66,761	3,130	38,510	57.7
1948	41,227	74,016	2,987	44,214	59.7

[a] Prior to 1939, *Statistics of Income* included intangible capital assets in "other assets." Estimates of intangible gross and net capital assets were made by assuming that the ratios of net and gross intangible capital assets to tangible net and gross capital assets, respectively, were the same in 1937 and 1938 as in 1939. These estimates were then added to the given net and gross tangible capital assets data for 1937 and 1938. The 1939 breakdown of fixed capital into intangible and tangible capital assets is available in *Statistics of Income for 1939*, Bureau of Internal Revenue (now Internal Revenue Serice), Part 2, p. 22.

Source: Columns 1 and 2: 1937–1947: *Statistics of income*: 1948 Treasury Department Release No. S-2808, Sept. 20, 1951, p. 13; column 3: see Appendix Table A-5, col. 4 less col. 9.

APPENDIX A

From 1937 on, data on gross fixed capital and its reserve for depreciation for corporations with balance sheets are available in *Statistics of Income*. Before 1937, data on net fixed capital only are available. We assumed that the relative importance of net fixed capital to gross fixed capital was roughly the same in 1929 as in the late thirties, namely, 56 to 58 per cent (Table A-7). To secure gross fixed capital under varying assumptions of the relationship of net to gross capital, our 1929 estimate of net fixed capital in 1929 prices for all manufacturing establishments was divided by 58, 57, and 56 per cent; for 1937 and 1948, net fixed capital (in 1929 prices) was divided by 57.4 and 59.7 per cent, respectively. Gross total capital in 1929 prices was computed for 1929, 1937, and 1948 by substituting gross fixed capital for net fixed capital in our (net) total capital data.

Data on net total and fixed capital in 1929 prices are from Appendix Tables A-8 and A-9, below.

3. ESTIMATE OF CURRENT VALUE OF TOTAL CAPITAL, ALL MANUFACTURING, 1880–1948

The current value (i.e., replacement cost) of total capital for all manufacturing was estimated by adding (1) working capital (cash, inventories, accounts and notes receivable, and miscellaneous assets) in current prices to (2) the book value of fixed capital (machinery and equipment, buildings, and land) deflated by an index of replacement cost. Indexes of replacement cost were computed for machinery and equipment and for land and buildings, and a weighted average of these two indexes was used to deflate fixed capital. Estimates of current value were not made for 1904 and 1914.

a. *Working Capital.* Working capital in current prices was derived by subtracting the book value of fixed capital from that of total capital. Since fixed capital was not available for 1880, 1909, and 1919, we made estimates for these years by applying the ratio of fixed to total capital in 1890, 1904, and 1929 to total capital in 1880, 1909, and 1919, respectively. Data on total and fixed capital are in Appendix I, Tables A-8 and A-9, respectively.

b. *Machinery and Equipment.* The method of computing an index of replacement cost was the same as that used in constructing the index for expressing book values in 1929 prices (see Appendix A, section B-1), with one exception—the price indexes of machinery and equipment were converted to a given year base. For example, to construct a replacement cost index for 1909, the price indexes were converted to a 1909 base. We estimated the average length of life of machinery and equipment for all manufacturing by weighting the average length of life of machinery and equipment of the fifteen major industrial groups by fixed capital in current prices for each group. Data on fixed capital are in Appendix Table A-9. For 1880–1919, the average life was 18 years; for 1929–1948, 17 years.

c. Buildings and Land. We used the method of section b, above, to compute an index of replacement cost for buildings and land. The length of life used was fifty years. In constructing the index of replacement cost for 1880, our first benchmark year, we should have used price and new construction data going back to 1831. However, since construction cost data are available from 1840 only, the index for 1880 was estimated for 1840–1880.

For 1840–1915, construction cost indexes are from unpublished tables of Simon Kuznets. For 1915–1948, price indexes were derived by dividing the value of nonresidential industrial construction in current prices by that in 1947–1949 prices [from "Construction Volume and Costs, 1915–1951," Statistical Supplement to *Construction and Building Materials*, May 1952 (Department of Commerce), pp. 6 and 48]. For 1840–1868, value of new construction in 1929 prices is from an unpublished table of Simon Kuznets; for 1869–1915, it is from Simon Kuznets, *National Product since 1869* (National Bureau of Economic Research, 1946), Table II-5, p. 99. For 1915–1948, the Department of Commerce series on nonresidential industrial construction in 1947–1949 prices in "Construction Volume and Costs, 1915–1951," *op. cit.*, p. 48 was used. The series were spliced in 1915.

We have computed the index of replacement cost for 1880, 1890, 1900, 1909, 1919, and 1937. Our indexes are about the same as Raymond W. Goldsmith's. Therefore, for 1929 and 1948, we used the implicit index derived by dividing his depreciated original cost by the current value of nonfarm, nonresidential structures [both are in his "A Perpetual Inventory of National Wealth," *op. cit.*, Table 1, pp. 18–19].

d. Fixed Capital. The index of replacement cost for fixed capital is a weighted average of the indexes constructed in sections b and c above. Weights used were the relative importance of the reported values of machinery and equipment and of buildings and land. Weights for the 1880 and 1890 indexes were the 1890 values taken from the *Census of Manufactures, 1890*; those for the 1900 index, 1900 values from the *Census, 1900*; and those for the 1909 index, 1904 values from the *Census, 1905*. For 1919–1948, the weights used were data on the reported value of improvements (i.e., buildings, additions, and alterations) and machinery and equipment, as of January 1, 1919 (in Simon Kuznets, *National Product since 1869, op. cit.*, Table IV-7, p. 220) and a rough estimate—5 per cent—of our total capital figure for land for 1919.

APPENDIX A

4. DERIVATION OF VALUE OF OUTPUT IN 1929 PRICES, MAJOR AND MINOR MANUFACTURING INDUSTRIES, SELECTED YEARS, 1879–1953

To deflate value of output data for minor industry groups for all censal years, 1879–1919, and for 1929, 1937, and 1948, we constructed indexes of wholesale prices on a 1929 base. The deflated components of a major group were added to obtain the deflated output of the major group. Weights used in constructing indexes of wholesale prices, unless it is otherwise indicated, were the relative importance of the value of output in the late twenties of commodities included in the indexes (see *Wholesale Price Bulletins* 493 and 572, Bureau of Labor Statistics). Arithmetic averages were used unless it is otherwise specified. The composition of the price indexes for minor groups are described below.

a. Food and Kindred Products

(*i*) *Bakery and confectionery products.* The following indexes were linked: 1926–1948: a weighted index combining the BLS wholesale price indexes for bread, N.Y.C.; bread, Chicago; soda crackers; sweet crackers; pretzels; and powdered cocoa; 1914–1926: a weighted index for bread, New York; bread, Cincinnati; and soda crackers (BLS); 1890–1914: a weighted index of bread, New York; bread, Washington, D.C.; and soda crackers (BLS); 1879–1890: unweighted average of all the bread and cracker series in *Wholesale Prices, Wages, and Transportation* (Senate Report 1934, Finance Committee, 52nd Congress, 2nd Sess., Part I, Washington, D.C., 1893), also known as the Aldrich Report.

(*ii*) *Canned products.* 1926–1948: BLS subgroup index for fruits and vegetables; 1914–1926: a weighted index of the BLS series for canned peaches, pineapples, corn, peas, tomatoes, and red salmon; 1908–1914: a weighted index of dried apples, prunes, and raisins, canned corn, peas, and tomatoes, and red salmon (BLS); 1890–1908: a weighted index of dried apples, prunes, and raisins and canned salmon (BLS); 1879–1890: a weighted index of dried apples and raisins (Aldrich Report).

(*iii*) *Packing-house products.* 1914–1948: BLS subgroup index for meats, poultry, and fish (fish was introduced into the index by the BLS in 1948); 1890–1914: a weighted index of the following BLS series: beef, fresh, native sides, New York; beef, salt, extra mess; hams, smoked; mutton, dressed; cured pork, (a) salt, mess, (b) rough sides, and (c) short, clear sides; and lard, prime contract; 1879–1890: an unweighted average of the eight meat and two lard series in the Aldrich Report.

(*iv*) *Grain-mill products.* 1914–1948: a weighted index consisting of BLS series for white and yellow corn meal; Blue Rose (begins in 1915)

NOTES ON ESTIMATES IN MANUFACTURING, 1880-1953

and Honduras-Rexora rice; cattle feed (subgroup index); wheat flour: hard winter, Buffalo, (a) standard patents and (b) first clears; winter, Kansas City, (a) patents and (b) straights; Minneapolis, (a) standard patents and (b) second-short patents; Portland, patents; soft winter, (a) St. Louis, patents and (b) Toledo, patents (ends in 1942); and rye flour; 1890-1914: a weighted index of white and yellow corn meal; domestic-Honduras rice; cattle feed; prime cottonseed meal; wheat flour: (a) winter, straights, New York-Kansas City and (b) spring, New York-Minneapolis, patents; and rye flour (BLS); 1879-1890: a weighted average of wheat and rye flour, yellow corn meal, and Carolina rice (Aldrich Report).

(v) *Sugar refining*. 1890-1948: BLS index for granulated sugar; 1879-1890: index for refined, crushed and granulated sugar (Aldrich Report).

(vi) *Beverages and liquors*. Index for "other food products" used. See a. viii, below. For deflation of components, see Addenda, section A, below.

(vii) *Tobacco manufactures*. 1929-1948: a weighted index of the following BLS series: cigarettes, cigars, plug and smoking tobacco, and snuff; 1879-1929: index of cigars, cigarettes and tobacco, in William Howard Shaw, *Value of Commodity Output since 1869, op. cit.*

(viii) *Other food products*. 1926-1948: a weighted index of BLS series for other food products (subgroup) after removing granulated sugar; dairy products (subgroup); corn and wheat cereal breakfast food; and oatmeal; 1914-1926: a weighted average of all series mentioned above except corn and wheat cereal breakfast food; 1890-1914: a weighted index of Rio coffee; black pepper; corn starch; Formosa tea; cottonseed oil; cider vinegar; butter, (a) creamery, extra, New York, (b) dairy, New York, and (c) creamery, Elgin; and cheese, whole milk, colored (BLS); 1879-1890: weighted index of butter, cheese, Rio coffee, corn starch, and spices (Aldrich Report).

b. Textiles and Textile Products

(i) *Cotton goods*. 1914-1948: BLS subgroup index for cotton goods; 1890-1914: a weighted index of the following BLS series: denims; brown drillings (two series); unbleached and colored flannel; ginghams (two series); muslin (four series); print cloths; brown sheetings (three series); thread; and white, mule-spun, Northern carded yarns (two series); 1879-1890: group index (unweighted) for cotton textiles (Aldrich Report).

(ii) *Woolen and worsted goods*. 1914-1948: BLS subgroup index for woolen and worsted goods; 1890-1914: a weighted index of white

APPENDIX A

flannel; Middlesex and serge suiting; trousering; all wool (three series) and cotton warp (two series) women's dress goods; and worsted yarns (two series); 1879–1890: suitings group index (unweighted) (Aldrich Report).

(*iii*) *Silk and rayon goods.* 1926–1948: a weighted average of BLS indexes for silk and rayon subgroups; 1914–1926: BLS index for silk and rayon subgroup; 1890–1914: a weighted index of raw silk: (a) Japanese, filiatures, Kansai, No. 1-Sinshiu, No. 1, and (b) Italian, classical; 1879–1890: silks group index (unweighted) in Aldrich Report.

(*iv*) *Hosiery and knit goods.* 1926–1948: BLS subgroup index for hosiery and underwear; 1914–1926: a weighted index of the following BLS series: women's cotton, full-fashioned-mercerized hosiery; women's silk full-fashioned hosiery; women's cotton union suits; men's woolen (a) shirts and drawers and (b) union suits; 1890–1914: men's cotton hosiery; women's cotton (a) full-fashioned and (b) single thread, combed yarn hosiery; men's woolen (a) shirts and drawers and (b) union suits; 1879–1890: underwear group index (unweighted) in Aldrich Report.

(*v*) *Carpets, floor coverings, etc.* 1926–1948: a weighted index of the following BLS series: Axminster, Brussels velvet broadloom, and Wilton carpets; floor coverings: felt base, printed and rugs; linoleum, inlaid and plain; 1919–1926: a weighted index of Axminster, Brussels, and Wilton carpets; 1879–1919: Shaw's index for floor coverings.

(*vi*) *Clothing.* 1919–1948: BLS subgroup index for clothing; 1879–1919: Shaw's index for clothing and personal furnishings. For deflation of components, see Addenda, section B.

(*vii*) *Other textile products.* 1914–1948: BLS subgroup index for other textile products; 1879–1914: Shaw's index for housefurnishings (semidurable).

(*viii*) *Cotton + silk and rayon + woolen and worsted goods + textiles, n.e.c.* For 1948, the "Source Book" of *Statistics of Income* gives a combined figure for cotton, silk and woolen yarn, thread, and narrow fabric mills and includes rayon and silk broad-woven fabric mills in textiles, n.e.c. The available 1948 combined output data for cotton, silk and rayon, and woolen and worsted goods were, therefore, deflated by a weighted price index of these three commodities. Textiles, n.e.c., including rayon and silk broad-woven fabric mills, was deflated by the 1948 price index for textiles, n.e.c. To achieve comparability with 1948, a separate industry—cotton + silk and rayon + woolen and worsted goods + textiles, n.e.c.—for earlier years was set up. The implicit index in Table A-12 for this group of industries was derived by dividing the sum of the output in current prices of its components by their output in 1929 prices.

c. Leather and Leather Products

(i) *Boots, shoes, slippers, etc. (leather).* 1914–1948: BLS subgroup index for boots and shoes; 1879–1914: Shaw's index for shoes and other footwear.

(ii) *Other leather products.* 1914–1948: a weighted average of the BLS subgroup indexes for leather and for other leather products; 1890–1914: a weighted index of the following BLS series: leather: (a) calf, (b) harness, oak, (c) sole, hemlock and scoured backs; 1879–1890: unweighted average of: 13 tanned calfskin series; harness and sole leather. For deflation of components, see Addenda, section C.

d. Rubber Products

Since a breakdown of the rubber products major group into (a) tires and tubes and (b) other rubber products is not available before 1914, the following indexes were used in constructing an index for this group for 1879–1914: 1900–1914: Shaw's index for tires and tubes; 1890–1900: BLS index for Para rubber; 1879–1890: index for Para rubber (Aldrich Report). The group index for 1879–1914 was linked to the implicit group index (1929 = 100) derived by dividing the sum of the output in current prices of the two components by the output in 1929 prices.

(i) *Tires and tubes.* 1914–1948: BLS subgroup index for tires and tubes; 1900–1914: Shaw's index for tires and tubes.

(ii) *Other rubber products.* 1927–1948: a weighted index of the following BLS series: men's and women's rubber heels; garden hose; and men's rubbers; 1919–1927: composite index for biennial censal years 1919–1927 (using value of output in each censal year as weights) derived from *Census of Manufactures* data on value and output (in pairs) of rubber shoes, boots, soles, and heels; 1900–1914: Shaw's index for tires and tubes.

e. Forest Products

(i) *Sawmill and planing mill products.* 1914–1948: BLS subgroup index for lumber; 1890–1914: unweighted average of hemlock, Northern, No. 1; maple, hard and soft; oak, white, plain, New York; oak, white, quartered, New York; white pine boards; yellow pine siding; poplar; spruce; cypress shingles; shingles, white pine—Michigan white pine—red cedar and white pine doors; 1879–1890: an unweighted average of pine doors; pine (six series), hemlock, maple, oak and spruce boards; pine flooring; and four pine shingles series (Aldrich Report).

APPENDIX A

(*ii*) *Other wood products.* 1914–1948: BLS subgroup index for furniture; 1879–1914: Shaw's index for household furniture. For deflation of components, see Addenda, section D.

f. Paper, Pulp, and Products

1914–1948: BLS subgroup index for paper and pulp; 1890–1914: Shaw's index for magazines, newspapers, stationery and supplies, and miscellaneous paper products; 1879–1890: unweighted average of pine and hemlock lumber, in the log, not sawed (Aldrich Report). For deflation of components, see Addenda, section E.

g. Printing, Publishing, and Allied Industries

1919–1948: a weighted average of BLS price indexes for book paper (begins in 1921) and newsprint, combined with the BLS index of union hourly wage rates in the printing trades (*Handbook of Labor Statistics, 1950 Edition*, BLS, p. 89); 1890–1919: an average of the following (equally weighted): (a) an index of wage rates derived from average hourly earnings data in Paul Douglas, *Real Wages in the United States, 1890–1926* (Houghton Mifflin, 1930), p. 96 for book and job and newspaper printing and (b) Shaw's price index for magazines, newspapers, stationery and supplies, and miscellaneous paper products; 1879–1890: an average of: (a) an unweighted average of wage rate indexes for various printing skills (Aldrich Report) and (b) an unweighted average of the price indexes for pine and hemlock lumber, in the log, not sawed (Aldrich Report). For deflation of components, see Addenda, section F.

h. Chemicals and Allied Products

(*i*) *Chemicals proper, acids, compounds, etc.* 1914–1948: BLS subgroup index for chemicals; 1890–1914: an unweighted index of muriatic acid; sulphuric acid; alcohol, wood, refined; bicarbonate of soda; sulphur; and alum, lumps (BLS); 1879–1890: an unweighted index of bichromate of potash; blue vitriol; crude brimstone; copperas; muriatic acid; soda ash; brown and white sugar of lead; sulphuric acid; rifle powder (two series); and alum, lump, crystal (Aldrich Report).

(*ii*) *Allied chemical substances.* 1914–1948: a weighted index of following BLS subgroups: (a) soap (subgroup index begins in 1926; for 1914–1926, a weighted index of two laundry soap series was computed): (b) drugs and pharmaceuticals; (c) oils and fats (subgroup index begins in 1926; for 1914–1926 a weighted index was computed using tallow, inedible, packer's prime; copra, South Sea; and crude cocoanut and palm, niger vegetable oils); and paint and paint materials; 1890–1914: a weighted average of Shaw's index for drug, toilet and household preparations; and paint materials (unweighted average of linseed oil, spirits of turpentine, white lead, and white zinc [BLS]); 1879–1890: an unweighted average of alcohol; calomel; refined glycerine; linseed oil, and castile soap (Aldrich Report). For deflation of components, see Addenda, section G.

(*iii*) *Fertilizers.* 1914–1948: a weighted average of the BLS subgroup indexes for fertilizer materials and mixed fertilizers; 1879–1914: index for chemicals proper, acids, compounds, etc. used (see h. *i*, above).

i. Petroleum Refining

1914–1948: BLS subgroup index for petroleum products; 1879–1914: Shaw's index for fuel and lighting products, manufactured.

j. Stone, Clay, and Glass Products

1914–1948: a weighted index of the following BLS series: plate glass, (a) 3 to 5 square feet and (b) 5 to 10 square feet; window glass, (a) single A and (b) single B; brick and tile (subgroup); Portland cement (subgroup); common and hydrated building lime; dinner sets, semivitreous (begins in 1924); pitchers—bowls, glass; plates; teacups and saucers; and tumblers; 1891–1914: F. C. Mills' unpublished index for stone, clay and glass products (unweighted geometric mean of appropriate BLS series); 1879–1891: a weighted index of: brick, common, domestic building; cement, Rosendale; lime, Rockland; window glass, American, 10 × 14, firsts, single; plate glass, polished, unsilvered (six series); glassware (five series) available in the Aldrich Report, using value of product weights in the 1914 *Census of Manufactures*. For deflation of components, see Addenda, section H.

k. Iron and Steel Products

(*i*) *Iron and steel.* 1914–1948: BLS subgroup index for iron and steel; 1890–1914: a weighted index of: bar iron, best refined, from store, Philadelphia; steel rails, Bessemer; fence wire, barbed, galvanized; pig iron, foundry, No. 1-basic; woodscrews; saws (two series); steel billets, Bessemer; and steel sheets (BLS); 1879–1890: a weighted index of: bar iron, best refined, rolled; iron rails (ends in 1882); standard; iron wire; nails, cut; pig iron, No. 1, anthracite, foundry; woodscrews; saws (three series); and iron rods (Aldrich Report). The value of product in the 1914 *Census of Manufactures* was used as the weight for 1879–1914. For deflation of components, see Addenda, section I.

(*ii*) *Metal building materials and supplies.* 1914–1948: a weighted index of the following BLS series: cast iron, black steel, and galvanized steel pipe; butts; concrete reinforced bars; structural steel (subgroup);

APPENDIX A

plumbing and heating; and stoves [1939–1948: a weighted average of coal, electric, gas and oil stoves (BLS); 1914–1939: Shaw's index for heating and cooking apparatus and household appliances, except electrical]; 1879–1914: index for iron and steel (see k. *i*, above).

(*iii*) *Hardware, tools, etc.* 1939–1948: a weighted index of machine, plow, stove, and track bolts; files; hammers; hatchets; axes; nails; woodscrews; cross-cut and hand saws; and planes (BLS); 1879–1939: Shaw's index for carpenters' and mechanics' tools.

l. Nonferrous Metals and Products

(*i*) *Precious metals products and processes; jewelry, etc.* 1879–1948: an unweighted index of (a) the price of silver [1879–1890: silver bullion, ounce fine, London (equivalent value in dollars, based on average price of exchange); 1890–1948: silver, bar, ounce fine, New York (BLS)]; and (b) the legal coinage value of gold per fine ounce. Data for the price of silver, 1879–1890, are from the *Report of the Director of the Mint upon the Production of Precious Metals in the United States, 1898*, pp. 252–255. Data for the price of gold are from *Minerals Yearbook Review* of 1940, Department of the Interior, p. 63.

(*ii*) *Other metals, products and processes.* 1914–1948: BLS subgroup index for nonferrous metals; 1890–1914: a weighted index of copper, ingot; copper, sheet, hot rolled (base sizes); bare copper wire; lead, pig; lead pipe; and zinc, sheet (BLS); 1879–1890: a weighted index of copper, ingot; copper, sheet; lead, pig; lead pipe; and zinc, imported, sheet. *Census of Manufactures, 1914* value of product data were used as weights.

In the Addenda to this Appendix the nonferrous metals and products group is broken down into four components. For deflation of these components, see Addenda, section J.

m. Machinery, Excluding Transportation Equipment

(*i*) *Electrical machinery and equipment.* 1938–1948: a weighted average of maintenance account indexes for: telephone and telegraph lines; signals and interlockers; power transmission systems; and power plant machinery (*Railroad Construction Indices, 1914–1950*, Engineering Section, Bureau of Valuation, Interstate Commerce Commission offset release, August 1, 1951); 1889–1938: Shaw's index for electrical equipment, industrial and commercial; 1879–1889: index for iron and steel (see k. *i*, above). Weights used for 1938–1948 were the relative values of the accounts in 1914–1921 (ICC).

(*ii*) *Agricultural machinery and equipment.* 1914–1948: BLS subgroup index for farm machinery; 1889–1914: Shaw's index for farm machinery and equipment; 1879–1889: index for iron and steel (see k. i, above).

(iii) *Office and store machinery and equipment.* Index for factory, household, and miscellaneous machinery used (see m. iv, below).

(iv) *Factory, household, and miscellaneous machinery.* 1939–1948: Department of Commerce implicit price index for investment in producers' durable equipment; 1915–1939: Lowell J. Chawner's implicit price index for new manufacturing capital expenditures for equipment (Lowell J. Chawner, "Capital Expenditures for Manufacturing Plant and Equipment—1915 to 1940," *Survey of Current Business*, March 1941); 1889–1915: Shaw's index for industrial machinery and equipment; 1879–1889: index for iron and steel (see k. i, above).

n. Transportation Equipment

(i) *Motor vehicles, complete or parts.* 1919–1948: BLS subgroup index for motor vehicles; 1899–1919: a weighted average of Shaw's indexes for (a) passenger vehicles, motorized, and (b) business vehicles, motorized (begins in 1904); 1879–1899: index for iron and steel (see k. i, above).

(ii) *Locomotives and railroad equipment.* 1938–1948: a weighted average of ICC indexes (*Railroad Construction Indices, 1914–1950*, op. cit.) for steam locomotives; other locomotives; freight-train cars; and passenger-train cars, using relative values of the accounts (ICC) as weights; 1889–1938: Shaw's index for locomotives and railroad cars; 1879–1889: index for iron and steel (see k. i, above).

(iii) *Aircraft.* 1914–1918: index for miscellaneous manufactures used (see o. below).

o. Miscellaneous Manufactures

1914–1948: BLS group index for manufactured products; censal years 1879–1909: implicit price index derived by dividing sum of value of product of fourteen major groups in current prices by value of product in 1929 prices. For deflation of components, see Addenda, section K.

ADDENDA

From the 1948 unpublished data furnished by the Internal Revenue Service, we were able to secure additional breakdowns of value of output for several of the major and minor industrial groups listed above. A comparable breakdown was made for the censal years 1879–1919, but it was not possible to make any for 1929 and 1937. Price indexes

APPENDIX A

used in deflating value of output for these additional breakdowns are described below.

A. Beverages and liquors (minor group)

    1. Nonalcoholic beverages.

1926–1948: a weighted index of ginger ale; grape juice; and plain soda (BLS); 1879–1926: index for beverages and liquors used (see a. *vi*, above).

    2. Malt liquors and malt.
    3. Wines.
    4. Distilled liquors.

1879–1948: index for beverages and liquors used (see a. *vi*, above)

B. Clothing (minor group)

    1. Hats, except cloth and millinery.
    2. Men's and boy's clothing, except fur and rubber.
    3. Women's clothing, children's and infants' wear, except fur and rubber.
    4. Millinery.

1879–1948: index for clothing used (see b. *vi*, above).

C. Other leather products (minor group)

    1. Leather, tanned, curried, and finished.

1914–1948: BLS subgroup index for leather; 1879–1914: index for other leather products used (see c. *ii*, above).

    2. Leather products, n.e.c.

1914–1948: BLS subgroup index for other leather products; 1879–1914: index for other leather products used (see c. *ii*, above).

D. Other wood products (minor group)

    1. Wooden containers.

1926–1948: a weighted index of the following BLS series: barrels, wooden, 50-gallon tierce; caskets, adult size, wood, covered; cigar boxes, cedar veneer; and shipping cases, casket pine, adult size; 1879–1926: index for other wood products used (see e. *ii*, above).

    2. Wood products, n.e.c.

1879–1948: index for other wood products used (see e. *ii*, above).

E. Paper, pulp, and products (major group)

    1. Paper, pulp, and paperboard mills.
    2. Paper bags, containers and boxes.
    3. Other paper products.

1879–1948: index for paper, pulp and products used (see f., above).

NOTES ON ESTIMATES IN MANUFACTURING, 1880–1953

F. Printing, publishing, and allied industries (major group)
  1. Book and job, including lithographing.
  2. Newspapers and periodicals.
  3. Allied industries.
1879–1948: index for printing, publishing, and allied industries used (see g., above).

G. Allied chemical substances (minor group)
  1. Drugs, medicines, and cosmetics.
1914–1948: BLS subgroup index for drugs and pharmaceuticals; 1889–1914: Shaw's index for drug, toilet, and household preparations; 1879–1889: an unweighted average of alcohol; calomel; and refined glycerine (Aldrich Report).
  2. Soaps, cleaning, and polishing preparations.
1926–1948: BLS subgroup index for soap; 1914–1926: a weighted index of 2 BLS laundry soap series; 1879–1914: index for allied chemical substances used (see h. *ii*, above).
  3. Paints and varnishes.
1914–1948: BLS subgroup index for paint and paint materials; 1890–1914: an unweighted average of four BLS paint materials series: linseed oil, spirits of turpentine, white lead, and white zinc; 1879–1890: index for allied chemical substances used (see h. *ii*, above).
  4. Other chemical substances.
1879–1948: index for allied chemical substances used (see h. *ii*, above).

H. Stone, clay, and glass products (major group)
  1. Cement, lime, and concrete products.
1914–1948: a weighted index of Portland cement (subgroup) and common and hydrated building lime (BLS); 1890–1914: a weighted index of Portland cement, New York, Chicago; common lime, Rockport, lump; 1879–1890: a weighted index of cement, Rosendale; lime, Rockland (Aldrich Report), using value of output weights in the 1914 *Census of Manufactures*.
  2. Clay and pottery products.
1914–1948: a weighted index of brick and tile (subgroup): dinner sets, semivitreous (begins in 1924); teacups and saucers, white granite (BLS); 1890–1914: a weighted index of brick, common, red, domestic; plates, white granite; and teacups and saucers, white granite (BLS); 1879–1890: index for brick, common, domestic, building (Aldrich Report).
  3. Glass and glass products.
1890–1948: a weighted index of plate glass, (a) 3 to 5 square feet and

APPENDIX A

(b) 5 to 10 square feet; window glass, (a) single A and (b) single B; pitchers and bowls, glass; and tumblers, glass (BLS); 1879–1890: a weighted index of window glass, American 10 × 14, firsts, single; plate glass, polished, unsilvered (six series); and glassware (five series). (Aldrich Report), using value of output weights in the 1914 *Census of Manufactures*.

    4. Cut stone and products.

    5. Stone, clay, and glass products, n.e.c.

1879–1948: index for stone, clay, and glass products used (see j., above).

I. Iron and steel (minor group)

    1. Tin cans and other tinware.

1914–1948: a weighted index of cans, sanitary No. 3 or No. 2 (begins 1926); terneplate; and tinplate (BLS); 1899–1914: BLS index for tinplate.

    2. Blast furnaces, steel works, and rolling mills.

    3. Ordnance and accessories.

    4. Iron and steel, n.e.c.

1899–1948: the index for iron and steel (see k. *i*, above) after removing cans, terneplate and tinplate was used; 1879–1899: index for iron and steel (k. *i*) used.

J. Nonferrous metals and products (major group)

    1. Clocks, watches, and parts.

1879–1948: implicit price index derived by dividing value of output of nonferrous metals and products group by output deflated by price indexes described in l. *i* and *ii* above.

    2. Jewelry, silverware, and plating.

1879–1948: index for precious metal products and processes; jewelry, etc., used (see l. *i*, above).

    3. Smelting, refining, and alloying.

    4. Nonferrous metal products, n.e.c.

1879–1948: index for other metals, products and processes used (see l. *ii*, above). Gold, silver, and platinum reducing and refining make up a very small part of the smelting, refining, and alloying group; thus, the index in l. *ii* was used rather than the major group index.

K. Miscellaneous manufactures

    1. Professional, scientific, photographic and optical instruments.

    2. Miscellaneous manufactures, n.e.c.

1879–1948: index for miscellaneous manufactures used (see o., above).

NOTES ON ESTIMATES IN MANUFACTURING, 1880–1953

C. Total Number of Persons Employed in Selected Manufacturing Industries, 1900–1953

For 1900–1919, the total number of persons employed is the sum of (1) proprietors and firm members, (2) salaried officers and personnel, and (3) the monthly average number of wage earners, as reported in the *Censuses of Manufactures*. For 1929–1948, Department of Commerce estimates of (1) the number of active proprietors of unincorporated enterprises and (2) the average number of full- and part-time employees were added to secure total persons employed. These data are from the *Survey of Current Business*, National Income Supplement, 1954, pp. 202–203, Table 28. The totals obtained from data in the census and the National Income Supplement are considered to be conceptually comparable.

In computing the number of persons employed in selected industries, we rearranged the census industries in a manner identical to that used in securing data for output and capital for 1880–1919. This rearrangement was made to bring about the same industrial coverage as that of the industries listed in *Statistics of Income*. For 1900, data are presented in Appendix Table A-16 both including and excluding custom and neighborhood shops. Custom and neighborhood shops are excluded after 1900. In the *Census of Manufactures, 1905*, Part I, Table 1, pp. 3–20, data for 1900 for wage earners and salaried officers and personnel employed in establishments are presented excluding custom and neighborhood shops, but no data are presented for firm members and proprietors. To estimate the latter we first subtracted the number of establishments excluding custom and neighborhood shops (in the census of 1905) from those including these shops (in the census of 1900). We then subtracted this difference from the number of firm members and proprietors in 1900 in establishments including custom and neighborhood shops. In making this computation, we assumed that there was only one firm member or proprietor per custom or neighborhood shop.

Since we have excluded ship and boat building and repairing from manufacturing, the data for transportation equipment excluding motor vehicles in the National Income Supplement had to be adjusted to exclude the former industry. For 1929 and 1937, we multiplied the ratio of the total number employed in ship and boat building and repairing to the total number employed in transportation equipment excluding motor vehicles (in the 1929 and 1937 *Censuses of Manufactures*) by the total number employed in transportation equipment excluding motor vehicles (from the National Income Supplement). The product was then subtracted from total personnel in transportation

APPENDIX A

equipment excluding motor vehicles (in the National Income Supplement) to give us an estimate of total personnel excluding those in ship building. For 1948, we applied the ratio of the number of wage earners and salaried personnel in 1948 to the number in 1947 in ship and boat building and repairing [from *Handbook of Labor Statistics, 1950 Edition* (BLS), p. 18, Table A-4] to wage earners and salaried personnel in that industry in 1947 (1947 census); we added the product to the number of proprietors and firm members in 1947 (1947 census) to obtain an estimate of total personnel in ship building. The same method was used to obtain an estimate of total personnel in transportation excluding motor vehicles which, for 1948, includes ship building. Since no census or BLS data are available for firm members and proprietors for 1948, we used 1947 census data and assumed that the change in their number from 1947 to 1948 was negligible. The ratio of estimated total personnel in ship building to total personnel in transportation equipment excluding motor vehicles (census data) was then applied to total personnel in transportation equipment excluding motor vehicles in 1948 (National Income Supplement). The estimate of total personnel in ship building, thus derived, was subtracted from total personnel in transportation equipment excluding motor vehicles in 1948 (National Income Supplement) to give us an estimate of total personnel in transportation equipment excluding those in ship building.

Although we have excluded coke-oven products from capital and output in manufacturing in all years except 1948 and from employment in all years before 1929, we did not exclude the number employed in coal products from the petroleum and coal products group in the National Income Supplement. We believe that this does not affect the trend in the ratios for petroleum refining in which total persons employed was used.

NOTES ON ESTIMATES IN MANUFACTURING, 1880–1953

D. Supporting Tables
TABLE A-8
Total Capital in Book Values and in 1929 Prices, by Major and Minor Manufacturing Industries, Selected Years, 1880–1948
(millions of dollars)

	1880a	1890a	1900a	1900b	1904b	1909b	1914b	1919b	1929c	1937c	1948c, d
All manufacturing											
Book values	2,718	5,697	8,663	8,168	11,588	16,937	20,784	40,289	59,072	50,166	113,394
1929 prices (sum of components)	4,821	11,157	18,626	17,452	23,295	31,563	36,737	46,094	63,022	55,319	77,982
Food and kindred products											
Book values	498	925	1,647	1,576	2,230	2,935	3,668	6,272	8,881	8,069	16,071
1929 prices	897	1,839	3,760	3,598	4,656	5,517	6,515	7,593	9,591	9,180	10,488
Bakery and confectionery products											
Book values	28	72	123	114	173	295	426	911	1,568	1,131	1,757
1929 prices	50	143	281	256	361	555	757	1,103	1,693	1,287	1,146
Canned products											
Book values	9	25	59	59	90	119	172	378	853	820	1,681
1929 prices	16	50	135	135	188	224	306	458	921	933	1,097
Mill products											
Book values	177	208	219	189	265	349	380	802	471	496	1,060
1929 prices	319	414	500	432	553	656	675	971	509	564	691
Packing house products											
Book values	49	117	189	189	238	378	537	1,185	1,385	1,114	1,975
1929 prices	88	233	432	432	497	711	954	1,435	1,496	1,267	1,288
Sugar refining											
Book values	28	24	204	204	221	283	316	473	1,053	599	780
1929 prices	50	48	466	466	461	532	561	573	1,137	681	509
Liquors and beverages											
Book values	135	310	534	516	660	873	1,016	782	692	1,371	3,158
1929 prices	243	616	1,219	1,178	1,378	1,641	1,805	947	747	1,560	2,061

(continued)

APPENDIX A

TABLE A-8 (continued)

	1880a	1890a	1900a	1900b	1904b	1909b	1914b	1919b	1929c	1937c	1948c,d
Other food products											
Book values	32	73	195	193	259	392	517	1,136	1,709	1,577	3,302
1929 prices	58	145	445	441	541	737	918	1,375	1,846	1,794	2,154
Tobacco products											
Book values	40	96	124	112	324	246	304	605	1,150	961	2,330
1929 prices	72	191	283	256	676	462	540	732	1,242	1,093	1,520
Textile products											
Book values	602	1,119	1,494	1,366	1,783	2,550	2,881	6,205	7,687	4,770	10,397
1929 prices	998	2,024	3,145	2,876	3,482	4,636	5,163	6,752	8,195	5,638	6,892
Cotton goods											
Book values	246	392	528	528	702	936	1,039	2,145	1,603	866	
1929 prices	408	709	1,112	1,112	1,371	1,702	1,862	2,334	1,709	1,024	
Silk and rayon goods											
Book values	19	51	81	81	110	152	210	533	869	441	3,693
1929 prices	32	92	171	171	215	276	376	580	926	521	2,447
Woolen and worsted goods											
Book values	117	203	264	264	313	429	403	868	601	415	
1929 prices	194	367	556	556	611	780	722	945	641	491	
Carpets, floor coverings, etc.											
Book values	25	43	53	53	69	97	112	179	262	199	483
1929 prices	41	78	112	112	135	176	201	195	279	235	320
Knit goods											
Book values	16	51	82	82	107	164	216	516	709	433	929
1929 prices	27	92	173	173	209	298	387	561	756	512	616
Clothing											
Book values	114	292	350	257	345	568	633	1,447	1,758	1,036	3,018
1929 prices	189	528	737	541	674	1,033	1,134	1,575	1,874	1,225	2,001

(continued)

NOTES ON ESTIMATES IN MANUFACTURING, 1880-1953

TABLE A-8 (continued)

	1880a	1890a	1900a	1900b	1904b	1909b	1914b	1919b	1929c	1937c	1948c, d
Textiles, n.e.c.											
Book values	65	87	136	101	137	204	268	517	1,887	1,380	2,253
1929 prices	108	157	286	213	268	371	480	563	2,012	1,631	1,493
Cotton+woolen and worsted +silk and rayon goods +textiles, n.e.c.											
Book values	447	733	1,009	974	1,262	1,721	1,920	4,063	4,960	3,102	5,946
1929 prices	741	1,325	2,124	2,051	2,465	3,129	3,441	4,421	5,288	3,667	3,940
Leather and products											
Book values	157	274	369	335	452	659	743	1,523	1,167	751	1,303
1929 prices	328	640	891	809	1,066	1,359	1,351	1,411	1,213	808	817
Boots and shoes											
Book values	43	95	102	100	123	197	255	581	625	410	710
1929 prices	90	222	246	242	290	406	464	538	650	441	445
Other leather products											
Book values	114	179	267	235	329	462	488	942	542	341	592
1929 prices	238	418	645	568	776	953	887	873	563	367	371
Rubber products											
Book values	9	37	78	78	99	162	268	960	1,088	795	1,791
1929 prices	10	36	74	74	93	139	265	704	1,131	816	1,422
Tires and tubes											
Book values	n.a.	n.a.	n.a.	n.a.	n.a.	n.a.	130	635	918	586	1,383
1929 prices	n.a.	n.a.	n.a.	n.a.	n.a.	n.a.	129	466	954	602	1,098
Other rubber products											
Book values	n.a.	n.a.	n.a.	n.a.	n.a.	n.a.	138	325	170	209	361
1929 prices	n.a.	n.a.	n.a.	n.a.	n.a.	n.a.	136	238	177	215	287
Forest products											
Book values	361	825	1,110	872	1,174	1,767	1,932	2,726	3,842	2,405	4,816
1929 prices	847	1,950	2,868	2,253	2,662	3,591	3,475	3,155	4,083	2,548	2,934

(continued)

APPENDIX A

TABLE A-8 (*continued*)

	1880[a]	1890[a]	1900[a]	1900[b]	1904[b]	1909[b]	1914[b]	1919[b]	1929[c]	1937[c]	1948[c,d]
Sawmill and planing mill products											
Book values	219	518	731	520	694	1,122	1,193	1,730	2,660	1,562	3,000
1929 prices	514	1,225	1,889	1,344	1,574	2,280	2,146	2,002	2,827	1,655	1,826
Other wood products											
Book values	142	307	379	352	480	645	739	996	1,182	843	1,805
1929 prices	333	726	979	910	1,088	1,311	1,329	1,153	1,256	893	1,099
Paper, pulp and products											
Book values	58	115	219	218	354	523	689	1,195	2,060	1,942	3,692
1929 prices	90	200	455	453	670	1,002	1,246	1,524	2,239	2,062	2,476
Printing, publishing, and allied industries											
Book values	80	234	342	342	450	611	745	1,189	2,622	2,320	3,984
1929 prices	144	466	801	801	939	1,265	1,444	1,556	2,737	2,505	2,571
Chemicals and allied products											
Book values	137	288	458	457	634	911	1,280	2,594	3,942	3,537	9,109
1929 prices	206	478	871	869	1,134	1,531	2,078	2,777	4,221	3,965	6,487
Fertilizers											
Book values	18	41	61	61	69	122	217	312	335	198	334
1929 prices	27	68	116	116	123	205	352	334	359	222	237
Chemicals proper, acids, etc.											
Book values	49	96	145	144	194	273	390	941	973	1,125	2,580
1929 prices	74	159	276	274	347	459	633	1,007	1,042	1,261	1,830
Allied chemical substances—drugs, oils, etc.											
Book values	70	151	252	252	371	516	673	1,341	2,634	2,214	5,917
1929 prices	105	251	479	479	664	867	1,093	1,436	2,820	2,482	4,196

(*continued*)

NOTES ON ESTIMATES IN MANUFACTURING, 1880–1953

TABLE A-8 (continued)

	1880a	1890a	1900a	1900b	1904b	1909b	1914b	1919b	1929c	1937c	1948c, d
Petroleum refining											
Book values	27	77	95	95	136	182	326	1,170	5,745	5,814	15,363
1929 prices	37	151	195	195	254	327	552	1,380	6,092	6,503	11,188
Stone, clay, and glass products											
Book values	83	217	351	336	554	860	990	1,267	2,351	1,825	2,934
1929 prices	156	408	741	709	1,138	1,755	1,937	1,676	2,592	1,975	2,128
Metal and its products											
Book values	655	1,463	2,332	2,327	3,477	5,366	6,679	14,181	17,517	16,746	40,253
1929 prices (sum of deflated components)	1,019	2,735	4,481	4,475	6,733	9,729	11,815	16,618	18,672	18,015	28,159
Iron and steel and products											
Book values	318	646	860	870	1,544	2,411	2,836	5,671	6,226	6,383	13,796
1929 prices	472	1,143	1,581	1,599	2,886	4,305	5,166	6,735	6,666	6,719	9,645
Iron and steel											
Book values	258	469	657	657	1,185	1,845	2,147	4,456	4,155	4,394	9,521
1929 prices	383	830	1,208	1,208	2,215	3,295	3,911	5,292	4,449	4,625	6,598
Metal building materials and supplies											
Book values	10	73	87	97	202	340	417	665	756	805	2,309
1929 prices	15	129	160	178	378	607	760	790	809	847	1,600
Hardware, tools, etc.											
Book values	49	104	117	116	156	225	273	549	1,315	1,184	1,177
1929 prices	73	184	215	213	292	402	497	652	1,408	1,246	816
Nonferrous metals and products											
Book values	86	187	381	360	455	705	827	1,484	2,194	2,090	3,401
1929 prices	116	276	646	610	804	1,203	1,365	1,808	2,364	2,338	2,520

(continued)

APPENDIX A

TABLE A-8 (continued)

	1880a	1890a	1900a	1900b	1904b	1909b	1914b	1919b	1929c	1937c	1948c, d
Precious metal products and processes											
Book values	29	70	97	97	126	181	196	315	352	247	515
1929 prices	39	103	164	164	223	309	323	384	379	276	379
Other metals, products, and processes											
Book values	57	117	284	263	329	524	631	1,169	1,842	1,843	2,663
1929 prices	77	173	481	446	581	894	1,041	1,424	1,985	2,062	1,960
Machinery excluding transportation equipment											
Book values	242	557	924	924	1,309	1,860	2,331	4,700	5,833	4,979	14,674
1929 prices	414	1,160	1,917	1,917	2,710	3,654	4,293	5,595	6,166	5,286	10,352
Electrical machinery and equipment; radios											
Book values	2	19	86	87	183	282	390	963	1,514	1,120	4,874
1929 prices	3	40	178	180	379	554	718	1,146	1,600	1,189	3,438
Agricultural machinery											
Book values	62	145	158	158	197	256	339	367	730	749	1,745
1929 prices	106	302	328	328	408	503	624	437	772	795	1,226
Office equipment, etc.											
Book values	6	8	24	24	41	72	95	167	430	413	815
1929 prices	10	17	50	50	85	141	175	199	455	438	573
Factory, household, and miscellaneous machinery											
Book values	172	385	656	655	888	1,250	1,507	3,203	3,159	2,697	6,962
1929 prices	295	802	1,361	1,359	1,839	2,456	2,775	3,813	3,339	2,863	4,892

(continued)

246

TABLE A-8 (concluded)

	1880[a]	1890[a]	1900[a]	1900[b]	1904[b]	1909[b]	1914[b]	1919[b]	1929[c]	1937[c]	1946[c,d]
Transportation equipment											
Book values	9	73	167	173	169	390	685	2,326	3,264	3,294	8,382
1929 prices	17	156	337	349	333	567	991	2,480	3,746	3,672	5,642
Motor vehicles											
Book values	n.a.	2	30	36	29	184	426	1,816	2,575	2,504	6,006
1929 prices	n.a.	4	60	73	57	267	616	1,936	2,742	2,792	4,016
Locomotives and railroad equipment											
Book values	9	71	137	137	139	206	259	491	578	610	927
1929 prices	17	152	276	276	274	299	375	523	616	680	618
Aircraft and parts											
Book values	n.a.	n.a.	n.a.	n.a.	n.a.	n.a.	n.a.	18	80	80	1,114
1929 prices	n.a.	n.a.	n.a.	n.a.	n.a.	n.a.	n.a.	19	118	201	743
Miscellaneous manufacturing											
Book values	51	123	168	166	245	411	583	1,007	2,168	1,192	3,681
1929 prices	89	230	344	468	468	712	896	948	2,256	1,304	2,420

n.a. = not available.
n.e.c. = not elsewhere classified.
[a] Includes custom and neighborhood shops.
[b] Factories producing annual value of $500 or more.
[c] Factories producing annual value of $5,000 or more.
[d] Some minor groups are not adjusted for accelerated depreciation of investment in emergency facilities or for intangible assets. Therefore, sum of parts does not always equal total.
Source: For derivation see Appendix A, section B, part 1.

APPENDIX A

TABLE A-9

Fixed Capital in Book Values and in 1929 Prices, by Major and Minor Manufacturing Industries, Selected Years, 1890–1948

(millions of dollars)

	1890[a]	1900[a]	1904[b]	1929[c]	1937[c]	1948[c, d]
All manufacturing						
Book value	2,646	4,223	5,596	27,410	23,282	45,727
1929 prices (sum of components)	5,553	9,651	12,316	30,853	25,851	36,526
Food and kindred products						
Book value	498	896	1,039	4,001	3,367	5,526
1929 prices	1,062	2,074	2,289	4,531	3,775	4,376
Bakery and confectionery products						
Book value	42	78	107	878	639	835
1929 prices	90	181	236	994	716	661
Canned products						
Book value	10	27	41	317	278	582
1929 prices	21	62	90	359	312	461
Mill products						
Book value	136	143	140	198	196	366
1929 prices	290	331	309	224	220	290
Packing house products						
Book value	45	67	87	568	447	632
1929 prices	96	155	192	643	501	500
Sugar refining						
Book value	14	100	97	612	311	356
1929 prices	30	231	214	693	349	282
Liquors and beverages						
Book value	190	316	378	315	639	1,222
1929 prices	405	731	833	357	716	968
Other food products						
Book value	41	136	152	993	762	1,435
1929 prices	87	315	335	1,125	854	1,136
Tobacco products						
Book value	19	30	36	120	95	188
1929 prices	41	69	79	136	107	149
Textiles and products						
Book value	491	667	825	2,932	1,928	2,923
1929 prices	1,004	1,533	1,825	3,339	2,126	2,390
Cotton goods						
Book value	251	334	440	864	500	
1929 prices	513	768	973	984	551	
Silk and rayon goods						
Book value	21	33	47	382	251	1,380
1929 prices	43	76	104	435	277	1,128
Woolen and worsted goods						
Book value	87	105	144	239	165	
1929 prices	178	241	319	272	182	

(continued)

NOTES ON ESTIMATES IN MANUFACTURING, 1880–1953

TABLE A-9 (continued)

	1890[a]	1900[a]	1904[b]	1929[c]	1937[c]	1948[c, d]
Carpets, floor coverings, etc.						
Book value	20	25	33	122	84	187
1929 prices	41	57	73	139	93	153
Knit goods						
Book value	24	37	50	290	189	329
1929 prices	49	85	111	330	208	269
Clothing						
Book value	48	68	58	301	171	369
1929 prices	98	156	128	343	189	302
Textiles, n.e.c.						
Book value	41	65	53	734	568	655
1929 prices	84	149	117	836	626	336
Cotton + silk and rayon + woolen and worsted goods + textiles, n.e.c.						
Book value	400	537	684	2,219	1,484	2,035
1929 prices	818	1,234	1,513	2,527	1,636	1,464
Leather and products						
Book value	75	104	127	269	159	235
1929 prices	160	240	280	308	179	186
Boots and shoes						
Book value	22	26	30	141	84	114
1929 prices	47	60	66	162	95	90
Other leather products						
Book value	53	78	97	128	75	126
1929 prices	113	180	214	147	85	100
Rubber products						
Book value	10	23	30	434	240	618
1929 prices	22	54	66	485	268	480
Tires and tubes						
Book value	n.a.	n.a.	n.a.	363	145	422
1929 prices	n.a.	n.a.	n.a.	406	162	328
Other rubber products						
Book value	n.a.	n.a.	n.a.	71	95	154
1929 prices	n.a.	n.a.	n.a.	79	106	120
Forest products						
Book value	346	584	504	2,001	1,336	2,021
1929 prices	716	1,224	1,115	2,261	1,473	1,638
Sawmill and planing mill products						
Book value	224	426	308	1,504	983	1,449
1929 prices	464	893	681	1,700	1,084	1,174
Other wood products						
Book value	121	158	196	497	353	554
1929 prices	251	331	434	562	389	449
Paper, pulp, and products						
Book value	73	143	240	1,196	1,099	1,900
1929 prices	153	331	527	1,345	1,218	1,526

(continued)

APPENDIX A

TABLE A-9 (*continued*)

	1890[a]	1900[a]	1904[b]	1929[c]	1937[c]	1948[c, d]
Printing, publishing, and allied industries						
Book value	139	191	246	974	792	1,442
1929 prices	295	449	538	1,043	865	1,135
Chemicals and allied products						
Book value	128	209	299	1,497	1,547	4,100
1929 prices	269	480	660	1,719	1,728	3,309
Fertilizers						
Book value	13	20	25	134	91	145
1929 prices	27	46	55	154	102	117
Chemicals proper, acids, etc.						
Book value	53	83	113	507	637	1,471
1929 prices	111	191	249	582	712	1,187
Allied chemical substances—drugs, oils, etc.						
Book value	61	106	161	856	819	2,360
1929 prices	128	244	355	983	915	1,905
Petroleum refining						
Book value	35	54	73	3,729	3,821	9,115
1929 prices	74	127	160	4,018	4,171	7,217
Stone, clay, and glass products						
Book value	129	222	368	1,451	1,091	1,462
1919 prices	275	509	811	1,685	1,238	1,158
Metal and its products						
Book value	680	1,072	1,756	8,294	7,505	15,281
1929 prices (sum of components)	1,435	2,495	3,854	9,389	8,363	12,236
Iron and steel and products						
Book values	346	462	920	3,786	3,507	6,438
1929 prices	738	1,087	2,013	4,235	3,892	5,146
Iron and steel						
Book value	264	364	750	2,914	2,699	4,618
1929 prices	563	856	1,641	3,260	2,996	3,691
Metal building materials and supplies						
Book value	30	41	88	297	331	638
1929 prices	64	96	193	332	367	510
Hardware, tools, etc.						
Book value	53	56	82	575	477	443
1929 prices	113	132	179	643	529	354
Nonferrous metals and products						
Book value	75	183	204	1,002	941	1,490
1929 prices	154	420	451	1,150	1,043	1,217
Precious metal products, and processes						
Book value	22	34	41	86	65	107
1929 prices	45	78	91	99	72	87

(*continued*)

NOTES ON ESTIMATES IN MANUFACTURING, 1880–1953

TABLE A-9 (concluded)

	1890[a]	1900[a]	1904[b]	1929[c]	1937[c]	1948[c, d]
Other metals, products, and processes						
Book values	53	149	163	916	876	1,176
1929 prices	109	342	361	1,052	971	962
Machinery excluding transportation equipment						
Book value	223	364	570	1,907	1,601	4,387
1929 prices	468	841	1,256	2,162	1,783	3,524
Electrical machinery and equipment; radios						
Book value	6	28	59	463	349	1,363
1929 prices	13	65	130	525	389	1,095
Agricultural machinery						
Book value	32	34	65	215	204	547
1929 prices	67	79	143	244	227	439
Office equipment, etc.						
Book value	3	9	15	106	129	310
1929 prices	6	21	33	120	144	249
Factory, household, and miscellaneous machinery						
Book value	182	292	431	1,123	919	1,959
1929 prices	382	674	949	1,273	1,023	1,573
Transportation equipment						
Book value	35	64	61	1,599	1,456	2,966
1929 prices	75	147	134	1,842	1,645	2,337
Motor vehicles						
Book value	1	15	13	1,232	1,040	2,153
1929 prices	2	35	29	1,419	1,175	1,705
Locomotives and railroad equipment						
Book value	34	49	48	307	351	303
1929 prices	72	113	106	354	397	240
Aircraft and parts						
Book value	n.a.	n.a.	n.a.	60	65	192
1929 prices	n.a.	n.a.	n.a.	69	73	152
Miscellaneous						
Book value	42	59	87	632	397	1,104
1929 prices	88	135	191	730	447	887

n.a. = not available.
n.e.c. = not elsewhere classified.
[a] Includes custom and neighborhood shops.
[b] Factories producing annual value of $500 or more.
[c] Factories producing annual value of $5,000 or more.
[d] Some minor groups not adjusted for accelerated depreciation of investment in emergency facilities or for intangible assets. Therefore, sum of the parts does not always equal totals.

Source: For derivation see Appendix A, section B, part 1.

APPENDIX A

TABLE A-10

Value of Output in Current and in 1929 Prices, by Major and Minor Manufacturing Industries, Selected Years, 1880-1948
(millions of dollars)

	1880[a]	1890[a]	1900[a]	1900[b]	1904[b]	1909[b]	1914[b]	1919[b]	1929[c,d]	1937[c,d]	1948[c,d]
All manufacturing											
Current prices	5,147	8,393	11,590	10,997	14,218	19,894	23,253	58,533	71,220	67,436	213,340
1929 prices (sum of deflated components)	8,820	15,274	23,182	21,984	26,136	32,648	36,434	45,090	71,220	74,687	128,124
Food products, total											
Current prices	1,442	2,188	3,001	2,857	3,709	5,072	6,139	14,193	15,014	15,881	45,273
1929 prices (sum of deflated components)	2,452	4,014	6,794	6,513	7,326	8,388	9,546	11,240	15,014	18,346	26,196
Bakery and confectionery products											
Current prices	93	188	267	246	371	554	755	1,979	2,171	2,023	5,090
1929 prices	174	349	529	487	695	949	1,206	1,730	2,171	2,083	3,111
Canned products											
Current prices	20	50	104	103	138	157	243	628	952	1,048	2,802
1929 prices	36	66	194	192	262	289	354	443	952	1,381	1,911
Mill products											
Current prices	505	514	561	501	713	884	878	2,052	1,555	1,313	4,643
1929 prices	499	582	1,055	898	969	1,055	1,183	1,185	1,555	1,379	2,364
Packing house products											
Current prices	304	562	786	784	914	1,856	1,665	4,288	5,403	4,677	13,181
1929 prices	1,034	1,719	2,646	2,604	2,589	2,819	2,901	3,978	5,403	5,151	6,080
Sugar refining											
Current prices	156	123	248	247	302	327	374	938	783	622	1,157
1929 prices	94	90	255	254	320	347	401	530	783	663	768

(continued)

NOTES ON ESTIMATES IN MANUFACTURING, 1880–1953

TABLE A-10 (*continued*)

	1880a	1890a	1900a	1900b	1904b	1909b	1914b	1919b	1929c, a	1937c, a	1946c, d
Liquors and beverages											
Current prices	167	341	425	383	500	675	772	603	505	2,035	5,902
1929 prices	283	508	940	847	1,033	1,108	1,216	452	505	2,599	3,610
Other food products											
Current prices	78	198	327	327	440	702	962	2,692	2,364	2,598	9,066
1929 prices	132	295	723	723	909	1,153	1,515	2,016	2,364	3,318	5,545
Tobacco products											
Current prices	119	212	283	266	331	417	490	1,013	1,284	1,309	3,183
1929 prices	200	405	502	472	549	668	770	906	1,284	1,484	2,670
Textiles and their products											
Current prices	989	1,530	1,955	1,673	2,218	3,165	3,519	9,442	10,528	8,249	24,636
1929 prices (sum of deflated components)	1,553	2,476	3,822	3,279	3,879	5,050	5,789	6,530	10,528	10,286	14,735
Cotton goods											
Current prices	243	298	384	384	501	712	810	2,520	1,420	1,026	
1929 prices	435	543	891	891	904	1,254	1,429	1,688	1,420	1,203	
Silk and rayon goods											
Current prices	41	87	107	107	133	197	254	688	1,016	533	7,060
1929 prices	23	65	103	103	156	215	286	380	1,016	1,306	4,083
Woolen and worsted goods											
Current prices	199	221	247	247	318	435	400	1,119	690	616	
1929 prices	295	349	454	454	534	632	699	795	690	597	
Carpets, floor coverings, tapestries											
Current prices	38	55	59	59	75	92	92	187	231	200	860
1929 prices	77	141	163	163	186	216	199	171	231	196	524
Knit goods											
Current prices	30	67	96	96	137	200	259	713	885	742	1,868
1929 prices	28	77	152	152	206	278	353	509	885	1,008	1,579
Clothing											
Current prices	322	679	889	628	839	1,256	1,369	3,348	3,866	2,985	9,715
1929 prices	486	1,079	1,703	1,203	1,506	1,972	2,289	2,376	3,866	3,055	5,927

(*continued*)

APPENDIX A

TABLE A-10 (*continued*)

	1880[a]	1890[a]	1900[a]	1900[b]	1904[b]	1909[b]	1914[b]	1919[b]	1929[c, d]	1937[c, d]	1948[c, d]
Textiles, n.e.c.											
Current prices	116	123	173	152	215	273	335	867	2,355	1,961	4,995
1929 prices	209	222	356	313	387	483	534	611	2,355	2,668	2,542
Cotton+silk and rayon+woolen and worsted goods+textiles, n.e.c.											
Current prices	599	729	911	890	1,167	1,617	1,799	5,194	5,481	4,136	12,055
1929 prices	962	1,179	1,804	1,761	1,981	2,584	2,948	3,474	5,481	5,774	6,625
Leather and its mfrs.											
Current prices	471	543	640	582	724	993	1,105	2,610	1,747	1,425	3,405
1929 prices (sum of deflated components)	1,013	1,310	1,569	1,435	1,747	2,043	1,959	1,854	1,747	1,510	2,008
Boots and shoes											
Current prices	166	221	261	259	320	443	502	1,155	1,049	838	1,920
1929 prices	350	552	694	689	816	943	947	912	1,049	848	1,076
Other leather products											
Current prices	305	322	379	323	404	550	603	1,455	689	572	1,439
1929 prices	663	758	875	746	931	1,100	1,012	942	689	646	904
Rubber products											
Current prices	25	43	100	100	148	197	301	1,138	1,102	1,103	3,415
1929 prices (sum of deflated components)	17	21	37	37	62	68	174	459	1,102	1,089	2,743
Tires and tubes											
Current prices	n.a.	n.a.	n.a.	n.a.	n.a.	197	146	753	868	767	2,657
1929 prices	n.a.	n.a.	n.a.	n.a.	n.a.	68	46	196	868	749	2,235
Other rubber products											
Current prices	n.a.	n.a.	n.a.	n.a.	n.a.	n.a.	155	385	200	280	688
1929 prices	n.a.	n.a.	n.a.	n.a.	n.a.	n.a.	128	263	200	285	451
Forest products											
Current prices	575	1,049	1,227	1,170	1,406	1,784	1,764	3,268	2,975	2,349	9,029
1929 prices (sum of deflated components)	1,615	2,749	3,476	3,314	3,267	3,554	2,925	2,710	2,975	2,398	4,161

(*continued*)

NOTES ON ESTIMATES IN MANUFACTURING, 1880–1953

TABLE A-10 (continued)

	1880[a]	1890[a]	1900[a]	1900[b]	1904[b]	1909[b]	1914[b]	1919[b]	1929[c,d]	1937[c,d]	1948[c,d]
Sawmill and planing mill products											
Current prices	307	622	735	723	827	1,080	1,032	1,898	1,583	1,214	5,149
1929 prices	948	1,723	2,070	2,037	1,892	2,093	1,940	1,575	1,583	1,142	1,543
Other wood products											
Current prices	268	427	492	447	579	704	732	1,370	1,392	1,135	3,880
1929 prices	667	1,026	1,406	1,277	1,375	1,461	985	1,135	1,392	1,256	2,618
Paper, pulp, and products											
Current prices	82	122	199	198	286	413	520	1,251	1,761	1,891	6,143
1929 prices (sum of deflated components)	90	134	334	332	388	666	794	966	1,761	1,834	3,242
Printing, publishing, and allied industries											
Current prices	119	328	410	410	574	767	937	1,764	3,122	2,699	6,974
1929 prices (sum of deflated components)	225	606	965	965	1,141	1,598	1,805	2,054	3,122	2,871	3,725
Chemicals and allied products											
Current prices	238	370	521	520	706	1,010	1,273	3,295	4,254	4,381	14,541
1929 prices (sum of deflated components)	286	485	829	829	1,032	1,365	1,713	2,128	4,254	4,911	9,054
Fertilizers											
Current prices	24	39	45	45	57	104	153	281	262	198	538
1929 prices	15	32	46	46	57	120	177	129	262	265	464
Chemicals proper, acids, compounds, etc.											
Current prices	57	88	97	95	135	196	250	796	788	994	3,327
1929 prices	35	69	93	91	128	215	275	547	788	1,123	2,618
Allied chemical products, paints, varnishes, etc.											
Current prices	157	243	379	380	514	710	870	2,218	3,061	3,030	10,567
1929 prices	236	384	690	692	847	1,030	1,261	1,452	3,061	3,344	5,903

(continued)

APPENDIX A

TABLE A-10 (*continued*)

	1880[a]	1890[a]	1900[a]	1900[b]	1904[b]	1909[b]	1914[b]	1919[b]	1929[c, d]	1937[c, d]	1948[c, d]
Petroleum refining											
Current prices	44	85	124	124	175	237	396	1,633	4,737	5,221	20,038
1929 prices (sum of deflated components)	28	138	173	173	200	277	429	910	4,737	6,150	12,532
Stone, clay, and glass products											
Current prices	108	230	294	271	392	533	616	1,088	1,655	1,624	4,391
1929 prices (sum of deflated components)	188	351	547	505	730	1,068	1,203	982	1,655	1,622	2,885
Metal and its products											
Current prices	954	1,715	2,900	2,878	3,569	5,226	6,079	17,504	21,991	21,057	68,789
1929 prices (sum of deflated components)	1,183	2,648	4,202	4,179	5,799	7,765	9,255	14,282	21,991	21,983	42,868
Iron and steel and products											
Current prices	430	782	1,158	1,171	1,496	2,264	2,269	6,225	7,627	6,769	23,184
1929 prices (sum of deflated components)	459	1,058	1,434	1,452	2,246	3,165	3,681	4,747	7,627	6,630	13,833
Iron and steel											
Current prices	342	558	929	929	1,146	1,736	1,671	4,822	5,269	4,199	16,382
1929 prices	341	679	1,050	1,050	1,626	2,293	2,583	3,520	5,269	4,057	10,026
Metal bldg. materials and supplies											
Current prices	21	113	117	130	218	344	398	810	918	1,039	4,588
1929 prices	24	161	154	172	362	531	718	670	918	1,037	2,525
Hardware, tools, etc.											
Current prices	66	112	111	111	133	182	199	592	1,319	1,464	1,976
1929 prices	94	218	230	230	258	341	380	557	1,319	1,473	1,144
Nonferrous metals and products											
Current prices	182	305	718	679	834	1,131	1,267	2,402	3,014	2,903	5,494
1929 prices (sum of deflated components)	160	274	801	757	1,116	1,499	1,681	2,030	3,014	3,265	3,677
Precious metal products and processing; jewelry, etc.											
Current prices	61	111	120	119	149	199	194	450	463	430	1,031
1929 prices	39	80	112	112	143	201	189	289	463	339	668

(*continued*)

NOTES ON ESTIMATES IN MANUFACTURING, 1880–1953

TABLE A-10 (continued)

	1880[a]	1890[a]	1900[a]	1900[b]	1904[b]	1909[b]	1914[b]	1919[b]	1929[c,d]	1937[c,d]	1948[c,d]
Other metal products and processing											
Current prices	121	194	598	560	685	932	1,073	1,952	2,503	2,399	4,591
1929 prices	121	194	689	645	973	1,298	1,492	1,741	2,503	2,842	3,094
Machinery excluding transportation equipment											
Current prices	314	527	859	859	1,022	1,408	1,639	5,017	5,985	6,043	23,747
1929 prices (sum of deflated components)	513	1,098	1,658	1,658	2,041	2,660	2,893	4,732	5,985	6,194	15,615
Electrical machinery and equipment; radios, etc.											
Current prices	3	19	93	94	151	233	362	1,157	1,735	1,632	8,381
1929 prices	6	43	188	190	316	459	627	1,102	1,735	1,801	5,902
Agricultural machinery and equipment											
Current prices	69	81	101	101	112	146	164	305	570	730	2,717
1929 prices	51	74	110	110	117	151	174	254	570	748	1,945
Office equipment, etc.											
Current prices	6	14	22	22	35	61	72	173	389	406	1,050
1929 prices	11	32	45	45	74	122	135	164	389	402	645
Miscellaneous; household; factory machinery											
Current prices	236	413	643	642	724	968	1,041	3,382	3,224	3,163	11,660
1929 prices	445	949	1,315	1,313	1,534	1,928	1,957	3,212	3,224	3,132	7,162
Transportation equipment											
Current prices	28	101	165	169	217	423	904	3,860	5,365	5,342	16,364
1929 prices (Sum of deflated components)	51	218	309	312	396	441	1,000	2,773	5,365	5,894	9,743
Motor vehicles, complete or parts											
Current prices	n.a.	3	32	37	35	260	655	3,133	4,765	4,696	13,699
1929 prices	n.a.	2	17	20	21	132	507	2,211	4,765	5,259	8,154

(continued)

APPENDIX A

TABLE A-10 (concluded)

	1880[a]	1890[a]	1900[a]	1900[b]	1904[b]	1909[b]	1914[b]	1919[b]	1929[a,d]	1937[a,d]	1948[a,d]
Locomotives and railroad equipment											
Current prices	28	98	133	133	182	164	248	713	458	473	1,312
1929 prices	51	216	292	292	375	309	492	552	458	450	788
Airplanes, airships, seaplanes, etc.											
Current prices	n.a.	n.a.	n.a.	n.a.	n.a.	n.a.	1	14	132	142	1,534
1929 prices	n.a.	n.a.	n.a.	n.a.	n.a.	n.a.	1	10	132	154	909
Miscellaneous											
Current prices	100	190	219	214	311	497	604	1,347	2,334	1,557	6,706
1929 prices (sum of deflated components)	170	342	434	423	565	806	842	975	2,334	1,687	3,975
Addenda:											
Index of physical output (1929 = 100) (Frickey-Fabricant-Federal Reserve Board)[e]	10	n.a.	28	28	n.a.	43	n.a.	61	n.a.	103	181
Value added[f] for total manufacturing											
Current prices	1,850	3,688	4,920	4,609	5,977	8,116	9,343	22,904	31,196	27,615	83,792
1929 prices	3,201	6,756	9,916	9,275	11,132	13,674	14,931	18,042	31,196	30,581	50,326

n.a. = not available.
[a] Includes custom and neighborhood shops.
[b] Factories producing annual value of $500 or more.
[c] Factories producing annual value of $5,000 or more.
[d] Some minor groups not adjusted for net physical change in inventories. Therefore, sum of the parts does not always equal total.
[e] Edwin Frickey, *Production in the United States, 1860–1914*, Harvard Economic Studies, 1947, Table 6, p. 54; Solomon Fabricant, *The Output of Manufacturing Industries, 1899–1937*, National Bureau of Economic Research, 1940, p. 44; Federal Reserve Board index is from Department of Commerce, *Business Statistics 1953, Biennial Edition*, p. 10.
[f] For 1880–1937 value added (value of output minus cost of purchased materials, fuels, and containers) is based on data from *Census of Manufactures*. Value added in 1948 was derived by extrapolating value added from the 1947 *Census of Manufactures* by the percentage change from 1947 to 1948 in income originating in manufacturing. The latter is from *National Income, 1954 Edition, A Supplement to the Survey of Current Business*, Table 13, pp. 176 and 177.

TABLE A-11

Price Indexes for Deflating Book Values of Fixed and Total Capital, by Major Manufacturing Industries, Selected Years, 1880–1948
(values in 1929=100)

Capital as Specified	1880	1890	1900	1904	1909	1914	1919	1929	1937	1948
All manufacturing[a]										
Fixed	n.a.	47.6	43.8	45.4	n.a.	n.a.	n.a.	88.8	90.1	124.8
Total	56.4	51.1	46.5[b] / 46.8[c]	49.7	53.4	56.6	87.4	93.7	90.7	146.1
Food and kindred products										
Fixed	n.a.	46.9	43.2	45.4	n.a.	n.a.	n.a.	88.3	89.2	126.3
Total	55.5	50.3	43.8	47.9	53.2	56.3	82.6	92.6	87.9	153.3
Textiles and products										
Fixed	n.a.	48.9	43.5	45.2	n.a.	n.a.	n.a.	87.8	90.7	122.3
Total	60.3	55.3	47.5	51.2	55.0	55.8	91.9	93.8	84.6	150.9
Leather and products										
Fixed	n.a.	46.9	43.3	45.4	n.a.	n.a.	n.a.	87.3	88.7	126.3
Total	47.8	42.8	41.4	42.4	48.5	55.0	107.9	96.2	92.9	159.5
Rubber products										
Fixed	n.a.	46.4	42.9	45.6	n.a.	n.a.	n.a.	89.4	89.4	128.7
Total	94.4	102.5	105.0	106.0	116.4	101.1	136.4	96.2	97.4	125.9
Forest products										
Fixed	n.a.	48.3	47.7	45.2	n.a.	n.a.	n.a.	88.5	90.7	123.4
Total	42.6	42.3	38.7	44.1	49.2	55.6	86.4	94.1	94.4	164.3
Paper, pulp, and products										
Fixed	n.a.	47.8	43.2	45.5	n.a.	n.a.	n.a.	88.9	90.2	124.5
Total	64.2	57.6	48.1	52.8	52.2	55.3	78.4	92.0	94.2	149.4
Printing, publishing, and allied industries										
Fixed	n.a.	47.1	42.5	45.7	n.a.	n.a.	n.a.	93.4	91.6	127.1
Total	55.7	50.2	42.7	47.9	48.3	51.6	76.4	95.8	92.6	155.0

(continued)

APPENDIX A

TABLE A-11 (concluded)

Capital as Specified	1880	1890	1900	1904	1909	1914	1919	1929	1937	1948
Chemicals and allied products										
Fixed	n.a.	47.6	43.5	45.3	n.a.	n.a.	n.a.	87.1	89.5	123.9
Total	66.5	60.2	52.6	55.9	59.5	61.6	93.4	93.4	89.2	141.0
Petroleum refining										
Fixed	n.a.	47.3	42.6	45.6	n.a.	n.a.	n.a.	92.8	91.6	126.3
Total	72.7	51.1	48.8	53.5	55.6	59.1	84.8	94.3	89.4	137.8
Stone, clay, and glass products										
Fixed	n.a.	46.9	43.6	45.4	n.a.	n.a.	n.a.	86.1	88.1	126.3
Total	53.2	53.2	47.4	48.7	49.0	51.1	75.6	90.7	92.4	138.0
Iron and steel and their products										
Fixed	n.a.	46.9	42.5	45.7	n.a.	n.a.	n.a.	89.4	90.1	125.1
Total	67.4	56.5	54.4	53.5	56.0	54.9	84.2	93.4	95.0	144.3
Nonferrous metals and their products										
Fixed	n.a.	48.6	43.6	45.2	n.a.	n.a.	n.a.	87.1	90.2	122.3
Total	74.4	67.8	59.0	56.6	58.6	60.6	82.1	92.8	89.4	135.9
Machinery excluding transportation equipment										
Fixed	n.a.	47.7	43.3	45.4	n.a.	n.a.	n.a.	88.2	89.8	124.5
Total	58.4	48.0	48.2	48.3	50.9	54.3	84.0	94.6	94.2	142.3
Transportation equipment										
Fixed	n.a.	46.9	43.4	45.4	n.a.	n.a.	n.a.	86.8	88.5	126.3
Total	53.7	46.7	49.6	50.8	68.8	69.1	93.8	93.9	89.7	149.9
Miscellaneous										
Fixed	n.a.	47.5	43.6	45.5	n.a.	n.a.	n.a.	86.6	88.9	124.5
Total	57.0	53.4	48.8	52.4	57.7	65.1	106.2	96.1	91.4	152.6

n.a. = not available.
a Implicit index derived by dividing the sum, for the fifteen major groups, of total or fixed capital in book values by total or fixed capital in 1929 prices.
b Deflator for total capital of all establishments including custom and neighborhood shops.
c Deflator for total capital of all establishments excluding custom and neighborhood shops.
Source: For derivation, see Appendix A, section B, part 1.

NOTES ON ESTIMATES IN MANUFACTURING, 1880–1953

TABLE A-12

Indexes of Wholesale Prices of Output, by Major and Minor Manufacturing Industries, Selected Years, 1880–1948

(values in 1929 = 100)

	1880	1890	1900a	1900b	1904	1909	1914	1919	1929	1937	1948
All manufacturing[c]	58.4	54.9	50.0	50.0	54.4	60.9	63.8	129.9	100.0	90.3	166.5
Food and kindred products[c]	58.8	54.5	44.2	43.9	50.6	60.5	64.3	126.3	100.0	86.6	172.8
Bakery and confectionery products	53.3	53.9	50.5	50.5	53.4	58.4	62.6	114.4	100.0	97.1	163.6
Canned products	54.8	75.9	53.6	53.6	52.6	54.4	68.6	141.9	100.0	75.9	146.6
Mill products	101.3	88.3	55.8	55.8	73.6	83.8	74.2	173.1	100.0	95.2	196.4
Packing house products	29.4	32.7	29.7	29.7	35.3	48.1	57.4	107.8	100.0	90.8	216.8
Sugar refining	166.8	136.2	97.3	97.3	94.4	94.2	93.2	176.9	100.0	93.8	150.7
Liquor and beverages	59.0	67.1	45.2	45.2	48.4	60.9	63.5	133.5	100.0	78.3	163.5
Nonalcoholic beverages	59.0	67.1	45.2	45.2	48.4	60.9	63.5	133.5	100.0	78.3	163.5
Malt liquors and malt	59.0	67.1	45.2	45.2	48.4	60.9	63.5	133.5	100.0	78.3	163.5
Wines	59.0	67.1	45.2	45.2	48.4	60.9	63.5	133.5	100.0	78.3	163.5
Distilled liquors	59.0	67.1	45.2	45.2	48.4	60.9	63.5	133.5	100.0	78.3	163.5
Other food products	59.0	67.1	45.2	45.2	48.4	60.9	63.5	133.5	100.0	78.3	163.5
Tobacco products	59.4	52.3	56.4	56.4	60.3	62.4	63.6	111.8	100.0	88.2	119.2
Textiles and their products[c]	63.7	61.8	51.2	51.0	57.2	62.7	60.8	144.6	100.0	80.2	167.2
Cotton goods	55.9	54.9	43.1	43.1	55.4	56.8	56.7	149.3	100.0	85.3	209.6[a]
Silk and rayon goods	178.0	134.8	103.9	103.9	85.5	91.6	88.8	181.2	100.0	40.8	56.8[a]
Woolen and worsted goods	67.5	63.3	54.4	54.4	59.5	68.8	57.2	140.8	100.0	103.2	176.2[a]
Carpets, floor coverings, etc.	49.4	39.0	36.1	36.1	40.4	42.5	46.3	109.5	100.0	101.9	164.0
Knit goods	106.0	86.6	63.3	63.3	66.4	71.9	73.4	140.0	100.0	73.6	118.3
Clothing	66.2	62.9	52.2	52.2	55.7	63.7	59.8	140.9	100.0	97.7	163.9
Hats, except cloth and millinery	66.2	62.9	52.2	52.2	55.7	63.7	59.8	140.9	100.0	n.a.	163.9
Men's and boys' clothing, except fur and rubber	66.2	62.9	52.2	52.2	55.7	63.7	59.8	140.9	100.0	n.a.	163.9
Women's clothing, children's and infant's wear except fur and rubber	66.2	62.9	52.2	52.2	55.7	63.7	59.8	140.9	100.0	n.a.	163.9
Millinery	66.2	62.9	52.2	52.2	55.7	63.7	59.8	140.9	100.0	n.a.	163.9

(continued)

APPENDIX A

TABLE A-12 (continued)

	1880	1890	1900a	1900b	1904	1909	1914	1919	1929	1937	1948
Textiles, n.e.c.	55.5	55.5	48.6	48.6	55.5	56.5	62.7	141.8	100.0	73.5	196.5f
Cotton+silk and rayon+woolen and worsted goods+textiles, n.e.c.c	62.3	61.8	50.5	50.5	58.9	62.6	61.0	149.5	100.0	71.6	182.0
Leather and leather productsc	46.5	41.5	40.8	40.6	41.4	48.6	56.4	140.8	100.0	94.4	169.6
Boots and shoes	47.4	40.0	37.6	37.6	39.2	47.0	53.0	126.7	100.0	98.8	178.5
Other leather products	46.0	42.5	43.3	43.3	43.4	50.0	59.6	154.4	100.0	88.6	159.1
Leather, tanned, curried, and finished	49.4	45.6	46.5	46.5	46.6	53.7	64.0	165.6	100.0	n.a.	166.3
Leather products, n.e.c.	37.3	34.4	35.1	35.1	35.2	40.5	48.3	125.1	100.0	n.a.	140.5
Rubber productsc	143.2	207.8	267.1	267.1	237.8	290.3	173.0	247.9	100.0	101.3	124.5
Tires and tubes	n.a.	n.a.	n.a.	n.a.	n.a.	n.a.	317.4	383.9	100.0	102.4	118.9
Other rubber products	n.a.	n.a.	n.a.	n.a.	n.a.	n.a.	120.9	146.3	100.0	98.1	152.5
Forest productsc	35.6	38.2	35.3	35.3	43.0	50.2	60.3	120.6	100.0	97.9	215.1
Sawmill and planing mill products	32.4	36.1	35.5	35.5	43.7	51.6	53.2	120.5	100.0	106.3	333.7
Other wood products	40.2	41.6	35.0	35.0	42.1	48.2	74.3	120.7	100.0	90.4	148.2
Wooden containers	40.2	41.6	35.0	35.0	42.1	48.2	74.3	120.7	100.0	n.a.	148.2
Wood products, n.e.c.	40.2	41.6	35.0	35.0	42.1	48.2	74.3	120.7	100.0	n.a.	148.2
Paper, pulp, and products	90.8	90.8	59.6	59.6	73.7	62.0	65.5	129.5	100.0	103.1	189.5
Paper, pulp, and paperboard mills	90.8	90.8	59.6	59.6	73.7	62.0	65.5	129.5	100.0	n.a.	189.5
Paper bags, containers, and boxes	90.8	90.8	59.6	59.6	73.7	62.0	65.5	129.5	100.0	n.a.	189.5
Other paper products	90.8	90.8	59.6	59.6	73.7	62.0	65.5	129.5	100.0	n.a.	189.5
Printing, publishing, and allied industries	52.9	54.1	42.5	42.5	50.3	48.0	51.9	85.9	100.0	94.0	187.2
Printing and publishing, including lithographing	52.9	54.1	42.5	42.5	50.3	48.0	51.9	85.9	100.0	n.a.	187.2
Book and job, including lithographing	52.9	54.1	42.5	42.5	50.3	48.0	51.9	85.9	100.0	n.a.	187.2
Newspapers and periodicals	f	54.1	42.5	42.5	50.3	48.0	51.9	85.9	100.0	n.a.	187.2
Allied industries	52.9	54.1	42.5	42.5	50.3	48.0	51.9	85.9	100.0	n.a.	187.2
Chemicals and allied productsc	83.2	76.3	62.8	62.7	68.4	74.0	74.3	154.8	100.0	89.2	160.6
Fertilizers	155.0	121.6	98.8	98.8	100.2	86.5	86.4	217.8	100.0	74.8	115.9
Chemicals proper, acids, compounds etc.	163.1	127.9	103.9	103.9	105.4	91.0	90.9	145.6	100.0	88.5	127.1

(continued)

NOTES ON ESTIMATES IN MANUFACTURING, 1880–1953

TABLE A-12 (continued)

	1880	1890	1900a	1900b	1904	1909	1914	1919	1929	1937	1948
Allied chemical substances	66.5	63.2	54.9	54.9	60.7	68.9	69.0	152.8	100.0	90.6	179.0
Drugs, medicines, and cosmetics	63.3	70.0	63.9	63.9	71.6	86.2	88.8	166.0	100.0	n.a.	229.6
Soaps, cleaning and polishing preparations	68.1	64.8	56.3	56.3	62.2	70.6	70.7	142.2	100.0	n.a.	164.1
Paints and varnishes	54.2	51.5	46.5	46.5	50.8	54.8	53.4	147.8	100.0	n.a.	168.2
Other chemical substances	66.5	63.2	54.9	54.9	60.7	68.9	69.0	152.8	100.0	n.a.	179.0
Petroleum refining	158.2	61.6	71.8	71.8	87.4	85.7	92.3	179.5	100.0	84.9	159.9
Stone, clay, and glass products	57.4	65.6	53.7	53.7	53.7	49.9	51.2	110.8	100.0	100.1	152.2
Cement, lime, and concrete products	91.1	79.4	78.0	78.0	58.2	58.7	59.9	112.9	100.0	n.a.	144.7
Clay and pottery products	31.9	54.9	44.0	44.0	57.2	49.0	42.9	104.8	100.0	n.a.	167.4
Glass and glass products	88.3	78.3	64.2	64.2	63.3	56.0	56.5	132.2	100.0	n.a.	123.7
Cut stone and products	57.4	65.6	53.7	53.7	53.7	49.9	51.2	110.8	100.0	n.a.	152.2
Stone, clay, and glass products, n.e.c.	57.4	65.6	53.7	53.7	53.7	49.9	51.2	110.8	100.0	n.a.	152.2
Iron and steel and their products[c]	93.7	73.9	80.8	80.6	66.6	71.5	61.6	131.1	100.0	102.1	167.6
Iron and steel	102.5	84.1	88.5	88.5	70.5	75.7	64.7	137.0	100.0	103.5	163.4
Blast furnaces, steel works, and rolling mills	102.5	84.1	90.5	90.5	71.5	77.1	65.0	137.8	100.0	n.a.	169.0
Ordnance and accessories	102.5	84.1	90.5	90.5	71.5	77.1	65.0	137.8	100.0	n.a.	169.0
Tin cans and other tinware	n.a.	n.a.	73.5	73.5	63.1	65.5	62.5	131.2	100.0	n.a.	121.1
Iron and steel, n.e.c.	102.5	84.1	90.5	90.5	71.5	77.1	65.0	137.8	100.0	n.a.	169.0
Metal building materials and supplies	85.8	70.4	75.8	75.8	60.3	64.8	55.4	120.9	100.0	100.2	181.7
Hardware, tools, etc.	70.2	51.4	48.3	48.3	51.5	53.3	52.4	106.2	100.0	99.4	172.7
Nonferrous metals and their products[c]	113.8	111.3	89.6	89.7	74.7	75.5	75.4	118.3	100.0	88.9	149.4
Precious metal products and processes, jewelry, etc.	156.3	138.6	106.7	106.7	104.2	98.9	102.8	155.6	100.0	126.9	154.4
Other metals, products, and processes	100.4	99.8	86.8	86.8	70.4	71.8	71.9	112.1	100.0	84.4	148.4
Clocks, watches, and parts	113.8	111.3	89.7	89.7	74.7	75.5	75.4	118.3	100.0	n.a.	149.4
Jewelry, silverware, and plating	156.3	138.6	106.7	106.7	104.2	98.9	102.8	155.6	100.0	n.a.	154.4

(continued)

263

APPENDIX A

TABLE A-12 (concluded)

	1880	1890	1900[a]	1900[b]	1904	1909	1914	1919	1929	1937	1948
Smelting, refining, and alloying	100.4	99.8	86.8	86.8	70.4	71.8	71.9	112.1	100.0	n.a.	148.4
Nonferrous metal products, n.e.c.	100.4	99.8	86.8	86.8	70.4	71.8	71.9	112.1	100.0	n.a.	148.4
Machinery excluding transportation equipment[c]	61.2	48.0	51.8	51.8	50.1	52.9	56.7	106.0	100.0	97.6	152.0
Electrical machinery and equipment; radios, complete or parts	53.8	44.1	49.5	49.5	47.8	50.8	57.7	105.0	100.0	90.6	142.0
Agricultural machinery and equipment	134.0	109.9	91.7	91.7	96.1	96.7	94.4	120.2	100.0	97.6	139.7
Office and store machines and equipment	53.0	43.5	48.9	48.9	47.2	50.2	53.2	105.3	100.0	101.0	162.8
Factory, household, and miscellaneous machinery and equipment	53.0	43.5	48.9	48.9	47.2	50.2	53.2	105.3	100.0	101.0	162.8
Transportation equipment	55.3	46.3	53.4	54.2	54.8	95.9	90.4	139.2	100.0	90.6	168.0
Motor vehicles, complete or parts	n.a.	172.9	186.3	186.3	168.1	196.6	129.1	141.7	100.0	89.3	168.0
Locomotives and railroad equipment	55.3	45.4	45.5	48.5	48.5	53.1	50.4	129.2	100.0	105.1	166.4
Aircraft and parts	n.a.	n.a.	n.a.	n.a.	n.a.	n.a.	71.7	138.2	100.0	92.3	168.7
Shipbuilding	n.a.	n.a.	n.a.	n.a.	n.a.	n.a.	n.a.	n.a.	100.0	n.a.	168.0
Miscellaneous	58.7	55.5	50.5	50.6	55.0	61.7	71.7	138.2	100.0	92.3	168.7
Professional, scientific, photographic, and optical equipment	58.7	55.5	50.5	50.6	55.0	61.7	71.7	138.2	100.0	92.3	168.7
Miscellaneous, n.e.c.	58.7	55.5	50.5	50.6	55.0	61.7	71.7	138.2	100.0	92.3	168.7

n.a. = not available.
n.e.c = not elsewhere classified.
[a] Price index for 1900 output comparable with output of preceding years.
[b] Price index for 1900 output comparable with output of following years.
[c] Implicit price index derived by dividing the sum of output of the major components of the industry (except rubber products, 1880–1809) in current prices by output in 1929 prices.
[d] A weighted index (172.9) of the price indexes for cotton, silk and rayon, and woolen and worsted goods was used to deflate the combined output data available for these three industries in 1948 (see Appendix A, section B, part 4b, viii).
[e] This index was used to deflate the output data available for textiles, n.e.c. which, in 1948, included rayon and silk broad-woven fabrics (see Appendix A, section B, part 4b. viii).
[f] Newspapers and periodicals excluded from 1880 census.
Source: For derivation, see Appendix A, section B, part 4.

NOTES ON ESTIMATES IN MANUFACTURING, 1880–1953

TABLE A-13

Ratios of Total Capital to Output by Major and Minor Manufacturing Industries, Selected Years, 1880–1948
(per cent based on values in 1929 prices)

	1880	1890	Comparable with— Preceding Years[a]	Comparable with— Following Years	1904	1909	1914	1919	1929[b]	1937[b]	1948[b]
All manufacturing	54.7	73.0	80.3	79.4	89.1	96.7	100.8	102.2	88.5	74.1	60.9
Food and kindred products	36.6	45.8	55.3	55.2	63.6	65.8	68.2	67.6	63.9	50.0	40.0
Bakery and confectionery products	28.7	41.0	53.1	52.6	51.9	58.5	62.8	63.8	78.0	61.8	36.8
Canned products	44.4	75.8	69.6	70.3	71.8	77.5	86.4	103.4	96.7	67.6	57.4
Mill products	63.9	71.1	49.8	48.1	57.1	62.2	57.1	81.9	32.7	40.9	29.2
Packing house products	8.5	13.6	16.3	16.4	19.2	25.2	32.9	36.1	27.7	24.6	21.2
Sugar refining	53.2	53.3	182.7	183.5	144.1	153.3	139.9	108.1	145.2	102.7	66.3
Liquors and beverages	85.9	121.3	129.7	139.1	133.4	148.1	148.4	209.5	147.9	61.2	57.1
Other food products	43.9	49.2	61.5	61.0	59.5	63.9	60.6	68.2	78.1	54.1	38.8
Tobacco products	36.0	47.2	56.4	54.2	123.1	69.2	70.1	80.8	96.7	73.7	56.9
Textiles and products	64.3	81.7	82.3	87.7	89.8	91.8	89.2	103.4	77.8	54.8	46.8
Cotton goods	93.8	130.6	124.8	124.8	151.7	135.7	130.3	138.3	120.4	85.0	
Silk and rayon goods	139.1	141.5	166.0	166.0	137.8	128.4	131.5	152.6	91.1	39.9	59.9
Woolen and worsted goods	65.8	105.2	122.5	122.5	114.4	123.4	103.3	118.9	92.9	82.2	
Carpets, floor coverings, etc.	53.2	55.3	68.7	68.7	72.6	81.5	101.0	114.0	120.8	119.9	61.1
Knit goods	96.4	119.5	113.8	113.8	101.5	107.2	109.6	110.2	85.4	50.7	39.0
Clothing	38.9	48.9	43.3	45.0	44.8	52.4	49.5	66.3	48.5	40.1	33.8
Textiles, n.e.c.	51.7	70.7	80.3	68.1	69.3	76.8	89.9	92.1	85.4	61.1	58.7
Cotton + silk and rayon + woolen and worsted goods + textiles, n.e.c.	77.0	112.4	117.7	116.5	124.4	121.1	116.7	127.3	96.5	63.5	59.5
Leather and leather products	32.4	48.9	56.8	56.4	61.0	66.5	69.0	76.1	69.4	53.5	40.7
Boots and shoes	25.7	40.2	35.4	35.1	35.5	43.1	49.0	59.0	62.0	52.0	41.4
Other leather products	35.9	55.1	73.7	76.1	83.4	86.6	87.6	92.7	81.7	56.8	41.0

(continued)

265

APPENDIX A

TABLE A-13 (continued)

	1880	1890	Comparable with— Preceding Years[a]	Following Years	1904	1909	1914	1919	1929[b]	1937[b]	1948[b]
Rubber products	58.8	171.4	200.0	200.0	150.0	204.4	152.3	153.4	102.6	74.9	51.8
Tires and tubes	n.a.	n.a.	n.a.	n.a.	n.a.	n.a.	280.4	237.8	109.9	80.4	49.1
Other rubber products	n.a.	n.a.	n.a.	n.a.	n.a.	n.a.	106.2	90.5	88.5	75.4	63.6
Forest products	52.4	70.9	82.5	68.0	81.5	101.0	118.8	116.4	137.2	106.3	70.5
Sawmill and planing mill products	54.2	71.1	91.3	66.0	83.2	108.9	110.6	127.1	178.6	144.9	118.7
Other wood products	49.9	70.8	69.6	71.3	79.1	89.7	134.9	101.6	90.2	71.1	42.1
Paper, pulp, and products	100.0	149.3	136.2	136.4	172.7	150.5	156.9	157.8	127.1	112.4	76.4
Printing, publishing, and allied industries	64.0	76.9	83.0	83.0	82.3	79.2	80.0	75.8	87.7	87.3	69.0
Chemicals and allied products	72.0	98.6	105.1	104.8	109.9	112.2	121.3	130.5	99.2	80.7	71.6
Fertilizers	180.0	212.5	252.2	252.2	215.8	170.8	198.9	258.9	137.0	83.8	51.1
Chemicals proper, acids, compounds, etc.	211.4	230.4	296.8	301.1	271.1	213.5	230.2	184.1	132.2	112.3	69.9
Allied chemical substances	44.5	65.4	69.4	69.2	78.4	84.2	86.7	98.9	92.1	74.2	71.1
Petroleum refining	132.1	109.4	112.7	112.7	127.0	118.1	128.7	151.6	128.6	105.7	89.3
Stone, clay, and glass products	83.0	116.2	135.5	140.4	155.9	164.3	161.0	170.7	156.6	121.8	73.8
Metals and metal products	86.1	103.3	106.6	107.1	116.1	125.3	127.7	116.4	84.9	81.9	65.8
Iron and steel and products	102.8	108.0	110.3	110.1	128.5	136.0	140.3	141.9	87.4	101.3	69.7
Iron and steel	112.3	122.2	115.0	115.0	136.2	143.7	151.4	150.3	84.4	114.0	65.8
Metal building materials and supplies	62.5	80.1	103.9	103.5	104.4	114.3	105.8	117.9	88.1	81.7	63.4
Hardware, tools, etc.	77.7	84.4	93.5	92.6	113.2	117.9	130.8	117.1	106.7	84.6	71.3
Nonferrous metals and their products	72.5	100.7	80.6	80.6	72.0	80.3	81.2	89.1	78.4	71.6	68.5
Precious metal products and processes, jewelry, etc.	100.0	128.8	146.4	146.4	155.9	153.7	170.9	132.9	81.9	81.4	56.7
Other metals, products, and processes	63.6	89.2	69.8	69.1	59.7	68.9	69.8	81.8	79.3	72.6	63.3

(continued)

TABLE A-13 (concluded)

	1880	1890	Comparable with— Preceding Years[a]	Comparable with— Following Years	1904	1909	1914	1919	1929[b]	1937[b]	1948[b]
Machinery, not including transportation equipment	80.7	105.6	115.6	115.6	132.8	137.4	148.4	118.2	103.0	85.3	66.3
Electrical machinery and equipment; radios, complete or parts	50.0	93.0	94.7	94.7	119.9	120.7	114.5	104.0	92.2	66.0	58.3
Agricultural machinery and equipment	207.8	408.1	298.2	298.2	348.7	333.1	358.6	172.0	135.4	106.3	63.0
Office and store machines and equipment	90.9	53.1	111.1	111.1	114.9	115.6	129.6	121.3	117.0	109.0	88.8
Factory, household, and miscellaneous machinery and equipment	66.3	84.5	103.5	103.5	119.9	127.4	141.8	118.7	103.6	91.4	68.3
Transportation equipment	33.3	71.6	109.1	111.9	84.1	128.6	99.1	89.4	64.8	62.3	57.9
Motor vehicles, complete or parts	n.a.	200.0	352.9	365.0	271.4	202.3	121.5	87.6	57.5	53.1	49.3
Locomotives and railroad equipment	33.3	70.4	94.5	94.5	73.1	96.8	76.2	94.7	134.5	151.1	78.4
Aircraft and parts	n.a.	n.a.	n.a.	n.a.	n.a.	n.a.	(54.5)	190.0	89.4	130.5	81.7
Miscellaneous	52.4	67.3	79.3	80.4	82.8	88.3	106.4	97.2	96.7	77.3	60.9

n.a. = not available.
n.e.c. = not elsewhere classified.
[a] Includes custom and neighborhood establishments which were included in the preceding census enumerations but excluded in the following enumerations.
[b] The output figures in these years are adjusted to include net changes in inventories as estimated by the Department of Commerce, National Income Division. This adjustment can be made only for major industry groups and for six minor industries, beverages and liquors, tobacco products, sawmill and planing mill products, other wood products, electrical machinery and equipment, and motor vehicles.
In 1948, the capital figures include an estimate of the investment in emergency facilities after "normal" depreciation. This adjustment is made only for major groups and the six minor industries mentioned above.
Source: Based on data in Appendix Tables A-8 and A-10.

APPENDIX A

TABLE A-14

Ratios of Fixed Capital to Output by Major and Minor Manufacturing
Industries, Selected Years, 1890–1948
(*based on values in 1929 prices*)

	1890[a]	1900[a]	1904[b]	1929[c]	1937[c]	1948[c]
All manufacturing	0.364	0.416	0.471	0.433	0.346	0.285
Food and kindred prod.	0.265	0.305	0.312	0.302	0.206	0.167
Bakery and confectionery prod.	0.258	0.342	0.340	0.458	0.344	0.212
Canned prod.	0.318	0.320	0.344	0.377	0.226	0.241
Mill prod.	0.498	0.329	0.319	0.144	0.160	0.123
Packing house prod.	0.056	0.059	0.074	0.119	0.097	0.082
Sugar refining	0.333	0.906	0.669	0.885	0.526	0.367
Liquors and beverages	0.797	0.778	0.806	0.707	0.275	0.268
Other food prod.	0.295	0.436	0.369	0.476	0.257	0.205
Tobacco prod.	0.101	0.137	0.144	0.106	0.072	0.056
Textiles and their prod.	0.405	0.401	0.470	0.317	0.207	0.162
Cotton goods	0.945	0.862	1.076	0.693	0.458	
Silk and rayon goods	0.662	0.738	0.667	0.428	0.212	0.276
Woolen and worsted goods	0.510	0.531	0.597	0.394	0.305	
Carpets, floor coverings, etc.	0.291	0.350	0.392	0.602	0.474	0.292
Knit goods	0.636	0.559	0.539	0.373	0.206	0.170
Clothing	0.091	0.092	0.085	0.090	0.062	0.051
Textiles, n.e.c.	0.378	0.419	0.302	0.355	0.235	0.132
Cotton+silk and rayon+ woolen and worsted goods+ textiles, n.e.c.	0.694	0.684	0.764	0.461	0.283	0.221
Leather and prod.	0.122	0.153	0.160	0.176	0.119	0.093
Boots and shoes	0.085	0.086	0.081	0.154	0.112	0.084
Other leather prod.	0.149	0.206	0.230	0.213	0.132	0.111
Rubber prod.	1.048	1.459	1.065	0.440	0.246	0.175
Tires and tubes	n.a.	n.a.	n.a.	0.468	0.216	0.147
Other rubber prod.	n.a.	n.a.	n.a.	0.395	0.372	0.266
Forest prod.	0.260	0.352	0.341	0.760	0.614	0.394
Sawmill and planing mill prod.	0.269	0.431	0.360	1.074	0.949	0.761
Other wood prod.	0.245	0.235	0.316	0.404	0.310	0.172
Paper, pulp, and prod.	1.142	0.991	1.358	0.764	0.664	0.471
Printing, publ., etc.	0.487	0.465	0.472	0.334	0.301	0.305
Chemicals and allied prod.	0.555	0.579	0.640	0.404	0.352	0.365
Fertilizers	0.844	1.000	0.965	0.588	0.385	0.252
Chemicals proper, acids, etc.	1.609	2.054	1.945	0.739	0.634	0.453
Allied chemical prod.	0.333	0.354	0.419	0.321	0.274	0.323
Petroleum refining	0.536	0.734	0.800	0.848	0.678	0.576

(*continued*)

NOTES ON ESTIMATES IN MANUFACTURING, 1880–1953

TABLE A-14 (concluded)

	1890[a]	1900[a]	1904[b]	1929[c]	1937[c]	1948[c]
Stone, clay, and glass prod.	0.783	0.931	1.111	1.018	0.763	0.401
Metal and prod.	0.542	0.594	0.665	0.427	0.380	0.285
Iron and steel and prod.	0.698	0.758	0.896	0.555	0.587	0.372
Iron and steel	0.829	0.815	1.009	0.619	0.738	0.368
Metal building materials and supplies	0.398	0.623	0.533	0.362	0.354	0.202
Hardware, tools, etc.	0.518	0.574	0.694	0.487	0.359	0.309
Nonferrous metals and prod.	0.562	0.524	0.404	0.382	0.319	0.331
Precious metal prod.	0.562	0.696	0.636	0.214	0.212	0.130
Other metals, prod.	0.562	0.496	0.371	0.420	0.342	0.311
Machinery excl. transp.	0.426	0.507	0.615	0.361	0.288	0.226
Electrical machinery and equipment	0.302	0.346	0.411	0.303	0.216	0.186
Agricultural machinery	0.905	0.718	1.222	0.428	0.303	0.226
Office equipment	0.188	0.467	0.446	0.308	0.358	0.386
Factory, household, etc.	0.403	0.513	0.619	0.395	0.327	0.220
Transportation equipment	0.344	0.476	0.338	0.343	0.279	0.240
Motor vehicles	1.000	2.059	1.381	0.298	0.223	0.209
Locomotives and railroad equipment	0.333	0.387	0.283	0.773	0.882	0.305
Aircraft and parts	n.a.	n.a.	n.a.	0.523	0.474	0.167
Miscellaneous	0.257	0.311	0.338	0.313	0.265	0.223

n.a. = not available.
n.e.c. = not elsewhere classified.
[a] Includes custom and neighborhood shops.
[b] Factories producing annual value of $500 or more.
[c] Factories producing annual value of $5,000 or more.
Source: Based on data in Appendix Tables A-9 and A-10.

APPENDIX A

TABLE A-15

Basic Data for Capital-Output Ratios in 1929 Prices, by Major Manufacturing Industries, 1948 and 1953
(dollars in millions)

	Capital					Indexes for Deflating Book Values in 1929 Prices		Output in 1929 Prices
	Total		Fixed					
	Book Values	1929 Prices[a]	Book Values	1929 Prices[a]		Total (1929=100)	Fixed	
All manufacturing								
1948	$113,956	$78,357	$45,913	$36,685		145.4	125.2	$128,604
excluding shipbuilding	113,394	77,982	45,727	36,526		n.c.	n.c.	128,124
1953	169,655	99,040	74,125	45,258		171.3	163.8	167,821
Food and kindred products								
1948	10,583	6,907	4,116	3,259		153.3	126.3	19,916
1953	13,195	7,703	5,080	3,146		171.3	161.5	23,458
Beverages								
1948	3,158	2,061	1,222	968		153.3	126.3	3,610
1953	3,900	3,222	1,551	960		121.0	161.6	7,802
Tobacco products								
1948	2,330	1,520	188	149		153.3	126.3	2,670
1953	2,826	1,906	184	114		148.3	161.4	2,893
Textile mill products								
1948	7,379	4,891	2,554	2,088		150.9	122.3	8,808
1953	8,153	5,205	3,196	2,055		156.6	155.5	8,251
Apparel								
1948	3,018	2,001	369	302		150.9	122.3	5,927
1953	3,924	2,638	516	332		148.7	155.4	7,717
Leather and products								
1948	1,303	817	235	186		159.5	126.3	2,008
1953	1,394	819	244	151		170.1	161.5	1,979
Rubber products								
1948	1,791	1,422	618	480		125.9	128.7	2,743
1953	2,614	1,652	767	466		158.3	164.6	3,241

(continued)

NOTES ON ESTIMATES IN MANUFACTURING, 1880–1953

TABLE A-15 (continued)

	Capital						Output in 1929 Prices
	Total		Fixed		Indexes for Deflating Book Values in 1929 Prices (1929=100)		
	Book Values	1929 Prices[a]	Book Values	1929 Prices[a]	Total	Fixed	
Lumber and basic timber products							
1948	3,398	2,069	1,599	1,293	164.2	123.4	1,861
1953	4,430	2,265	2,089	1,331	195.7	156.9	1,996
Furniture and finished lumber products							
1948	1,422	865	426	345	164.2	123.4	2,300
1953	1,917	980	479	305	195.7	156.9	2,273
Paper, pulp, and products							
1948	3,692	2,476	1,900	1,526	149.4	124.5	3,242
1953	5,499	3,074	3,053	1,925	178.9	158.6	4,082
Printing, publishing, and allied industries							
1948	3,984	2,571	1,442	1,135	155.0	127.1	3,725
1953	5,202	2,606	1,918	1,180	199.4	162.5	3,898
Chemicals and allied products							
1948	9,109	6,487	4,100	3,309	141.0	123.9	9,054
1953	16,286	9,662[b]	9,665	5,614[b]	160.5	157.8	11,515
Petroleum and coal							
1948	15,363	11,188	9,115	7,217	137.8	126.3	12,532
1953	19,960	12,367	12,650	7,833	161.4	161.5	16,221
Stone, clay, and glass products							
1948	2,934	2,128	1,462	1,158	138.0	126.3	2,885
1953	4,482	2,615	2,181	1,350	171.0	161.5	3,814
Primary metals industries							
1948	11,217	7,922	6,052	4,838	141.6	125.1	11,154
1953	16,696	9,521[b]	9,483	5,977[b]	174.2	158.2	12,468
Fabricated metals							
1948	5,047	3,564	1,713	1,369	141.6	125.1	6,202
1953	7,821	4,449	2,674	1,686	174.2	158.2	8,265

(continued)

APPENDIX A

TABLE A-15 (concluded)

	Capital							Output in 1929 Prices
	Total		Fixed		Indexes for Deflating Book Values in 1929 Prices (1929=100)			
	Book Values	1929 Prices[a]	Book Values	1929 Prices[a]	Total	Fixed		
Machinery except electrical								
1948	9,800	6,914	3,024	2,429	142.3	124.5		9,713
1953	15,170	8,239[b]	4,544	2,857[b]	183.9	158.6		12,549
Electrical machinery								
1948	4,874	3,438	1,363	1,095	142.3	124.5		5,902
1953	8,929	5,505	2,297	1,448	162.1	158.6		10,449
Transportation equipment except motor vehicles								
1948	2,938	2,001	999	791	149.9	126.3		2,069
1953	2,376	1,626	813	632	n.c.	n.c.		1,589
Excluding shipbuilding								
1953	7,994	3,987[a]	2,859	1,478[a]	195.1	161.5		5,992
Motor vehicles and equipment								
1948	6,006	4,016	2,153	1,705	149.9	126.3		8,154
1953	9,982	5,367	3,774	2,337	183.8	161.5		12,639
Professional, scientific, photographic, and optical equipment								
1958	1,221	800	337	271	152.6	124.5		1,125
1953	2,501	1,468[b]	705	444[b]	170.0	158.6		2,240
Miscellaneous manufacturing								
1948	3,050	2,009	904	726	152.6	124.5		3,004
1953	5,970	3,216[b]	3,317	1,695[b]	170.0	158.6		4,080

[a] Totals are not the sum of the components because the adjustments for the excess of accelerated amortization over normal depreciation, and for privately operated, government-owned facilities were made only for those industries in which the amounts involved were important.
[b] Privately operated, government-owned facilities were not necessarily deflated by the price indexes shown.

Source: See Appendix A, sections A and B.

NOTES ON ESTIMATES IN MANUFACTURING, 1880–1953

TABLE A-16

Total Number of Persons Employed, by Major Manufacturing Industries, Selected Years, 1900–1953
(thousands)

	1900[a]	1900[b]	1909	1919	1929	1937	1948	1953
All manufacturing[c]	5,457	5,063	7,226	9,665	10,497	10,615	15,333 15,468[d]	17,414[d]
Food and kindred products	521	476	681	1,026	1,078	1,254	1,559	1,583
Tobacco products	168	157	198	184	147	112	100	104
Textile mill products	763	728	980	1,179	1,264	1,265	1,370	1,192
Apparel	596	380	610	643	793	855	1,203	1,264
Leather and leather products	329	296	344	399	372	377	406	388
Rubber products	39	39	56	206	176	154	254	279
Lumber and basic timber products	525	545	746	645	620	467	1,222	1,167
Furniture and finished lumber products	374	342	418	384	442	402		
Paper, pulp, and products	103	102	159	235	285	326	471	532
Printing, publishing, and allied industries	273	273	406	475	630	619	744	814
Chemicals and allied products	139	139	205	370	401	434	696	810
Petroleum refining[c]	13	13	17	74	128	132	243	256
Stone, clay, and glass products	276	258	387	346	402	359	533	555
Iron and steel and their products	416	421	692	1,051	1,219	1,319	2,525	3,057
Nonferrous metals and products	200	170	237	323	330	316		
Machinery, except electrical	456	456	586	962	769	795	1,554	1,741
Electrical machinery	48	49	112	306	519	461	877	1,222
Transportation equipment except motor vehicles	58	58	68	95	91	100	337[d]	
Motor vehicles	20	22	90	408	541	580	472[d] 767	1,017[d] 922
Miscellaneous	140	138	233	353	290	288	472[e]	511

[a] Includes custom and neighborhood shops.
[b] Excludes custom and neighborhood shops.
[c] Coal products excluded for 1900–1919, included for 1929–1953.
[d] Includes shipbuilding.
[e] Not comparable with series before 1948.
Source: Appendix A, section C.

APPENDIX B

Notes on Estimates of Capital, Output and Employment in Mining, 1870–1953

A. Census Remarks and Definitions on Capital Invested in Mining

In the censuses of 1850, 1860, and 1870, the inquiries relating to mining were contained in the general industry schedule covering manufacturing, mining, and fisheries. All three censuses were carried out in accordance with the census law of May 23, 1850, which was recognized as being entirely inadequate to meet the changed conditions of 1870. Thus,

"... the machinery of enumeration provided by the census law of 1850 was created without consideration of certain of the great mining industries of the country (some of which, indeed, at the date of the passage of the act had scarcely come into existence within the United States, and none of which were then of great importance) and cannot be applied to them with any degree of success. It may fairly be taken for granted that an attempt to enumerate cotton spinning, coal mining, and cod fishing, on one and the same schedule, will always result in returns unsatisfactory in respect to one, if not two, of the three industries so widely diverse in character and condition."[1]

To these objections, relating to the statistics of mining as a whole, may be added the highly unfavorable appraisal of the capital figures for both mining and manufacturing, already noted in Appendix A, section A.

No definition was furnished by the 1870 census. However, it can be assumed from the statement following, in the succeeding census in 1880, that the capital values reported by this census do not include the value of leased property.

"The largest part of the increase of capital [1880 over 1870] is due to the fact that we have included the coal lands not owned by the mining companies, but worked on royalty. Mineral lands are clearly a part of the capital of the mining industry, whether owned or leased or mortgaged."[2]

In the census of 1880, for the first time, special schedules were used to collect the data for mining. Also for the first time, a separate report

---

[1] Census of 1870, Volume VIII, *Statistics of Industry and Wealth*, p. 748.

[2] Census of 1880, *Report on the Mining Industries of the United States, 1880*, p. 639.

on mining industries, exclusive of precious metals, was published. Although here, too, no clear definition of capital is given, some explanatory remarks distributed through the book help to clarify the meaning of the capital figures; for example:

"What the present investigation has sought to ascertain is the value of the mineral property of the country as a producer of actual values, that it might be ranked with the other great divisions of productive energy with regard to its real importance. From this point of view the question of ownership and indebtedness which occupies the most important place in the mind of the operator, may be disregarded. If the mine is worked on a royalty, the operator would, naturally, omit the real estate in estimating his assets. Whereas, it is in reality the most important part of mining capital. The questions should therefore be framed with a view to ascertaining the value of the entire mining establishment, and not merely the mercantile capital of the lessee. They were: what is the value of the mineral real estate attached to the mine? What is the value of the plant? How much is usually employed as working capital? The result of this form of inquiry has been to increase very greatly the amount returned as "capital of the mining establishments," without including anything of a speculative or artificial value, nor the great body of mineral producing land which is not productive at present and is in reality the property of the next generation."[3]

Plant, real estate, and working capital are defined in statements for the particular industries. In connection with copper we read:

"The plant means all machinery, improvements, personal property (not supplies), animals, fixtures, etc. An estimate of this should be based on *actual values*, not cost, and should exclude all antiquated and idle machinery.

Real estate... as in iron ore, and anthracite coal, means the mine itself as a mineral producer. Its value depends of course, on the average price of copper during a term of years, and on the reasonable expectation of productive life for each mine."[4]

"... the term 'working capital' means the sum of money necessarily advanced for wages and supplies during the interval between production and the receipt of returns from sales. It is represented in actual property by the unsold product on hand and in transit.... As the sum is equal to, but little more than the value of product for 60 days...."[5]

[3] *Ibid.*, p. xxvi ff.
[4] *Ibid.*, p. 801.
[5] *Ibid.*, p. 640.

APPENDIX B

The census of 1880 did not present an appraisal of its data. Some suggestions in this respect can be derived from a statement in the census of 1902. The latter refers only to the failure of the 1880 census of precious metals, but it throws some light on the difficulties which must have been encountered by the census in other industries. The reason for the failure is stated as follows:

"After the work had been some time under way, it was found ... that it was impossible to find the number of men required who were in every respect fitted for it by education and experience; and that among owners and superintendents of mines and reduction works, while with a very few unimportant exceptions the greatest willingness was shown to grant us all the information they possessed, it was often found that they were themselves unable to answer the questions we asked, either through want of system in keeping records, or because they had never thought of the importance or bearing of certain facts."[6]

In the instructions on special schedules for the census of mining for 1890 we read:

"In stating the amount of capital there should be included not only the amount of capital actually invested in the business, as in lands, leases, mineral rights, rights of way, private railroads, buildings, tools, and all other forms of property, but also that used in carrying on business. This statement, to be complete, should include as capital all money borrowed, as well as accounts having a long time to run. The idea is to get returned as capital all money invested and used in the business whether owned by the party making the return or borrowed. The value of land, fixtures, etc., should be estimated at what they are worth or would cost in 1890."[7]

The items tabulated are: (1) land; (2) buildings and fixtures; (3) tools, implements, livestock, machinery, and supplies on hand; and (4) cash. Some difficulties encountered in connection with a proper evaluation of the capital invested in iron mining can be regarded as inherent in other mining industries:

"The inquiry concerning the capital invested in iron-ore mines has presented difficulties which made it practically impossible in many cases to obtain valuations on the basis of the questions presented in the schedules prepared by the Census Office. In the Lake Superior region a large proportion of the mines are leased, and in other districts mines are worked under leases, a stipulated sum per ton, with a minimum yearly royalty provision, being paid to the owners of the fee. The

[6] *Special Report on Mines and Quarries, 1902,* pp. 6–7.
[7] *Report on Mineral Industries in the United States, 1890,* p. 789 ff.

lessor in a majority of instances owns tracts of greater or less extent as yet unproved, of which the mines occupy but a limited portion. Some of the large deposits in other sections have been in the hands of the present owners for a number of years, and have grown from small operations to great enterprises. During this time no actual appraisement of values has been made, as the properties have not been offered for sale, nor have propositions of purchase been entertained. In these instances the assessors' valuation gave an approximate basis for formulating an estimate.

"A number of iron-ore mines are connected with blast furnace plants, and the properties are valued as entire enterprises, no division of the capitalization being attempted by the owners. Other properties have the ore distributed over large areas, from which it is won by stripping or benching, and in some of these the value is partly dependent upon a deposit of coal lying close to the iron ore. Similarly, the timber upon some areas worked for iron ore affects the valuation. An attempt has been made, where valuations could not be reported, to arrive at a basis of estimate by using the rate of tax assessment, or by calculating a value by capitalizing an assumed royalty, necessarily depending upon the location and character of the ore, multiplied by the product for the year 1889. This explanation will indicate that the capital invested, as reported in the table, is considerably less than that actually employed in the mining of iron ore, but it is as close an approximation as can be made."[8]

The census of 1902, in comparing its figures with those in the 1890 census states:

"In addition to the mining statistics, the Census of 1890 included statistics for smelting and refining of gold, silver, copper, lead, and zinc. The statistics apparently included all reduction works, though the general line of demarcation between manufacturing and mining agrees very closely with that followed in the canvass of the Twelfth Census."[9]

The schedule for the 1902 census of mining industries did not include an inquiry on invested capital. The reasons for not securing capital statistics are stated as follows:

"It has been the practice at prior censuses to include in the report on mining industries statistics concerning capital invested. The subject was to ascertain the value of all mining properties and money invested or used in the business, whether owned or borrowed. In order to

[8] *Ibid.*, pp. 15 ff.
[9] *Special Report on Mines and Quarries, 1902*, pp. 8–9.

APPENDIX B

develop these amounts the inquiries called for the value of the mine and improvements, including land, buildings, fixtures, tools, implements, livestock, machinery, etc., and were in harmony with those concerning capital included in the schedule for the manufacturing and mechanical industries, but the statistics for both branches of industry have frequently been referred to as untrustworthy and delusive. It is evident from the various inquiries made at the Eleventh Census that uniform amounts were not reported for capital invested in all branches of the mining industry, and the statistics can not be accepted as representing the actual value of the mining properties or the amount of capital invested in the industry.

"All of the objections to the statistics for capital in manufactures apply with greater force to the statistics for mines and quarries, and they may be summarized as follows:

"1. It is impossible to define the word "capital" for statistical measurement so that it shall be tangible, restricted, and uniform.

2. The inquiry creates more prejudice and arouses more opposition to the progress of the enumeration than all of the other inquiries united.

3. The value of "fixed capital"—land and building—is dependent upon conditions of which a census can take no cognizance.

4. The difficulties attending the collection of statistics for live capital —"cash on hand, bills receivable, unsettled accounts, etc."—preclude the possibility of reliable results.

5. It is impossible to eliminate the duplication in gross assets and credit capital.

6. Good will, patents, mining rights, etc., are forms of capital for which no satisfactory value can be obtained.

7. Many mining companies have investment other than of the amounts required to carry on their business and yet constituting a part of their capital, such as railroads, steamships, and timber lands, and it is impossible to segregate the capital that pertains strictly to mining.

8. A number of mines are operated under leases. The lessees furnish the Census reports, but have no knowledge of the value of the mine or the capital invested by the lessor in land, shafts, machinery, etc.

9. The value of a mine is due chiefly to the character and amount of ore supposed to be in the earth, and is, therefore, largely speculative."[10]

For the census of 1902, the amount of bonds and capital stock of incorporated mining companies was requested, rather than the value

[10] *Ibid.*, pp. 74–75.

of the mining properties. The reasons given were that, exclusive of the products of natural gas and petroleum wells, 85.9 per cent of the mining products of the country during 1902 was produced by incorporated companies, and that inquiries concerning bonds and stocks could be readily answered.

The general schedule of the census of 1909 asked merely for the book value of the total amount of capital owned and borrowed by the operator:

"The answer should show the total amount of capital owned and borrowed, invested by the operator in the enterprise on the last day of the business year reported, as shown in his books. Do not include securities and loans representing investments in other enterprises."[11]

The census instructions to the special agents contain additional information on what should be included or excluded from the reported figures:

"The purpose of this inquiry is to determine the value of property employed by the establishment for the purposes of its productive operation, but not including rented property. Therefore both capital owned by the operator and capital borrowed by him is to be included; in other words, no deduction is to be made from the value of the assets by reason of liabilities for money due to others.

"If the books of the establishment show specifically an item of *depreciation* charged against land, buildings, machinery, and tools, deduction of such depreciation should be made and the net value resulting after such deduction be given. If, however, the books are not kept so as to show clearly this item of depreciation, then this item should be disregarded and no deduction made.

"*Patent rights and good will* must not be considered as a part of the capital, except in so far as the value of these items may be included in other items as carried on the books of the establishment. If the books of the establishment, however, in any way segregate or report separately the value of such patent rights and good will, such value must not be included in any of the answers called for by Inquiry 3, but should be reported separately under 'Remarks' "[12]

In the appraisal of its capital figures the census states:

"The census schedule required every operator to state the total amount of capital invested in the enterprise on the last day of the business year

---

[11] Thus, no information was obtained on the principal types of capital or on the value of leased land, *Census of Mines and Quarries, 1909,* General Schedule, pp. 351–352.

[12] *Ibid.,* p. 358.

APPENDIX B

reported, as shown by his books. There is however, a great diversity in the methods of bookkeeping in use by different operators. As a result, the statistics for capital lack uniformity. Some of the reported figures apparently represent capital stock at face value; others include large investments in mineral lands which are not at present being actively mined, but are held in reserve; still others may include expenditures for unproductive mining ventures in no way related to the operations carried on during the census years.

"For the reason stated, schedules in which the inquiry in relation to capital remained unanswered, notwithstanding every effort made to secure the information required, were included in the general tabulation."[13]

The instructions and formulations for the 1919 census of mining were identical with those employed for the census of 1909. The census appraisal of its capital figures appears in the following statement:

"The reports received in respect to capital ... at both Censuses [1919, 1909], have in so many cases been defective that the data compiled are of value only as indicating very general conditions. While there are some enterprises maintaining accounting systems such that an accurate return for capital could be made, this is not true of the great majority, and the figures therefore do not show the actual amount of capital invested."[14]

B. Coverage

The list of minerals (Table B-1) indicates only that the census authorities attempted to canvass mines producing those items. It does not mean that all the items requested were reported, or that totals for the industry were presented. In some cases, the census authorities attempted to estimate totals if the reported figures were incomplete; but in other cases they did not.

For some of the minerals, for some of the years, the Bureau of Mines has figures on value of production. Apart from the valuation problem (the Bureau of Mines frequently reports value after some processing), there is the question of their production as by-products of operations of other mineral enterprises.

In 1870, 1880, and 1890, we can assume that nonproducing mines, in so far as they came to the attention of the interviewers, were included in the totals. One exception noted is for anthracite coal in 1880, except for the capital item (*Report on the Mining Industries of the United*

---

[13] *Ibid.*, p. 18.
[14] *Census of Mines and Quarries, 1919*, p. 15.

NOTES ON ESTIMATES IN MINING, 1870–1953

TABLE B-1
Industry Coverage of Mining Data, Selected Years, 1870–1919

	1870	1880[a]	1890	1902	1909	1919
Anthracite coal	x	x	x	x	x	x
Bituminous coal	x	x	x	x	x	x
Petroleum	x	x	x	x }	x	{ x
Natural gas	n.a.	n.a.	x	x }		{ x
Iron	x	x	x	x	x	x
Copper	x	x	x	x	x	x
Lead and zinc	x	x	x[b]	x	x	x
Precious metals						
Deep	x }	x[c]	x	{ x	x	x
Placer	x }			{ x	x	x
Miscellaneous						
Slate	x	x	x	x	x	x
Marble	x }	x	{ x	x	x	x
Limestone			{ x	x	x	x
Granite		x }	x }	x	{ x	x
Basalt					{ x	x
Bluestone			x }		{ x }	x
Sandstone		x[d] }	n.a. }	x	{ x }	
Grindstone[e]	x }	x	x	x	x	n.a.
Barytes		x	x	x	x	x
Clay	f	x	g	x	x	x
Mica		x	x	x	x	x
Ochre (mineral pigment)		x	x	x	x	x
Silica quartz			{ h	x	x	x
Feldspar	n.a. }	x	{ h	x	x	x
Millstones and buhrstones	n.a.	n.a.	x	x	x	x
Corundum	n.a.	x	x	x	x }	
Garnet	n.a.	x	n.a.	x	x }	
Oilstones and whetstones	n.a.	x[i]	x	x	x }	x
Infusorial earth	n.a. }				{ x }	
Tripoli	n.a. }	x }	x }	x	{ x }	
Pumice	n.a. }				{ x }	
Peat	x	n.a.	n.a.	n.a.	x	n.a.
Manganese	n.a.	x	x	x	x	x
Quicksilver	j	n.a.	x	x	x	x
Bauxite	k	k	x	x	x	x
Asbestos	n.a.	x	x	x	x	x
Asphalt	j	x	x	x	x	x
Fluorspar	k	l	x	x	x	x
Fuller's earth	k	k	k	x	x	x
Graphite	n.a.	x	x	x	x	x
Gypsum	n.a.	m	x	x	x	x
Pyrite	n.a.	x	x }	x	{ x	x
Sulphur	n.a.	n	x }		{ x	x
Phosphate rock	n.a.	o	x	x	x	x
Talc and soapstone	n.a.	x	x	x	x	x
Marl	n.a.	n.a.	p	x	x	n.a.
Monazite	l	l	l	x	x	n.a.
Precious stones	n.a.	n	n	x	x	n.a.

(continued)

APPENDIX B

TABLE B-1 (concluded)

	1870	1880ᵃ	1890	1902	1909	1919
Magnesite	l	l	l	p	×	×
Chromite	n.a.	×	×			×
Nickel and cobalt	×	×	×	×	q	n.a.
Molybdenum	n.a.	n.a.	n.a.			
Rutile (titanium)	n.a.	n.a.	n			×
Uranium and vanadium	n.a.	n.a.	n.a.	×	×	
Tungsten	n.a.	n.a.	n.a.	×	r	
Antimony	n.a.	n.a.	×	n.a.		n.a.
Tin	n.a.	n.a.	×	n.a.		n.a.
Manganiferous iron	n.a.	n.a.	n.a.	n.a.	×ˢ	n.a.
Bismuth	n.a.	n.a.	n.a.	n.a.		n.a.
Borax	n.a.	n	n	×		n.a.
Platinum	n.a.	n.a.	p	×	n.a.	n.a.
Lithium	n.a.	n.a.	n.a.	×	n.a.	n.a.

n.a. = not available.

Note: Cement, reported for 1880 and 1902, and lime, reported for 1880, are assumed to be processed items not belonging in mining.

ᵃ Magnesian limestone and shoemakers' sandstone reported separately.
ᵇ Total for value of output only. Partial coverage for other items.
ᶜ Very rough estimate. (Value of output for both).
ᵈ Glass sand, reported separately, is assumed to be included in sandstone in other years.
ᵉ Value of output given separately in 1880 and 1890.
ᶠ Fire clay only.
ᵍ Value of output from Bureau of Mines is reasonable.
ʰ Value of output only.   ⁱ Scythestones reported separately.
ʲ Only very suspicious figures available.   ᵏ Production starts later.
ˡ Negligible.
ᵐ Value of output reasonable according to *Historical Statistics of the United States, 1789–1945*, Bureau of the Census, 1949, p. 147.
ⁿ Value of output reasonable according to figures in Bureau of the Census, *Special Report for Mines and Quarries, 1902* (1905).
ᵒ Value of output only.   ᵖ Value of output available.
ᵠ Included below.   ʳ Also shown separately.
ˢ Includes chromite and nickel.

Source: *Census of Mines and Quarries* (variously titled) for the given years.

States, 1880, p. 631); another is copper (*ibid.*, p. 802). In 1902, which contains probably the most detailed industrial breakdown, the nonproducing mines are shown separately for several of the groups and we are probably justified in assuming that nonproducing mines were not being worked in the others. In 1909 and 1919, the data on nonproducing mines are reported for much broader mineral groups.

For a few minerals, e.g., coal and iron, there is some production by "irregular" or "small surface mines." For some of them, not only value of product, but also wage earners, wages, and, sometimes, materials are reported. Since their methods of production are probably not those

NOTES ON ESTIMATES IN MINING, 1870-1953

typical of the industry as a whole, their inclusion in the capital-output analysis is, perhaps, questionable.

Before 1909 the items detailed in Table B-2 were not necessarily

TABLE B-2
Items Transcribed from the *Census of Mining*, Selected Years, 1870–1919

	1870	1880	1890	1902	1909	1919
Number of:						
Wage earners	x [a]	x	x	x	x	x
Salaried workers	n.a.	x	x	x	x	x
Corporations	n.a.	n.a.	n.a.	x	n.a.	n.a.
Value of:						
Wages	x	x	x	x	x	x
Salaries	n.a.	x	x	x	x	x
Supplies	n.a.	n.a.	n.a.	n.a.	x	x
Fuel	x	x	x	x	x	x
Power						x
Contract work	n.a.	[b]	x	x	x	x
Royalties and rents	n.a.	n.a.	x	x	x	x
Taxes	n.a.	n.a.	x	x	x	x
Other expenses	n.a.	n.a.	x	x	x	x
Output	x	x	x	x	x	x
Land		x [c, d]	x [d]	n.a.	x	x
Building and fixtures	x	x [e]	x	n.a.	x	x
Tools and machinery			x	n.a.	x	x
Cash and inventories	n.a.	x [f]	x	n.a.	n.a.	n.a.
Stocks at par	n.a.	n.a.	n.a.	x	n.a.	n.a.
Bonds at par	n.a.	n.a.	n.a.	x	n.a.	n.a.
Dividends paid	n.a.	n.a.	n.a.	x	n.a.	n.a.
Interest paid	n.a.	n.a.	n.a.	x	n.a.	n.a.

n.a. = not available.
[a] Called "hands employed."
[b] For petroleum only.
[c] Called "real estate."
[d] Includes value of leased land.
[e] Called "plant."
[f] Called "working capital."
Source: Same as Appendix Table B-1.

reported for all the mineral groups covered. Furthermore, for any particular mineral group, all establishments may not have reported all the items, e.g., in the 1880 census, capital is not reported for some districts for coal and copper, but totals of the reported capital appear in the summary tables in juxtaposition to total value of product.

In the early years, also, central offices were not canvassed; and salaried workers included only the office force at the mine. As mentioned above, salaried workers were not always tallied; but, since their total number is limited, we can assume that the error owing to omissions is slight.

APPENDIX B

Sometimes, the figure for wage earners is the average for the year. At other times, the largest number employed is reported. Full-time employment also presents a problem, since the number of days the mine is operated varies from mineral group to mineral group and from geographic region to geographic region within any one mineral group.

Frequently, if items were not reported, the census authorities made estimates and included them in the totals.

C. Level of Business Activity in Year of Census Canvass

Period Covered by Census	Level of Business Activity According to National Bureau of Economic Research Business Cycles Chronology
6/1/69–5/31/70	A peak was reached in June 1869 and the next trough occurred in December 1870. The censal year, therefore, covers the first year of an 18-month business contraction.
6/1/79–5/31/80	A trough occurred in March 1879, terminating a depression of 65 months. The subsequent peak is dated March 1882. This censal year represents the first third of a business expansion.
6/1/89–5/31/90	Between this census and the preceding one there had been two complete cycles and the expansion phase of a third, with a peak in July 1890. This censal year covers the last half of a two-year expansion.
1/1/02–12/31/02	A peak occurred in September 1902. This censal year represents the last nine months of a 21-month-long business expansion, and the first three months of a 23-month business contraction.
1/1/09–12/31/09	In the five years between this and the preceding census there was one business cycle and an expansion phase of another, with a peak in January 1910. This censal year spans the last two-thirds of that expansion phase.
1/1/19–12/31/19	The expansion phase initiated in December 1914 extended to August 1918. The next contraction was brief, ending in April 1919. It was followed by an equally brief expansion ending January 1920. This censal year covers the last stages of contraction and virtually the entire subsequent expansion.

D. Estimate of the Value of Leased and Total Land Used in Mining, 1909 and 1919

The capital figures from the censuses of 1909 and 1919 do not include the value of rented land. Hence, these figures are incomplete, since both owned and leased productive property are equally significant in any analysis of capital requirements. In order to complete the figures, the value of rented land has to be estimated and included. The estimate of the value of rented land is directly connected with the estimate of total land employed in the given industry. The latter estimate is especially needed when we deflate the capital figures.[15]

1. AVAILABLE ESTIMATES OF THE VALUE OF MINING LAND

The censuses of 1880 and 1890 reported the value of mineral land separately. The only other estimate available is that by R. R. Doane, who places the value of mining real estate for 1922 at $4,482 million,[16] of which 75 per cent, or $3,362 million, consists of land. Doane's method of estimation was as follows:

The census of 1919 puts the capital employed in mining at $7 billion. Using the ratio of working to total capital in mining corporations (16 per cent),[17] the Federal Trade Commission report on *National Wealth and Income* estimates the 1922 value of real estate in mining, including land, improvements and equipment, at $6 billion.[18] Doane distributed the sum among the individual states. The allocation was controlled by an over-all figure for taxed real property excluding personal equipment. As a result, Doane had to reduce the FTC estimate by $1,518 million. Therefore, he obtained $4,482 million for the value of real estate (excluding personal equipment). Doane does not furnish the distribution of this value by individual industries.

a. Trends Indicated by the Available Figures. For all mining, the Doane estimate indicates a decline in the relative importance of the money value of land as a capital component. If we exclude the value of leased land from the capital values in 1890 and take the Doane figure as equal to the value of land owned by establishments, we find that the ratio of land value (excluding leased land) to capital for all mining fell from 57.4 per cent in 1890 to 48 per cent in 1922. An even larger decline is registered when we consider the Doane figure as representing the value of total land[19] (from 64.4 per cent in 1890 to 48 per cent in 1922). This change was consistent with the development

---

[15] For some mining industries, data for the acreage of mineral land employed are available beginning 1880. Estimates in constant prices used in Part 1 above exclude land.

[16] R. R. Doane, *The Anatomy of American Wealth* (Harper, 1940, p. 209). This estimate is used by Simon Kuznets in *National Product since 1869* (National Bureau of Economic Research, 1946), and is published in Bureau of the Census, *Historical Statistics of the United States*.

[17] *National Wealth and Income*, a report by the Federal Trade Commission in final response to Senate Resolution No. 451 (1926), pp. 134 and 138.

[18] *Ibid.*, p. 29.

[19] The figure obtained from tax reports includes leased land. The census figure, however, includes only the value of land owned. Adding the estimated value of leased land to the census figure and proceeding as Doane did, we would have to add approximately $2 billion to the $1,518 million assumed as the value of equipment. Such a figure is undoubtedly too high. Therefore, it seems more reasonable to consider the Doane estimate as representing the value of land owned by establishments.

APPENDIX B

shown by the two censuses—1880 and 1890—in which land values were reported. Thus, the ratio of land value (including leased land) to total capital, 1880–1890, decreased from 68.1 to 64.4 per cent.

At first glance, an extrapolation of the indicated trend appears to be justified not only for all mining, but also for each industry group. A stricter examination, however, reveals that the shift in the land-capital relationship for total mining occurred because of changes in the weights for individual industries. The industries where the value of land played a relatively smaller role than in all mining, e.g., the petroleum industry, developed faster than the other industries. If we keep constant the land-capital ratio for the individual industries, the share of land in all mining fell from 64.4 per cent in 1890 to 55.7 per cent in 1919. If, to make it comparable with Doane's estimate,[20] we take the ratio of owned land to capital excluding leased land, the share was reduced from 57.4 to 41.7 per cent. This decline is even sharper than that indicated by Doane—41.7 per cent against 48 per cent, or, in absolute figures, $2,967 million against $3,361.5 million.

2. POSSIBLE METHODS OF ESTIMATING LAND VALUE IN 1909 AND 1919

We have available two ways of estimating the value of land for mining industry groups for 1909 and 1919. One makes use of estimates available in previous years. The other capitalizes the royalties which would have to be paid out of the given level of production if all the land is leased. The second method is identical with an estimate of the value of subsoil minerals of the given industry. The market value of mining land should approximate the value of its mineral content, assuming, of course, that the surface value can be neglected.

a. *Estimate Based on Data in Previous Years.* As mentioned above, the figure for the value of total land employed in mining, obtained on the assumption of a constant ratio of land to capital within the single industries, is smaller than Doane's estimate. When two reproducible capital components are considered one would expect an increase in the relative importance of a certain capital component in physical terms to move parallel with such an increase in money terms. The figure obtained on the assumption of a constant ratio of land to capital could be regarded as a maximum figure, since the relative importance of land in physical terms undoubtedly becomes smaller. However, the value of land as a nonreproducible good is more exposed to market influences than the value of reproducible capital components. Therefore, it is as likely that the ratio of the value of land to other capital components would rise as that it would fall or that it would remain constant. The

[20] See note 19.

NOTES ON ESTIMATES IN MINING, 1870-1953

assumption of constancy leads to an average figure which, at least when several industries are added together, should approximate the desired value.

(*i*) *Formulas used and difficulties encountered.* The censuses of 1880 and 1890, which included the value of leased land in the capital figures, gave a breakdown of capital into its components. They did not, however, report separately the value of leased and owned land for the individual industries.[21] The censuses of 1909 and 1919 reported only the amount of capital invested, owned, and borrowed excluding rented property. These censuses reported the total acreage of mineral land operated, and distinguished between leased and owned land. However, they did not give a breakdown of capital. There are two possible methods of estimating the value of total land in 1909 and 1919, if we assume a constant ratio of land to capital: We could estimate the value of leased land in 1890 using the ratio of total acreage to leased acreage in whichever year—1909 or in 1902—these data were reported. Having excluded the value of leased land from the capital figures for 1890, we could obtain the ratio of owned land to capital excluding leased land. We could then use this ratio to estimate the value of owned land in 1909–1919. Finally, we could raise the last-mentioned figure by the ratio of total acreage to owned acreage to get the value of total land.

This method of estimation implies two additional arbitrary assumptions. One, which the second method cannot avoid (although the effect is lessened), is that the value of a unit of leased land is equal to the value of a unit of owned land. Another assumption, which the second method avoids completely, is that the distribution between owned and leased land in 1902 (or in 1909) is the same as in 1890. It is obvious that the error introduced by these assumptions could be considerable. Therefore, although the second assumption had to be made in order to separate leased from owned land in 1880 and 1890, it appeared undesirable to base further estimates on figures so obtained.

The second method is to calculate the value of leased land from an estimate of the value of owned and leased land reduced by the ratio of leased acreage to total acreage; the ratio of the estimated value of owned and leased land to total capital must be equal to that for 1890. In other words, the total value of land has to satisfy two conditions: (1) to be so much larger than the value of leased land as the total acreage is larger than the leased acreage, that is,

$$\frac{x}{y} = t$$ where x = value of leased land
y = value of total land
t = ratio of leased acreage to total acreage

---

[21] These data are available in 1890 for only a few industries.

APPENDIX B

(2) to be in identical relation to the value of leased land as the total acreage is to leased acreage, that is,

$$\frac{y}{c+x} = z$$

where c = value of capital excluding leased land
z = ratio of total land to capital including value of leased land in 1890

Solving,

$$x = \frac{tzc}{1-tz}$$

$$y = \frac{x}{t}$$

As we have mentioned, this preferred method involves only one assumption (other than the basic assumption expressed by z), namely, that the value of a leased acre is equal to the value of an owned acre. However, since both derived values are dependent variables, the error will be smaller in the second method than in the first. In the latter, we estimate the value of owned land only, on the basis of certain data, and raise the figures so obtained by some ratio.

b. Estimate of the Value of the Subsoil Minerals.

(*i*) *Previous estimates*. So far as we can learn, two attempts have been made to estimate the subsoil value of the different minerals. One is the 1922 report of the Federal Trade Commission, which presents estimates for iron, petroleum, coal and copper; the other is in "Subsoil Wealth," by H. F. Bain (in *Studies in Income and Wealth, Volume Twelve*, National Bureau of Economic Research, 1950) and includes estimates for coal, oil and gas, iron, copper, and gold for 1929, 1939, and 1946. The method of estimation used by the Commission was simple. The Commission addressed schedules to all listed companies calling for data on the value per quantity unit and on the size of the mineral reserve remaining on land owned or controlled by the company. The Commission computed an average value per quantity unit. This was multiplied by the total quantity of reserves, obtained by making adjustments for nonreporting establishments.

It is evident that the values so obtained are much too high, because values accruing in the future are counted as equal to values due at the present. For this reason, the Commission was unable to reconcile its estimates with the figures reported by the census.[22] In bituminous coal, the estimated values are five times the census figures; in iron, seven times; and in anthracite, copper and petroleum, twice as large. The census figures, moreover, include capital values other than land.

The figures estimated by H. F. Bain are superior to those published by the Commission in that they were obtained by discounting future

[22] *National Wealth and Income, op. cit.*, pp. 71 ff.

values. Nevertheless, we find them unacceptable because of an error in estimating the "years purchase factor" (the factor by which a prospective annuity must be multiplied in order to obtain the present value of the total income to be received). This will be made clear in the following comments.

The value of a resource which produces a royalty can be viewed theoretically in two ways. It can be seen as a sum of annuities occurring during the lifetime of the resource. As such, it would equal the discounted value of these annuities. It can be seen also as a capital fund yielding dividends. These consist of interest on the capital fund plus a part repayment of capital at a compound interest rate such that the repayments will equal the capital fund by the time the last dividend is paid. Practically, both approaches yield identical results if the respective interest rates are the same.

For obvious reasons, there is no question about the equivalence of the discount rate and the rate by which a sinking fund can be increased. Both result from capital productivity in a given period. The rate of interest on the capital fund also must be equivalent to these two rates, since it is a "pure" interest rate which makes no allowance for entrepreneurial activity and risk and is, therefore, identical to the discount rate on royalties and the interest rate on sinking funds.

If, however, the estimate of the value of mining land is based on profits including royalties, the interest rate on the capital fund ought to differ from the rate by which the sinking fund must increase. In these circumstances, the Hoskold formula[23] helps us to find the cash price which an entrepreneur should be ready to pay for mining land. This formula can be used only under these circumstances: (1) there is a net profit after allowing for depreciation and for interest on capital; (2) the entrepreneur has decided what profit (including royalties) he expects to earn from his invested capital. That is, royalties plus profits

---

[23] 1. $(r \neq r')$
$$V = \frac{A}{\left[\frac{r}{(1+r)^n - 1}\right] + r'}$$

2. $(r = r')$
$$V = \frac{A[(1+r)^n - 1]}{r(1+r)^n}$$

where: V = value of land
A = profit per year including royalties
r = rate of increase of the sinking fund
r' = entrepreneur's expected rate of profit (including royalties)

Formula 2 was used in our estimates.

The Hoskold formula is given in Charles Homer Baxter and R. D. Parks, *Mine Examination and Valuation* (1st ed., Michigan College of Mining and Technology, 1933), p. 125.

APPENDIX B

(as defined above) are kept constant, and the equation is solved for the value of land. When the estimate is based on royalties, these only are kept constant; and the interest rates on the sinking fund and on the capital fund are identical.

Bain does not make clear when he is dealing with profits including royalties and when he is dealing with royalties only. In the case of petroleum and natural gas, however, Bain's estimates of 12.5 per cent and 10 per cent, respectively, of output as the land owners' share in these industries (the percentages remained fairly constant in the census reports) must refer to royalties alone (the designation used in the article is "royalties"). The application of the Hoskold formula to arrive at the years purchase factor appears, from the above considerations, to be incorrect.

A mistake of another sort seems to have happened in the estimation of the value of gold reserves. In discounting the value of the gold reserves (in the article, this is called the "nationalistic method") by $1/(1+r)^n$,[24] the assumption was made that total output will accrue to the end of the nth year. Actually, however, the production is current, and the common formula for the present value of an annuity divided by n years should have been used.

(ii) *Formula used and difficulties encountered.* The attempt we made to estimate the value of subsoil minerals for each reported industry is based on the amount of royalty paid by the given industry. We first obtained the amount of royalty which would have to be paid if total employed land is leased. We then raised this amount by a years purchase factor.[25] In this procedure, many arbitrary decisions had to be made, and it is hardly necessary to emphasize the roughness of the estimates. In the following, we restrict ourselves to a review of only the major difficulties.

The census reports are for royalties including rents. However, it is emphasized that, in most cases, the amount of rent is so small that it can be neglected.[26] Nevertheless, in some industries, the figures estimated on the basis of royalties are too high. For the others, the small amount of rent, although neglected when the royalty figure alone is examined, plays a more important role when multiplied by a years purchase factor. Besides this technical obstacle, there is the theoretical difficulty of replacing an unknown distribution of unknown future amounts by a uniform distribution of an amount which occurred in one year.

A further source of arbitrariness is connected with the determination

---

[24] A printing mistake put n in the same line with $(1+r)$.
[25] See note 23, above.
[26] *Census of Mines and Quarries, op. cit.*, pp. 284, 323, 349, and 377.

of the average length of life of the resources at the disposal of the establishments. The length of life we used is based on estimates of the amount of economically available mineral reserves in the United States.[27]

These estimates include the total of all economically worthwhile reserves available, not merely the part at the disposal of active enterprises. The difference is mainly accounted for by mining land in the hands of the government and by land that, for lack of sufficient demand, is still "wild" even though production costs would not be prohibitive. The total available reserves and those at the disposal of active enterprises will, of course, differ in different industries. In dealing with each industry, we have made an effort to take these differences into account and to reduce accordingly the length of life of the resources. Obviously, it could be done only in a very arbitrary manner. Another unsatisfactory solution had to be made for industries for which no data concerning economic reserves were published prior to 1943. In these cases, we had to assume that the ratio of depletion to new discovery remained constant.

Two other deliberate choices had to be made. We have some freedom in the choice of an interest rate for discounting future royalties to obtain the present value. With the aid of the series on yields of sixty high-grade bonds, we chose a 4.5 per cent discount for 1919 and a 4 per cent rate for 1909; evidently, other rates could have been selected.

Secondly, the census did not report for every industry the average amount of royalties paid per quantity or per value of product. In order to arrive at the total of royalties which would have to be paid if all land were leased, we were obliged to multiply the amount of royalty paid by the ratio of total to leased land. As in the first approach, we thus assume that leased and owned land are equally productive. Fortunately, this lack of data is largely restricted to industries of minor importance.

3. COMPARISON OF ESTIMATES OBTAINED BY BOTH APPROACHES

In spite of all these inadequacies, a comparison of the figures obtained by both approaches—(1) keeping constant the ratio of land to total capital and (2) capitalizing royalties—is possible and revealing. The figures obtained by the first approach, reflecting certain past

[27] We relied on figures in the following publications: (1) *Papers on Conservation of Mineral Resources*, United States Geological Survey *Bulletin* No. 394, 1909; (2) *The Mineral Reserves of the United States and Its Capacity for Production* (National Resources Committee, 1936, mimeograph), prepared for the Planning Committee for Mineral Policy by Kenneth Leith and Donald M. Lindell; (3) *Investigation of National Resources*. Hearings before a subcommittee of the Committee on Public Lands of the United States Senate, 80th Congress, 1st Session, May 1947.

APPENDIX B

conditions, can be taken as approximating book values. The census of 1890 reported capital figures at market prices. A mining establishment founded in 1890, which did not make any changes in its capital

TABLE B-3

Assumed Average Length of Life for Royalties on Leased Mineral Lands, by Mineral Groups, 1919 and 1909

	Length of Life (years)	
	1919	*1909*
Anthracite coal	40	40
Bituminous coal	50	50
Petroleum and natural gas	15	20
Iron ore	40	40
Copper	25	25
Lead and zinc	10	10
Precious metals	40	50
Limestone	50	50
Granite	40	40
Sandstone	40	40
Basalt	40	40
Slate	25	25
Marble	50	50
Manganese	35	–
Quicksilver	30	30
Rare metals	8	–
Abrasive materials	20	40
Asbestos	40	–
Asphalt	10	40
Barytes	10	15
Bauxite	40	40
Chromite	15	–
Clay	20	20
Feldspar	50	50
Fluorspar	50	50
Fuller's earth	50	50
Graphite	50	50
Gypsum	30	40
Magnesite	13	–
Mica	25	30
Millstones	50	–
Mineral pigments	20	40
Phosphate rock	10	10
Pyrite	50	50
Silica	50	50
Sulphur	–	–
Talc and Soapstone	50	50
Grindstones	–	50

– No estimate.
Source: See Appendix B, particularly note 27.

composition after that date, would report the same figures to the census of 1909, which asked for book values. The figures obtained by the second approach reflect the market conditions in the given year. For total mining, the value of land in 1919 would amount, according to the first approach, to $5,208 million; according to the second, to $5,065 million. The comparable estimates of owned land would be $2,968 million and $2,644 million, respectively (compared with R. R. Doane's $3,361.5 million). For particular industries, the figures obtained by both approaches are sometimes surprisingly close.[28] In other cases, the deviation reflects some special circumstances. For instance, in the anthracite coal industry, the value obtained for land by the second approach is much higher than by the first. Actually, the recent prices of undeveloped land were high in comparison with prices in the earlier years, when reserves of land were surveyed. Similarly, the petroleum industry shows some difference, probably as a consequence of the increased demand for oil land. A reverse situation is indicated by the figures for precious metals and bituminous coal mining.

E. Notes on the Statistical Reliability of the Major Findings

Our estimates have two types of deficiency. One arises from differences in definition, coverage, classification, etc.; the other, because the capital data are based on accounting records and are affected, therefore, by changes in accounting practices (e.g., in the treatment of capitalization, depletion, and depreciation) and by revaluations stemming from changing market conditions, tax regulations, waves of company mergers, etc. The second type of deficiency was partly explored in the text in the discussion of limitations of the inferences. We shall add here a brief discussion of the more important deficiencies of the first type and concentrate on those of the second which were omitted from the text.

1. No clear-cut definition of capital is given in the *Report on Mineral Industries in the United States* for 1880 and 1890. From explanatory remarks, we gather that these censuses tried to ascertain the current value of the total amount of business assets in use, whether owned or leased, distinguishing, thereby, between such types of assets as land and plant. In order to make the capital figures of these censuses comparable with those of other censuses, we estimated and excluded the value of leases. We made no adjustment for the fact that the figures represent current, instead of depreciated original, cost, since, to judge

---

[28] For iron, for example, the estimates are $701,477 thousand by the first method and $672,026 thousand by the second. However, it should be emphasized that the assumption of equal productivity of leased and owned land was not necessary, because the production of leased land is reported in 1909.

APPENDIX B

by evidence for the later years,[29] the two valuation bases would yield identical results in 1880 and 1890.

The censuses of 1909 and 1919 asked for the "total amount of capital, owned and borrowed, invested by the operator in the enterprise on the last day of the business year reported as shown in the books," excluding securities and loans representing investments in other enterprises. Capital according to this definition should approximately equal the sum of cash, notes, and accounts receivable minus reserves for bad debts, inventories, and net capital assets including land as reported by *Statistics of Income*, from which we derive our capital data for the years following. A formal difference between the censuses and *Statistics of Income* exists in the treatment of patent rights and good will. According to the census instruction to its agents, these were not to be considered a part of capital. However, in *Statistics of Income* beginning with 1939 they are entered as intangible assets under capital assets. This conceptual difference makes the capital figure taken from *Statistics of Income* slightly higher than that taken from the census and thus imparts a slightly conservative bias to our findings.

The change from census to *Statistics of Income* data gives rise to other discrepancies. First, we do not use the amount of capital reported by *Statistics of Income* directly; we apply the ratio of assets to output from *Statistics of Income* to output as reported by the census in order to obtain capital comparable with the latter. Our output figures from *Statistics of Income* consist of the sum of gross sales and gross receipts from operations. This differs from our working definition of industrial output by the total of output produced and used by the operating company plus net changes in inventories. This discrepancy makes the denominator based on *Statistics of Income* somewhat lower in years when production exceeds sales and somewhat higher in years when sales exceed production. Hence, the opposite is true of the capital-output ratio.

Second, *Statistics of Income* covers only corporations, whereas the census includes all establishments. Corporations are generally larger establishments, e.g., in 1919 they produced 94 per cent of total output, although they constituted only 51 per cent of total enterprises.[30] Since, according to our statistical evidence, the capital-output ratio rises with the size of enterprise, one would expect estimates of capital based on *Statistics of Income* to be somewhat high. On the other hand, this bias is counterbalanced by the fact that data for many of the large,

---

[29] See Raymond W. Goldsmith, "A Perpetual Inventory of National Wealth," *Studies in Income and Wealth*, Volume 14, National Bureau of Economic Research, 1951, Table 1.

[30] *Census of Mines and Quarries: 1919, op. cit.*, Table 13.

integrated concerns, particularly those engaged in oil production, appear in *Statistics of Income* under the manufacturing classification. The ratios derived from the latter may, therefore, underweight those of large corporations. One might have assumed that the effect of such classification on the oil industry is greater than has been previously mentioned and, therefore, that our capital estimates for this industry derived from *Statistics of Income* ratios have a downward bias. This is not the case, however, if we judge by the comparison of our capital estimates for this industry with estimates by others.[31]

A third and related inconsistency arises from the fact that the census reports draw a sharper demarcation line between mining and manufacturing than does *Statistics of Income*. This is particularly true for metals and oil—industries in which mining and manufacturing operations are very frequently performed by a single corporation. As a result, *Statistics of Income* data for these industries include some figures pertaining to manufacturing processes. According to our work sheets, the ratios of total capital and of capital to value added are higher in petroleum refining than in petroleum producing. Hence, any bias for this industry resulting from the change from census data to *Statistics of Income* data would be in the direction of overstatement of the capital-output ratios. Similarly, the ratio of capital to value added is higher in smelting and refining of metals than in metal mining. However, if we include the value of land in the numerator, the total amount of capital used per unit of value added is higher in metal mining than in smelting and refining. As a result, our ratios derived from *Statistics of Income* for this industry may be somewhat low.

Formally, the capital definition used by the censuses of 1909 and 1919 is well matched by the corresponding assets items from *Statistics of Income*. However, the balance sheet data from *Statistics of Income* may be net of depreciation and depletion to a greater extent than the census data. In order to ascertain whether there actually is continuity between the capital figures derived from the two sources, we reconciled *Statistics of Income* and census figures for 1919 for total

[31] Joseph E. Pogue and Frederick G. Coqueron [*Financial Analysis of Thirty Oil Companies for 1949* and *Supplement* (Chase National Bank of the City of New York)] estimate the value of net investment in oil and natural gas producing facilities (property, plant, and equipment) in 1949 at $6,050 million. The ratio of this aggregate to the 1949 value of net investment in the domestic producing facilities of thirty oil companies when applied to the 1948 value of the latter yields the sum of $5,124 million. This sum represents the net value of fixed assets invested in the oil and gas industry in 1948. Our estimate for 1948 was $5,513 million. Similarly, the ratio of the 1949 aggregate to the total value of domestic *and* foreign producing facilities of the thirty companies applied to the 1940 value of the latter yields $3 billion. This compares with our estimate of $3,582 million. Another estimate for that year sets the figure at $3,440 million (John D. Gill, taken from *Petroleum Facts and Figures, 1947*, American Petroleum Institute, p. 197).

manufacturing and mining and found no significant difference between the capital figures reported. We conclude that "the allegations of gross inaccuracy made against the reports of capital in the *Census of Manufactures* appear to be without foundation for the aggregate in 1919."[32] A similar reconciliation for the mining figures alone would be difficult, because the corporation returns to the Internal Revenue Service for 1919 were filed on a consolidated basis, and many of the mining activities classified as such by the census appear in *Statistics of Income* under manufacturing. This is particularly true for metal mining in that year. However, the close agreement found for aggregate mining and manufacturing and for those manufacturing groups where multi-industry activity is less widespread is evidence that the capital-output ratios derived from census and *Statistics of Income* data are closely comparable.

2. The limitations imposed on our data by the second type of deficiency are of a more serious character. Accounting practices vary among individual enterprises and have varied considerably over time. There is no way to ascertain trends with respect to certain aspects of accounting treatment, and we have to rely on suppositions which, often, are not universally accepted by the accounting profession.

There is a strong case for assuming that a trend toward wider recognition of depreciation allowances began with the period studied. With the inception of the corporation income tax in 1909, this trend was strengthened. The high taxes during World War I completed the process, so that by 1919 depreciation accounting was used by virtually all mining firms. If this assumption is valid, the growth of capital depicted by our figures should tend to be understated prior to 1919 and correctly reflected in subsequent years. This would imply a conservative bias in our finding concerning the increase in the capital-output ratio during the earlier period.

It is also conceivable, however, that the effect of wider acceptance of depreciation accounting was counterbalanced by other factors. One such factor is the tendency toward less conservative accounting with regard to capitalization of betterments and other types of capital expenditure. Before formal depreciation accounting was adopted, many expenditures on buildings and equipment may have been

[32] See Appendix A, section A. It should be noted that the census authorities have frequently referred to the reported capital figures as being liable to a wide margin of *error*. Examination of the figures has shown that this may indeed have been true in the case of some minor mining industries. (For this reason, we work with the combined group of other nonmetal mining.) With regard to major industries, however, the figures have proved to be consistent enough to serve as indicators of the very general patterns of growth. Our reconciliation suggests that the appraisal of reported capital figures given by the census authorities, at least that given by the census of 1919, may have been based on preconceived ideas.

treated as current operating expenses. The introduction of depreciation accounting effected a more proper allocation of these expenditures over time, but it may have had little influence on the net capital values kept on the books, particularly if industry aggregates and changes over long periods of time are considered. Second, as already stated, early censuses did not ask for book values but for the "actual value" of plant and equipment. It is possible that, in estimating this actual value, many operators took into account cost, as well as wear and tear. The figures thus reported are, in a way, net of depreciation and should be comparable with the figures of the later censuses.

The effect of changes in depletion allowances was dealt with in the text and needs little further elaboration here. Provisions for depletion were less common than provisions for depreciation before the inception of corporation taxes in 1909. Although depletion accounting spread in the years following, it is even today, less widespread than depreciation accounting. Thus, unlike changes in depreciation accounting, changes in depletion accounting should have tended to introduce a downward bias in our total capital estimates throughout the period investigated. As a consequence, our finding of an increase in the total capital-output ratio in the earlier period would be strengthened. However, our finding of a decline in the total capital-output ratio in the later period, particularly during the forties when depletion charges were high, could be questioned. If we grant that our net total capital estimates (including land) are understated during the later period as a result of high depletion (and depreciation) allowances,[33] the movement of the gross total capital-output ratio (including reserves for depletion and depreciation) becomes even more interesting. Fortunately, we are able to trace this movement between 1937 and 1948.[34] For total mining, in 1937 and 1948, the ratios based on book values of gross total capital (total capital plus depreciation and depletion reserves) to output are

[33] This should not be true of our estimates excluding land. High depletion, depreciation, or amortization allowances during the forties could not have had a depressing effect on our capital estimates excluding land, since high depreciation charges, by our method of deriving the value of improvements and equipment, should have the effect of overstating the capital value. (The method is described in the source note to Table B-11.) Our estimates of the value of improvements and equipment for this period are based on the value of depreciation charges. The underlying idea is that, with the prevailing methods of straight-line depreciation, the depreciation charges should remain in a constant relationship to the gross value of depreciable assets, provided, of course, that no changes occurred in the average length of life and in depreciation practices.) Since the assumption that depreciation practices remain constant irrespective of the level of employment is not quite justifiable, our estimates of depreciable assets in the forties may be overstated rather than understated.

[34] 1937 is the first year for which reserves for depreciation and depletion are reported by *Statistics of Income*.

APPENDIX B

3.03 and 1.79, respectively. When based on values in 1929 prices, they are 3.10 and 2.63, respectively.[35] Thus, they, too, declined, though not so markedly as the net total capital-output ratios. Hence, the decline in the latter was not merely an effect of high depreciation, depletion, or amortization allowances.

The statistical evidence available for appraising the degree of distortion in our capital estimates attributable to revaluations, for the period during which our estimated ratios of capital to output were declining, is given in the text (Chapter I). Unfortunately, this evidence is restricted to 1925–1934. In the latter half of the thirties, further downward revaluations presumably took place, with the result that our figures for 1940 may be understated. Downward revaluations of assets were restricted to the thirties, however, and cannot be held responsible for the decline in the capital-output ratio during the twenties and forties. Moreover, it should be noted that downward revaluations are relevant for our study only if they exceed the "real" shrinkage of capacity which has occurred. The cases in which downward adjustments were accompanied by the closing of mines and the reduction of capacity do not distort the behavior of the capital-output ratios. It is entirely possible that downward revaluations during the thirties did not exceed the actual shrinkage of capacity that occurred during that period. Reduction of capacity was also large even where no actual closing of mines took place. We point, in particular, to the abandonment that occurs at times of low production levels of the relatively older but still efficient types of equipment.

There is no accurate way to ascertain the impact on our data of upward revaluations. There were apparently two waves of such revaluations. One, 1889–1893 and 1897–1904, (much stronger in the second cycle than in the first), was a result of the merger movement. The other, from 1915 to 1925, was presumably a result of tax regulations and price increases. It is our belief (1) that the effect of the revaluations during and after World War I was largely counterbalanced by the spread of depreciation, and particularly depletion, accounting at the same time and (2) that revaluations connected with mergers were largely excluded by the *Census of Mines and Quarries: 1909* when it called for the exclusion of good will and similar items. This latter supposition can be supported as follows: The *Census of Mines and Quarries: 1902* asked, not for the value of assets, but for the amount of

---

[35] The book values of gross fixed assets (improvements, equipment, and land before reserves for depreciation and depletion) were obtained by adjusting the values reported by *Statistics of Income* to census coverage. The values in 1929 prices were obtained by adjusting the estimated book values by indexes for equipment and improvements used in our estimate of plant in 1929 prices (see source note to Table B-11).

"capitalization," i.e., the par value of outstanding capital stock (common and preferred) and bonded indebtedness of incorporated mining companies. The reported figure for total mining is $3.2 billion. This is equivalent to about $3.7 billion of "watered" capital assets, estimated on the assumption that the 1909 ratio of "capitalization" to current and fixed assets[36] applies in 1902. For 1909, the comparable census figure for total capital of all mining corporations is $3.1 billion. This sum is $0.6 billion lower than the figure implicit in the 1902 census report, in spite of the fact that total value of mining output in 1929 prices rose about 55 per cent between 1902 and 1909. It is evident that such a discrepancy cannot be attributed, as one might like, entirely to the fact that the 1902 census data on capitalization include some figures pertaining to manufacturing. It can be explained only by assuming that the 1909 census managed to exclude from its returns most, if not all, extravagant valuations.

F. Notes on the Comparability of the Benchmark Years With Regard to Employment Levels

A problem in the comparability of the capital-output ratios, as well as of the rates of growth of capital and output, is created by the fact that output is more sensitive to business cycles than is the book value of capital. Years of comparatively low employment and output levels are characterized by comparatively high capital-output and capital-wage-earner ratios. Therefore, in selecting the benchmarks, we must consider the level of activity of the given industry in that year. However, business fluctuations in single industries do not always conform exactly to cycles in general business; probably no two years in recent economic history could be chosen which are exactly comparable with respect to their position in the cycle. Moreover, we have no freedom of choice in the selection of benchmarks prior to 1929, since our data are derived from the *Censuses of Mines*. We are, therefore, obliged to check the degree to which our analysis is distorted by differences in the level of activity in the benchmark years.

Such a check may be made by comparing the actual output of a given industry in a given benchmark year with the average output of the five years centered on the benchmark year (Table B-4). Although output in some benchmark years was above the average and in others, below, differences in employment levels were not very great except in 1919, when output was generally below the five-year average, and in 1929, when output was considerably above. If we adjust our

---

[36] The ratio is around 85 per cent in 1909, according to a sample of mining corporations drawn from *Moody's Manual*.

APPENDIX B

TABLE B-4

Value of Output: Benchmark-Year Estimate as Percentage of Five-Year Average,[a] by Major and Minor Mining Industries, Selected Years, 1870–1948
(*per cent based on values in 1929 prices*)

	1870	1880	1890	1909	1919	1929	1940	1948
All mining	98[b]	96[b]	97	100	93	113	101	107
Metals	104	97	100	107	93	130	104	108
Iron	110	109	106	107	101	128	105	113
Copper	106	94	96	110	90	144	105	106
Lead and zinc	100	93	99	103	91	113	103	102
Precious metals	100	93	100	105	93	104	111	102
Anthracite coal	100	97	98	95	94	103	97	109
Bituminous coal	87	90	93	98	90	111	100	110
Petroleum and natural gas	97	110	94	97	96	111	102	106
Other nonmetals	n.a.	n.a.	104	102	91	113	95	104

n.a. = not available.
[a] Average is centered on benchmark year.
[b] Excluding other nonmetals.
Source: Value of output for benchmark years as in Appendix Table B-8. The five-year moving averages are calculated from the series described in the source notes to Chart 1.

capital-output ratios by those presented in Table B-4, i.e., if, in the denominator, we substitute the five-year average of output for the output of the given year, a rise and decline similar to those described in the text are evident (Table B-5). However, such an adjustment shifts the turning point for total mining from 1919 to 1929.

Is there a reason for substituting averages of output for the output of a given year when we compare capital with output? Although,

TABLE B-5

Capital: Ratio of Benchmark-Year Estimate to Five-Year Average[a] of Output, by Major Mining Industries, Selected Years, 1870–1948
(*based on values in 1929 prices*)

	1870	1880	1890	1909	1919	1929	1940	1948
All mining	0.70	1.11	1.32	1.79	2.10	2.42	1.60	1.42
Metals	1.34	2.22	2.74	2.68	2.02	2.22	1.29	1.09
Anthracite coal	0.42	0.61	0.49	0.48	0.50	0.85	0.53	0.47
Bituminous coal	0.79	0.62	0.64	1.04	1.16	1.18	0.88	0.95
Petroleum and natural gas	1.71	2.26	3.56	4.88	5.63	3.98	2.30	1.88
Other nonmetals	n.c.	n.c.	1.20	1.31	1.10	1.32	0.89	0.58

n.c. = not comparable.
[a] Average is centered on benchmark year.
Source: Capital figures as in Appendix Table B-11. Averages of ouput as in Appendix Table B-4.

ordinarily, the secular trend in output is perhaps better represented by five-year averages than by single-year observations, the five-year averages, too, have certain deficiencies. For example, low levels of output in 1930 and 1931 heavily depress the average centered on 1929, while our capital estimate for this year remains unaffected by the considerable disinvestment which occurred afterward. Thus, if we assume that the five-year average of output centered on 1929 correctly describes the secular trend of output, we must question whether the single-year capital estimate for 1929 correctly describes the secular trend of capital. On the other hand, let us assume that the developments in the thirties were an interruption, rather than a continuation, of the long-term secular trend. In that case, the figure for 1929 alone may be considered a closer approximation to the secular trend position of capital and output in that year than an average affected by consecutive depression years; if so the output average has to be considered as an understatement.

G. General Remarks on Table B-6

In general, we tried to preserve as much industry detail as possible. Some exceptions, however, had to be made. Changes in census classifications made it necessary to group some industries together, as in the case of feldspar and quartz, or certain stones. Further regrouping was necessary because of very low values for certain industries, e.g., abrasive materials. Some industries have not been covered regularly. Where possible, estimates were made to replace the missing figures. Two catch-all groups—"rare metals" and "other nonmetals"—had to be established. The census-to-census changes in the composition of those catch-all groups are so numerous that no comparison of the data is sensible. The only function of the catch-all groups is to make the table totals agree with the totals reported by the census. Subtotals are estimated, where possible, for kindred products, as follows:

A. METALS
I. *Non-precious*
  Iron
  Copper
  Lead and Zinc

II. *Precious*
  Gold and silver lode mineral
  Gold placer mineral

B. NONMETALS
I. *Fuel*
  Anthracite Coal
  Bituminous Coal
  Petroleum and Natural Gas

II. *Stone*
  Granite and Basalt
  Marble and Limestone
  Sandstone and Bluestone
  Slate

APPENDIX B

A. Metals	B. Nonmetals
III. *Rare*	III. *Abrasive Materials*
Antimony	Corundum and Emery
Bismuth	Garnet
Chromite	Infusorial Earth
Lithium	Oilstones
Manganiferous Iron	Pumice
Molybdenum	Tripoli
Nickel and Cobalt	Whetstones
Platinum	
Rutile	
Tin	
Tungsten	
Uranium and Vanadium	
IV. *Other*	IV. *Miscellaneous*
Bauxite	Asbestos
Manganese	Asphalt
Quicksilver	Barytes
	Clay
	Feldspar and Silica
	Fluorspar
	Fuller's earth
	Graphite
	Grindstones
	Gypsum
	Mica
	Millstones and Buhrstones
	Mineral pigments
	Phosphate rock
	Pyrite and Sulphur
	Talc and Soapstone
	V. *Other*
	Borax
	Magnesite
	Marl
	Monazite
	Precious Stones

The figures in row (a) represent the value of capital excluding leased land. In order to make the capital figures for 1880 and 1890, which originally included leased land, comparable with the other figures, the value of leased land had to be separated. The census of 1890 reported the value of leased land for some industries only. For 1880, no such data were available. In order to estimate the missing figures, we used the ratio of leased to total land for the given industry in the earliest available year. Thus, we assume that forms of land holding did not change between 1880 (or 1890) and the year for which we could compute the estimating ratio. When we compare the figures in this row, we should bear in mind that such an assumption may lead to error.

The figures in row (b) for 1880 and 1890 have been separated from reported capital by the method described above. For 1909 and 1919, the figures for this row are obtained by the formula $[x = tzc/(1-tz)]$ described earlier (section D, part 2.a.i.). For 1869, for which no land holdings data are available, the method is reduced to taking the ratio of leased land to capital in 1880.

The figures in row (c) are obtained by multiplying the royalties paid in the given year by a years purchase factor. The rate of discount used is 4 per cent in 1909 and 4.5 per cent in 1919. In the determination of the length of life, account has been taken of the economically available mineral reserves in the United States (see notes on estimation, Section D, part 2.b., and Appendix Table B-3 on the average length of life of the royalty sources). In examining the capital data, one should remember that the data for 1880 and 1890 are reported at replacement values, whereas the data for 1909, 1919 are book values. In the census of 1870, the values intended (book or replacement) were not stated. In the special census report for 1902, no capital data were reported, and no estimates were made.

Since 1902, the figures do not include the nonproductive enterprises. The census of 1919 did not report the figures for these in enough detail for every industry. Only the totals for metals and nonmetals could, therefore, be made strictly comparable.

Estimated figures are placed in parentheses in order to distinguish them from reported figures, with the exception of the figures in row (b) and (c), all of which are estimates. In those cases where the value of materials used had to be estimated, the figures for value added have been put in parentheses.

H. Supporting Tables

TABLE B-6
Capital, Value of Output, and Related Measures, by Major and Minor Mining Industries, Selected Years, 1870–1919
(thousands of dollars)

	1870	1880	1890	1902	1909	1919
All mining						
a. Capital excluding leased land	211,674	557,955	1,066,942		3,279,679[a]	6,955,877[a]
b. Capitalized value of lease land	61,448	128,231	210,927		1,011,388[a]	2,196,478[a]
c. Alternate estimate					1,116,555[a]	2,377,085[a]
d. Value of ouput	152,598	253,025	418,516	772,558	1,186,231	3,123,066
e. Value added	138,320		344,279	657,840	969,728	2,481,250
Total metals						
a. Capital excluding leased land	79,885	309,407	595,167		1,181,941[a]	1,877,326[a]
b. Capitalized value of leased land	7,638	27,575	57,483		368,524[a]	608,094[a]
c. Alternate estimate					375,270[a]	536,042[a]
d. Value of output	47,225	111,243	144,055	215,712	354,294	544,660
e. Value added	41,182		120,108	176,025	269,922	414,738
Nonprecious metals						
a. Capital excluding leased land	28,592	83,108	143,554		665,260	1,552,259
b. Capitalized value of leased land	5,399	17,924	38,428		305,113	543,120
c. Alternate estimate					346,990	508,671
d. Value of output	19,930	36,826	56,904	131,243	263,317	473,121
e. Value added	17,984	32,208	47,053	108,642	201,809	365,811
Iron						
a. Capital excluding leased land	17,774	45,852	74,610		300,736	501,396
b. Capitalized value of leased land	4,660	15,930	35,156		287,789	479,810
c. Alternate estimate					300,356	459,028
d. Value of output	13,204	23,157[b]	33,352	65,465	109,881	218,218
e. Value added	11,924	20,263	28,353	56,459	92,652	180,736

(continued)

304

TABLE B-6 (continued)

	1870	1880	1890	1902	1909	1919
Copper						
a. Capital excluding leased land	7,789	30,875	60,719		301,896	853,639
b. Capitalized value of leased land	235	932	1,904		7,899	25,043
c. Alternate estimate					27,963	7,963
d. Value of output	5,201	9,832c	(18,748)	51,178	124,020	179,730
e. Value added	4,614	8,440	(14,680)	40,095	86,978	130,589
Lead and zinc						
a. Capital excluding leased land	3,029	6,381	(8,225)		62,628	197,224
b. Capitalized value of leased land	504	1,062	(1,368)		9,425	38,267
c. Alternate estimate		d			18,671	41,680
d. Value of output	1,525	3,837	4,804	14,600	29,416	75,173
e. Value added	1,446	3,505	(4,020)	12,088	22,179	54,486
Precious metals						
a. Capital excluding leased land	50,043	(225,785)	447,028		500,556	304,963
b. Capitalized value of leased land	2,123	(9,568)	18,933		63,006	51,427
c. Alternate estimate					28,056	20,279
d. Value of output	26,453	74,127	(85,615)	82,482	87,671	63,533
e. Value added	22,389	(61,637)	(71,797)	65,782	65,595	43,144
Gold and silver lode mines						
a. Capital excluding leased land	42,531	(193,956)	(388,096)		443,715	280,389
b. Capitalized value of leased land						
c. Alternate estimate						
d. Value of output	16,678	62,031		77,154	77,434	54,164
e. Value added	14,472			61,245	58,228	37,164
Gold placer mines						
a. Capital excluding leased land	7,512	(31,829)	(58,932)		56,841	24,574
b. Capitalized value of leased land						
c. Alternate estimate						
d. Value of output	9,775	12,096		5,328	10,237	9,369
e. Value added	7,917			4,537	7,367	5,980

(continued)

APPENDIX B

TABLE B-6 (*continued*)

	1870	1880	1890	1902	1909	1919
Rare metals [e]						
a. Capital excluding leased land	60	442[f]	1,182[f]		9,423	6,463
b. Capitalized value of leased land	0	83	3			(349)
c. Alternate estimate						349
d. Value of output	24	193	103	131	1,747	1,825
e. Value added	22		70	124	1,204	1,150
Other metals [g]						
a. Capital excluding leased land	1,190	72	3,403		6,702	13,641
b. Capitalized value of leased land	116		119		405	13,198
c. Alternate estimate					224	6,743
d. Value of output	818	97	1,433	1,856	1,559	6,181
e. Value added	787	85	1,188	1,477	1,314	4,633
Bauxite						
a. Capital excluding leased land					3,023	1,950
b. Capitalized value of leased land					(138)	(2,815)
c. Alternate estimate					138	2,815
d. Value of output			2	128	671	2,190
e. Value added			2	88	615	1,748
Manganese						
a. Capital excluding leased land		72	2,189		960	7,268
b. Capitalized value of leased land		0	0		0	9,300
c. Alternate estimate					0	3,195
d. Value of output		97	241	178	20	2,188
e. Value added		85	(216)	161	17	1,642
Quicksilver						
a. Capital excluding leased land	1,190[h]		1,214		2,719	4,423
b. Capitalized value of leased land	116		119		267	1,083
c. Alternate estimate					86	733
d. Value of output	818		1,190	1,550	868	1,803
e. Value added	787		970	1,228	682	1,243

(*continued*)

TABLE B-6 (continued)

	1870	1880	1890	1902	1909	1919
Total nonmetals						
a. Capital excluding leased land	131,789	248,548	471,775		2,097,738[a]	5,078,551[a]
b. Capitalized value of leased land	53,810	100,656	153,444		642,864[a]	1,588,384[a]
c. Alternate estimate					741,285[a]	1,841,043[a]
d. Value of output	105,373	141,782	274,461	556,846	831,937	2,578,406
e. Value added	97,138		224,171	481,815	699,804	2,066,512
Fuel [1]						
a. Capital excluding leased land	120,054	222,100	381,269		1,890,485	4,759,804
b. Capitalized value of leased land	50,621	95,236	135,327		603,898	1,536,467
c. Alternate estimate					705,787	1,800,442
d. Value of output	92,829	120,351	214,513	469,297	726,042	2,412,608
e. Value added	85,758	105,579	172,995	407,368	612,606	1,944,101
Anthracite coal						
a. Capital excluding leased land	50,937	100,441[l]	104,995		246,713	433,868
b. Capitalized value of leased land	28,195	53,959[j]	56,789		66,932	85,984
c. Alternate estimate					157,749	216,532
d. Value of output	38,437	42,173	71,948[k]	76,174	148,958	363,651
e. Value added	34,841	35,441	61,126	63,433	122,296	290,607
Bituminous coal						
a. Capital excluding leased land	59,071	78,551[j]	145,932		960,504	1,904,450
b. Capitalized value of leased land	18,552	24,664[j]	35,041		245,251	481,481
c. Alternate estimate					258,796	440,594
d. Value of output	35,088	53,577	94,505	290,858	401,556	1,145,978
e. Value added	33,015	48,711	86,499	266,059	356,174	966,368
Petroleum and natural gas						
a. Capital excluding leased land			130,342		683,268	2,421,486
b. Capitalized value of leased land			43,497		291,715	969,002
c. Alternate estimate					289,242	1,143,316
d. Value of output			48,060	102,265	175,528	902,979
e. Value added			25,370	77,876	134,136	687,126

(continued)

307

APPENDIX B

TABLE B-6 (continued)

	1870	1880	1890	1902	1909	1919
Petroleum						
a. Capital excluding leased land	10,046	43,108	82,396[l]			
b. Capitalized value of leased land	3,874	16,613	31,761			
c. Alternate estimate						
d. Value of output	19,304	24,601	26,963			
e. Value added	17,902	21,427	17,457			
Natural gas						
a. Capital excluding leased land			47,946[l]			
b. Capitalized value of leased land			11,736			
c. Alternate estimate						
d. Value of output			21,097			
e. Value added			7,913			
Total stone[m]						
a. Capital excluding leased land	4,055	20,728	74,643		132,642	148,759
b. Capitalized value of leased land	995	4,283	14,846		25,888	35,329
c. Alternate estimate					28,259	25,841
d. Value of product	2,115	18,141	52,596	70,462	75,992	101,685
e. Value added	1,958		44,724	59,722	63,710	75,763
Slate						
a. Capital excluding leased land	2,738	2,544	8,192		12,177	6,923
b. Capitalized value of leased land	793	784	2,378		3,529	2,042
c. Alternate estimate					4,234	2,343
d. Value of output	1,311	1,530	3,483	5,696	6,054	5,721
e. Value added	1,191		3,201	5,016	5,205	4,671
Marble and limestone	m					
a. Capital excluding leased land	1,317	8,750	35,863		64,362	91,158
b. Capitalized value of leased land	202	1,815	6,252		12,943	21,558
c. Alternate estimate					11,536	13,911
d. Value of output	804	6,857	22,583	35,486	36,071	57,342
e. Value added	767		17,700	29,256	30,003	41,421

(continued)

TABLE B-6 (continued)

	1870	1880	1890	1902	1909	1919
Granite and basalt						
a. Capital excluding leased land		4,178	15,094		34,168	31,723
b. Capitalized value of leased land		1,113	4,021		6,948	7,393
c. Alternate estimate					9,421	7,158
d. Value of output		5,189	14,464	18,258	24,576	27,937
e. Value added			13,018	15,765	20,600	21,498
Sandstone and bluestone[n]						
a. Capital excluding leased land		4,889	15,494		17,058	18,955
b. Capitalized value of leased land		687	2,195		2,468	4,336
c. Alternate estimate					3,068	2,429
d. Value of output		4,280	12,066	11,022	9,291	10,685
e. Value added			10,806	9,685	7,902	8,173
Abrasive materials[o]						
a. Capital excluding leased land		302	235		1,068	1,443
b. Capitalized value of leased land		117	91		415	320
c. Alternate estimate					237	338
d. Value of output		107	219	408	498	722
e. Value added		100	205	362	437	550
Total miscellaneous[p]						
a. Capital excluding leased land	7,680	5,418	15,628		73,543	168,545
b. Capitalized value of leased land	2,194	1,020	3,180		12,663	16,268
c. Alternate estimate					7,002	14,422
d. Value of output	10,429	3,183	7,133	16,679	29,405	63,391
e. Value added	9,422		6,246	14,363	23,051	46,098
Asbestos						
a. Capital excluding leased land		6	25		88	772
b. Capitalized value of leased land		4	18		66	57
c. Alternate estimate						37
d. Value of output		4	2	46	65	250
e. Value added			1	38	42	198

(continued)

APPENDIX B

TABLE B-6 (*continued*)

	1870	1880	1890	1902	1909	1919
Asphalt						
a. Capital excluding leased land	514	(38)	1,585		2,557	3,171
b. Capitalized value of leased land	299	(22)	1,066		1,491	43
c. Alternate estimate					39	103
d. Value of output	450	4	172	237	466	750
4. Value added	423		158	215	386	349
Barytes						
a. Capital excluding leased land		12	249		473	2,290
b. Capitalized value of leased land		4	102		193	180
c. Alternate estimate					156	356
d. Value of output		37	106	203	225	1,575
e. Value added			98	195	197	1,287
Clay						
a. Capital excluding leased land		368	(1,230)		6,780	17,645
b. Capitalized value of leased land		68	(214)		(1,155)	(6,049)
c. Alternate estimate					1,155	6,049
d. Value of output		200	636	2,061	2,946	10,086
e. Value added			553	1,788	2,557	8,216
Feldspar and Silica						
a. Capital excluding leased land		320	(209)		850	1,391
b. Capitalized value of leased land		220	(131)		(257)	(395)
c. Alternate estimate					257	395
d. Value of output		104	88	437	502	956
e. Value added			75	367	416	745
Fluorspar						
a. Capital excluding leased land			174		195	8,047
b. Capitalized value of leased land			18		21	2,899
c. Alternate estimate					42	1,996
d. Value of output			46	276	289	3,335
e. Value added			41	245	230	2,538

(*continued*)

TABLE B-6 (continued)

	1870	1880	1890	1902	1909	1919
Fuller's earth						
a. Capital excluding leased land					1,362	1,877
b. Capitalized value of leased land					(21)	(118)
c. Alternate estimate					21	118
d. Value of output				98	316	2,019
e. Value added				69	232	1,381
Graphite						
a. Capital excluding leased land		237	220		1,506	3,755
b. Capitalized value of leased land		43	39		274	60
c. Alternate estimate					128	59
d. Value of output		50	73	228	344	869
e. Value added			65	176	238	538
Grindstones						
a. Capital excluding leased land		(505)	(559)		304	(411)
b. Capitalized value of leased land		(149)	(164)		(64)	(87)
c. Alternate estimate					64	(87)
d. Value of output		500	440	667	413	(506)
e. Value added			389	636	299	(386)
Gypsum						
a. Capital excluding leased land		(1,036)	1,980		10,213	13,542
b. Capitalized value of leased land		(258)	493		2,543	1,100
c. Alternate estimate					1,484	1,123
d. Value of output		400ʳ	764	2,089	5,813	6,806
e. Value added			635	1,747	4,253	4,616
Mica						
a. Capital excluding leased land		256ˢ	524		1,262	699
b. Capitalized value of leased land		82ˢ	168		406	373
c. Alternate estimate					104	282
d. Value of output		128	52	119	207	607
e. Value added			45	107	185	476

(continued)

311

APPENDIX B

TABLE B-6 (continued)

	1870	1880	1890	1902	1909	1919
Millstones and buhrstones						
a. Capital excluding leased land			50		10	53
b. Capitalized value of leased land			5		1	44
c. Alternate estimate						40
d. Value of product			35	60	34	65
e. Value added			34	58	34	47
Mineral pigments						
a. Capital excluding leased land		154	721		387	816
b. Capitalized value of leased land		27	127		68	100
c. Alternate estimate					59	104
d. Value of output		136	464	361	151	481
e. Value added			379	303	128	367
Phosphate rock						
a. Capital excluding leased land		(2,264)	5,926		30,643	72,734
b. Capitalized value of leased land		(82)	206		(2,806)	(1,661)
c. Alternate estimate					2,806	1,661
d. Value of output		1,124	2,938	4,923	10,781	10,300
e. Value added			2,621	4,124	8,522	6,319
Pyrite and sulphur						
a. Capital excluding leased land		54	1,490		7,011	32,503
b. Capitalized value of leased land		2	190		279	1,697
c. Alternate estimate					21	850
d. Value of output		26	210	947	5,109	20,345
e. Value added			166	730	3,925	15,291
Talc and soapstone						
a. Capital excluding leased land		168	686‡		8,660	6,226
b. Capitalized value of leased land		59	239‡		3,018	950
c. Alternate estimate					666	707
d. Value of output		121	476	1,138	1,175	2,302
e. Value added			404	1,012	913	1,802

(continued)

TABLE B-6 (continued)

	1870	1880	1890	1902	1909	1919
Other[a]						
a. Capital excluding leased land	13				1,242	2,613
b. Capitalized value of leased land						(455)
c. Alternate estimate						455
d. Value of output	8	349	631	2,789	569	2,139
e. Value added	7		582	2,554	494	1,542

Note: Figures in parentheses in rows (a), (d), and (e) are estimates. Blank spaces indicate data not available.
a For strict comparability the following figures ('ooo omitted) for nonproducing enterprises should be added:

All mining
1909   Capital excluding leased land $282,001
          Value of leased land   16,600
1919   Capital excluding leased land   153,157
          Value of leased land   43,550

All metals
1909   Capital excluding leased land   239,043
          Value of leased land   6,234
1919   Capital excluding leased land   116,147
          Value of leased land   26,974

All nonmetals
1909   Capital excluding leased land   42,958
          Value of leased land   10,366
1919   Capital excluding leased land   37,010
          Value of leased land   16,576

b Including irregular production.
c Including value of output of $975,000 of the western states and Tennessee, for which other items are not available.

(continued)

APPENDIX B

Notes to TABLE B-6 (*concluded*)

d For 1880, the figures refer to areas east of longitude 100 degrees East only.
e The coverage is as follows: 1870: nickel only; 1880: nickel, cobalt, and chromite; 1890: chromite, nickel and cobalt, antimony, platinum, tin, and rutile; 1902: chromite, magnesite, molybdenum, nickel and cobalt, rutile, platinum, lithium, uranium, and tungsten. Magnesite could not be separated and added to nonmetals; 1909: tungsten, molybdenum, rutile, titanium, uranium, vanadium, chromite, nickel and cobalt, antimony, bismuth, tin, manganiferous iron, and borax (the latter could not be separated and added to nonmetals); 1919: chromite, molybdenum, rutile, tungsten, uranium, and vanadium.
f Includes the value of some leased land for which no basis for separation could be found.
g Not including quicksilver in 1880.
h Census reports $11,900 thousand. We assumed there was a printing mistake and dropped the zero.
i Excluding natural gas in 1870 and 1880.
j Not including small surface mines (value of output is $56,000 for anthracite and $1,092,000 for bituminous).
k Value of anthracite used for steam is added to the census figures
l Census claims that this figure is too low.
m Totals for 1870 are for slate and marble only; marble only in "marble and limestone." For 1880, the totals include "other stones," that could not be distributed among the individual industries. For 1909 the capital figure includes $4,876 thousand which the census could not distribute among the individual industries.
n The figures for 1880 and 1890 represent sandstone after removing grindstones, which have been included in this group by the census.
o Includes: tripoli, infusorial earth, pumice, oilstones, whetstones, garnet, corundum, and emery.
p In 1870 includes barytes, silica fire clay, mica, mineral pigments, and unspecified stone. The census called this group "stone."
q Two mines did not report capital; their value of output is not stated.
r Figure is taken from *Historical Statistics of United States 1789–1945*, Bureau of the Census, 1949, p. 147.
s Seven mines did not report capital.
t Does not include capital of talc.
u 1870: peat only; 1880 and 1890: marl, precious stones, and borax; 1902: marl, precious stones, borax, and monazite; 1909: marl, precious stones, monazite, magnesite, and peat; 1919: magnesite only.
Source: See Appendix B, section G.

TABLE B-7

Value of Output, in Current Prices, by Major Mining Industries,
Selected Years, 1870–1953
(*millions of dollars*)

	All Mining[a]	Metals	Coal		Petroleum and Natural Gas	Other Non-metals
			Anthracite	Bituminous		
1870	153	47	38	35	19	13
1880	253	111	42	54	25	21
1890	419	144	72	95	48	60
1902	773	216	76	291	102	88
1909	1,186	354	149	402	176	106
1919[b]	3,123	545	364	1,146	903	166
1919[c]	3,204	545	364	1,146	903	247
1929	3,979	635	385	967	1,563	430
1937	3,680	615	199	866	1,697	304
1939	3,222	515	190	731	1,472	314
1940	3,592	631	208	882	1,540	330
1948	11,082	1,040	473	3,003	5,792	773
1952	11,813	1,386	385	2,297	6,632	1,113
1953	12,690	1,615	303	2,255	7,334	1,183

Note: The industries included in the major groups shown in the tables are:

Metals: Iron, copper, lead, and zinc; gold and silver (placer and lode); other metals. The composition of other metals changes from census to census before 1919. Beginning with 1919 it includes antimony, bauxite, chromite, manganese, molybdenum, quicksilver, rutile, tungsten, uranium, and vanadium.

Anthracite: Pennsylvania anthracite.

Bituminous: bituminous coal, lignite, and non-Pennsylvania anthracite.

Petroleum and natural gas: crude petroleum, natural gas, and natural gasoline.

Other nonmetals: until 1919, stone quarrying industries—basalt, bluestone, granite, limestone, marble, sandstone, and slate; industries supplying other construction materials—asphalt, gypsum, and magnesite; industries supplying chemicals—barite, fluorspar, phosphate rock, pyrites, and sulphur; abrasive materials—corundum, garnet, grindstones, infusorial earth, pumice, oilstones, whetstones, and tripoli; miscellaneous industries—asbestos, clay, feldspar, Fuller's earth, graphite, marl, mica, millstones, mineral pigments, silica, talc, and soapstone. Beginning with 1919, the list was widened by the inclusion of sand and gravel, sand glass, sand molding, natural sodium compounds, potash, rock salt, and the production of limestone mines and quarries operated in conjunction with cement and lime plants. The inclusion of these industries from 1919 on renders the figures for the earlier and later years noncomparable for this group and somewhat restricts the comparability of the figures for total mining. (In all cases where a continuous series is used in the text, we inflate the figures for the period before 1919 by the ratio of the two appropriate sets of figures in 1919.)

[a] Because of rounding, details may not add to total.
[b] Comparable with earlier years.
[c] Comparable with later years.

Source: 1870, 1880, 1890, 1902, 1909, 1919, 1929, and 1939; Census figures, supplemented by estimates for industries not included in a given census canvass but included in census reports for other years. The estimates were derived by adjusting Bureau of Mines data for comparability with census reports. Where necessary and possible, census data were also adjusted for comparability.

1937: Interpolated between 1929 and 1939 by Bureau of Mines data.

1940, 1948, 1952, and 1953: Extrapolated from 1939 by Bureau of Mines data.

APPENDIX B

TABLE B-8

Value of Output in 1929 Prices, by Major Mining Industries,
Selected Years, 1870–1953
(*millions of dollars*)

	All Mining[a]	Metals	Coal		Petroleum and Natural Gas	Other Non-metals
			Anthracite	Bituminous		
1870	176[b]	29	91	35	7	n.c.
1880	354	76	148	77	33	20
1890	673	131	235	172	65	71
1902	1,248[b]	297	214	468	129	n.c.
1909	1,933	437	418	676	250	152
1919[c]	2,439	465	456	829	535	155
1919[d]	2,507	465	456	829	535	223
1929	3,979	635	385	967	1,563	430
1937	3,939	596	269	803	1,917	353
1939	3,798	517	268	715	1,908	390
1940	4,206	643	269	832	2,051	411
1948	5,808	649	298	1,086	3,174	601
1952	6,332	681	211	845	3,810	785
1953	6,460	731	161	828	3,939	801

n.c. = not comparable.

Note: The figures for total mining can be readily converted to an index of mining output constructed by the use of fixed value weights. Since our estimates are derived largely from census data, while other indexes are based on figures reported by the Bureau of Mines, a comparison with other indexes appears of interest. We find a close agreement between the index of total mining output implicit in this table and the two most comprehensive estimates so far available. A comparison with the Barger and Schurr index (Harold Barger and Sam H. Schurr, *The Mining Industries, 1899–1939: A Study of Output, Employment and Productivity*, National Bureau of Economic Research, 1944 for 1902–1939 shows that the largest difference found—that in 1919—does not exceed three index points. A comparison with Leong's index (Y. S. Leong, "Index of Mineral Production," *Journal of the American Statistical Association*, March 1950) for 1880–1948 shows similarly small differences except in 1948, when our figure is significantly lower. This difference is probably explained by the fact that Leong uses 1935–1939 weights for this segment of his series, while we use 1929 weights.

[a] Because of rounding, details may not add to total.
[b] Includes the value of other nonmetals deflated by the price deflator implicit in the figures for total mining less other nonmetals.
[c] Comparable with earlier years.
[d] Comparable with later years.

Source: Output values in current prices were adjusted to a 1929 price base by price indexes derived from the quantities and prices reported by the Census Bureau. For years not covered by Census Bureau reports, indexes were interpolated or extrapolated by Bureau of Mines price data.

TABLE B-9

Book Value of Capital (Including Land), by Major Mining Industries, Selected Years, 1870–1953

(*millions of dollars*)

	All Mining[a]	Metals	Coal		Petroleum and Natural Gas	Other Non-metals
			Anthracite	Bituminous		
1870	212	80	51	59	10	12
1880	558	309	100	79	43	26
1890	1,067	595	105	146	130	91
1909	3,280	1,182	247	961	683	207
1919[b]	6,956	1,877	434	1,904	2,421	319
1919[c]	7,112	1,877	434	1,904	2,421	475
1929	11,448	2,335	585	2,116	5,491	921
1940	7,828	1,251	289	1,278	4,476	534
1948	11,998	1,142	319	1,784	8,089	664
1952	13,639	1,702	297	1,746	9,006	888
1953	14,739	2,000	243	1,840	9,696	960

Note: Whenever we adjusted the output figures reported by the Census Bureau for comparability with other census reports, we also adjusted the capital figures. In such cases a straight-line interpolated ratio of capital to output at earlier and later benchmarks was applied to the value of output in the given year.

[a] Because of rounding, details may not add to total.
[b] Comparable with earlier years.
[c] Comparable with later years.

Source: 1870: Census figures.

1880 and 1890: Census figures adjusted to exclude the value of leased land. The value of total land including leased land was reported by the censuses of 1880 and 1890. For some industries the census of 1890 reported the value of leased land separately. For the other industries, and for 1880, this value was obtained by applying the ratio of leased land to total land (acreage or value) in the next available year to the value of total land in the given year. The value of leased land thus estimated was subtracted from the value of total land.

1909 and 1919: Census figures for producing enterprises. The 1919 capital figure for other nonmetals comparable with the figure for later years was obtained by applying the ratio of capital to value of output implicit in the figures comparable with earlier years to the value of output comparable with later years.

1929: 1930 estimates (described below) extrapolated by the percentage change in total capital (cash, notes and accounts receivable, inventories, and net capital assets including land) for total mining from 1929 to 1930 as reported by *Statistics of Income*, Bureau of Internal Revenue (now called Internal Revenue Service). The same percentage was used for each industry. For 1930 estimate, see below.

1930, 1940, 1948, 1952, and 1953: Obtained by applying the ratio of the sum of cash, notes and accounts receivable, inventories, and net capital assets including land to the sum of gross sales and gross receipts reported by *Statistics of income, ibid.* (or its Source Book), to the output figures consistent with census reports (Table B-7 and work sheets).

The ratios for 1930 were adjusted for consolidated returns. For years in which sales and receipts of corporations submitting balance sheets are not reported by industries, they were estimated using either (a) the raising ratio, for the next available year, of the value of sales and receipts of all corporations in the industry to the total value of sales and receipts for those corporations in the industry submitting balance sheets or (b) the average ratio for total mining. We refrained from making adjustments for the accelerated depreciation of emergency defense facilities which began in 1940. (Accelerated amortization is a small item in mining, amounting to only 5 per cent of normal depreciation at its peak in 1943.)

APPENDIX B

TABLE B-10

Book Value of Plant and of Working Capital, by Major Mining Industries, Selected Years, 1870–1953
(millions of dollars)

	All Mining[a]	Metals	Coal		Petroleum and Natural Gas	Other Non-metals
			Anthra-cite	Bitumi-nous		
1870						
Plant	65	19	19	15	8	4
Working capital	19	4	5	8	1	1
1880						
Plant	187	79	41	22	36	9
Working capital	32	9	8	9	3	3
1890						
Plant	385	149	51	48	107	30
Working capital	70	28	7	10	13	12
1909						
Plant	1,450	398	89	299	586	76
Working capital	386	206	22	76	54	28
1919[b]						
Plant	3,277	460	133	590	1,993	100
Working capital	1,049	452	51	223	269	54
1919[c]						
Plant	3,325	460	133	590	1,993	148
Working capital	1,076	452	51	223	269	81
1929						
Plant	5,624	630	154	628	3,943	270
Working capital	2,291	382	144	326	1,235	204
1940						
Plant	4,325	350	84	408	3,318	166
Working capital	1,701	348	47	240	894	172
1948						
Plant	6,527	429	91	637	5,137	234
Working capital	4,121	503	91	737	2,542	249
1953						
Plant	8,743	897	83	954	6,386	422
Working capital	4,766	813	91	657	2,801	403

[a] Because of rounding, details may not add to total.
[b] Comparable with earlier years.
[c] Comparable with later years.
Source: See source notes to Appendix Table B-11.

NOTES ON ESTIMATES IN MINING, 1870–1953

TABLE B-11
Book Value of Capital (Excluding Land) in 1929 Prices, by Major Mining Industries, Selected Years, 1870–1953
(millions of dollars)

	All Mining[a]	Metals	Coal Anthracite	Coal Bituminous	Petroleum and Natural Gas	Other Non-metals
1870	127	38	38	32	13	8
1880	410	174	93	54	68	21
1890	918	357	117	118	244	83
1909	3,476	1,093	211	713	1,264	194
1919[b]	5,596	1,004	240	1,036	3,133	184
1919[c]	5,686	1,004	240	1,036	3,133	274
1929	8,532	1,086	318	1,026	5,601	502
1940	6,699	798	148	730	4,637	386
1948	7,773	651	129	959	5,696	338
1952	7,683	878	126	915	5,319	445
1953	8,127	1,019	103	966	5,550	489

[a] Because of rounding, details may not add to total.
[b] Comparable with earlier years.
[c] Comparable with later years.

Source: All figures were obtained by adjusting the estimates in book values to a 1929 price base. This was done separately for equipment and improvements, and for working capital, after deduction of the estimated value of land owned by the establishment. The following price indexes were used:

1. *Equipment.* 1870–1940: Price index implicit in Raymond W. Goldsmith's estimates of producers' durable equipment valued at original cost and in 1929 prices (Raymond W. Goldsmith, "A Perpetual Inventory of National Wealth," *Studies in Income and Wealth,* Volume 14 (National Bureau of Economic Research, 1951, Table I) extrapolated by the price index for this group estimated by Simon Kuznets (Simon Kuznets, *National Product Since 1869,* National Bureau of Economic Research, 1946, Table 4, line 7, p. 216);

1948, 1952, and 1953: Price index for producers' durable equipment weighted by the private purchase of mining and oilfield machinery depreciated over 15 years. (*National Income, 1954 Edition, A Supplement to the Survey of Current Business,* pp. 210, 216, and 217.) Since this index for 1948 is close to Goldsmith's, the extrapolation of the latter seemed inappropriate.

2. *Improvements.* 1870–1940: Goldsmith's implicit indexes for underground mining structures and for nonfarm nonresidential structures (*op. cit.*) combined with equal weights and extrapolated by Kuznets' index for all construction (*op. cit.*);

1948, 1952, and 1953: Index used to deflate book values of structures in manufacturing. For its derivation see Appendix A, section B, part 1.

3. *Working capital.* Bureau of Labor Statistics index of wholesale prices (*Historical Statistics of the United States, 1789–1945,* Census Bureau, 1947, pp. 233 ff. and *Statistical Abstract 1953,* Census Bureau, p. 303) converted from the 1926 to a 1929 base. (Since the censuses of 1870, 1880, and 1890 covered June 1, 1869–May 31, 1870, etc., we used averages of the indexes for pairs of calendar years.)

Value of land: 1870: Estimated by the formula $x = \dfrac{cvz}{1 - z(1-v)}$

(continued)

APPENDIX B

Notes to Table B-11 (*continued*)

where x = value of land owned by establishment
c = capital excluding value of leased land
v = ratio of value of owned to total land in nearest available year
z = ratio of value of total land to capital including value of leased land in 1880.

See also Appendix B, section D, part 2. a. i.

1880: Estimated by applying the ratio of owned to total land (either acreage or value) in 1890 or the next available year to the value of total land reported by the census.

1890: Reported for some of the major industries; for the others estimated as for 1880.

1909 and 1919: Arithmetic mean of two estimates. One estimate was obtained by the formula used for 1870, but with v taken from the census data for 1909 and 1919 and z taken as the ratio of the value of total land to capital including the value of leased land in 1890. The other was obtained by (a) inflating the amount of royalties paid, as reported in the censuses of 1909 and 1919, by the ratio of total to leased acreage, as reported; (b) multiplying the hypothetical royalties by a "years purchase factor" using a 4 per cent rate of discount in 1909 and a 4.5 per cent rate in 1919, and assuming, for each minor industry, different lengths of life of the royalty according to information on available reserves; and (c) subtracting from the given totals the capitalized value of royalties actually paid.

1929, 1940, 1948, 1952, and 1953: The residual after deducting the estimated value of improvements and equipment, and working capital from the reported values of total capital presented in Table B-9.

Book value of working capital: 1870: Estimated by solving the equations

$$x + y + z = a$$
$$\frac{x}{x_i} \div \frac{y}{y_i} = b_i$$
$$\frac{z}{z_i} \div \left(\frac{x}{x_i} + \frac{y}{y_i}\right) = c$$

where x = book value of improvements
y = book value of equipment
z = book value of working capital
x_i, y_i, z_i = price deflators in given year for above three series
a = capital excluding value of land
b_i = ratio of improvements to equipment in 1929 prices
c = ratio of working capital to improvements and equipment in 1929 prices in nearest available year (1880).

For x and y, see notes to estimates of value of plant, below.

1880 and 1890: As reported.

1909: Same method as for 1870, but the 1919 ratio was used for c.

1919: Estimated by applying the ratio of working capital to total capital. For coal, petroleum, and other nonmetals, the ratios used are based on *National Wealth and Income*, Federal Trade Commission, 1926, p. 138, a report in response to Senate Resolution 451; for iron, copper, lead, zinc, and precious metals, the ratios are based on a sample taken from *Moody's Manual of Industrials, 1919*. (A small correction was made to adjust the ratio for total metals in the Moody sample to the ratio for metals in the FTC report.)

1929: The 1930 ratio of working capital (described below) to total capital was applied to estimated total capital in 1929.

1930, 1940, 1948, 1952, and 1953: The ratio of the sum of inventories plus cash, notes and accounts receivable minus reserves for bad debts to this sum plus net fixed capital assets as reported in *Statistics of Income*, Bureau of Internal Revenue (now called Internal Revenue Service), was applied to estimated total capital.

Book value of plant (improvements and equipment): 1870, 1909, and 1919: Estimated by deducting the estimated value of land owned plus working capital from the value of capital as reported.

(*continued*)

NOTES ON ESTIMATES IN MINING, 1870–1953

Notes to Table B-11 (concluded)

1880 and 1890: Values as reported. For 1890, the value of improvements and of equipment was reported separately.

1929, 1940, 1948, 1952, and 1953: The ratio of the value of improvements and equipment to fixed assets was assumed in each industry to be the same in 1929 and in 1930 as in 1919. This ratio was divided by the ratio of depreciation charges to fixed assets in 1930 as given in *Statistics of Income, ibid.* The figure obtained (the implicit average length of life of improvements and equipment) was multiplied in each of the years following 1930 by the ratio of depreciation charges to net fixed assets as secured from *Statistics of Income, ibid.* These annual estimates of the ratio of improvements and equipment to total assets were then averaged by periods, the averages being centered on the benchmark years. Finally, by straight-line interpolation between the given benchmark years, "smoothed" ratios of the value of improvements and equipment to net fixed assets were obtained; these in turn were applied to the estimated value of net fixed assets in each year. Estimated book values of plant were adjusted to a 1929 price base by combining the price indexes for improvements and equipment with varying weights. The weights were obtained on the assumption that the ratio of improvements to equipment in constant prices changed by 1 per cent per decade in favor of equipment for the years before 1890 (when improvements were reported by the census) and by 0.5 per cent per decade in the years following in each of the industries.

TABLE B-12
Indexes for Deflation of Output, by Major Mining Industries, Selected Years, 1870–1953
(values in 1929 = 100)

	All Mining	Metals	Coal		Petroleum and Natural Gas	Other Non-metals
			Anthracite	Bituminous		
1870	87	162	42	101	270	n.a.
1880	71	146	28	70	75	105
1890	62	110	31	55	74	85
1909	61	81	36	59	70	70
1919[a]	128	117	80	138	169	107
1919[b]	128	117	80	138	169	111
1929	100	100	100	100	100	100
1937	93	103	74	108	89	86
1939	85	100	71	102	77	81
1940	85	98	77	106	75	80
1948	191	160	159	277	182	129
1953	196	221	188	272	186	148

n.a. = not available.

[a] Comparable with earlier years.
[b] Comparable with later years.
Source: See source note to Appendix Table B-8.

APPENDIX B

TABLE B-13

Indexes for Deflation of Book Values of Mining Capital, by Components, Selected Years, 1870–1953
(*values in 1929 = 100*)

	Improvements	Equipment	Working Capital
1870	50	87	95
1880	46	65	65
1890	48	48	60
1909	50	49	71
1919	61	73	145
1929	86	94	100
1940	91	96	82
1948	118	128	169
1953	156	165	178

Source: See source note to Appendix Table B-11.

TABLE B-14

Implicit Price Indexes for Deflation of Capital (Excluding Land), by Major Mining Industries, Selected Years, 1870–1953
(*values in 1929 = 100*)

| | All Mining | Metals | Coal | | Petroleum and Natural Gas | Other Non-metals |
			Anthracite	Bituminous		
1870	67	61	63	72	68	71
1880	53	51	53	57	56	59
1890	50	50	49	50	49	51
1909	53	55	54	53	51	54
1919	77	91	77	78	72	84
1929	93	93	94	93	92	94
1940	90	87	89	89	91	88
1948	137	143	141	143	135	143
1953	166	168	168	167	166	169

Source: Based on values in Appendix Tables B-11 and B-9.

NOTES ON ESTIMATES IN MINING, 1870–1953

TABLE B-15

Employment and Man-Hours, by Major Mining Industries, Selected Years, 1880–1953

(*numbers*)

	1880	1890	1909	1919	1929a	1929b	1939	1948	1953
All miningc									
Total employees (*thousands*)d	n.a.	521	988	1,056	1,002	1,040	813	895	n.a.
Wage earners (*thousands*)e	329	507	944	981	921	954	736	804	642
Man-hours (*millions*)	709	1,202	n.a.	2,052	1,933	2,027	1,224	1,557	1,273
Metals									
Total employees (*thousands*)d	n.a.	115	159	141	119	119	99	100	102
Wage earners (*thousands*)e	98	113	150	131	110	110	88	90	87
Man-hours (*millions*)	207	244	n.a.	333	275	275	188	197	197
Anthracite									
Total employees (*thousands*)d	n.a.	124	174	155	151	151	88	79	54
Wage earners (*thousands*)e	70	122	169	147	143	143	83	75	50
Man-hours (*millions*)	143	239	320	329	273	273	123	148	79
Bituminous coal									
Total employees (*thousands*)d	n.a.	175	506	579	482	482	390	438	290
Wage earners (*thousands*)e	109	169	488	546	459	459	371	410	267
Man-hours (*millions*)	201	413	976	980	892	892	545	741	498
Petroleum and natural gas									
Total employees (*thousands*)d	n.a.	15	43	111	176	176	146	161	n.a.
Wage earners (*thousands*)e	8	13	37	93	142	142	113	126	130
Man-hours (*millions*)	28	45	111	230	328	328	207	238	254
Other nonmetals									
Total employees (*thousands*)d	n.a.	92	106	70	74	112	90	117	125
Wage earners (*thousands*)e	44	90	100	64	67	100	81	103	108
Man-hours (*millions*)	130	261	n.a.	180	165	259	161	233	245

n.a. = not available

a Comparable with earlier years.
b Comparable with later years.
c Because of rounding, details may not add to total.
d Includes wage earners and salaried employees.
e Average per year including inactive periods. The figures for 1880 and 1890 presumably represent an average for active periods only. Those for 1880 include some salaried employees.

(*continued*)

APPENDIX B

Notes to Table B-15 (*concluded*)

Source: Salaried employees and wage earners, 1870–1939, based on census reports (except wage earners in the petroleum and natural gas industry, 1890–1929); 1948 and 1953, estimated by linking Bureau of Labor Statistics employment data to the census figures for 1939. Wage earners in petroleum and natural gas, 1890–1929, taken from O. E. Kiessling and Others, *Technology, Employment and Output per Man in Petroleum and Natural Gas Production*, Works Project Administration, National Research Project Report No. E-10, Philadelphia, 1939; salaried employees for the same industry in 1948 and 1953 were estimated on the basis of the ratio of wage earners to salaried employees in 1939.

Man-hours, 1880–1890, from V. E. Spencer, *Production, Employment and Productivity in the Mineral Extractive Industries*, 1880–1938, Works Project Administration, National Research Project Report No. S-2, Philadelphia, 1940, after making minor adjustments in coverage; 1909–1929, from Harold Barger and Sam H. Schurr, *The Mining Industries, 1899–1939: A Study of Output, Employment and Productivity*, National Bureau of Economic Research, 1944, after adjusting to census coverage; 1939, as reported by the census; 1948 and 1953, except for bituminous coal in 1948, estimated from the number of wage earners and average weekly hours [both reported by Bureau of Labor Statistics, *Monthly Labor Review* (various issues)] assuming 52 weeks worked per year. 1948 estimate of bituminous coal based on Bureau of Labor Statistics index of man-hours worked.

I. Adjustment of Capital Estimates for Manufacturing and Mining to Eliminate Duplication

For 1919 and earlier, the capital estimates for both manufacturing and mining are based on reports by establishments to the Bureau of the Census. Accordingly, there is no duplication when the two estimates are combined for those years. After 1919, however, the estimating procedures are such that the simple addition of the two sector totals entails some duplication. This follows from the method of derivation of capital estimates for mining—the ratio of total capital to sales and receipts, as reported in the *Statistics of Income*, was applied to output reported by (or estimated to correspond to) the census. The capital figures attained in this way are more comparable to the estimates for 1919 and earlier than they would be if we had used the data exactly as given in *Statistics of Income*. In certain cases, the data on output (sales and receipts) appearing in *Statistics of Income* differ substantially from the census figures. Thus, for instance, on the returns—largely consolidated—to the Internal Revenue Service, some oil output appears as sales of corporations engaged mainly in oil processing. This output is, therefore, included with manufacturing, instead of in mining where it properly belongs. On the other hand, in certain years, the value of output of metal mining is exaggerated by the inclusion of smelting and refining activities. In general, this estimating procedure tends to overstate the amount of capital in mining. As a result, there is some duplication when the capital estimates of the two sectors are combined. This duplication is, of course, immaterial as long as we are concerned only with ratios of capital to output. An adjustment for it becomes necessary as soon as a single total of the capital invested in the two sectors is desired.

The amount to be subtracted from manufacturing capital in reported values is simply the difference between the capital reported for each of the mining industries in *Statistics of Income* and that estimated as being comparable to the census coverage. We obtain the same amount in 1929 prices by applying a price deflator to the amount of duplication in reported values. The implicit deflators in Table B-14 are used.

For 1929, only aggregate figures for mining are available in *Statistics of Income*. We derive the data on total capital and on sales plus receipts for each of the major mining industries in that year on the assumption that the share of each major industry in total mining was the same as it was in 1930. These estimates are then used to derive the amount of duplication using the method just described.

TABLE B-16

Unduplicated Total of Capital (Including Land), in Book Values and in 1929 Prices, in All Manufacturing and Mining, Selected Years, 1880–1953
(*millions of dollars*)

	Total Capital Including Land					
	1929 Prices			Book Values		
	Mfg.	Mining	Mfg. and Mining	Mfg.	Mining	Mfg. and Mining
1880	4,821	1,029	5,850	2,718	558	3,276
1890	11,157	2,116	13,273	5,697	1,067	6,724
1900[a]	18,626 / 17,452	3,134	21,760 / 20,586	8,663 / 8,168	1,563	10,226 / 9,731
1904	23,295	4,404	27,699	11,588	2,218	13,806
1909	31,563	6,538	38,101	16,937	3,280	20,217
1914	36,737	7,577	44,314	20,784	4,115	24,899
1919	46,094	9,720	55,814	40,289	7,112	47,401
1929	60,944	12,336	73,280	57,161	11,448	68,609
1937	54,702	7,701	62,403	49,601	7,008	56,609
1948[b]	73,920 / 74,295	8,758	82,678 / 83,053	107,915 / 108,477	11,998	119,913 / 120,475
1953	95,326	8,868	104,194	163,503	14,739	178,242

[a] For manufacturing and for manufacturing and mining combined, the larger figures (upper row) are comparable with preceding years; the smaller figures (lower row) are comparable with following years.

[b] The smaller figures (upper row) exclude shipbuilding; the larger ones (lower row) include shipbuilding.

Source: See Appendix B, section I.

APPENDIX C

Financial Series: Notes and Supporting Tables

A. Estimates of External Financing by Manufacturing and Mining Corporations, 1900–1953

1. CAPITAL STOCK ISSUES

a. 1900–1949. Our estimates of the value of net capital stock issues of manufacturing and mining corporations for 1900–1949 are based on the data on preferred and common stock issues of industrial corporations in Raymond W. Goldsmith's *A Study of Saving in the United States*, Princeton University Press, 1955, Volume I (see, in particular, Tables V-9, V-17, and V-18, pp. 482, 492, and 494 for preferred stock issues and Table V-19, p. 496 for common stock issues).

Goldsmith's "industrials" group contains not only manufacturing and mining, but also trade, service, agriculture, shipping, and construction. Therefore, to estimate the value of net capital stock issues of manufacturing and mining corporations for 1919–1948, we multiplied his "industrial" issues by annual ratios of net capital issues in manufacturing and mining (from the *Commercial and Financial Chronicle* [*CFC*]) to the *CFC* stock issues data for shipping, land and buildings, mining and manufacturing, and miscellaneous (adjusted as explained below). The *CFC* "miscellaneous" category contains commercial banks and insurance companies as well as trade, service, and agriculture. However, commercial banks and insurance companies are not in Goldsmith's "industrials" category. Therefore, to eliminate their net issues from the *CFC* "miscellaneous" group, we multiplied the *CFC* "miscellaneous" net issues by an average of the ratios of capital stock outstanding as of the end of 1939 and 1950 in trade, service, and agriculture to capital stock outstanding in these industries plus commercial banks and insurance companies. (Data on outstandings are from *Statistics of Income*, 1939 and 1950, Bureau of Internal Revenue [now Internal Revenue Service], Part 2.)

Estimates of the value of net capital stock issues of manufacturing and mining corporations for 1900–1918 were then made by multiplying Goldsmith's "industrial" stock issues for these years by an average of the 1919–1929 ratios of our final estimates of net capital stock issues of manufacturing and mining corporations to Goldsmith's "industrial" stock issues.

Since Goldsmith presents separate data on preferred and common stock issues of new incorporations in all industries, we assumed that Goldsmith's small-issues data for industrials, included in his estimates of stock issues, do not, however, include new corporations. To estimate the value of stock issues of new incorporations in manufacturing, we first secured the annual average value ($233 million) of such issues during 1946–1948 from Lawrence Bridge's "The Financing of Investment by New Firms" (Conference on Research in Business Finance, National Bureau of Economic Research, 1952) Table 1, p. 68. To the $233 million we then added an estimate of the annual average value of capital stock issued by new mining corporations. The latter estimate ($35 million) was computed by multiplying $233 million by the 1948 ratio of capital stock outstanding in mining to that in manufacturing for corporations with an asset-size of less than $1 million (*Statistics of Income* data). The 1946–1948 average value of stock issues for new manufacturing and mining corporations was multiplied by an annual index (1946–1948 = 100) of the value of capital stock issued by all new corporations. This gave us estimates of the value of issues of new manufacturing and mining corporations for 1900–1949. (The index of stock issues is from Raymond W. Goldsmith, *op. cit.*, Table V-43, p. 525.) The sum of the value of capital stock issues of new plus existing manufacturing and mining corporations gives us a final series on funds received from capital stock financing in 1900–1949.

b. 1950–1953. Our 1900–1949 series was extrapolated to 1953 as follows: (1) we computed an average of the 1948–1949 ratios of our estimates of the value of manufacturing and mining net capital stock issues to Securities and Exchange Commission estimates of the value of manufacturing net capital stock issues; (2) we multiplied this average ratio by SEC data, 1950–1953, on annual manufacturing net capital stock issues. (The SEC data are from the *Survey of Current Business*, April 1954, Table 3, p. 16.)

2. BOND ISSUES

a. 1900–1943. Since it was not possible to obtain a series on net cash proceeds through flotation of manufacturing and mining bond issues for 1900–1943, we used a series on the annual change in bonds outstanding. Changes in bonds outstanding and cash flows originating in bonds transactions are, however, similar with respect to relative magnitude, cyclical amplitude, and timing at cyclical turning points (see W. Braddock Hickman, *The Volume of Corporate Bond Financing since 1900*, Princeton University Press for the National Bureau of Economic Research, 1953, pp. 220–227). Data on changes in manufacturing and mining bonds outstanding are from unpublished tables supplied by Hickman.

b. 1944–1953. For 1944–1953, SEC data on net debt issues were used. The SEC published no data for mining for this period and initiated a series for manufacturing net debt issues in 1948; thus, estimates were made for manufacturing and mining for 1944–1947 and for mining for 1948–1953. Mining is in the SEC "commercial and miscellaneous" group. Hence, to estimate mining net debt issues for 1948–1953, we multiplied the net debt issues of the "commercial and miscellaneous" group, 1948–1953, by an average of the annual ratios, 1941–1943, of mining bonds outstanding to the bonds outstanding of industries represented in the "commercial and miscellaneous" group. (Data on outstandings are from Hickman's unpublished tables.) The value of mining debt issues thus estimated plus the SEC data on net debt issues available for manufacturing, 1948–1953, give us annual estimates for this period.

To secure estimates of net debt issues, 1944–1947, for mining and manufacturing, we first took an average over 1948–1950 of the annual ratios of SEC manufacturing and estimated mining (as described above) net debt issues to the issues of the SEC "manufacturing" plus "commercial and miscellaneous" group. We then applied this average to the net bond issues of Hickman's "industrial" group in 1944–1947. Hickman's "industrial" group is comparable in industrial coverage with the SEC "manufacturing" and "commercial and miscellaneous" groups combined. (SEC net debt issues data are from *Survey of Current Business, op. cit.* Hickman's "industrial" net debt issues data for 1944–1947 are from his study, cited above, Table 26, p. 230.)

B. Estimates of Internal Financing by Manufacturing and Mining Corporations, 1900–1953

In this study we have utilized the net and gross concepts of internal financing. Net internal financing or retained net profits is defined as net income after subtracting depreciation, depletion, taxes and cash dividends paid out by corporations. Gross internal financing is derived by adding back depreciation and depletion expenses to retained net profits.

1. RETAINED NET PROFITS

Data for retained profits for 1900–1915 are from Raymond W. Goldsmith's *A Study of Saving in the United States*, Princeton University Press, 1955, Volume I, Table C-4, p. 917; 1916–1922: *ibid.*, Table C-27, p. 939; 1923–1948: *ibid.*, Table C-32, p. 943. Since Goldsmith's data for 1923–1948 are from *Statistics of Income*, Part 2, the series was continued to 1953 using this source. Retained net profits were derived by subtracting dividends paid in "cash and other assets other than own stock" from "compiled net profits less tax" of all manufacturing and mining corporations filing tax returns.

NOTES AND SUPPORTING TABLES

2. DEPRECIATION AND DEPLETION

Data for depreciation for 1900–1947 are from Raymond W. Goldsmith, *op. cit.*, Table C-42, p. 957, and for 1948–1953, from *Statistics of Income*, Part 2. Data for depletion for 1900–1924 are from Goldsmith, *op. cit.*, Table C-46, p. 963, and for 1925–1953, from *Statistics of Income*, Part 2. Since Goldsmith's data for depletion cover all industries, we estimated depletion of manufacturing and mining corporations at 90 per cent of the total. Amortization (accelerated depreciation) of emergency facilities as reported in *Statistics of Income*, Part 2, are also included in depreciation and depletion for 1940–1953.

C. Estimates of Expenditures for New Plant and Equipment by Manufacturing and Mining Corporations, 1900–1953

1. 1919–1953

Expenditures for new plant and equipment by manufacturing and mining corporations were estimated for 1919–1953 by adjusting available annual data on expenditures of all manufacturing and mining establishments to a corporation level. The adjustment was made by applying to the establishment data ratios of net fixed capital of all manufacturing and mining corporations to that of all manufacturing and mining establishments.

For 1919–1938, capital expenditures of all manufacturing and mining establishments are from George Terborgh, "Estimated Expenditures for New Durable Goods, 1919–1938," *Federal Reserve Bulletin*, September 1939, Table 2, p. 732. Data for 1939–1950 (which are a continuation of the Terborgh series) are from *The Midyear Economic Report of the President*, July 1952, Table B-18, p. 159. New plant and equipment expenditures data for 1950 and for 1951–1953 for manufacturing are from the *Survey of Current Business*, September 1953, p. 4, Table 3, and September 1954, p. 4, Table 2, respectively. Since the 1950 figure for mining in the *SCB*, September 1953, was not identical with that in *The Midyear Economic Report, op. cit.*, the data in the *SCB, op. cit.*, for mining were used to extrapolate the 1939–1950 data from *The Midyear Economic Report* to 1953. Ratios of net fixed capital of corporations to that of all establishments are from worksheets used for Part I of the present study.

2. 1900–1918

Estimates of capital expenditures were made for 1900–1918 by converting annual data on the value of domestic consumption of (1) construction materials and (2) industrial machinery and equipment

APPENDIX C. FINANCIAL SERIES

into weighted index numbers (1919 = 100) and extrapolating the 1919–1953 series back to 1900 using these indexes.

The two annual domestic consumption series are from William H. Shaw, *Value of Commodity Output since 1869, op. cit.*, Table I-1, pp. 52–53 and Table I-2, p. 69. Weights used in constructing the index numbers are based on the relative importance of expenditures for plant and for equipment by all manufacturing establishments during 1915–1919. (Expenditures are from Lowell J. Chawner, "Capital Expenditures for Manufacturing Plant and Equipment—1915 to 1940," *Survey of Current Business*, March 1941, Department of Commerce, Table 1, p. 10.)

D. Ratios of Selected Balance Sheet Items To Total Assets of Manufacturing and Mining Corporations, By Asset Size, 1937 and 1948

The balance sheet ratios presented in Table C-4 are based on data in *Statistics of Income, op. cit.*, for 1937 and 1948, and its unpublished "Source Books." Ratios were calculated for corporations in the following ten asset-size groups (in thousands of dollars):

1. Under $50
2. $50 and under $100
3. $100 and under $250
4. $250 and under $500
5. $500 and under $1,000
6. $1,000 and under $5,000
7. $5,000 and under $10,000
8. $10,000 and under $50,000
9. $50,000 and under $100,000
10. $100,000 and over

Since data for all balance sheet items of mining corporations and for government securities in the current assets account of manufacturing corporations are not available separately for income-size groups 9 and 10, a combined ratio for these groups could be calculated only for the combined mining and manufacturing industries shown in Table C-4, Panel A.

In order to make data as presented in *Statistics of Income for 1948* comparable with those in 1937, we subtracted the "oil and gas field contract services" minor industry from mining in 1948 and added to mining for this year the "lessors of mining, oil and similar properties" minor industry (the latter being in the "finance, insurance, real estate and lessors of real property" major group in 1948). Data for the minor industries are available in the "Source Book" to *Statistics of Income for 1948*.

NOTES AND SUPPORTING TABLES

E. Supporting Tables

TABLE C-1

External Financing through Net Capital Stock and Net Bond Issues,
All Manufacturing and Mining Corporations, 1900–1953
(*millions of dollars*)

	Type of Issue		
	Net Capital Stock (1)	Net Bond (2)	Net Security (Col. 1) + (Col. 2) (3)
1900	128	37	165
1901	256	557	813
1902	141	151	292
1903	119	252	371
1904	103	74	177
1905	118	122	240
1906	165	113	278
1907	168	125	293
1908	136	107	243
1909	183	139	322
1910	178	124	302
1911	203	206	409
1912	288	50	338
1913	185	−10	175
1914	120	66	186
1915	146	−32	114
1916	567	130	697
1917	396	126	522
1918	307	129	436
1919	1,145	13	1,158
1920	917	575	1,492
1921	281	544	825
1922	328	266	594
1923	518	244	762
1924	336	136	472
1925	696	163	859
1926	591	500	1,091
1927	505	362	867
1928	1,196	−182	1,014
1929	1,727	−528	1,199
1930	398	141	539
1931	81	−168	−87
1932	25	−347	−322
1933	142	−305	−163
1934	99	−287	−188
1935	13	−458	−445
1936	171	−155	16
1937	553	−304	249
1938	107	382	489
1939	131	−86	45

(*continued*)

APPENDIX C. FINANCIAL SERIES

TABLE C-1 (concluded)

	Type of Issue		
	Net Capital Stock (1)	Net Bond (2)	Net Security (Col. 1)+(Col. 2) (3)
1940	118	−135	−17
1941	103	−146	−32
1942	59	109	168
1943	38	−36	2
1944	192	−231	−39
1945	543	−303	240
1946	1,271	830	2,101
1947	1,008	974	1,982
1948	549	1,610	2,159
1949	472	750	1,222
1950	206	205	411
1951	1,378	1,796	3,174
1952	1,117	2,741	3,858
1953	174	1,349	1,523

Source: See Appendix C, section A.

TABLE C-2

Internal Financing, All Manufacturing and Mining Corporations, 1900–1953
(millions of dollars)

	Retained Net Profit (1)	Depreciation and Depletion (2)	Gross Internal Financing (Col. 1+Col. 2) (3)
1900	351	219	570
1901	396	238	634
1902	594	258	852
1903	544	281	825
1904	252	306	558
1905	374	333	707
1906	540	362	902
1907	495	394	889
1908	263	428	691
1909	534	467	1,001
1910	574	509	1,083
1911	368	551	919
1912	590	595	1,185
1913	512	645	1,157
1914	338	666	1,004

(continued)

TABLE C-2 (concluded)

	Retained Net Profit (1)	Depreciation and Depletion (2)	Gross Internal Financing (Col. 1 + Col. 2) (3)
1915	1,054	713	1,767
1916	2,912	1,087	3,999
1917	3,189	1,317	4,506
1918	1,209	1,672	2,881
1919	2,614	1,459	4,073
1920	1,032	1,680	2,712
1921	−2,207	1,630	−577
1922	870	1,856	2,726
1923	1,121	2,041	3,162
1924	470	2,017	2,487
1925	1,269	2,068	3,337
1926	998	2,265	3,263
1927	174	2,281	2,455
1928	790	2,340	3,130
1929	1,048	2,489	3,537
1930	−2,042	2,434	392
1931	−3,199	2,148	−1,051
1932	−3,248	1,955	−1,293
1933	−1,187	1,899	712
1934	−687	1,784	1,097
1935	−282	1,778	1,496
1936	23	1,878	1,901
1937	−24	2,039	2,015
1938	−629	1,957	1,328
1939	613	2,002	2,615
1940	1,220	2,136	3,356
1941	2,571	2,394	4,965
1942	2,847	2,757	5,604
1943	3,388	3,106	6,494
1944	2,596	3,381	5,977
1945	1,284	3,926	5,210
1946	3,626	2,846	6,472
1947	6,359	3,706	10,065
1948	6,934	4,692	11,626
1949	3,908	4,856	8,764
1950	7,116	5,411	12,527
1951	4,941	6,373	11,314
1952	3,082	7,150	10,232
1953	3,144	8,251	11,395

Source: See Appendix C, section B.

APPENDIX C. FINANCIAL SERIES
TABLE C-3

Expenditures for New Plant and Equipment, All Manufacturing and Mining Corporations, 1900–1953
(*millions of dollars*)

Year	Value	Year	Value	Year	Value
1900	746	1920	3,131	1940	2,922
1901	743	1921	1,808	1941	3,797
1902	842	1922	1,935	1942	2,953
1903	875	1923	2,396	1943	2,432
1904	760	1924	2,112	1944	2,689
1905	906	1925	2,456	1945	4,128
1906	1,115	1926	2,865	1946	6,857
1907	1,173	1927	2,589	1947	8,770
1908	870	1928	2,777	1948	9,271
1909	1,060	1929	3,283	1949	7,355
1910	1,159	1930	2,325	1950	7,628
1911	1,090	1931	1,316	1951	10,966
1912	1,192	1932	855	1952	11,746
1913	1,280	1933	915	1953	12,370
1914	1,090	1934	1,349		
1915	1,181	1935	1,658		
1916	1,806	1936	2,276		
1917	2,489	1937	3,100		
1918	2,808	1938	1,704		
1919	2,753	1939	2,164		

Source: See Appendix C, section C.

TABLE C-4

Selected Balance Sheet Items as Percentages of Total Assets All Manufacturing and Mining Corporations, 1937 and 1948
(per cent)

A. ALL RETURNS WITH BALANCE SHEET

1937

	All Classes	Asset-size Class									
		1	2	3	4	5	6	7	8	9	10
Assets											
Total	100.0	100.0	100.0	100.0	100.0	100.0	100.0	100.0	100.0	100.0	100.0
Current	37.6	50.5	47.6	46.4	45.1	43.1	41.5	37.5	36.9	33.2	33.2
Fixed	42.1	37.6	39.7	40.7	42.3	43.2	43.2	43.7	42.9	41.0	41.0
All other	20.3	11.9	12.7	12.9	12.6	13.7	15.3	18.8	20.2	25.8	25.8
Debt and net worth	100.0	100.0	100.0	100.0	100.0	100.0	100.0	100.0	100.0	100.0	100.0
Total debt	26.2	57.7	44.0	38.8	32.9	30.4	26.8	24.9	23.5	23.3	23.3
Short-term	16.9	48.9	36.6	31.2	24.8	22.3	18.4	14.6	13.8	13.5	13.5
Bonds, notes and mortages payable—less than one yr.	4.6	12.8	10.9	10.1	8.9	8.0	6.3	4.3	3.5	2.5	2.5
Accounts payable	8.2	25.0	17.5	13.8	11.0	9.4	7.7	5.9	5.9	8.0	8.0
Other liabilities	4.2	11.1	8.1	7.4	4.9	4.9	4.4	4.5	4.4	3.0	3.0
Long-term	9.3	8.8	7.4	7.5	8.1	8.1	8.4	10.3	9.7	9.8	9.8
Net worth	73.8	42.3	56.0	61.2	67.1	69.6	73.2	75.1	76.5	76.7	76.7
Capital stock	46.9	83.9	62.1	58.2	53.1	49.8	46.2	44.8	44.6	44.7	44.7
Preferred	9.3	5.8	5.8	7.5	8.4	9.1	9.6	10.5	8.8	9.6	9.6
Common	37.6	78.0	56.3	50.7	44.7	40.6	36.6	34.4	35.8	35.0	35.0
Surplus	26.9	−41.6	−6.1	3.1	14.1	19.1	27.0	30.3	31.9	32.0	32.0
Current ratio[a]	2.22	1.03	1.30	1.48	1.82	1.93	2.25	2.56	2.67	2.46	2.46

(continued)

TABLE C-4 (continued)

A. ALL RETURNS WITH BALANCE SHEET

1948

	All Classes	Asset-size Class									
		1	2	3	4	5	6	7	8	9	10
Assets											
Total	100.0	100.0	100.0	100.0	100.0	100.0	100.0	100.0	100.0	100.0	100.0
Current	53.5	55.0	56.8	57.5	58.6	59.7	58.9	58.1	55.4	54.0	48.6
Fixed	34.9	36.7	35.6	35.0	33.9	32.9	32.7	32.7	34.2	32.5	37.1
All other	11.6	8.3	7.6	7.5	7.5	7.4	8.4	9.2	10.4	13.5	14.3
Debt and net worth	100.0	100.0	100.0	100.0	100.0	100.0	100.0	100.0	100.0	100.0	100.0
Total debt	30.9	54.4	43.1	39.8	36.6	33.5	30.4	27.9	29.9	29.7	30.1
Short-term	21.0	41.7	32.9	30.4	28.2	26.5	23.5	20.7	20.1	19.6	18.4
Bonds, notes and mortgages payable—less than one yr.	3.1	9.4	7.4	6.8	6.0	6.1	5.0	3.6	3.0	1.5	1.8
Accounts payable	9.2	20.2	15.9	14.4	12.5	10.6	8.8	8.0	7.6	8.6	9.1
Other liabilities	8.7	12.1	9.5	9.3	9.8	9.8	9.7	9.1	9.5	9.4	7.5
Long-term	9.9	12.7	10.2	9.3	8.3	7.0	6.9	7.2	9.8	10.2	11.7
Net worth	69.1	45.6	56.9	60.2	63.4	66.5	69.6	72.1	70.1	70.3	69.9
Capital stock	27.8	62.3	42.6	35.4	30.9	27.3	24.7	23.1	23.9	26.4	29.9
Preferred	5.3	3.5	3.2	3.3	3.5	3.9	4.2	4.1	5.4	8.3	5.9
Common	22.5	58.8	39.4	32.1	27.4	23.4	20.5	19.0	18.6	18.1	24.1
Surplus	41.3	−16.7	14.3	24.8	32.5	39.2	44.8	49.0	46.2	43.9	40.0
Current ratio[a]	2.55	1.32	1.73	1.89	2.07	2.25	2.51	2.81	2.75	2.76	2.65

(continued)

NOTES AND SUPPORTING TABLES

TABLE C-4 (continued)

B. RETURNS WITH NET INCOME
1937

| | All Classes | \multicolumn{10}{c}{Asset-size Class} |
		1	2	3	4	5	6	7	8	9	10
Assets											
Total	100.0	100.0	100.0	100.0	100.0	100.0	100.0	100.0	100.0	100.0	100.0
Current	39.2	55.4	52.9	51.6	49.9	47.7	45.7	41.7	39.6	41.1	33.5
Fixed	39.6	34.9	36.1	36.9	38.3	39.4	39.2	39.2	39.7		39.9
All other	21.2	9.7	11.0	11.5	11.8	12.9	15.1	19.1	20.7		26.3
Debt and net worth											
Total	100.0	100.0	100.0	100.0	100.0	100.0	100.0	100.0	100.0	100.0	100.0
Total debt	22.4	39.9	34.0	31.7	27.1	24.4	22.4	20.5	20.6	22.1	21.6
Short-term	14.9	34.9	28.9	26.2	21.2	19.1	16.6	13.7	12.9	10.7	13.7
Bonds, notes and mortgages payable—less than one yr.	3.6	8.2	8.3	7.9	7.2	6.3	5.3	3.8	3.2	2.0	2.2
Accounts payable	7.4	18.5	14.0	11.6	9.4	8.3	6.9	5.5	5.2	6.0	8.5
Other liabilities	3.9	8.2	6.6	6.7	4.6	4.5	4.4	4.4	4.5	2.7	3.0
Long-term	7.5	5.0	5.1	4.5	5.9	5.3	5.8	6.8	7.7	11.4	7.9
Net worth	77.6	60.0	66.0	68.5	72.8	75.5	77.4	79.5	79.3	77.8	78.3
Capital stock	45.6	67.7	55.6	52.2	48.2	46.2	44.3	43.4	45.1	38.9	46.9
Preferred	9.3	3.6	4.7	6.4	7.6	8.7	9.4	10.1	9.1	8.8	10.1
Common	36.3	64.0	50.9	45.7	40.6	37.6	35.0	33.3	36.0	30.1	36.8
Surplus	32.0	−7.7	10.4	16.3	24.6	29.3	33.1	36.1	34.2	38.9	31.4
Current ratio[a]	2.63	1.58	1.83	1.97	2.35	2.50	2.75	3.04	3.07	3.84	2.91

(continued)

TABLE C-4 (continued)

B. RETURNS WITH NET INCOME

1948

	All Classes	Asset-size Class									
		1	2	3	4	5	6	7	8	9	10
Assets											
Total	100.0	100.0	100.0	100.0	100.0	100.0	100.0	100.0	100.0	100.0	100.0
Current	53.9	59.3	60.6	60.5	61.2	61.6	60.5	59.2	56.1	53.8	48.5
Fixed	34.4	33.7	32.8	32.8	31.8	31.4	31.3	31.7	33.5	32.6	37.1
All other	11.7	7.0	6.6	6.7	7.0	7.0	8.2	9.1	10.4	13.6	14.4
Debt and net worth	100.0	100.0	100.0	100.0	100.0	100.0	100.0	100.0	100.0	100.0	100.0
Total debt	29.6	39.4	34.8	34.3	32.8	30.7	28.5	26.8	29.4	29.4	29.8
Short-term	20.2	31.2	27.9	27.5	26.4	25.2	22.7	20.2	20.1	19.2	18.3
Bonds, notes and mortgages payable—less than one yr.	2.6	5.6	5.3	5.3	4.9	5.1	4.2	3.3	2.7	1.4	1.7
Accounts payable	8.8	14.7	13.4	12.6	11.2	9.7	8.4	7.6	7.7	8.4	9.1
Other liabilities	8.8	10.9	9.2	9.6	10.3	10.4	10.1	9.3	9.7	9.4	7.5
Long-term	9.4	8.2	6.9	6.8	6.4	5.5	5.8	6.6	9.3	10.2	11.5
Net worth	70.4	60.6	65.2	65.7	67.3	69.5	71.7	73.2	70.7	70.6	70.0
Capital stock	27.4	50.2	37.1	31.9	29.0	25.7	24.0	23.2	24.1	26.7	30.0
Preferred	5.3	2.2	2.2	2.5	3.1	3.4	4.1	4.2	5.4	8.4	5.8
Common	22.0	48.0	34.9	29.4	25.8	22.2	19.9	19.0	18.7	18.3	24.2
Surplus	43.0	10.4	28.1	33.9	38.3	43.8	47.7	50.0	46.6	43.9	40.0
Current ratio[a]	2.67	1.90	2.17	2.20	2.32	2.44	2.67	2.93	2.79	2.80	2.65

(continued)

TABLE C-4 (continued)

C. RETURNS WITHOUT NET INCOME

1937

	All Classes	Asset-size Class									
		1	2	3	4	5	6	7	8	9	10
Assets											
Total	100.0	100.0	100.0	100.0	100.0	100.0	100.0	100.0	100.0	100.0	100.0
Current	30.9	47.3	41.6	38.9	36.0	33.6	30.2	24.6	23.6	28.3	28.3
Fixed	52.6	39.3	43.7	46.2	50.0	51.1	53.7	57.5	58.8	52.6	52.6
All other	16.5	13.4	14.7	14.9	14.0	15.3	16.1	17.9	17.6	17.1	17.1
Debt and Net worth	100.0	100.0	100.0	100.0	100.0	100.0	100.0	100.0	100.0	100.0	100.0
Total debt	42.6	69.0	55.1	49.5	43.6	42.5	38.2	38.4	37.6	43.4	43.4
Short-term	25.5	57.8	45.2	38.9	31.3	28.7	22.9	17.6	18.1	17.1	17.1
Bonds, notes and mortgages payable—less than one yr.	8.8	15.6	13.8	13.3	11.9	11.6	8.8	5.6	4.9	6.7	6.7
Accounts payable	11.4	29.2	21.5	17.0	14.0	11.6	9.9	7.2	9.1	6.7	6.7
Other liabilities	5.3	13.0	9.9	8.6	5.4	5.5	4.2	4.8	4.1	3.7	3.7
Long-term	17.1	11.2	9.9	10.6	12.3	13.8	15.3	20.8	19.5	26.3	26.3
Net worth	57.4	30.9	44.7	50.5	56.5	57.5	61.9	61.5	62.3	56.6	56.6
Capital stock	52.3	94.2	69.5	67.1	62.1	57.0	51.1	49.1	41.9	35.2	35.2
Preferred	8.9	7.2	7.0	9.0	9.9	10.1	10.1	11.6	7.3	6.8	6.8
Common	43.4	87.0	62.4	58.1	52.2	46.9	41.0	37.5	34.6	28.4	28.4
Surplus	5.1	−63.3	−24.7	−16.6	−5.6	0.5	10.8	12.4	20.4	21.4	21.4
Current ratio[a]	1.21	0.81	0.92	1.00	1.15	1.17	1.32	1.40	1.30	1.65	1.65

(continued)

APPENDIX C. FINANCIAL SERIES

TABLE C-4 (concluded)

C. RETURNS WITHOUT NET INCOME
1948

	All Classes	\multicolumn{10}{c}{Asset-size Class}									
		1	2	3	4	5	6	7	8	9	10
Assets											
Total	100.0	100.0	100.0	100.0	100.0	100.0	100.0	100.0	100.0	100.0	100.0
Current	47.3	50.2	49.6	48.7	47.4	49.1	45.7	42.5	40.2	67.1	58.3
Fixed	42.4	40.0	41.0	41.5	42.8	40.9	43.7	47.5	49.4	25.5	27.3
All other	10.3	9.8	9.4	9.8	9.8	10.0	10.6	10.0	10.4	7.4	14.4
Debt and net worth	100.0	100.0	100.0	100.0	100.0	100.0	100.0	100.0	100.0	100.0	100.0
Total debt	50.6	70.9	59.2	56.3	53.1	49.5	47.5	42.7	42.2	55.4	49.3
Short-term	33.0	53.3	42.7	39.5	36.5	34.3	30.7	26.6	22.4	48.3	16.9
Bonds, notes and mortgages payable—less than one yr.	11.0	13.5	11.6	11.3	10.7	11.8	12.1	8.5	9.2	8.4	11.0
Accounts payable	14.7	26.3	21.0	19.8	18.2	15.8	12.0	12.6	6.7	25.9	4.6
Other liabilities	7.3	13.5	10.1	8.4	7.6	6.7	6.6	5.5	6.5	14.0	1.3
Long-term	17.6	17.6	16.5	16.8	16.6	15.2	16.7	16.1	19.8	7.1	32.4
Net worth	49.4	29.3	40.8	43.7	46.9	50.6	52.6	57.3	57.8	44.7	50.7
Capital stock	34.9	75.7	53.3	45.7	39.3	36.1	31.0	22.4	20.7	3.1	16.5
Preferred	5.5	5.1	5.2	5.4	5.4	6.5	5.5	3.6	4.4	0.0	11.8
Common	29.4	70.6	48.2	40.3	33.9	29.6	25.5	18.8	16.3	3.1	4.8
Surplus	14.5	−46.4	−12.5	−2.0	7.6	14.5	21.6	34.9	37.1	41.6	34.2
Current ratio[a]	1.43	0.94	1.16	1.23	1.30	1.43	1.49	1.60	1.79	1.40	3.45

Note: Data do not add to total due to rounding. For asset-size classes, see Appendix C, section D.
[a] Current assets divided by current liabilities (short-term debt).
Source: *Statistics of Income, 1937* and *1948*, Part 2 and their unpublished "Source Book," Bureau of Internal Revenue (now Internal Revenue Service).

INDEX

Accounting: depreciation, 13–14, 44–46, 82, 130–132; LIFO, 76; practices, 78, 293; reporting deficiencies, 12, 44; social-accounting approach, 80

Accounts: payable, 118, 156, 182–183; receivable, 224

Alexander, Sidney S., 198

Amortization: and capital-output ratios, 45; and fixed-capital assets, 89; and operational capacity, 79

Arnold, John R., 204

Asset expansion, 113–119, 189

Assets: capital, 44, 45, 78; current, 186, 189; financial, xxxvi, xli, 110, 111–112; fixed, xxix f., 88–89, 124, 127, 129–130, 133–134, 153, 186, 189; intangible, 45, 220–221; net, 116; nonreproducible, 79; operating, xlviii, 156–158, 159, 169f.; physical, 110, 112, 118, 119, 148f., 151, 153; short-term, xliv, xlix–l; total, xxix f., xliv, 5, 14–15, 44, 45, 158, 170, 172, 182–183, 186, 189, 330

Bain, Foster H., 82n., 290

Bank term loans, 145–146, 156, 167, 179–183

Benchmark years: and employment levels, 299–301; selection of, 17–18

Bonds, xlviii, 123, 145, 161–170, 172, 181, 327–328

Burns, Arthur F., 11

Capacity utilization, xxxvii–xxxix, 38, 91, 94

Capital: and capacity, xxxvii–xxxix; consumption, 130, 132; data, xxiv, 11, 12, 44, 45, 324–325; defined, 12–15, 197–207, 274–280; deflation of, 19–20, 31, 39; depreciation, 13–14, 44–46, 130, 132; per employed, 94–101, 105–106; fixed, xxxiii, xxxvii–xxxix, 91; growth, xxix f., 38, 40; inflation of, 53; innovations, xxv ff.; measurement of, 38; and money markets, 111; net inflow of, 110–111; and output, xxiv, xxxi f.; and prices, xxix, 19–21, 39, 47, 53; real, 110–111, 130; retardation, xxix f.; total, xxx, xxxiii, 55; working, xxxiii, xlix–l; see also Capital-output ratios; Financing

 manufacturing: and asset size, 61–65; data, 67–68, 88, 195–207; defined, 45, 197–207; deflation, 39; depreciation, 89, 218–220; efficiency, 72, 94, 95f.; expenditures, 44, 329–330; fixed, xxvii, xxxiii, 67, 71f., 83f., 88–91, 96, 220–227;

Capital—*cont.*
 manufacturing—*cont.*
 and GNP, 24; growth, 22–31, 83, 103–105; by industries, 24–31, 53, 88, 207–208, 217–221; inflation, 38; innovations, 41–42, 63, 89, 94; and output, xxiv, 38, 41–42, 53, 63, 91, 94, 96, 99; and prices, 19–20, 38, 39, 44, 47, 51–52, 53; total, xxx, 221–227; working, xxxiii, 67, 71, 72, 77, 83, 85–88, 91, 226; *see also* Capital-output ratios

 mining: data, 74, 274–299; defined, 274–280; growth, xxx, 31–36, 78, 103–105; efficiency, 102; by industries, 31, 55, 88; land, 31, 59, 77, 79–81, 284–293; and labor, 99–102; and mineral resources, 103; and output, 33–36, 55, 58ff., 78, 301–303; plant, xxxiii, 31, 74, 76, 78, 80, 88; and plant capacity, 78; and prices, 42, 44, 103; retardation, 11, 31, 78; and tax liabilities, 76; total, 31; working, xxxiii, 31, 74, 76–78; *see also* Capital-output ratios

Capital-output ratios: and asset size, xxxiv f., 60–65; average, xlvi, 38; and capacity, xxxviii–xxxix; data, xxiv, xxxi, 12, 43–46; and depreciation, xxxv, 14, 44–46, 89; discussed, xxiv, xxx–xlii, 5, 17, 43–46; and employment levels, 299ff.; and fixed capital, xxxvii–xxxix, xl–xli, 67f., 71f., 83–84, 89, 90–91, 96; hypothetical, 53ff., 60; and internal financing, xlvi; marginal, xxxii, xlvi, xlvii, 38; and output, xl, 7, 53–55, 94; peak year of, 65; and plant capital, 74, 76, 80, 88; and prices, xxxi, 38, 43–44, 47, 51–53, 65, 76, 80, 92, 103; and technological changes, 11, 65, 79, 94; trends in, 62, 92; in unincorporated firms, 45; and working capital, 67f., 71f., 74, 76f., 83–88, 91; *see also* Capital; Output

 manufacturing: xxxi, xxxiii–xxxiv, xxxviii, 11, 14–15, 38–42, 44–47, 51–55, 60–65, 67f., 71–72, 76, 83–87, 88–91, 93–99, 103–105

 mining: xxxi, xxxiii–xxxiv, 7, 11, 42–43, 55–60, 74, 76–79, 80, 87f., 99, 101–105

Carson, Daniel, 19, 207

Cash and receivables, 127, 224

Census, Bureau of, 14, 16, 33n., 195, 201

Census of Manufactures, 11, 12–13, 14n., 15f., 20, 44, 45n., 65n., 169n., 196

Census of Mining, 15, 16

341

INDEX

Chawner, Lowell J., 24
Claims, financial, 110, 111
Coal, xxvii, xxx, 9, 55, 59, 76, 102, 177
Commerce, Department of, 15n., 72n., 113, 177
Consumption, xxvii, 7, 9–10
Corey, Raymond E., 174n.
Corporate financing; *see* Debt financing; Equity financing; Financing
Corporate saving, defined, 109n.
Credit: long-term, 118; medium-term, 118; short-term, xxxvi; trade, 111, 156

Data: adjustments for price changes, 19–21, 195–196, 198–201, 226–228; coverage, 196–197, 201, 280–284, 293; reliability, 195–196, 203, 293–296
Debt, total, 156–161, 189
Debt-asset ratio, xlviii, l, 161, 169, 172, 189
Debt financing: and asset size, 159–161, 172; and assets, l; bank loans, 145–146, 156, 167, 179–183; bonds, xlviii, 123, 145, 161–170, 172, 181, 327–328; data, 141, 145, 146, 156–158, 161–164, 172; debt issues, 177; and financial intermediaries, 172, 173–174; long-term, l, 145–146, 161–166, 167–169, 172, 179–180; operating assets, ratio to, xlviii, l; short-term, l, 183; sources of funds, 156; stocks, xlviii, 167–169; and total financing, 168–169
Depletion, 82–83, 113, 120–122, 130, 132n., 329; *see also* Depreciation
Depreciation: accelerated, 218–220; accounting, 13–14, 44–46, 82, 130–132; and capital estimates, 13, 14, 88–89; and capital-output ratios, xxxv, 14, 44f., 46, 89; data, 113, 120–122; and fixed assets, 88–89, 133–134; and gross internal financing, 130–134, 329; manufacturing, 88–89, 218–220; mining, 78–79; and output, 120–122; and prices, 130; and retained net profits, 132–134, 135–136; and technological changes, 78; *see also* Depletion
Depression (1930's), xxv, 3, 31, 78, 127
Dispersion, 93–94, 105
Dissaving, net, 115, 132, 136–138, 140
Doane, R. R., 285–286

Employment: levels of, 299–301; number of persons, 5, 65, 239–240; *see also* Labor
Equity, l, 156, 166
Equity financing: and asset size, 159–161; and bond issues, 166–169; external, 166; internal, 166; and long-term debt

Equity financing—*cont.*
financing, 168–169; stocks, 111f., 141, 156, 164–169, 326–327; *see also* Financing, internal; Profits, retained
Excess profit tax, 138, 144
Expenditures: capital, 44; and financial assets, 111; and internal financing, 124–130, 148f., 151, 153; plant and equipment, xlvi–xlvii, 113, 120, 124–130, 134, 329–330

Fabricant, Solomon, 15, 21, 41
Federal Reserve Board (FRB), 89n., 141, 179–180
Federal Trade Commission, 88, 288
Financial statements, corporate, 112
Financing: and bank term loans, 156, 167, 179–183; and capital-output ratios, xlvi, li; components of, 113; data, xxiv, xliii, 112–113; future prospects, l–liv; long-term, xxv, 115–116, 127, 129–130, 141, 144, 145–146, 149, 153, 172–174, 176–177, 179–182; ratio of internal to external, 130, 142–143; "self-liquidating," 179; short-term, xliv-xlv, xlvii–l, 116, 141, 144ff., 149, 151–153, 156, 182–186, 189; trends, xliii–l; *see also* Capital; Debt financing; Equity financing
external: and assets, 182–183, 186; defined, 109; and excess profit tax, 144; and financial assets, 111; and fixed assets, 127; gross, 141–146; and income tax, xliv-xlv, xlix, 116, 144f., 149, 151, 183–186; and internal financing, 130, 142–143; and liabilities, 111, 132, 156, 182–183, 186, 189; loans, 145–146, 153; long-term, 127, 141, 144, 145–146, 149, 153; net, 149; net balance of, xliii, 111, 146–149, 151–153; and retained income, 127; security issues, 113, 146, 153, 168, 326–328; short-term, xliv-xlv, xlvii–l, 141, 144ff., 149, 151–153, 156, 182–186, 189; and total financing, xliv, 119, 145f., 182; and total new financing, 119, 145f., 183; trade credits, 111, 156; trends, xliii–l
internal: and capital-output ratios, xlvi; data, 111, 113, 328–329; defined, 109; and equity, 156; and expenditures, xliii-xliv, 124–130, 151; and external financing, 130, 142–143, 153; and external funds, xliii, 151; gross, xliii–xlv, 109, 120, 122–124, 124–130, 130–141, 143, 146, 148f., 151, 153; long-term, 116, 153; net, 109, 115, 143–144; and net assets, 116; net balance of, 111–112;

342

INDEX

Financing—*cont.*
  internal—*cont.*
    retention ratios, 118–119; and security issues, 138; short-term, 116; and total financing, xlv; and total new financing, 143–144, 146; trends, xliii–l; *see also* Profits, retained
      total, xliv ff., 119, 127, 145f., 168–169, 182
      total new, 109–110, 115, 119, 143–144, 145f., 153, 182
Frickey, Edwin, 21, 41
Friend, Irwin, 179–180
Fuel, 10
Fund inflow, 111, 141, 143
Fund outflow, 111–112, 141, 143
Funds: external, xliii, 118–119, 127, 136, 138–141, 149, 151, 153; internal, xliii f., xlvi–xlvii, 112, 118, 119, 124, 127, 136, 138–141

Goldsmith, Raymond W., 326–327
Gross National Product (GNP), xxvi–xxvii, 7, 9–10, 24

Hale, E. V., 176–177
Hoskold formula, 289–290

Income retention; *see* Profits, retained
Income tax, 11, 13, 14, 44f., 76, 82, 116–117, 132, 144, 149, 151, 166, 183–186
Industrial classifications, 18–19, 52–53
Internal revenue data, 11, 52–53
Internal Revenue Service, 11, 12–13, 16, 19, 20, 159n., 201–
Inventories, 220, 224
Inventory-output ratio, xl–xli

Korean War, 87n., 117, 144, 176, 220
Kuznets, Simon, 38n.

Labor: and capital, 94–101, 105–106; and output, 94–96, 99, 102; past labor, 79; and plant size, xxxvi; *see also* Employment
Land, mining, 31, 59, 77, 79–81, 82, 284–293
Land-output ratios, 79–81
Last-in, first-out (LIFO), 76
Liabilities: accrued, 156, 182, 189; current, 182–183, 186, 189; long-term, 156; net balance of, 111; short-term, 156, 182, 183

Man-hours, 94–96, 99, 101

Manufacturing: and asset size, xxxiv, 60–65, 330; capacity utilization, 38, 91, 94; composition of, 53–55; debt-asset ratios, 161, 172; GNP, xxvi–xxviii, 24; growth, xxvii–xxviii, xlii, 3–5, 27; by industries, xxviii, 24–31, 46–47, 51–55, 61, 71f., 83–84, 104; merger movements, 14f., 44–45; and prices, xxvii, 19–20, 47, 51–52; retardation, xxvii–xxx, 78; securities, 123–124, 173, 174–177; and total debt, 156–159; *see also* Capital; Capital-output ratios; Output
Measurement, 11, 38
Merger movements, 14–15, 44–45
Metals, xxvii, xxx, 9, 10, 76, 102
Mineral coefficient, 7–9
Minerals; *see* Mining
Mining: accounting practices, 76, 78; and asset size, 330; by categories, xxvii–xxviii, 9, 31, 88; composition of, 55–60; depletion, 82–83, 132n.; development, xxvii–xxviii, xlii, 7–11, 101f.; land, 31, 59, 77, 79–81, 82, 284–293; mineral coefficient, 7–9; and national product, xxvi–xxviii, 7, 9–10; and prices, xxvii, 76, 79, 80; production, 9–10, 59, 79, 102; retardation, xxvii–xxx, 7, 11, 31, 78; securities, 123–124, 174; technological changes in, 78f., 103; and total debt, 158; *see also* Capital; Capital-output ratios; Output
Money markets, 111
Moody's, 76, 198, 203

National Bureau of Economic Research, xxiii, 18, 141, 207
National income, xxvii, xlii, 3, 113
National product, xxiii, xxvi–xxvii, xxxi, 7, 9–10, 24
Natural gas industry, xxviii, xxx, 7, 9, 58f., 76, 80, 88, 102
Net National Product (NNP), xxvi, 7, 9–10
Nonmetals, 7, 9f., 76, 102

Obsolescence; *see* Depreciation
Oil industry, 10n., 31, 58, 82, 88, 102, 104
Output: and capital, xxiv, xxvi–xxxi, xli, 38, 47, 53–55, 60, 85ff., 88, 91, 94, 113; data, 11, 223, 228–238; defined, 15–17; and depreciation and depletion, 120–122; and employment levels, 299–301; land-output ratios, 79–81; and labor, 94–96, 99, 102; manufacturing, xxiv, xxvii–xxviii, xxxiii, 38f., 41–42, 53–55, 67, 72, 78, 83ff., 89, 90–91, 94–96, 99, 103ff., 113, 228–238; mining, xxiv, xxvi–

343

INDEX

Output—*cont.*
xxviii, xxxiii, 7, 9–11, 33–36, 55, 58, 60, 74, 76, 78–80, 99, 101ff., 113; and national product, xxvi–xxvii; and prices, xxvii, 19, 20–21, 38, 39–40, 47, 53f., 94, 228; and retained profits, xlvii, 120–122; total value of, 112–113; *see also* Capital-output ratios

Past labor, 79
Petroleum industry, xxviii, xxx, 7, 9, 59, 76, 80, 88, 102–104, 164, 177
"Predominant operation" principle, 16
Price indexes, 19–21, 41, 47, 221–225, 226–228, 228–238
Prices: adjustments, 19–21, 43, 47; and capital, 19–21, 39, 53, 79, 91; and capital-output ratios, xxxi, 38, 47, 51–52, 53, 76, 80; constant, 42, 47, 51–52, 53, 65, 79, 91, 103, 228; and depreciation, 130; fluctuations in, 19–21; inflation, 43; and LIFO accounting, 76; manufacturing, xxvii, 19–20, 44, 47, 51–52, 53, 228; mining, 42, 44, 76, 79, 80, 103; and output, xxvii, 19, 20–21, 38–40, 47, 53f., 94, 228; relative, 205–207; reported, 42, 44, 47, 65, 92, 103; and total assets, xxix, 14–15; and total debt, 158
Production, 9–10, 83
Profits, retained: changes in, 115ff., 123; and debt financing, 168–169; gross, 124; and income tax, 116f.; net, xlvii, 132–133, 134–136, 136–141, 143–144, 166f., 328; and output, xlvii, 120–122; retention ratios, 118–119; and stock issues, 166–167
Projections, future, l–liv

Retained profits; *see* Profits
Retardation, xxvii-xxx, 7, 11, 31, 78

Schor, S. Stanley, 61, 63
Scitovsky, Tibor, 61–63

Securities: and assets, 112, 115–116; data, 113, 120; and debt issues, 177; dividends, 123; and external financing, 113, 146, 153, 168, 326–328; and gross internal financing, 120, 122–124, 125; and internal funds, 112, 136, 138; and long-term financing, 127, 129, 146, 153; market, 122, 124; net, defined, 123; and net retained profits, 116, 136–141; net transactions, 141; and plant and equipment expenditures, 125–127; and plant expansion, 140; private placement of, 172–179; and total financing, 127; *see also* Bonds; Stocks
Securities and Exchange Commission, 88, 173f.
"Self-generating" liquidity, 78
Stocks, 111f., 141, 156, 164–169, 326–327
Surplus, earned, 111–112

Tax: excess profit, 138, 144f.; income, xliv–xlv, xlvii f., 11, 13f., 44f., 76, 82, 116–117, 132, 144f., 149, 151, 166, 183–186
Tax liabilities, 76
Technological innovations: capital-output ratios, xxxv ff., xli, 11, 65, 79, 94, 101n.; and depreciation, 78; and financial assets, xxxvi; and fixed capital, 89; and industrial growth, xxxvi–xxxvii; manufacturing, 89; mining, 78, 79, 103; and retardation, xxviii
Terborgh, George, 111, 149
Term loans, 156, 167, 179–182
Trade credits, 111, 156

U.S. Steel Corporation, 124, 164

Value added, 104–105

Wage-earners; *see* Employment; Labor
Working capital, defined, 12

GPSR Authorized Representative: Easy Access System Europe - Mustamäe tee 50, 10621 Tallinn, Estonia, gpsr.requests@easproject.com